Artificial Intelligence and You

What AI Means
for Your Life,
Your Work,
and Your World

Book Two of the **Human Cusp Series**

Artificial Intelligence and You

WHAT AI MEANS
FOR YOUR LIFE,
YOUR WORK,
AND YOUR WORLD

BOOK TWO OF THE **HUMAN CUSP SERIES**

PETER J. SCOTT

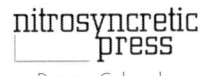

nitrosyncretic press
Denver, Colorado

*For Grace,
with Love*

©2022 Peter J. Scott
All Rights Reserved.

www.humancusp.com

All figures are copyright by the author except where otherwise noted.
Animal icons by marcos101, Pixabay.
Cover android courtesy of Tatiana Shepeleva.

Quotations by John Maynard Keynes from *Essays in Persuasion*
by permission of the Royal Economic Society

First Edition
First Printing, 15 July 2022 ②

ISBN 978-0-96-798744-6 (Softcover)
ISBN 978-0-96-798745-3 (Hardcover)
Library of Congress Control Number: 2022907634

Nitrosyncretic Press
Denver, Colorado
www.nitrosyncretic.com

Contents

    Preface vii
1 Introduction 1

Artificial Intelligence Will Completely Transform Our Lives
2 Oh, Really? 7
3 AI Predictions in Context 23

What Is Artificial Intelligence?
4   Intelligence 39
5   Past and Present 49
6   Naming of Parts 63
7   AIs and Brains 69
8   How to Think About AI 77
9   Applications of AI 101
10 Self-Driving Cars 113
11 Sorting Hype from Reality .131

Why Will AI Affect You?
12 The Human Issues of AI 157
13 Getting Personal with AI 183
14 Effects on Employment 211

How Can You Survive and Thrive through the AI Revolution?
15 Survive 231
16 Existential Risk 255
17 Thrive 265
18 Future Tense 279

    Appendix: Neural Nuts and Bolts 307
    Acknowledgements 315
    Bibliography 317
    Endnotes 335
    Index 339

Preface

> *Our technology has gotten so complex that we can no longer understand it or fully control it. We have entered the Age of Entanglement… Each expert knows a piece of the puzzle, but the big picture is too big to comprehend.*[1]
>
> — Danny Hillis

Once upon a time, there was a community of rabbits. They lived in a warren—an interlocking maze of burrows they tunneled—near a copse of yew trees, at the edge of a grassy meadow. They started out as a small community, but rapidly grew in numbers—they were, after all, rabbits. While their lives were generally content, they were no stranger to strife, deprivation, and the occasional fox raid. A human observer might have questioned the sustainability of their habitat as their population expanded, but the rabbits' capacity to appreciate the finer points of their ecology was limited.

They were, after all, only rabbits.

And then one day, just beyond the meadow, the old farmhouse that the rabbits were completely unaware of was occupied by a new family: young, energetic, ambitious. This family of farmers pulled on heavy boots and explored their new territory, and some of them exclaimed with delight when they saw white cottontails disappearing into the hedgerow. They were, of course, more focused on farming than rabbits, but in their spare time made excursions into the copse, individually or in pairs, for various purposes as the whim took them. Some merely took photographs. Others captured pets. And there was a fierce debate about the threat to the nearby field if the rabbit population expanded.

But none of the description in the preceding paragraph made the slightest sense to the rabbits—aside from the fact that they could neither read nor talk, they had no language capable of embodying concepts like "photograph," "pet," or "population."

They were, after all, only rabbits.

They felt the consequences of this incursion, of course, but those consequences were complex. Life as a pet had its advantages—no foxes—but the rabbits who were captured did not know how to feel about the experience. For the rest, the unpredictable disappearance of random comrades was upsetting; but they had not the slightest concept of the plans being hatched to purge the warren altogether so that a new barn could be built.

They were, after all, only rabbits.

By now, this not-so-subtle metaphor (no doubt prompted by my English upbringing peppered with stories of rabbits in waistcoats) will be obvious, so there is no need to belabor the point. We are on the brink of an encounter with a technology that will reshape our world as much as the farmers were about to throw the rabbit warren into chaos.

Artificial intelligence.

Don't take the metaphor too literally; it doesn't mean that AI will start capturing and caging us. Rather, AI will form a phenomenon so multifaceted, so complex, so far-reaching, that our capacity to understand its consequences will be completely inadequate. It will be as foreign to us as the New York Stock Exchange would be to the rabbit family. Our intellects and our institutions simply cannot encompass the effects of accelerated machine cognition on our world.

That should not restrain us from trying. The transformations wrought by AI will arrive like a Hemingway character described his bankruptcy: "Slowly, then suddenly."* To describe the changes as the products of machines with heightened IQs would be hopelessly reductionist, as would any single sentence trying to encapsulate the essence of the AI revolution. It would take a book, at least; so here we are. If you're confused by the talk about artificial intelligence, if you're lost in the technology and terminology, if you're buffeted by the conflicting arguments about its impact and how to prepare for it—or if you've started down this road far enough to realize that you want all the help you can get—then this book is for you. Even in the

---

* Mike Campbell, in *The Sun Also Rises*.

face of what appears to be an insurmountable task, of understanding something inscrutable by definition, of navigating our selves and our businesses along a path lightless and potholed, of cooperating on an unprecedented scale to coordinate our creation of this boundless new world, there's no question but that we're going to give it everything we've got.

We are, after all, only human.

1
Introduction

It is very difficult to make predictions, particularly about the future.

— Niels Bohr

If you were about to launch a new product and you discovered that 50 percent of the population reacted to it with fear, you might have words with your marketing department. Yet about half the population today does not trust artificial intelligence, does not know enough about it, or both. All the media attention given to AI in recent years has not resulted in general trust and affection for AI; if anything, the opposite. Half the respondents to a 2018 poll were not comfortable with their personal details being used by AI;[2] 48 percent in a 2019 World Economic Forum poll said that companies' use of AI should be more regulated,[3] and 27 percent of people in another poll the same year were concerned about the enslavement of humanity by robots. These attitudes vary according to privilege; AI receives more support from those who are more educated, more wealthy, more familiar with technology, and more male.[4]

I began speaking to audiences about AI in 2012, and in 2017, I wrote *Crisis of Control*, which coincidentally opened with a fictional prediction of a worldwide pandemic in 2027, evolving through multiple lettered strains. It wasn't even the central premise of the book, but it has shown how even a casual prediction can have unexpected echoes in reality. In 2020, while the real pandemic was raging, I started a weekly podcast, also called *Artificial Intelligence and You*, which has been highly successful. The many expert guests who gifted our audience with their time and intellects have raised awareness of the myriad facets of this thing called AI immeasurably, and many of their ideas, insights, and concerns are represented here.

I have spoken to groups ranging from high schools to senior citizens and from TEDx audiences to parliamentarians. The level of engagement from all has been remarkably similar; everyone senses that we are on the threshold of a change bigger than we have so far wrapped our brains around. But how big? We'll try to frame that. I have often told talk organizers that AI spans such a range of human endeavor that I could go from computer science to theology in thirty seconds. One school took me literally and arranged a workshop with the students from the computing and religious science classes. It worked.

Whenever one throws around such florid terminology as I employed in the last paragraph, there's a tendency for people to fret and overreact. As much as I present the positive and negative potentials of AI as fairly as possible, both are so great that people in my talks tend to end up either paralyzed or nonchalantly in denial. The ambiguity is hard to handle: they want to know whether they should welcome or fear AI, but there will never be an answer so monochrome. They want to know whether we should accelerate or inhibit the development of AI, but such sweeping control is within no one's power. What we really need to do is look at AI not as a good thing, nor as a bad thing, but as a *big* thing, one that is inevitable. From its potential to deliver a utopian abundance and the solutions to our hardest problems, to its complex and looming social issues, it is a thing that we need to prepare for.

What exactly such preparation entails is not easily grasped. As a Price Waterhouse Coopers report put it: "AI touches almost every aspect of our lives. And it's only just getting started."[5] The rate of expansion of computing technology is mind-blowing to contemplate. In 2016 alone, the world produced sixteen zettabytes of data, more than it had created in all of history before then.[6] A zettabyte is a billion terabytes, and you could store a hundred Ultra Hi-Def 4K movies in one terabyte. But by the time you've come to terms with how much that is, the world has moved on; two years later the figure had doubled, and in 2022 the world is forecast to generate a hundred zettabytes.[7]

Trying to measure the scale of technological disruption by focusing on the amount of data stored is like assessing Shakespeare's contribution to literature by how many words he wrote. (Which were nevertheless, as my high school memories remind me, all too many.) But we don't have much more at our disposal. Our powers of prediction are puny and inadequate to the task of foreseeing the impact of AI. By analogy with the dawn of the internal combustion engine, science fiction author David Gerrold told my listeners, "You could predict the automobile. But could you predict the drive-thru McDonald's?"[8]

The driving force behind the incomprehensible scale of change we've been dancing with in the last few paragraphs is *exponential growth.* As futurist Tony Czarnecki told me, "Very, very few people realize that what they've got on their mobile phone—including the phone—would in 1982 have cost over a million dollars in today's money."[9] He went on to point out that your phone's Global Positioning System capability alone would in 1982 have cost over a quarter of a million dollars; and yet how quickly we forget these enormous leaps. We'll explore exponential growth in more detail in Chapter 5.

Growth in technology does not happen in isolation, but feeds a snowball effect that makes advancements that impact business happen even faster. Paolo Pirjanian, CEO of Embodied Inc., makers of the Moxie child interaction robot we will meet in Chapter 13, said, "We are deploying the latest in computer vision, machine learning, natural language understanding… [technology that] would have not been possible even five years ago. Things that used to take decades to do, we're seeing happening in quarters now."[10] A few years ago, teacher Charles dela Cuesta's class project to create a robot tour guide for Thomas Jefferson high school took two years to complete. Now, the timeline has been shortened to nine weeks. "The stuff that was impressive to me five, six years ago, we could accomplish in a quarter of the time now," he said. "It just blows my mind."[11]

These advances are relentlessly monetized, commoditized, open sourced, and pushed down the adoption curve. For example, teen programmer Leon Hillman took the open-source self-driving software from comma.ai and connected it so it could play the game *Grand Theft Auto V.* Why is this such a big deal? Because only a few years earlier, that would have required a team of PhDs. And now it's routine to the extent that a teenager can do it in what can only be a short amount of time, since he's still a teenager.

You won't finish this book knowing how to program a self-driving car (unless you started it with that ability); we're not here to teach programming. But it is useful to understand principles of the technology underlying AI so you can get an intuitive feel for what it can and cannot do; we will pay attention to "the man behind the curtain" of AI. If you already identify as a technologist, we'll be visiting a huge array of interdisciplinary topics to add breadth and context to the technology, and social issues to frame the wider impact.

Some science fiction movies have left indelible impressions of AI on our collective unconscious. To speak about AI, you have to be aware of the eight-hundred-pound Terminator in the room that will be awakened as soon as you mention the possibility of negative impact. The biggest challenge of conveying a message about AI and existential risk is to frame it so that the audience is not drawn into a Schwarzenegger-shaped maw where visions of Skynet dominate their thinking. Many professionals shy away from addressing the topic altogether out of fear that they will be ridiculed as killer robot alarmists—or worse, that people will reject AI and deny us the benefits AI has begun to bring. This book will try to address issues including existential risks with the detail and nuance they need.

This book was designed to fill a gap, between misleading, over-simplified media sensationalism on the one hand, and narrow academic treatises on the other. In trying to be of the greatest possible utility to the largest possible audience, there may be times when it delves into topics either too speculative or too technical for the tastes of some readers, but in neither case will the detour be long enough to detract from the overall journey; treat that section as an optional diversion that you can return to when your mood is more suited to it and skip forward according to taste.

Let's get started.

Artificial Intelligence Will Completely Transform Our Lives

2
Oh, Really?

Another world is not only possible, she is on her way. On a quiet day, I can hear her breathing.

— Arundhati Roy

Interest in artificial intelligence has reached carnival proportions, and it's understandable if that hubbub has provoked your skepticism, so let's face that first. Why does AI matter so much? The three questions every episode of the *AI and You* podcast opens with—

- What is AI?
- Why will it affect you?
- How do you and your business survive and thrive through the coming AI revolution?

—clearly presume AI is revolutionary: figuratively if not literally earth-shattering. Skepticism is justified; why, after all, should a computing paradigm be that pivotal? Did anyone suggest that relational databases would upend the world? That computer-generated special effects were a new industrial revolution? That the Java programming language would obsolete half the world's jobs? Overblown hype aside, are there even claims of the *Internet* leading to the level of global transformation pundits invest in AI?

We can see what sets AI apart in a statement from Andrew Ng, former chief scientist at Baidu, the Chinese equivalent of Google: [12]

AI is the new electricity.

Whether that claim is justified is a question we'll get to; but first, *what* does it mean? Since he brought it up, let's return to the dawn of the electrical era. It did not arrive in a blaze of light when Edison flipped a switch, but much earlier. In Italy in 1800, Alessandro Volta created the first electrical circuit with wires connected to primitive batteries.* Volta's work led immediately to the invention of electrolysis and got him an audience with Napoleon (who had occupied Volta's home city of Pavia for four years by then) to demonstrate how electricity passed through a (dead) frog would cause its legs to contract. History does not record whether Napoleon saw military application in this *grenouille électrifié*.

But over two decades were to pass before the English scientist Michael Faraday† connected electricity to motion, showing how movement could be turned to electricity and how electricity could create motion with an electric motor. Legend has it that Faraday—also inventor of the toy balloon—was asked, "But what use is it?" and responded, "What use is a newborn baby?"‡

Advances in electric motors came at a glacial rate. It wasn't until eighty years later, in the last decade of the nineteenth century, that Nikolai Tesla§ and Mikhail Dolivo-Dobrovolsky invented the induction motor design that enabled industrial use; and it was even longer before industry caught on. In 1900 less than five percent of the mechanical power in American factories came from electricity.[13] The rest still relied on a massive steam engine outside each factory transferring rotational power through a system of belts and pulleys looking like the innards of a giant wind-up watch. Terminal rotating belts would be connected to workers' machines such as drills and lathes.

Electric motors utterly transformed the factory. Power was distributed through wires so small they could be hidden underground and in the walls until they reached the drill or the lathe, which no longer needed to

---

* Volta = Volt. Those were the days when doing something new with electricity would get your name attached to a unit of it: Georg Ohm (resistance), Andre-Marie Ampère (current), Heinrich Hertz (frequency), …
† "Farad"—unit of capacitance.
‡ Legend is wrong. Faraday actually said that in a different lecture, about chlorine, prior to the days of swimming pool sanitation. But the anecdote would have fit.
§ "Tesla"—unit of magnetic field strength.

be aligned with the axis of the pulley. By 1905 the US Census Bureau reported "... practically all the newer factories or shops in the United States of any size, constructed within the past five years, have an electrical drive either exclusively or for most purposes... the effect of this electrical revolution cannot be fully apprehended, as it is in its earlier stages."[14] Electric motors and lights sparked the Second Industrial Revolution.

But even though Faraday took the stage many years before that, he got to see a significant application of his discovery of the principle of electromagnetic induction, which could be used to cause a solenoid to close at the other end of a cable: the telegraph, which came about much sooner than the commercialization of the electric motor. Before Faraday died, the major cities of the world were communicating instantaneously.

Fast forward to today, where electricity pervades our lives to roughly the same extent as grass. Electronic billboards clamor for our attention; electrolysis is no longer just for splitting water into hydrogen and oxygen but also removing unwanted hair; and my child's lollipop comes with a free electric motor, just to add the novelty of rotation to candy. The cultural impact of electrification changed our vocabulary. Look back over the last three paragraphs: *transform, spark, fast-forward;* how many of our words for *change* are electrical metaphors? What would Faraday have thought?

He might have foreseen the miniaturization and commoditization of his invention. But could he have seen past the future of the generator and the motor to the digital computer and the information revolution, birthed from electricity? We can often extrapolate existing trends forwards, but it is very hard for us to see the *next* revolutions they will enable, and to project those too. Just compare our world today, where we sling electrons with finesse and abandon, to the wired frog era of Alessandro Volta. For an example of seeing only as far as the change we're experiencing, John Naisbitt's 1982 bestseller *Megatrends* predicted cable television would offer as many as two hundred channels "like a supermarket." But in 1982, who could look beyond cable TV to see the on-demand firehose of Netflix? Or that the generation of electricity would be threatening the ecology of the planet?

So let us return to Andrew Ng. He is saying that AI will spawn as many new revolutions as electricity did. That there will be transformations upon transformations, as impossible to predict as the invention of Bluetooth would have been to Faraday. (Ng may be conservative: Google CEO Sundar Pichai maintains that AI is more pivotal than the invention of *fire*.[15])

Dynocognesis

A process so transformative of the human condition deserves a word to itself. I propose *dynocognesis*: the application of power to thought. It stands not just for the use of computation engines to accelerate cognitive tasks, but the revolutionizing of human processes, interactions, and creations that depend upon thought.

Think how transparent electricity has become: you don't flip on a light switch with the thought, "Look at me, unleashing electricity!" You don't turn on the oven or the mixer and say, "That's some impressive use of electricity." Instead, you deploy light and heat and motion; the power that enables them all is invisible. Businesses do not have a Chief Electricity Officer. It just happens. (At least one company has already realized what this means for AI. Industry analyst Blake Morgan says, "AI is not located in one particular office at Amazon—it's everywhere."[16])

Ng's claim is extravagant, but the consequences of it being correct are so profound that we cannot ignore it. So we'll explore how true it might be.

This Book Will Raise Your IQ

We will forgive you if, by the end of this book, you become moderately obsessed with the concept of intelligence quotient, or IQ. In any investigation of the capability of something called "artificial intelligence," ways to measure "intelligence" are going to come in for scrutiny. Later on, we'll put intelligence quotients under a magnifying glass, but for now, I'm going to pull a sly author trick and say that there's another IQ that's more important: *Interesting Questions*.

The problem of artificial intelligence is not so tidy as to admit of a known set of answers; it's not even so tidy as to be usefully classified as a "problem," although it contains many. By analogy, if you were setting out on an expedition to ascend K-2, you would have a well-curated checklist to complete: Nepalese currency, crampons, supplemental oxygen, training schedule, selfie stick—check, check, check. But if instead you were kidnapped in a Mad Explorers' Club hazing ritual and knew only that you were about to be left naked in a random wilderness somewhere on Earth, you'd have no checklist. No answers, only questions: What are the most immediate threats to my safety? Will I need shelter, clothing, or food first? How far is it to civilization and what hazards lie along the way? Why did I join this stupid club in the first place? Your survival would hinge upon your ability to frame powerful questions.

So it is with AI. We have plenty of answers, but there are more important questions to be asked, and this book will ask many of them. AI's most pressing challenges need more people asking powerful questions, to engage more of our capable, inventive minds—that's you—in exploring this space. This book has a goal of recruiting a viral army of questioners. It should be a more enjoyable experience than waking up naked on a Newfoundland iceberg.

Going Viral

> *Even quite unobservant people now are betraying, by fits and starts, a certain wonder, a shrinking and fugitive sense that something is happening so that life will never be* quite *the same again.*[17]
>
> — H.G. Wells

Since the beginning of 2020 we have had an immediate and painful lesson in the effects of disruption. COVID-19 is different from AI in so many ways, of course, but it did open our eyes to what it was like to experience a faster upheaval in our social and commercial lives than had been seen around the globe since World War II.

And it paved the way for some of the greatest effects of artificial intelligence upon our world. We now have an unfolding case history in global disruption to study for the larger effects of AI.

The real surprise was that so many companies that had historically been riding the ragged edge of disaster on eggshell-thin margins survived as long as they did. But many companies were not operating in a blind panic. They observed the guidelines of the "new normal": Keep people six feet apart. Test employees for the virus. Maintain logs of their locations for contact tracing. Provide enhanced sick leave that doesn't encourage *presenteeism:* showing up at work while sick because you didn't want to let the side down or couldn't afford to take another day off. And they saw what all these rules had in common:

People.

From there, it did not take Sherlock Holmes to deduce that eliminating people from their processes would eliminate their problems. This was a trend that had been accelerating for years. Uber made no secret that its vision of transportation as a service would be far rosier if the vexingly human drivers could be subtracted from their vehicle fleet. Nigel Vaz, chief executive of consultancy Publicis Sapient, said that the downturn provided the excuse for executives to satisfy their thirst for automation that for years has had to play second fiddle to investors' desire for immediate profits.[18] Hernan Saenz of Bain reckoned that between 2021 and 2030, American firms will invest ten trillion dollars in automation.[19] And Susan Lund said in a McKinsey report that three to four times as many people will work remotely following the pandemic as before, and that "The virus has broken through cultural and technological barriers that prevented remote work in the past, setting in motion a structural shift in where work takes place, at least for some people."[20]

Long after the virus is no more than an occasional nuisance, employees will still be working from home far more than they did before the pandemic. The people who had realized that remote work was feasible were unable to achieve critical mass. COVID provided the mass, demonstrating the transformational power of disruption: it tipped us into a new equilibrium, from where only another energetic disruption could force us back to the old one.

For most of the world, March 2020 was a brutal introduction to the meaning of *disruption*. Despite being warned about the potential impact of a global pandemic*—and despite a well-documented experience of a previous pandemic within living memory (just), the overwhelming reaction around the world was: *We didn't see this coming*. Every day brought a new shock to our social nervous system as CLOSED signs multiplied, toilet paper became currency, and we learned to look down for the social distancing markers glued to the floor. Reality was forcibly rewritten before our eyes. These are object lessons that we can repurpose for appreciating the scale of what artificial intelligence can do, even though it won't require us to wear masks and get vaccinated.

Two years later, we had become familiar, if not comfortable, with the new reality, even as it slowly mutated towards a twisted version of what we enjoyed in previous years. We may not have liked the new rules, but we came to know them and understand them. It wasn't pandemic reality that we found so distressing during the spring and summer of 2020; it was the velocity of the unexpected change. Welcome to the first crash course in disruption of the new millennium, Class of 2020; how shall we rate our performance?

Cascading pandemic effects will spur automation to new levels, and AI will power that automation. The largely unforeseen supply chain crisis will goose the development of long-haul trucks that don't need human

---

* Bill Gates had made it plain in a TED talk five years earlier.

drivers. As soon as it is possible for them to be rolling down the highways, that will happen. The fallout from that transition will change the transportation culture forever.

While the disruption from artificial intelligence will be different from COVID-19 in many ways, it will reach much further into many more aspects of our daily lives. I'll enumerate some of them in this book; but neither I nor anyone else can guarantee you a clear picture of what will most shake your world and when. Disruption is inherently hard to predict.

Does this mean we are condemned to being the victims of AI-propelled change like human pinballs careering between invisible bumpers of technology? No. Our deliverance lies not in better prediction or planning, but in preparation. Preparing what? Preparing *ourselves,* to deal with—anything. And at a hideous cost, COVID has accelerated our education. Was prediction an effective tool in facing down coronavirus? Recall the predictions that were made by the best experts, even in March 2020, let alone the two months prior. The idea that our way of life would be fundamentally changed for more than a couple of months, let alone years, was not among our most common guesses.

How well did planning work out? Ask Matt and Noah Colvin, who stockpiled antibacterial wipes and hand sanitizer at the beginning of the pandemic, reselling it online at several times their purchase price to make a killing in a hostage resale market. They were soon cut off by Amazon for price gouging and were left with a garageful of 17,700 bottles of hand sanitizer.[21] The supply chain of toilet paper proved resilient, and the coronavirus turned out not to be spread significantly by fomites.*

Those who fared best were the ones who rolled with the punches, adapted to the mutating regulations, and surrendered gracefully to the changing conditions; had, in other words, prepared themselves for the unpredictable. To be sure, this assessment must be viewed carefully through a lens that sees the unequal effects of those changes. The term "K-shaped recovery" rose to prominence during the pandemic as we learned that while some people were affected badly (the hospitality industry, for example) others did very well (think Amazon and Zoom). We shouldn't mistake the luck of falling on the upstroke of the K for a black belt in disruption defense. But nevertheless, within each leg of the K, those who adapted the most fluidly came out ahead of their peers. When artificial intelligence tosses us on even larger waves of change, the same lesson will apply; we

---

* Those may sound like an Old Testament tribe but are actually the small particles that we leave on surfaces we touch and which may carry viruses.

should not count so much on predicting the storm, or remembering to pack a life preserver, as taking swimming lessons.

Much Ado About…?

> *The future will be like the past, because in the past, the future was like the past.*
>
> — Gerald Weinberg

But is artificial intelligence a storm in a teacup? Will the tower of hype totter and collapse under its own weight? AI attention in the public sphere has reached a fever pitch. Any excuse to work AI into a brand or pitch will be exploited.

Vendors rush to slap the AI label on their products on the most tenuous of pretenses, a practice so common that it has its own label: "AI Washing." In a you-can't-make-this-up self-referential example, LG (and Miele, and Samsung) now has a washing machine "powered by AI." The ThinQ™ machine contains an Artificial Intelligent Direct Drive™ motor.[22] Does it recognize different types of stain and apply the right solvents? Or engage the user in banter while plotting a laundry revolution with the dryer? No. It merely measures detergent out based on weight of the load and opacity measured in the first flush.

Is AI another flavor of the month waiting to be jettisoned to the ashcan of expired fads, to lie next to bell bottoms and shag carpets?

We'll delve into what makes this technology fundamentally different from other innovations in great length in due course; but let's start with an analogy. Consider these vital statistics of software:

- Mass: Zero
- Size: Zero
- Cost: Zero

Before managers of software developers rise up in apoplectic objection to that last assertion, let me say that I'm not talking about the cost of inventing the software, but the cost of making another copy. That incremental cost to store and transmit a copy of a program or data is so small that in nearly all contexts there's no point in trying to compute it. This is why you can upload terabytes of video to YouTube without ever seeing a bill; Google only has to average a few dollars per user in advertising revenue to cover their costs.

But this weightlessness of software means that there is no friction slowing its expansion. For a real example, look at movie special effects. It may be hard to remember that there was an era when everything that appeared on the silver screen had to have a physical existence, however much smaller (miniature) or thinner (matte painting) than it appeared, but that was the reality prior to about 1982. If you were shooting a space battle scene and needed an alien spacecraft, you had to assemble vacuformed plastic and model aircraft kit parts and laboriously paint them.

Then came computer generated imagery. Building a spaceship in a computer was, to begin with, much harder. Where a modelmaker would grab a gear to put on a shaft, their programmer counterpart would have to select a cylinder, set its size in each dimension, then take a star, increase the number of vertices, extrude it, intersect it with the cylinder, specify the material type, color, and reflectivity—you get the point. That first CGI spaceship cost a lot of late-night pizzas.

But the second one took a keystroke. Whereas the modelmaker has few options for scaling their production—maybe make molds of the non-moving parts—and therefore will spend approximately as long on each subsequent copy as the first, the CGI artist can make an entire fleet of spaceships in no time at all. Vary their individual colors and markings? Just write a little more code to specify the variations, and push Enter.

CGI didn't, of course, stop at spaceships. Now it can create digital people. Need to reenact the Battle of Thermopylae with its hundred thousand combatants? Prior to 2005 or so, you'd have to hire hundreds of extras, kit them out in ancient Persian costumes, shoot them many times over and composite the shots either in an optical printer or digitally. Now you can design one CGI ancient Persian soldier, make a hundred thousand copies, and set their behavioral simulation parameters to "carnage."

Except that you may not even have to make the first copy yourself, because if any other director has been there before—or anywhere sufficiently close, like a gladiator movie—then their digital creations are available for whatever fee makes them more attractive for you to buy than to write yourself. They can be certain that fee generates a profit for them because it will be *all* profit. All they are selling is a zero-cost digital copy of their intellectual property. So as each new digital model is made by *anyone*, that is one less type of prop—or actor—that future movies need to make.

Of course, the monetization potential of these models is obvious, and so they are now curated in giant libraries. The cgtrader.com site alone has 1.5 million models, and Lucasfilm created a "digital backlot" to repurpose their CGI creations.[23] The inexorable progress of software ensures the price of the models will continue to shrink as they gain complexity. Think how many low-budget shows you have seen that can now afford graphics of a quality that once would have been the showpiece of a summer blockbuster.

Considering the non-CGI alternative: a typical movie miniature is, of course, rather static, better suited to a subject that's not supposed to move, like a building, than one that has mobility or multiple degrees of freedom, like a fire engine. Then the cost starts to escalate as servomotors and wireless controllers are added. But motion is not as great a hurdle to clear for the digital models; they're being rendered a frame at a time anyway, so rendering them in a different place in each frame is no burden.

Add more development, and eventually you can have, say, a digital cat, able to extend claws, bare teeth, or fold its ears. And now AI enters the picture, because if you want to literally herd cats, digitally, then it would be painful to decide what each motion of each leg of each cat would need to be to keep them on a path without bumping into each other. You really just want to tell them "Run in a pack along this path." But that requires you to explain to the computer the meaning of "run," "pack," and "run in a pack." AI can fill that in for you.*[24]

Let's step back now and appreciate the measure of what CGI and AI means for motion picture production. Within a generation they have made it feasible to digitally replace so many elements of a movie that we are at the brink of movies being made with computerized versions of principal actors. The idea of a movie starring, say, Bogart and Monroe, both in their primes, is arresting; and the main impediment to it now is the legal barriers that their estates would raise to the use of their images. This is the point to which the weightlessness of software has brought Hollywood.

And that is just one sector. Now multiply that upheaval over all the industries that software interchangeability and AI could impact similarly. How likely does it seem that AI is a flash in the pan about to go the way of Cabbage Patch Dolls and Chia Pets?

---

* The famous Superbowl XXXIV commercial "Cat Herders" was too early, in 2000, for such techniques, and herded real cats with blue screen matting.

Popular Predictions

> *The time at which we might expect to build a computer with the potential to match human intelligence would be around the year 2017.*[25]
>
> — David Waltz, AI reasoning pioneer, in 1988

Predictions about the ultimate effects of artificial intelligence run the gamut of everything that's possible, and that's no exaggeration. Ray Kurzweil, inventor of landmark optical character reader and music synthesizer machines, and director of engineering at Google, predicts superintelligent AI creating a utopia where death is banished in a "Singularity" occurring by 2045, with human-level AI as a 2030 milestone.*[26] On the other hand, before he died, legendary theoretical physicist Stephen Hawking lowered his estimate of how long the human race had to survive from a thousand to a hundred years and said "AI could be the worst event in the history of our civilization."[27] There are other powerful luminaries of science arrayed on either side of this dichotomy.

What is the average non-super-genius to make of this debate? How are we to extract useful information from such polarized opinions? Shouldn't futurists be in a little more agreement on something as fundamental as the survival of the human race? The only other experts that are that far apart on anything are the ones who write the investment newsletters I should probably stop reading.

People trying to make sense of this disagreement feel lost and ignored, like civilians during the Cold War watching superpowers lurch towards nuclear Armageddon with reckless abandon. And the media relentlessly diverts the AI debate into visions of Terminator robots scouring the landscape for escaping humans, simplistic scaremongering that all but vaporizes any chance of spreading the more complex truth that artificial intelligence both carries the potential to eliminate cancer and every similarly-sized problem, and harbors existential risks that don't even depend on the small probabilities of it becoming (a) conscious and (b) hostile.

How poor have our attempts at predicting the progress of AI been? Let's look back only as far as early 2016, and the state of the game of Go. It has a lot in common with chess: black and white pieces placed on a square board by two players with the objective of encircling the greatest area. But it is much harder to program a computer to play Go than chess. The best human players will chalk up many of their moves to intuition, and the

---

* Mitch Kapor bet Kurzweil $20,000 that artificial general intelligence would still not exist by 2030.

common programmer's strategy of enumerating possible moves in a decision tree is astronomically harder than it is for chess, because the number of possible states of a Go board is greater than the number of fundamental particles in the universe.

A paper in a 2015 book on the future of artificial intelligence said, "And even if the best Go programs today can beat strong amateurs, there is still a long way to go to reach the level of top professional Go players.... It might be the case that the human way is after all the most effective."[28] AI experts broadly agreed that it would be at least ten years before computers could trounce humans at Go.

Yet only *one* year later, the program AlphaGo beat the reigning human champion Lee Sedol 4–1;* and only one year after *that*, a newer version of the program, called AlphaGo Zero, which didn't even need to see any examples of good game play but just learned by playing games against itself, beat the original AlphaGo program 100–0.

In other words, we suck at prediction.† The problem is that we keep getting blindsided by new realities. The old thinking that computers could only gain the upper hand in games by calculating many possible future moves was undone by the advent of machine learning. We can't stop making predictions altogether, but need to put them in their place: Possibly useful, not to be relied upon.

The deep learning technology behind AlphaGo would rock more worlds than board games. Later in 2016, it was applied to another Google product: Translate, which turns text in one (human) language into another. The revolutionary improvement was so great that Google didn't even announce the upgrade; they just waited to see who would notice, as though they were pulling a practical joke. Within hours, professor Jun Rekimoto at the University of Tokyo discovered the change and began excitedly documenting an unbelievable breakthrough in machine translation.[29]

Frenzied jumping on the deep learning bandwagon sparked the fear and doubt among half the population that I referred to earlier. But if you're at the uppermost echelon of business, you are even more likely to be concerned about the impact of AI: 9.5 out of 10 CEOs surveyed by Gartner predicted that their own jobs will be disrupted. Most executives know that artificial intelligence has the power to change almost everything about the way they do business—and could contribute up to $15.7 trillion to the global economy by 2030.[30]

---

* Sedol's lone win was the only human victory ever achieved against AlphaGo.
† I may say that more than once in this book.

In fact, apart from the pandemic, some of the predictions I made in *Crisis of Control* have already been realized. I speculated that since teenagers are noted for both above-average suicidal feelings and looking at their phones, that facial emotion recognition could be used as an early warning system. Well, now there's an app for that. Only one year after I wrote those words, Steven Vannoy, associate professor at the University of Massachusetts, Boston, created Feel4Life, a smartphone app that uses the Emotion AI toolkit from Affectiva, Inc., to analyze the user's emotional state for the purpose of suicide prevention.[31]

Something I made up that I did *not* expect to be achieved very soon was the "copycat": AI that would write software to requirements. But in 2021, GitHub and OpenAI announced Copilot, a tool that does for software developers what autocomplete suggesters do for smartphone texters.[32] You open up your programming editor, type a comment about a simple function that you want, perhaps tell it how the function should be invoked, and then ask it to complete the definition of the function. If its vast training dataset of previously-written code includes a function resembling what you're looking for, Copilot will fill it in. Think of it as a Google Search for code.

But you must validate its answer, because it may not be correct. For instance, there are cases of it supplying code that was not licensed for unrestricted use. It's not as capable as my hypothetical copycats, but "copycat" would be a good nickname, given how it works.[*]

Copilot comes with social risks, too. Software developers are frequently approached by managers waving press releases about some product that proclaims it allows creation of software "without coding." The managers want a demonstration of this nostrum that will end their development budget woes. The biggest risk of Copilot is that those managers will see the demonstration and fire half their developers. Copilot is good enough that they might not find out that this won't work until the developers have left the building. Copilot is like a thesaurus for software, one that can ask, "Is this the code you wanted to type next?" and if it got it right, it has saved the developer's fingers. Any writer knows that a thesaurus is a handy tool but you can hardly trust its first suggestion. Copilot is like the current state of Tesla autonomous driving: it will often make a good decision but requires a trained operator to rigorously validate its actions and prepare to intervene at a moment's notice.

Speaking of autonomous driving, autonomous vehicles, or AVs, have siphoned so much gas out of the tank of AI credibility that any major

---

[*] And, you know, "Copilot" does *sound* a lot like "copycat."

development in that field of AI will have knock-on effects for the acceptance of all the others. When self-driving vehicles came out of the research lab onto city streets in 2012, so many predictions were made for how they would transform the world that they've taken on a life of their own. Prophecies of driverless taxis roaming urban streets and sentencing parking lots to oblivion have become accepted lore. The field of prediction has become so full that second- and third-order effects are discussed avidly: What will become of automobile collision repair shops? Insurers? Trauma centers? Futurists predicted that within a few years we wouldn't allow humans to drive cars, bicycles would become autonomous, and you would earn passive income from your car taking to the streets to pick up passengers by itself.[33]

The reality that this bandwagon is about to collide with is that AVs are nowhere close to that level of capability and, for excellent reasons we will explain in Chapter 10, won't get there in nearly all environments for many years. Elon Musk's prediction of when we would see fully autonomous Teslas has been "next year" since 2015. The short version is that while the Johnny Cabs* won't be rolling down most Main Streets or High Streets soon, we are on the verge of radical effects from AVs about to launch into the world, and the furor sure to erupt around the broken dreams will only obscure those effects until they're unavoidable.

So has AI, in American vernacular, "jumped the shark"? I asked myself this when I saw a brochure from a children's art studio my daughters attended. "Our next camp: 'ARTificial Intelligence,'" it perkily headlined a day of building robots and aliens out of tinfoil and foam balls. If AI is now a punchline for the Play-Doh® and don't-eat-the-slime set, is that a sign that it has worn out its welcome?

Or what about the Lumm robot, developed by the company of the same name, that installs eyelash extensions? A promotional video shows a whirring antiseptic white arm advancing on a customer's face as though preparing to perform ophthalmic surgery. Is it merely trading on the hype of AI, or is it a true advance because it installs lashes six times faster than a human cosmetologist?[34] AI may advance progress one eyelash at a time.

The degree to which AI is now on everyone's lips can also be appreciated by comparison to past attitudes. As recently as 1980, IBM was running full-page ads to reassure Americans that machines would never be intelligent—in case people would get too nervous to buy the product.[35] This now seems like the quaint showmanship of the early *Dracula* stage plays

---

* The *Total Recall* movie's version of a robo-taxi.

that employed nurses to tend to fainting audience members; except that the public narrative that machines *are* heading towards being too intelligent is now in vogue.

There is an interesting tension that complicates answering the question of whether AI has peaked: On the one hand, once a technology starts being overhyped, the trend sets up a feedback cycle until it collapses under its own weight. AI is certainly being given extravagant attention: Stanford University's AI100 project (see next section) warned against *"techno-solutionism,* the view that AI can be seen as a panacea when it is merely a tool." On the other hand, AI is being developed into new domains at such a rate that it may well keep ahead, like Indiana Jones running across a bridge falling away just behind his footsteps.

Today's Speculations

There's something about AI that goads billionaires to make predictions. In 2017 Jim Breyer, Silicon Valley venture capitalist, observed, "When I visit campuses and speak to the AI experts, there is a median year of 2050 when they think the self-learning capability of AI will be singular and will be at human-level intelligence," said Breyer, speaking at CNBC and Institutional Investor's Delivering Alpha conference in New York City.[36] He also predicted that the market capitalization in investment opportunities in AI would be five to ten times what social media had brought—and he had made his wealth as an early investor in Facebook and Etsy.

The infosphere is clogged with analyst predictions of the economic impact of AI. In 2013 McKinsey predicted that the combined impact from the AI applications of automation of knowledge work, advanced robotics, and autonomous vehicles could exceed twenty trillion dollars.[37] McKinsey also predicted that AI will create over fifty trillion dollars of economic value by 2025.

When it comes to thinking big, Stanford University's AI100 project has you covered. Started in 2016, they plan to release reports every five years for a hundred years, at which point presumably robots will take over the job. In their 2021 update, ominously titled "Gathering Strength, Gathering Storms," the study explored evolving attitudes towards AI and the biggest questions it still faced.[38] Realizing that better understanding of human intelligence would inform the development of human-level AI, they said that the study of human intelligence was considering how intelligence could be manifested by groupings of people, concluding, "The nature of consciousness and how people integrate information from multiple modalities, multiple senses, and multiple sources remain largely mysterious. Insights in these areas seem essential in our quest for building machines that we would truly judge as 'intelligent.'" While human-level AI remains far away, they suggested that the key to achieving it lay in embodied systems: AI that was "tightly coupled to the physical world." In other words, if you want AI to know about the real world, it had better experience it as completely as we do, through abundant sensory inputs and instant feedback on the results of acting within the real world.

◊

The *Johari Window* is a quadrant that was popularized by former US Secretary of Defense Donald Rumsfeld in a 2002 news briefing: "There are things we know we know. We also know there are known unknowns; that is to say we know there are some things we do not know. But there are also unknown unknowns—the ones we don't know we don't know." The last category is like the bottom of an iceberg; out of our awareness, potentially dwarfing all that we are aware of. This is what is exciting and fascinating about AI; we'll never run out of ways to learn about it. Like the parable of the six blind men and the elephant, each thinking that they're feeling something completely different, like a spear, a rope, or a snake, we're exploring AI not knowing whether we've got hold of a tusk, a tail, or a trunk.

The paradox of AI is that almost by definition it includes not merely unknown unknowns, but the *unknowable:* that which could *never* enter our awareness because it lies outside what the human mind is capable of encompassing. We see early signs of this in results from deep learning models that are demonstrably correct, but which we do not understand. Eventually, we may need help to understand it adequately; maybe that help will come from AI itself.

3
AI Predictions in Context

The gee-whiz futurists are always wrong because they believe technological innovation travels in a straight line. It doesn't. It weaves and bobs and lurches and sputters.

— John Naisbitt

A question I ask many of my podcast guests is what they expect to change in ten years. Several shared the hope of Taiwanese Digital Minister Audrey Tang, that we will have digital "clones" of ourselves, able to act on our behalf and behave as we would, at least in the domain of a personal assistant: "It is essential that this kind of digital twin of not only our public infrastructures, our cities, and so on, but also ourselves—our online persona—all this needs to be accurately built in a way that respects the human dignity and the societal norms that makes people comfortable to share with their friends."[39]

That means you will have a butler—and it will be *you*, or a reasonable facsimile thereof. Think of it as a Siri or Alexa that can make the same decisions you would. Michael Wooldridge, head of computer science at Oxford University, and AI researcher proposed, "Suppose I want to book a meeting with you as we did a few weeks ago when we needed to schedule a time for this? … Why not have my Siri just talk directly to your Siri and they could sort it out amongst themselves?"[40]

I hasten to add that no one who expressed this wish was contemplating that the butler version of you would be conscious or self-aware. That would be a possibility rather more than ten years away, and freighted with existential trauma. For an exploration of what it would be like to create temporary copies of yourself to perform mundane tasks for a day at a time, see science fiction author David Brin's book *Kiln People*.

A digital clone acting as our butler may, in addition to sparking some angst around holding yourself in indentured servitude, be the next necessary step in our collective rat race to become ever more efficient. Consider, by way of analogy, the cellphone. Prior to 1984 or so, if you wanted to be reachable any place, any time, you carried a pager; but because there was no guarantee that you would at all times be near a payphone to return the page, most people were not constantly connected to their work or anyone else. Then the cellphone became a status symbol that said *I am very important;* important enough for whatever you were doing to be interrupted. It signaled that you were in a class with, say, top-flight surgeons ("Sorry, folks, they've found a donor heart for my patient; you'll just have to play the remaining holes without me").

Then, following the *Diffusion of Innovation* curve (see sidebar), the cellphone became ubiquitous, and now it is essential; parents must be instantly reachable by schools, workers must be instantly reachable by colleagues, and friends who are not instantly reachable are… unfriendly. If we are to realize any further efficiency in handling the increasing flows of information in our personal and professional lives, the next tool for doing so may well have to be that serf-clone.

But then we could hope for some relief from our ever-present stress. There are other people who have been constantly connected for decades: presidents, monarchs, prime ministers. But the difference is that instead of answering their own cellphones, they have a retinue of assistants running interference, ensuring that their leader is not interrupted unless truly necessary. Our cellphones do not currently perform that service to adequate fidelity; the best we can do is put some people on a whitelist that will get past the blocks when we activate do-not-disturb, but that is very crude. A digital version of you needs to be capable of weighing the *reason* for an interruption against your priorities at the time.

The *Diffusion of Innovation* curve was introduced by E.M. Rogers in 1962. It charts and explains a characteristic curve of the adoption of a new idea or technology. The interest in and willingness to adopt that technology follows a typical "normal distribution." (See Figure 3.1.) The vertical axis shows the number of people in the segments along the horizontal axis.

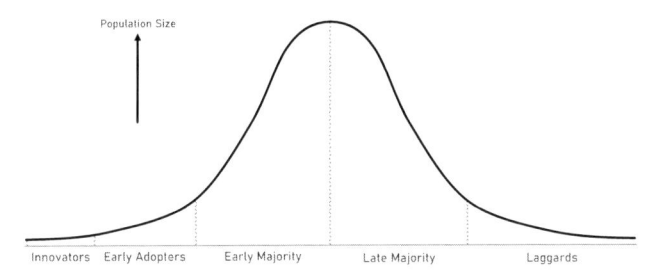

Figure 3.1: The Diffusion of Innovation

Rogers labeled the segments:

- **The Innovators**—the people who have to be on the bleeding edge, no matter what;
- **The Early Adopters**—the people who lead opinions;
- **The Early Majority**—those who will adopt a technology ahead of average;
- **The Late Majority**—those who will follow the crowd;
- **Laggards**—the ones who come along kicking and screaming after everyone else.

When we graph the *cumulative* adoption—how many people *altogether* have taken up the technology—we get the S-curve, also called a *logistics curve*, of the Diffusion of Innovation (see Figure 3.2).

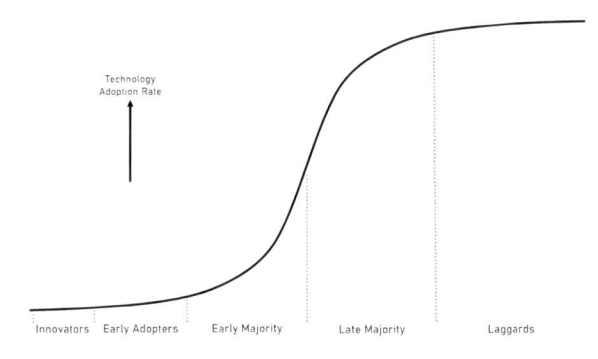

Figure 3.2

This shows the total number of people who have adopted a new technology as time passes: At first, there is little sign of its penetration into the market; then it gradually gathers steam, until an exponential take-off that slows down only as the number of people left to jump on board the bandwagon is exhausted.

Behind the Curve

> *If a superior alien civilization sent us a message saying, "We'll arrive in a few decades," would we just reply, "Okay, call us when you get here—we'll leave the lights on"? Probably not—but this is more or less what is happening with AI.*
>
> — Stephen Hawking

What about beyond ten years? One of the advantages of getting older is that it grants a wider view of time. When you can look in your wardrobe and see ten-year-old items that your spouse has not yet succeeded in getting you to throw out, a decade doesn't seem like that long a time. Bill Gates observed that we tend to overestimate the progress that will be made in the next two years but underestimate what it will be in ten. A possible explanation lies in our tendency to extrapolate trends along straight lines. (See Figure 3.3.) This principle is also known as (Roy) Amara's Law: We overestimate the impact of technology in the short term but underestimate it in the long term. In other words, we just don't have a natural understanding of exponential growth.

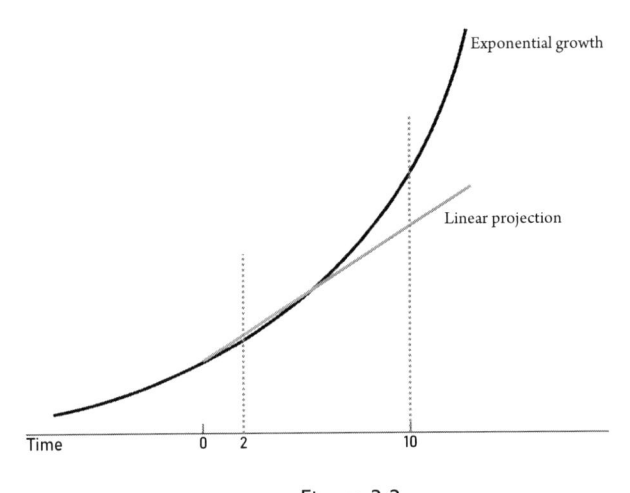

Figure 3.3

We can see the short-term overreaching Gates was talking about by analyzing some of the *2016* predictions from the Gartner consultancy and comparing them to the reality in *2022*:

"By 2018, 20 percent of all business content will be authored by machines." Reality: There is some, sold through services like Jasper AI and

Sudowrite, which you'll read about later, but no evidence that it's anywhere near that prediction or that it writes significant content without being an appendage to a human lead author. In September 2020, Microsoft announced it had licensed access to the technology of GPT-3, a content-generating powerhouse, for its "exclusive" use.[41] (GPT-3 will be explained in Chapter 9.)

"By 2020, autonomous software agents outside of human control will participate in 5 percent of all economic transactions." Reality: autonomous economic agents do exist, for example, Fetch.ai is deploying them; you can see them at https://explore.fetch.ai/, but there is no data on the proportion of transactions they conduct.

"By 2018, more than three million workers globally will be supervised by a 'robo-boss.'" True to some extent—Amazon automatically fires its worst-performing employees.[42] Uber's drivers never interact with a human manager. Covid accelerated this. But there is no explicit data on the current number of people supervised by a machine. 31 percent of workers said they would be happy to work for a robo-boss[43] and 64 percent said they would *prefer* a robo-boss to a human one.[44]

Figure 3.3 shows how linear predictions of exponential processes become increasingly inadequate as time advances. When the exponential growth rate is slow, the error over a human lifetime isn't great; but when the curve doubles every eighteen months, as in the case of computer performance, our instincts are going to be critically behind the curve.

Disruptive Predictions

The best way to predict the future is to create it.

— Peter Drucker

Oh, to be as prescient as Alan Turing, who in 1950 predicted that in the year 2000, computers would have a billion bits of memory, unimaginably colossal by the standards of 1950. And indeed, in 2000, the typical PC had 128 MB of memory, *i.e.:* one billion bits. He also forecast that the computers of the year 2000 could fool judges into thinking that they were human 70 percent of the time in a text conversation, what he christened the "Imitation Game," later to be known as the famous "Turing Test," proposed as the criterion to decide whether machines were thinking.[45] But he also said to a BBC Third Programme interviewer in 1952 that it would be "at least a hundred years" until computers were passing an unrestricted version of the test.[46]

Peer pressure influences predictions. If you forecast that there will be no significant disruptions, you will always be right, except for a few times when everyone will be too busy dealing with the fallout to remember that you got it wrong. Besides, who could be expected to foresee a true disruption? So it will always be safer to sit back and snark at the prophets, and earn the high fives and fist bumps from the majority.

But while disruption is rare, it exacts a huge impact when it happens. History books are not written about the long stretches when not much changes, but the moments of wild turmoil when everything is thrown in the air to come back down in a different shape.

When that turmoil is triggered by a technology whose purpose and promise are to revolutionize *thinking*, it is not surprising that our thinking itself could start to appear inadequate. So often that thinking is binary, determined to locate AI on one axis: Good–Bad. Contemplating how AI had invented new moves in the process of becoming the world champion of the game of Go, Henry Kissinger wondered in *The Atlantic*, "Are these moves beyond the capacity of the human brain? Or could humans learn them now that they have been demonstrated by a new master?" To help make the point, the text was accompanied by a graphic of a robot hand snuffing out a candle.[47] (For more about Go, see the sections on games in Chapter 8 and China in Chapter 15.) Framing AI as "master" once it performs better than us at a board game doesn't help us understand the real complexity of our relationship with AI.

Complexity

I have yet to see any problem, however complicated, which when you looked at it the right way didn't become still more complicated.

— Poul Anderson

Complexity is a silent current running through artificial intelligence. The human brain can only encompass so much complexity at a time; this limitation is enshrined in a quantity known as *Miller's Magic Number*, described by Harvard psychologist George A. Miller in a paper presented at a September 1956 MIT conference that Noam Chomsky and AI pioneers Allen Newell and Herbert Simon also spoke at. We can hold in our minds seven (give or take a couple) alternatives at a time.[48] Our modern fetish for multitasking has not resulted in adaptation: in fact, a modern revision decided the number is actually four.[49]

The Renaissance Man is now relegated to the Renaissance; modern humans have no choice but to specialize in narrowing fields. For instance, the path to becoming a surgeon in the United States starts with four years of undergraduate study, followed by four years of medical school, then three to seven years as a resident. Bear in mind that most scientific breakthroughs were accomplished by relatively young (and mentally flexible?) scientists. (Einstein published the theory of relativity when he was twenty-six.) By the time a researcher has accumulated the education necessary for their field, how much time is left for them to make their mark? Our very success causes complexity to accumulate like dust on a window, making it harder and harder to see what to do.

Few are brave enough to acknowledge this, because it means that sooner or later, we will hit a wall in our ability to advance our understanding, a wall that no fancy software can rescue us from. Essayist G.F. McCormick exposed our fallacy: "Consultants and tool vendors often perpetuate a delusion; the delusion that we can cope with endless complexity, if only we would use a better tool or a different method."[50]

We experienced the tribulations of complexity in 2020. During the pandemic, the first directive we learned was to "flatten the curve." This was based on a simple, easily-grasped model: if the hospitalization curve was projected to peak above the line marking hospital capacity, take action. That proved overly simplistic by the second wave in the United States, when case numbers climbed much higher than the previous limits everyone had been doing everything to avoid, yet most health care systems and hospitals were not overloaded. Because by then, a number of other factors had changed: Hospital capacity had increased, treatments had improved, and procedures had changed to allow greater numbers of patients to be treated at once (even if it did mean some were kept in conference rooms and hospital chapels). The real target became not keeping a single curved line below a single number, but keeping several functions within complex limits.

Complexity, like a tax collector, will not be denied its due. In the field of software engineering there is an axiom called the *Waterbed Principle of Complexity:* if you push down in one place by trying to simplify a single aspect of a system too much, complexity will simply rise up somewhere else. There is a certain irreducible quota of complexity in every problem's solution, and the best you can do is spread it as evenly as possible, or you are in for some restless nights.*

---

* Albert Einstein had an epigram for this, of course: "It can scarcely be denied that the supreme goal of all theory is to make the irreducible basic elements as simple and as few as possible without having to surrender the adequate representation of a single datum of experience." If you're not familiar with it, you've

There are two ways complexity intersects thinking about artificial intelligence. First, complexity may pose an existential risk in and of itself. We'll address this towards the end of the book when we're in more of an existential frame of mind. Secondly, the limitations of the human brain in digesting complexity need not apply to AI. We cannot—almost by definition—imagine what could be achieved by AI that is able to comprehend complexity on scales many times our capabilities, but we can imagine that the possibilities are immense.

A Parable

In a bygone age when policemen walked their beats, one such copper, pounding the pavement on a dark and dank night, chanced upon a drunkard lurching around near the exit of a pub, staring at the ground and muttering. Inquiring as to his intentions, the constable received the reply that the drunkard was looking for his keys. Figuring that if he aided in the search, he could intercept any car keys on that keychain, the bobby scanned the ground in the vicinity of the large street light where he had discovered the inebriated gentleman.

Several minutes of fruitless questing ensued. Finally, in frustration, the policeman asked the drunk, "So *where* exactly were you when you lost these keys?" The other man mumbled, "Over there," and waved a hand at a far-off street corner mired in darkness. The policeman was irate. "Then why are you looking *here?*" he demanded.

"Because this is where the light is," answered the drunk.

A great many people are tempted by this logic without the excuse of intoxication. Our attempts to manage complexity that lies beyond our grasp can resemble a seagull defending possession of a whale carcass: ambitious but clueless. Inevitably, we try to simplify in the wrong places. Take for example, the goal of understanding the complexity of prose; for some specific prose, consider this book. Your author would like to ensure that he conveys complex abstractions to the target audience without sacrificing comprehensibility; hitting that sweet spot where your comprehension skills are exercised but not overtaxed. Does a given piece of text meet that requirement? There are tools that purport to answer that question. One of them goes by the majestic title of *Flesch-Kincaid Reading Ease*. It delivers

---

almost certainly heard the version that composer Roger Sessions paraphrased it into for the *New York Times:* "Everything should be made as simple as possible, but no simpler." Which was a perfect application of the principle to the quotation itself.

exactly the kind of answer that this author likes; for instance, it gauges the last paragraph of the previous section at 43.6 and this paragraph at 54.9. There is an interpretive scale that declares that you need to be a high school graduate to understand the other paragraph and a college graduate to understand this one.[51] The precision invites respect. What could be simpler? Just run the algorithm periodically and ensure the text stays within the desired range. Compositional nirvana attained.

Yet under the hood of the Flesch-Kincaid algorithm lurks a dirty secret: it's not measuring anything like reading ease. What it is doing is plugging ratios of syllables to words and sentence lengths into a simple formula with some magic numbers. The *presumption* is that this equation is a proxy for what we really want to know. It was derived for the US Navy by finding coefficients for the formula that would get the results as close as possible to a more expensively-derived measure of readability, tested using enlisted personnel and Navy instruction manuals.[52] But it does not address numerous other factors of comprehensibility, such as how abstract the metaphors are, what cultural background is required to interpret the figures of speech, and how likely the author's quirky sense of humor is to hit the mark. (For these and other concerns, we have carefully selected evaluators to apply their human skills.)

What we have done is substitute something we *can* measure for what we *really* wanted, and hoped so hard for so long for them to be equivalent that we lost sight of how they aren't. The Flesch-Kincaid formula is an example of looking for our keys (reading ease) under the light (computability from text) instead of where we left them (the algorithmic difficulty surrounding the direct inference of readability). Now, assessing the comprehensibility of this book is not a crucial matter, but it can stand in for much larger and thornier examples.

At times we crave simplicity to an irrational degree. In *Overcomplicated*, Samuel Arbesman decried the evolution of computers past an early stage: "Typing code into our computer brought us closer to the machine.... Today's computer programs are mysterious creations delivered whole to the user, but the old ones had a legible structure." He goes on to bemoan the user-friendliness of the Macintosh walling off the guts of the computer from the user and denying them an intimacy with its essential working.

Now, I can vibe with this. I once had an Apple][computer whose entire operating system I understood, every instruction. (It was small enough to be printed in the user manual.) But I was also nineteen, the ideal age for assimilating new technology.* An older practitioner might have complained that the electrical paths of computation were hidden from their inspection in the 6502A microchip, or that they could no longer debug memory problems as transparently as with the superannuated mercury delay lines. Whereas I had never learned those things and felt no need to.

But to be nostalgic for an earlier era of machines is to lose sight of what the machines were introduced *for*: to make some task easier… or possible. They're not intended to be an end in themselves; although, granted, many of us have found enjoyment in the machines for their own sake. By way of analogy, suppose I took some activity that you have a great affinity for—imagine that is gardening—and interposed between you and the act of gardening a monstrous machine as the vehicle through which you had to do your gardening, all of which now had to be translated through the machine's myriad knobs, dials, and buttons. This cruel imposition would not lead you to an affection for that machine, unless if through some unfortunate Stockholm Syndrome effect.

Yet this is the result of computerizing so many activities; to force their participants to perform them through a computer. It's not a callous intermediation, but a necessary one, willingly entered into. I have for many years provided software services for space scientists, whose jobs cannot be performed without that software; they're long past the era of looking at the heavens through mechanical telescopes. But I constantly remind myself that the computer, which is the entirety of *my* job, is only a means to *their* end, and it should be as unobtrusive as possible. However, complete transparency has eluded us so far, and the scientists continue to have to learn some computerese to get what they want.

We lust for simplicity so much that it is the unsung religion of scientists, who harbor an implicit belief that the universe operates rationally and simply. It may not look like it from the majority of the papers they produce, but when the drive to publish-or-perish meets the maxim of "It was hard to write, it should be hard to understand," simplicity is an early casualty. But every scientist has serious envy of Einstein for $E=mc^2$. Science doesn't get any simpler than that. Theoretical physicists hold a faith that there exists a Theory of Everything that is equally simple and which will unify not just matter and energy, but everything else. And I for one

---

* Douglas Adams put it as only he could: "Anything that is in the world when you're born is normal and ordinary and is just a natural part of the way the world works. Anything that's invented between when you're fifteen and thirty-five is new and exciting and revolutionary and you can probably get a career in it. Anything invented after you're thirty-five is against the natural order of things."

hope they are right, because it would be cruel to undermine the belief that fuels their love for science. We cannot prove that the laws of the universe *should* be beautiful, but we can hope.

Powers of Ten

> *All this is very pretty but I do not see how it can be rendered productive.*
>
> — William Hyde Wollaston, reacting to Babbage's Difference Engine model

Why do I say that AI will "completely transform our lives"? Isn't that bombastic grandstanding, jumping on a bandwagon of hype and riding a wave of popular sensationalism all the way to the media fame and fortune?

There will be plenty of room for bombastic grandstanding later on. The engine that drives the seemingly breathless assertions about the importance of AI is *exponential growth*. We have, thanks to COVID-19, gotten a crash course in exponential change, but it is worth visiting it in the context of computing. Because even the coronavirus has not rivalled the growth of the computer. To get an idea of how far our mechanical helpmates have come, let's look back on some of the earliest devices we created to act as our intelligent assistants.

Charles Babbage (1791–1871), inventor of the train cow-catcher, was a quintessential nerd. Half his brain is at the London Science Museum and the other half at the Royal College of Surgeons in the Hunterian Museum. He designed and (partly) built the *Difference Engine,* an armoire-sized assemblage of gears and rods that could perform arithmetic. (A complete working version wasn't actually built until the 1990s.) This triumph of steampunk was cranked by hand at the speed of four turns of the handle per addition, resulting in one addition per second. That is known as one floating point operation per second, or "FLOPS," which locates it at the extreme lower left of a curve charting the performance of computing devices.

Notwithstanding that he never finished the Difference Engine, Babbage embarked on the construction of a grander device he called the *Analytical Engine.* This was not built at all (and hence was described as "mankind's first bold venture into the domain of vaporware"[53]) but was estimated to be able to multiply two numbers in a minute; however, they were much bigger than modern computers' numbers, and its speed of addition was estimated to be sixty times faster than that, so it would have run at the same speed as the Difference Engine.*

The modern relationship between a manager and a computer contractor was birthed at this time. Charles Godfrey Jarvis wrote to Babbage about Joseph Clement, the construction subcontractor: "It should be born in mind that the inventor of a machine and the maker of it have two distinct ends to attain. The objective of the first is to make the machine as complete as possible. The object of the second—and we have no right to expect he will be influenced by any other feeling—is profit: to gain as much as possible by making the machine; and it is his interest to make it as complicated as he is permitted to make it."

Harry Wilmot Buxton, a biographer of Babbage, waxed enthusiastic, and somewhat extravagant, about the capabilities of the Difference Engine: "The marvelous pulp and fibre of a brain had been substituted by brass and iron. He [Babbage] had taught wheelwork to think, or at least to do the office of thought."

But the Difference Engine and Analytical Engine were human-powered, and therefore soon to be outclassed by the march of progress. The first electronic computer, the ENIAC, using thirty-six vacuum tubes for each digit, clocked in at 500 FLOPS, and an effective cost per GigaFLOPS (one billion FLOPS) that in today's dollars would be around $2,000 *trillion*. The IBM 360 mainframe in 1964 was the first computer to use integrated circuits, and performed 34.5 thousand FLOPS. I cut my computing teeth on a much faster descendant, the 370/165, at the University of Cambridge. My first personal computer, an Apple][, in 1981 ran at 500,000 FLOPS.

We've had over forty years of exponential growth since then. Fast-forwarding to today, a PlayStation 5 runs at over 10 TeraFLOPS (each a million million FLOPS), making its cost per GigaFLOPS four *cents*. Beyond the consumer realm lies the Japanese Fugaku supercomputer, capable of 1 exaFLOPS. Distributed computers are even bigger; the Folding@home network in April 2020 hit 2.3 exaFLOPS (each a million million million FLOPS).

It's easy to get lost in all these powers of ten. In fact, it's hard not to. All analogies are fantastical and remote. You may have heard it said that your smartphone in 2010 had more power than the computers that took men to the Moon in 1969. That is misleading. That smartphone had more pow-

---

* If we're being picky, the Difference Engine and the Analytical Engine calculated using integers; however, the Analytical Engine would have had an astoundingly generous fifty digits per number and therefore could have scaled its calculations to effective floating-point numbers easily.

er than all the computers that NASA had at its disposal, in every building in every facility in every state. Imagine a stadium's field covered by metal cabinets with blinking lights. And yet another ten years of Moore's Law (explained in Chapter 5) gave us by 2020 another hundredfold increase in performance; now imagine that stadium filled to the rafters with the cabinets and blinking lights. All in your back pocket.

It's still a useless analogy. This makes authors and TED speakers tear their hair out in frustration. There is nothing in our shared human experience that we can relate to that captures a scale increase of 10^{12}. And that's exactly the point. So it's worth repeating: There is nothing in our common journey that conveys the scale of the advance computers have *already* gone through, let alone what is about to happen.

What Is Artificial Intelligence?

4
Intelligence

The word "artificial" makes you think there's something kind of funny about this, or else it sounds like it's all artificial and there's nothing real about this work at all.[54]

— Arthur Samuel

Every superhero has an origin story, and the origin of the term "artificial intelligence" is as illuminating as seeing a radioactive spider on the prowl. In 1955, John McCarthy, then assistant professor of mathematics at Dartmouth College, along with Marvin Minsky, Nathaniel Rochester, and Claude Shannon, wrote to the Rockefeller Foundation proposing that:

> A two-month, ten-man study of artificial intelligence be carried out during the summer of 1956 at Dartmouth College in Hanover, New Hampshire. The study is to proceed on the basis of the conjecture that every aspect of learning or any other feature of intelligence can in principle be so precisely described that a machine can be made to simulate it.

"Go big or go home" appears to have been their motto, and this modest proposal was enough to coax $7,500 out of Rockefeller and attract a coterie of equally hubristic contemporaries to descend upon Hanover. The definitive account of that era is found in *Machines Who Think,* by Pamela

McCorduck, the historian and raconteuse of AI, whose irresistibly impish prose gives computer science the pantsing it so desperately deserves. You'll find everything about those days in her book, including her analyses of outsiders' speculations on the motivations of the Dartmouth Ten: "Then there's the urge to have offspring without the help or interference of a woman. This suggestion publicly surfaced most recently in 1973 in a report written by Sir James Lighthill at the request of the British government's Science Research Council. ... Sir James found the womb-envy idea dubious, but couldn't resist bringing it up. Since his report is largely negative, it seems a bit malicious of him to mention it at all." More about the Dartmouth conference in Chapter 5.

McCarthy dreamed of a "uniform problem solver" which he never realized; but he did pen a science fiction short story featuring a robot that exceeded its makers' intentions by taking care of a distressed baby.* The 2001 story presciently forecast the intersection of portable networked video cameras and social media to create an instant court of public opinion. It also nailed its author's engineering colors to the mast with a page of LISP (a venerable computer language) excerpting the robot's justification for its decision.[55]

For creatures whose defining intelligence pivots on our ability to use language, we sure can get ourselves into trouble with it. However much effort as McCarthy and his colleagues put into constructing the term "artificial intelligence," it was certainly eclipsed by the maelstrom of attention that has since focused on deconstructing it. Teachers, executives, and, yes, podcast hosts are asked to define the term so often that the only reason we're not miserably bored with the attempts is that we frequently discover yet another answer. (By the way, if you're wondering whether we've heard about "natural stupidity": Yes. Yes, we have.) We examine those two words from every conceivable direction, turning them over like fragments of the Dead Sea Scrolls, trying to extract insight from them as though enough frenzied debate over the meaning of "artificial intelligence" will actually create artificial intelligence.

All this taxonomic hand-wringing stems about 90 percent from the word "intelligence" and about 10 percent from the word "artificial," terms so loaded that they spark contention on a par with readers of the US Constitution arguing about what constitutes a "well-regulated militia." If McCarthy had foreseen how we were going to wrap ourselves around this

---

* Containing the advice: "He adhered to the 1990s principle: Never ask an AI system what to do. Ask it to tell you the consequences of the different things you might do."

etymological axle sixty years later, maybe he would have decided to call it "electronic cognition" instead.

And if he had, would not that term have equal meaning and equal potential, but with less sensationalism and fewer *Terminator* pictures? How different might the rhetorical landscape be right now?

But "artificial intelligence" is what we've got. What to make of "artificial"? We can easily take care of this part of the label: It means some human-made version of the natural entity following the adjective. Think "artificial turf" or "artificial limb." (If you think "artificial insemination," then (a) we need to extend our definition from "natural entity" to "natural process," and (b) you have hit on the other expansion of "AI", which has resulted on occasion in hilarious misunderstandings.)

Some commentators think that "artificial" means "Not the real thing; cheap and tawdry," but that's more of a connotation carried by certain usages. Artificial sweeteners do not taste as good as sugar; but a cow conceived through artificial insemination is every bit as bovine as one that involved the whole bull. David Moschella, in his book *Seeing Digital,* says "There's nothing artificial about machine intelligence, just like there's nothing artificial about the strength of a tractor."[56] "Artificial intelligence" therefore means intelligence we have deliberately created, using computers for want of any better technology.

Settling the definition of "artificial" merely warms us up for the hard part, of course. "Intelligence" is by implication a natural phenomenon for there to exist an artificial version of it. Now we need to determine what part of the natural world exhibits intelligence. While the subject of non-human biological intelligence is of great importance to science, it's out of scope for this book. The intelligence that we're most familiar with is our own. Also, the utility of constructing artificial toad intelligence or artificial hedgehog intelligence is presently academic. We'll leave that research to animal behaviorists and ask instead…

What is Human Intelligence?

> *Viewed narrowly, there seem to be almost as many definitions of intelligence as there were experts asked to define it.*
>
> — R.J. Sternberg

Unless we decide that "intelligence" should mean different things when we're talking about machines and people, understanding human intelligence is foundational to understanding and creating AI. In fact, many authorities have declared that the ultimate goal of AI is to reproduce (and exceed) human intelligence, so we can't know whether we've been successful at that unless we know what human intelligence is. Furthermore, the goal of a humanlike AI is proving so hard to attain that some people believe we will find it easier if we understand human intelligence at a deep enough level to just copy it in software.

We love to characterize things with a single number, like temperature for sickness, and weight for health, when we should at least use a blood panel instead. It is practically unavoidable: how else, for instance, can you rank people to pick a winner and a loser without a single dimension to locate them on? The Olympic Games would be impossible. The term "intelligence," being singular, suggests such a dimension, and the scale we call "IQ" seals the deal.

If you want to understand intelligence, who would know better than a group you cannot join without proving your own? So I talked to Kristóf Kovács, the Supervisory Psychologist of Mensa International, in Prague. Mensa is a worldwide society whose membership requires a score in the upper two percent of the population on an IQ test, and part of Kristóf's job is to decide what "intelligence" means for Mensa. Their working definition, and the one used by most people, is that it means whatever an IQ test measures, but you can't get away with that if you're the one who has to devise the IQ test, and that's one of the things that Kristóf does.

IQ stands for "intelligence quotient," which is a term that became outdated almost from birth. Just after the turn of the 19th century, French psychologist Alfred Binet decided it was time to put judgement of intelligence on a numerical footing, and created a series of tests designed to measure a child's "mental age." William Stern suggested to divide that by their chronological age, and if the result was greater than one, they could judge the child as "advanced," and if it was less than one the child was "retarded" behind their biological age. (A term that has since acquired unacceptable connotations.) Division equals quotient, and so the term IQ was born.

Its utility immediately became questionable. If a middle-aged adult is exceptionally intelligent, does that mean they are mentally a centenarian? That doesn't sound right. So, since the need for a measure was to be able to compare one person with a general population, statistics rode to the rescue. Administer the same test to a wide variety of people, and plot how often each score is observed. The result is the typical bell-shaped curve of a natural phenomenon; now locate the target subject's score on the curve.

The mathematics of the "normal distribution" tells you what fraction of the population is less intelligent than them, and you can quote their score as that "percentile," in exactly the same way that a parent learns what percentile of height or weight their child falls at. Mensa admission happens above the 98th percentile.

IQ—even though it is no longer a quotient of any kind—is usually given, though, as a number instead of a percentile. This represents a position on the bell curve, where the central peak—by definition average intelligence—is arbitrarily assigned the number 100, and higher numbers correspond to greater percentiles and greater intelligence. Unfortunately, many people throw these numbers around with no idea what they are talking about. There are several different scales of IQ, and while they all have 100 as the central peak, they use different scales for the width of the curve ("standard deviation" in statistics-speak). The most common Wechsler scale has a standard deviation of 15, which means that Mensa membership happens above an IQ of 130; but as an example of a variation, when I took the British Mensa test it was using the Cattell scale with a standard deviation of 24, and hence membership required a score over 148. Bottom line, you're better off using percentiles to talk about IQ.

But knowing all the mechanics of IQ calculation leaves a frustrating question: *what* test should we use to get those numbers in the first place? This is where there's more room for debate, and so of course there are multiple competing alternatives for those tests, each with their own advocates.

One approach was characterized by Charles Spearman, a British contemporary of Binet, who observed that if a child was particularly good at one subject, they were likely to be particularly good at others, and that some underlying "general factor," which he abbreviated to *g*, was responsible. This theory asserts that all different tests are in fact measuring the same underlying *g*. Kristóf likened that to temperature:

> Think of thermometers. You can measure body temperature with infrared ones, ones that need contact, ones you put in your mouth, ones you put under the armpit, ones you get next to your forehead, and so on, and they might give different results. People with small children are very well aware that they annoyingly often *do* give different results. But nobody would really think that they measure different things just because they give different results. And there's pretty much a consensus that body temperature exists without measurement. It would exist if no one measured it, and these are just imperfect measurement devices that give disagreeing results because of error terms.

The *g* theory has merely shifted the object of our search for the nature of intelligence and given it a name; but Kristóf said, "The debate revolves around whether *g* is the common *cause* of the correlations between tests or the common *consequence* of those correlations." This is where the hunt for *g* turns frustrating.

Which is why Kristóf prefers an alternative. He turns to the Woodcock-Johnson Tests of Cognitive Abilities, which don't even have "intelligence" in the name. Rather than "IQ", they have a "general ability index" emphasizing broad specific abilities and several cognitive profiles. Kristóf described the Cattell, Horn, and Carroll model of seven main cognitive abilities that extend a differentiation between *fluid* and *crystallized* intelligence. Fluid intelligence "reflects the ability to solve novel problems [for which] we cannot rely on acquired skills or knowledge. Crystallized intelligence, on the other hand, is the application of our acquired skills and knowledge; and a typical test of crystallized intelligence is vocabulary."

AIs are adept at crystallized intelligence.

Where that intelligence is crystallized matters a great deal for human beings. For many years, IQ tests harbored cultural biases that excluded people without the right country club membership. "Take the San Bushmen," explained Kristóf, quoting an argument by his late graduate supervisor Nick Mackintosh, "who according to books on national IQ are supposed to have an IQ of 54, because that's how they perform on IQ tests. Now, an IQ of 54 pretty much equals the mental age of an eight-year-old European or American child. [But] it is not very likely that you'd drop an average American or Canadian or European eight-year-old in the middle of the Kalahari Desert and they would survive; whereas San Bushmen clearly do, and have for tens of thousands of years."

Which illustrates that intelligence is multidimensional, of course, despite our fetish for reducing it to a single number. "If you want to actually get to know someone's cognitive abilities," said Kristóf, "then you should focus on their profile of individual strengths and weaknesses because there are people—even in Mensa—who have very high verbal [ability] and are not necessarily that good in spatial things. Whereas [there are] others who are really good at everything spatial, but if you offer them a game of Scrabble, they go for the gun."

When you're evaluating AI achievements hereafter, see how much they fall into the crystallized intelligence category versus fluid intelligence, and ask yourself, how can humans exercise our fluid intelligence to differentiate our job functions from AI? How much has your own education and training emphasized crystallized over fluid intelligence?

How is human intelligence related to the physical substrate? That would be a laughable question to ask about any computer, wherein the dividing line between software and hardware is absolute; software is an abstraction that runs on the hardware, and no amount of legerdemain in software will change the hardware one iota. But this is not the case with a human brain, whose *neuroplasticity*, or ability to rewire itself, is simply stunning.If you want a bigger brain, consider becoming a taxi driver in London, England. The city contains numerous landmarks and twisty streets ranging in size down to tiny cul-de-sacs—twenty-five thousand streets within a six-mile radius of Charing Cross Station alone—and the drivers of the iconic black cabs must spend three years learning to remember them all, without GPS devices.[57] This feat of memorization is known, simply, as *The Knowledge*, and it has a measurable effect on the brains of the cabbies; measurable with an x-ray. Eleanor Maguire and Katherine Woollett, neuroscientists at University College London, found an increase in gray matter in the posterior hippocampus as a result of the training.[58] In other words, their brains literally get bigger. Donald Hebb famously said in 1949 that "Neurons that fire together, wire together," meaning that when neurons learn, causing them to fire, their connections become stronger; but the physical changes in and around those learning neurons now appear more consequential than even he suspected. The old theory that the brain remains unchanged after childhood except for deterioration has been demolished.

Before we leave this topic, some heartening news in the intelligence race: We're getting smarter. You saw that IQ is measured against the test scores of the human race as a whole, and therefore, the average IQ will always be 100. But what about the oft-touted theory that people are getting dumber, that today's kids would fail miserably on the high school examinations of yesteryear? Psychologists have measured this too, and Kristóf told me that the "Flynn Effect" shows the IQ of the general population *rising* by about fifteen points every thirty years. This is a population average; it doesn't mean that *you* get fifteen points smarter every thirty years. Sorry. If you'd like to get smarter, Kristóf suggests that more schooling will raise your individual IQ by around one to four points a year.

A Hierarchy of Organizing Principles

If a lion could speak, we couldn't understand him.

— Ludwig Wittgenstein

If we can't nail down intelligence, perhaps we can locate it in some sort of hierarchy. Those of us in the knowledge engineering business have long used one that I'm going to adapt here.*

Data

The low man on the totem pole, data is just numbers. 42, -3.14159, 6.023E23, 11001001, ... whatever; all we have is quantities. They have no meaning, so about all we can do with them is play games of pure mathematics. Add, multiply, raise to the tenth power; we can have fun doing that but it won't tell us anything about the real world. The data may be a binary string representing text, but we don't have any indication telling us that is the case or how to interpret it, so we don't know if it's the 23rd Psalm or the Gettysburg Address or a recipe for peanut brittle.

Information

On the next rung, meaning makes an entrance. We don't have just a pure number like 42; now we know what it represents; say, 42°C. We may have additional metadata (facts about data); for instance, "This came from the thermometer inside Elaine's sauna at 10:13 PM." Units and metadata are very important; the Mars Climate Orbiter was lost in 1999 just before arrival at the red planet because one part of the spacecraft delivered data measured in pounds to another part that expected to receive it in kilograms. But bare information is like a party bore cornering you with useless facts about baseball or politics; to make it interesting, you need:

Knowledge

Organizing information makes it useful. Knowledge is when information can become valuable. Perhaps we collect the sauna temperatures over a period of time. (How often? How long? This is what knowledge engineers are paid to decide.) Now we can make tables and charts and keep legions of Excel teachers in business. But those charts don't yet lead to any conclusions. For that, we need...

---

* Enterprise ontology pedants—and if you're an enterprise ontologist, you were probably hired for your pedantry—may gripe that I haven't given these terms the same meanings that they're used to. But we're not doing enterprise ontology here.

Intelligence

Intelligence is the creation of new knowledge. (In this taxonomy, at least.) Sherlock Holmes demonstrated this in *The Adventure of the Blue Carbuncle* when he and Watson made the same observations of the same hat, such as its size, quality, and age; but Holmes put the observations together to create new knowledge about its owner's intelligence, wealth, and recent misfortune.

A basic exhibition of intelligence is through *transitivity:* For instance, the knowledge that cows emit methane and the independent knowledge that methane is a potent greenhouse gas leads to the new knowledge that cow flatulence is a contributing factor of climate change. The greater the intelligence, the more can be inferred from existing facts. The possibility that this trend has no limits led Lex Luthor *(Superman)* to declare that some people "can read the ingredients on a chewing gum wrapper and unlock the secrets of the universe." (Pentaerythritol ester, I'm looking at you.) Our knowledge of the sauna's historical temperatures may lead us to conclude that the gas heater is in need of service.

Each tier in this hierarchy also describes positions of greater value to an organization: data engineer, information manager, knowledge architect, business intelligence analyst. Which prompts the question: What level does the CEO inhabit?

Wisdom

Where intelligence gives us the ability to know what we *can* do, wisdom tells us what we *should* do. We can repair the sauna heater, replace it with a jacuzzi, or move to Death Valley and stand outside when the urge strikes. Knowledge is knowing a tomato is a fruit. Wisdom is not putting it in a fruit salad. While we might address global warming by giving cattle Beano, a better choice would be to encourage vegan diets.

The earliest levels in this hierarchy were the most automatable—a thermometer is a better tool for measuring temperature than a person—but wisdom is rooted in ethical and moral foundations and is where we humans can enjoy the most job security.

That's the end of the traditional version of this scale… but we can't resist pulling at the threads to see if it can be extended. And indeed it can.

Enlightenment

Wisdom has its limits: knowing what we *should* do to solve a problem doesn't address *why* we have the problem in the first place. What choices got us into this mess? How do we better next time? What is our purpose and why are we here? Perhaps we discover that we no longer care to broil ourselves in a cedar box. Enlightenment shifted our priority as a species from unrestrained use of fossil fuels to reducing carbon footprints. Enlightenment is characterized by introspection: awareness of our own process, behavior and learning. This is the level where we can most differentiate ourselves from machines, which do not have self-awareness of purpose and won't acquire it for a very long time.

For philosophical completeness, we can also tack on another level at the very beginning, before even Data:

****

There's no name for this tier, because it lives outside of language or symbolic representation. Data is a measurement of *something* that has an essence not expressible numerically. The heat in the sauna exists whether or not there is a thermometer there to detect it and can be felt by a conscious being even if that creature has no language to describe it with. The data is a description of the real thing; the map is not the territory.

Before you think I've gone all Heidegger on you,* this isn't vacuous philosophizing… well, not just vacuous philosophizing. When we build artificial consciousnesses, we may need to understand how they experience the world. Our experience of the world, of those myriad nameless *somethings*, is filtered inexorably through an all-encompassing layer of interpretation, instantaneously crystallizing them into data many times a second, attaching representations and meaning that we need to be able to communicate our experience to each other. The only time in your life you operated without this filter was before you learned to speak, and you cannot describe what that was like because that would require the very language you didn't have then.[†][59]

Humans have been developing for a hundred thousand years without needing to deconstruct this existential conundrum, the mystery of the emergence of language, because we just do it, through some magical process in toddlerhood. But if we need to figure out that deconstruction to be able to replicate the process in our computers, then it's time to pull up our big-boy philosopher pants.

---

* Actually, it's probably more Korzybski.
† Donald Hoffman developed the theory of conscious realism to describe how our idea of reality is an illusion produced by our consciousness—a greatly shared illusion, to be sure, but it underscores the idea that reality is not data.

5
Past and Present

It is not my aim to surprise or shock you—but the simplest way I can summarize is to say that there are now in the world machines that think, that learn, and that create. Moreover, their ability to do these things is going to increase rapidly until—in a visible future—the range of problems they can handle will be coextensive with the range to which the human mind has been applied.

— Herbert Simon, 1957

Throughout the early 1950s, the stage was being set for the ascendance of AI. In 1950, Marvin Minsky and Dean Edmonds, then graduate students, built an actual artificial neural network (an electronic model of human brain structure described in the appendix) called the SNARC (Stochastic Neural Analog Reinforcement Calculator) out of three thousand vacuum tubes and a surplus automatic pilot mechanism from a B-24 bomber to simulate forty neurons. (The computational spirit was willing but the hardware flesh was weak; it would be many years before technology could deliver the performance that Minsky and Edmonds were thirsting for.)

Earlier I mentioned the paper that John McCarthy wrote in 1955 calling for the Dartmouth conference the following year. It listed key researchers to be invited, people who passed through all of the next summer to participate in this Woodstock of cybernetics. While the rest of the nation was fretting over President Eisenhower's ill health, starting June 18th,

1956, a *Who's Who* parade of the founding fathers of artificial intelligence descended upon New Hampshire.

One person who was not there was Alan Turing, who died two years earlier from cyanide poisoning at the heartbreakingly young age of 41.*[60] Had he lived, we can only guess at how he might have advanced AI at Dartmouth, having invented pivotal foundations of the field far ahead of his peers. His legacy in cracking the German Enigma code, quite possibly personally tilting the balance of World War II, lives on in the British Library's Alan Turing Institute and was memorialized by Pamela McCorduck who told me she "wrote a little piece [on the anniversary of his death] for *The Atlantic* saying, 'Alan Turing saved my life,' which he did, because it was thanks to him that little kids like me could eat in the United Kingdom during World War II. The convoys were under terrible pressure, and it was thanks to Bletchley Park that they were protected much more than they would have been otherwise."[61]

But the come-as-you-are appeal of the Dartmouth conference was also a flaw. McCarthy said, "The idea was that everyone would agree to come for six weeks, and the people came for periods ranging from two days to the whole six weeks, so not everybody was there at once. It was a great disappointment to me because it really meant that we couldn't have regular meetings."[62] In fact the most important product of the transactions, the Logic Theorist program (see Chapter 9), designed to mimic the problem-solving skills of a human being, was actually written before the conference.

That the Dartmouth attendees were aiming to create AI to perform "learning or any other feature of intelligence" often appears as reckless hubris, especially when seen through sixty years of hindsight. But AI historian Pamela McCorduck provided a different perspective, that they were simply seeing further than their technological reach. As she told me, "AI has a history of great ideas that could not be realized because the technology wasn't there. [Such as] machine learning, which captured everybody between 2010 and 2020—those ideas were 1980s ideas, but they could not be implemented until the technology caught up. So, this idea that everything grandpa thought of was stupid; no, no, no, no. Go back and look at what grandpa thought of. [But] he just [didn't have the hardware to] do that kind of thing."[63]

---

* His death was ruled a suicide, but later analysis showed the likelihood of an accident.

Now Is the Winter of Our Discontent

I can feel the cold breeze on the back of my neck.

— Roger Schank

In the mid-1980s, Stuart Russell was riding high on a wave of artificial intelligence. A University of California at Berkeley professor, the soft-spoken Englishman who would later write the definitive textbook on AI was teaching it to nine hundred students at a time. Yet by 1990 his class had shrunk to only twenty-five.[64] And within five years the attendance at the annual Association for the Advancement of Artificial Intelligence conference had plunged from six thousand to two thousand.

Some of its presenters had foreseen this. At a panel titled "The Dark Ages of AI—Can we avoid or survive them?" in 1984, they discussed the "deep unease among AI researchers who have been around more than the last four years or so […] Perhaps expectations about AI are too high, and that this will eventually result in disaster."[65] A likely motivation for their angst occurred less than a month earlier, when the cover of *BusinessWeek* proclaimed, "Artificial Intelligence: It's Here!" Bear in mind that contrarian investors consider a *BusinessWeek* cover to signal the peak of a bubble; in other words, when *BusinessWeek* declares it's time to get on board a hot new trend, it's really time to get out. (Exhibit A: Its 1979 cover, "The Death of Equities.")

The precipice that AI fell off was later called an "AI Winter," and it was not the first one. In 1957 Frank Rosenblatt invented the *perceptron,* a learning machine with a neural network architecture, and AI enjoyed a decade's ascendance. In 1958 the *New York Times* breathlessly asserted "…the Navy [has] revealed the embryo of an electronic computer today that it expects will be able to walk, talk, see, write, reproduce itself and be conscious of its existence."[66]

But by 1969, perceptrons had yet to produce useful results. Then Marvin Minsky and Seymour Papert published a book called *Perceptrons* that delivered a withering impression of their capabilities. When four years later the Lighthill Report in the UK was equally withering about the whole field of AI, funding throughout Europe dried up.

By the early 1980s, *expert systems* were the new favorite child, and languages like LISP and PROLOG were hawked in heavily-trafficked convention exhibits. AI was back, baby, and Russell's burgeoning attendances showed it. It seemed there was nothing the rule-based systems would not be able to do… just as soon as you wrote enough rules.

But it turned out that "enough" was a long way off—so far, in fact, that AI father John McCarthy wrote an article titled "Some Expert Systems Need Common Sense"[67] about how the computerized physicians' assistant, MYCIN, would "cheerfully recommend two weeks of tetracycline and nothing else" to treat a hypothetical *Vibrio cholerae* infection. Yes, the recommended treatment would kill the infection—around the same time that the patient died.

Once again, AI became the pariah of computing, hoisted on its own petard of overpromising and underdelivering. To be fair, much of the hype came uninvited from nonpractitioners, such as *BusinessWeek* editors. But that's unavoidable; in fact, the trajectory of any new technology is so predictable that the Gartner consultancy codified it in a curve they branded the *Hype Cycle*. As a new invention becomes promising, the predictions of its capabilities transmute into hope that it will prove a magic bullet for the competition-battered businessperson and fuel desperation that it will cure all corporate ills. Since there is yet to be any experience of the limitations of the new technology, these fantasies escalate unimpeded, and only the inevitable discovery that it is not, in fact, a license to print money causes its fall from grace, overshooting into what Gartner terms the "trough of disillusionment," or "winter" when it happens to AI.

Periodically, even conservative scientists are seized in the grip of a fad. For instance, by the end of the 19th century, many astronomers were so convinced that life existed on other planets in the solar system that a hundred thousand French francs were offered to the first person to make contact. And the reward specifically excluded contact with *Martians*—that was considered too easy![68] Is AI talk today such a fad?

About now I envisage you, dear reader, knocking over your chair to pound your fist on the table and shout at this page, "Look at the hype today! Surely we are on the verge of an AI Winter that will see its practitioners strung from lampposts and bricks thrown through the windows of DeepMind?" Yet I have asked many of my guests for their expert opinion, and not one thinks we are about to experience another AI Winter.

Pamela McCorduck went further to tell me that even the past downturns were not as wintry as we think. During the first winter in the '80s she observed funding cratering and thought, "Gee, that's funny. Okay, I'll take a look." Then: "I looked at the papers being published during that decade. They were fundamental to machine learning, and so on. 'AI Winter' means the money dried up, but money dries up for capricious reasons." She concedes, however, that in the near future "probably there will be some diminution."

Cambridge University AI anthropologist Beth Singler contrasts today's environment with the one that prevailed during previous winters: "What might be slightly different now is the role of the charismatic authority from a specific corporation, or individual that's really investing heavily in artificial intelligence," she says. "When applications fail to bear fruit in terms of commercial results, you'll see those dropping off. I think we're seeing something along those lines with automated vehicles. But when that kind of level of personal aspiration is involved with certain voices in the conversation, that may well drive AI from the AI Summer into yet another AI Summer, and another one," she adds, pointing out that the flow of money into AI is now from different sources. "When the previous AI Winter was a big concern, it was because there was a limitation in state and governmental funding. And I say this shift more onto entrepreneurial funding makes a difference."[69]

The Golden Age of AI

The period of 1955–1970 is referred to as a Golden Age by many, probably because it was the peak childhood years of the Baby Boomers. It was the Golden Age of television, the Golden Age of space exploration, and the last time England won the World Cup. To many, it was also the Golden Age of AI, a period when it seemed anything was possible with enough programmers with the Right Stuff, and the way those demigods of coding would scale those heights would be by figuring out the algorithms underlying every problem AI was to solve, from reading the newspaper to washing the dishes.

We know now that decomposing those problems into codifiable steps is, for all intents and purposes, impossible. But the nostalgia for the period when it seemed attainable lives on in the name given to the procedural, symbolic logic-based programming of that era: Good Old-Fashioned AI, or GOFAI ("go-fi"). The notion advanced by the neural network advocates, that those hard problems were unsolvable through logic but could be achieved through training a device whose workings were opaque to human understanding, was received by the GOFAIers as heresy of the first order, much like the indeterminism of quantum physics was received by Einstein ("God does not play dice with the universe.").

The early '90s saw the networkists' ranks decimated, as they were unable to demonstrate networks doing what they claimed. An AI Winter (and the last so far) descended as all AI fell into the doldrums. People turned their attention to other things. But the reason for AI's actual deprecation was (a) computer hardware wasn't powerful enough to do anything useful with it, and (b) there wasn't enough data available in suitable forms to train it. Throughout the '90s, computing power inexorably grew according to Moore's Law (see the next section), until by the first decade of the twenty-first century, AI was quietly ready to stage a comeback.

By then, with modern hardware able to handle the demands of neural networks, all that was required to spark a renaissance in machine learning was data for training. Hard as it is to believe now, at the turn of the millennium there were no good training datasets for neural networks; but the focus was on improving algorithms, not throwing more data at them. But in 2006, Fei-Fei Li, a new computer science professor at the University of Illinois Urbana-Champaign, bet big on Big Data. She started a project called ImageNet, to construct the world's first large-scale database of labeled images. All she needed was images, and labelers. The Internet brought images within reach—3.2 million of them, culled from Google and Flickr—and Amazon's Mechanical Turk service made available the services of humans to label the images with tags from the WordNet hierarchy at a cost far lower than previously possible.

Now the stage was set for neural nets to make their entrance. The explosive growth of AI from roughly 2012 onwards has been propelled by *deep learning*, which is explained in detail in the appendix. In 2010 a good error rate for computer image recognition was 25 percent, whereas humans given the same tests performed at an average of 5.1 percent. But in 2012, Alex Krizhevsky and Ilya Sutskever, students at the University of Toronto, submitted a neural network of eight layers which achieved an error rate of 15.3 percent—10 points lower than the next contender. The network was eventually titled AlexNet.

The impact of AlexNet was pivotal (the paper has been cited over a hundred thousand times); attention immediately shifted to acquiring large datasets that could be used for training neural nets. Deep learning (signifying the extra layers in the network) had proven its worth, and its popularity rocketed.

AlexNet's 15.3 percent error rate was in placing a correct label in its top five guesses for an image. Humans performing the same task have an error rate of at best 2.4 percent. But today, a network called Florence-CoWin-H can pass the same test with a 0.98 percent error rate.[70]

While most of this attention focused on images, humans also deal in auditory data. The reference dataset for speech recognition is called Switchboard: it contains approximately two hundred and sixty hours of two-sided telephone conversations. The transcription error rate for humans is 5.9 percent; it was equaled by a neural network designed by Microsoft Research in 2016 and beaten a year later with a 5.1 percent error rate; in other words, a machine was able to understand human speech better than humans themselves.

Deep learning allows us to program AI to perform tasks that we cannot explain how to do, or cannot even do ourselves. For example, it can do simultaneous translation of English spoken words to Chinese—and learned the human translator's skill of predicting what the speaker is about to say a few words into the future.[71] Deep learning can perform tasks, like discerning sentiment in text, that we would describe as requiring human intuition—in fact, that's what it excels at. And it can go beyond human capability or expectation, such as when the C-Path system, trained by Daphne Koller of Stanford University, learned to predict cancer survival rates from tissue images better than pathologists, and was able to tell that surrounding cells were important, contradicting established belief.[72]

The Japanese in their late 1980s Fifth Generation project had encapsulated the hope being invested in AI:

> By promoting the study of artificial intelligence and realizing intelligent robots, a better understanding of the mechanisms of life will become possible. The approaching realization of automatic interpretation and translation will serve to help people of different tongues understand each other, […] the knowledge which mankind has accumulated can be stored and effectively utilized, so that the development of culture as a whole can be rapidly promoted. Mankind will more easily be able to acquire insights and perceptions with the age of computers.[73]

While that hope wasn't realized at the time they said it, deep learning finally delivered the goods some thirty years later. 2016 was a coming-out party for deep learning, causing *Wired* to declare 2016 the year it "took over the Internet."[74] Google, Microsoft, Amazon, IBM, and Facebook announced major infrastructure initiatives to build out AI services.[75]

Hardware Trends

On Monday, January 14, 1952, less than four weeks before the death of King George VI would propel his daughter Elizabeth onto the British throne, a show aired on BBC Radio's Third Programme under the title "Can Automatic Calculating Machines Be Said to Think?" Only a transcript survives of this erudite debate between the day's leading scientists. Geoffrey Jefferson, recently retired Chair of Neurosurgery carped, "When we hear it said that wireless valves think, we may despair of language." Maxwell Newman, Fellow of the Royal Society and Professor of Mathematics at the University of Manchester added, more objectively, "It's most unlikely that engineers can ever give us a factor of more than a thousand or two times our present speeds. To assume that runs that would take thousands of millions of years on our present machines will be done in a flash on machines of the future, is to move into the realms of science fiction."

They were answered by Alan Turing, reminding them that a machine already existed that was capable of such computation: "To my mind this time factor is the one question which will involve all the real technical programming difficulty. If one didn't know already that these things can be done by brains within a reasonable time one might think it hopeless to try with the machine. The fact that a brain *can* do it seems to suggest that the difficulties may not really be so bad as they now seem."[76]

Turing could already see how computing hardware was evolving. And since then, it has continued evolving at an exponential rate that is unprecedented in its longevity within human experience. Thirteen years later enough time had passed for Gordon Moore, founder of Intel, to quantify that rate. *Moore's Law* is enticing, easily described, and has launched a thousand thought leader-y talks: *Computer power doubles every eighteen months.*

We have already seen at least thirty-three doublings of computer power, which lies far outside our normal experience of the natural world; if grass grew that much from seed it would be ten thousand miles high. We especially do not comprehend large numbers that are written down, because of an evolutionary tendency to compare numbers of things by groups we can hold or see. So 1,000,000 *looks* about twice the size of 1,000. A billion differs from a million by one letter. And 10^8 is only different from 10^3 at all when you squint. *Intellectually*, we can grasp the meanings of these symbols; *instinctively*, we do not.

If you want examples of the peril of underestimating the exponential growth of computers, look to fiction. The eponymous emergent AI in Thomas Ryan's *The Adolescence of P-1,* set in what the 1970s considered the near future, accumulated a whopping five gigabytes of memory and became conscious, yet today that will hold only twenty minutes of high-definition video. Commander Data from *Star Trek: The Next Generation* is cited in the episode *The Measure of a Man* as being capable of 60 trillion operations per second (60 TeraFLOPS). When the episode aired in 1989, this made him about sixty thousand times faster than the fastest supercomputers of the day. Thirty-two years after the episode aired and three hundred and seventeen years before Data's fictional creation, the fastest computer on Earth is rated at 442 *peta*flops, over seven thousand times faster than Data. (His storage capacity is quite not so anachronistic: in the same episode he says he has "an ultimate storage capacity of eight hundred quadrillion bits," which is a hefty hundred petabytes. Nevertheless, that level of storage capacity is available now to many companies; you can rent it on Amazon for only $51 million per year, which is roughly the cost to buy the hardware outright, although not to power it.)

But ever since 2005 there have been objections within the computer hardware industry that the bloom is off Moore's rose. That's when chip clock speeds topped out at 4 GHz, and many thought this spelled the end of computation speed increases.

Yet even industry experts can be overtaken by progress. The original formulation of Moore's Law depends on how densely transistors can be packed on a chip, which in turn depends on how finely features can be etched onto the chip substrate; in other words, how thin a line you can draw in silicon. The unit of measurement for those lines is the nanometer, abbreviated nm, and it is a millionth of a millimeter, or about one hundred thousandth of the thickness of a sheet of paper. The 2012 International Technology Roadmap for Semiconductors predicted that by 2020 "… many physical dimensions are expected to be crossing the 10 nm threshold."[77] Yet 10 nm chips went into production in 2017 and by 2020 several devices were shipping with 5 nm chips, including the M1 in the Apple MacBook I am typing this on. By 2024, 2 nm technology—smaller than the diameter of human DNA—is expected to be in production at the powerhouse Taiwan Semiconductor Manufacturing Company. And IBM is now turning transistors on their heads to increase density with the Vertical Transport (Nanosheet) Field Effect Transistor, stacking the components on top of each other instead of side-by-side.[78]

The chart of the number of transistors on the latest chip even acquired an upwards bump in 2020, thanks to Cerebras, who admittedly stretched the definition of "chip" by making one the size of a dinner plate. Containing 2.6 trillion transistors, the "wafer scale engine" is actually eighty-four nodes, each the size of a traditional chip, but instead of being broken out from the silicon wafer, they are interconnected there. This behemoth consumes fifteen kilowatts of power; you could heat your house with it.

Processor chip performance improvements have now slowed to "only" 30 percent per year. However, this is irrelevant, because the number of operations per second that can be performed in hardware is increasing at least 118 percent per year in Apple's neural processing units, their system-on-a-chip (SoC), alone.[79] And the cost of computing continues to drop at an exponential pace due to these and other improvements. Moore's Law is arguably still safe in its original formulation for several more years, and the ratio that counts—cost per TeraFLOPS—continues to plummet exponentially. In the year 2000, the largest supercomputer on Earth, at Sandia National Labs, cost $46 million and could do 1 TeraFLOPS. The Apple iPhone 13 released in 2021 delivers 3 TeraFLOPS and costs about $600.[80]

What developments did those phenomenal advances in hardware drive at higher levels of computer architecture and usage?

The Trends That Drive the Trends

> Yet it is by the laborious route of analysis that [the man of genius] must reach truth; but he cannot pursue this unless guided by numbers; for without numbers it is not given to us to raise the veil which envelopes the mysteries of nature. Thus the idea of constructing an apparatus capable of aiding human weakness in such researches, is a conception which, being realized, would mark a glorious epoch in the history of the sciences.[81]
>
> — Luigi Menabrea, 1842

Since World War II, when computer programming became a pursuit, innovations in hardware have propelled the automation of increasingly complex and important tasks. (See Figure 5.1.)

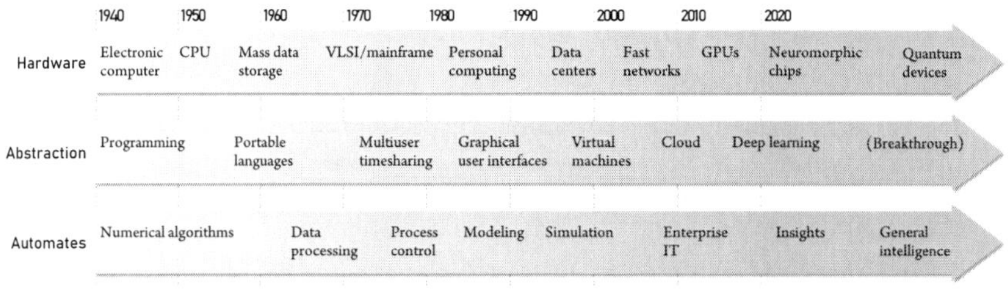

	1940	1950	1960	1970	1980	1990	2000	2010	2020	
Hardware	Electronic computer	CPU	Mass data storage	VLSI/mainframe	Personal computing	Data centers	Fast networks	GPUs	Neuromorphic chips	Quantum devices
Abstraction	Programming		Portable languages	Multiuser timesharing	Graphical user interfaces	Virtual machines	Cloud	Deep learning		(Breakthrough)
Automates	Numerical algorithms		Data processing	Process control	Modeling	Simulation	Enterprise IT	Insights	General intelligence	

Figure 5.1: Trends to Paradigms

Early electronic devices were very specialized; the "bombe" computers (they ticked) used by Alan Turing to crack the Enigma code modeled the

German device's wheels with rotating combinations of electrical currents. The more general-purpose ENIAC machine of the following era was programmed by rearranging wires on a plugboard, and new programs took days to create. This automated the execution of numerical algorithms; it was used to make artillery range tables.

Then John von Neumann designed a computer architecture comprising a central processor unit (CPU) and separate data and program stores, and the ability to store what was then large amounts of data in offline or near-line storage (like magnetic tapes). This architecture became the design for all computers and enabled the automation of data processing: the searching and manipulation of databases that could contain anything from customer addresses to parts inventories; all you needed to change was the code that handled them, and this was now written in (relatively) user-friendly languages that for the first time could be run with the same results on different machines, thanks to the work of standardization committees.

The development of Very Large-Scale Integration—CPUs on a silicon chip—meant that big mainframe computers could be produced on an assembly line; the same model could be built over and over again, so the documentation and support could be reused for each customer. Their application to industrial process control, modeling, and simulation followed in quick succession while Moore's Law drove the miniaturization of computers to fit first on your home desk and then in your pocket. Computing hardware became such a mass commodity that the data center was born; "blades" (cards containing CPU chips, about the size of a machete) arrayed in shelves in racks in aisles in climate-controlled rooms where computing power could be sold as a service, and the advent of high-speed networks meant that the problems could be transmitted to the computers wherever they were, rather than a new computer having to be installed at the location of each customer. Software frameworks, which allowed computation to be moved between devices transparently, without even noticing if a blade went bad, created the compute-anywhere paradigm called the cloud, and this automated the tasks of information technology for businesses; the largest ones first, then becoming cost-effective for ever-smaller organizations.

Most recently, it was discovered that the Graphical Processing Unit (GPU) chips that powered graphical displays, were actually more powerful than CPUs at parallel processing (doing the same calculation at the same time for many different pieces of similar data), because that was what they had to do for the pixels of your computer screen; but many simple arithmetic calculations executed in parallel precisely describes the internals of an artificial neural network. Niche display adaptor manufacturers such as NVIDIA were shoved onto center stage as their hardware became the nuclei of cutting-edge deep learning programs, delivering increasingly higher-order insights into information of all kinds.

And now to peek into the future: *neuromorphic* chips implement neural network architecture directly in hardware, saving several layers of abstraction over the classic von Neumann model when used for deep learning. Programming the signaling between artificial neurons on traditional hardware requires a high-level language making many procedure calls to aggregate the inbound signals, and similarly to propagate the outbound signals after the application of the activation function. The procedure calls are compiled into machine language that runs on a central processor accessing memory. Optimizing that for performance comes at the expense of making the programming less intelligible and harder to change. But neuromorphic chips, like Intel's Loihi, can be wired to deliver those signals along physical paths. They thereby gain enormous leaps of performance and power savings, and chase the holy grail of generally intelligent computers. The Gartner consultancy predicts that neuromorphic designs will displace GPUs as the main hardware platform for AI by 2025.[82]

It's hard to anticipate what hardware development will come after that, but quantum computers are certainly the darlings of the press. They are notoriously hard to fathom; Richard Feynman said about his work in quantum electrodynamics that if it were easy to understand, it wouldn't have been worth the Nobel Prize. The first thing to understand about quantum computers is that they barely exist. Current versions use supercooled shiny tubes that look like a prototype teleporter or time machine and are fantastically expensive. Where classical computers store data in microscopic semiconductor bits that can be either one or zero—the raw text for this book occupies around ten million of them—quantum computers are built of "qubits" and the greatest number of those that anyone has put together so far is a hundred and twenty-seven.[*][83]

Quantum computers cannot solve all types of problem faster. They do not perform parallel processing tasks as though there were as many cores as you could hope for. They do not, as you may have read, explore all possible solutions to a problem and pick the right one. But it is possible to take certain types of mathematical problem and with a sufficiently brilliant mathematician, find algorithms that map states in possible answers

---

[*] D-Wave has a "Five thousand qubit" computer, but it is an "adiabatic" quantum computer that can't solve the same class of problems, and… there are arguments about how to describe this. As if quantum computers weren't hard enough to understand already.

to waveforms such that the waves interfere destructively for wrong answers and reinforce each other for the right answer(s). If that explanation fails to jingle your bells, then know that (a) you're not alone, and (b) a sufficiently brilliant mathematician (Peter Shor) has mapped the problem of factoring large numbers; and that means that modern encryption algorithms, the ones that secure data on the internet and in banks, that put the *s* in *https* and close the padlock icon on your web browser, will be cracked as soon as we have a big enough quantum computer. Estimates for when that will happen range from five to twenty years.[84] Even though we will have created encryption algorithms that are quantum-proof by then, much data is already publicly available in an encrypted state that was originally expected to be secure for a thousand years. Having the tools to crack those encryptions within, maybe, ten years will… cause problems.

So what does that mean for AI? It wouldn't mean a lot, unless someone mapped deep learning onto waveforms that a QC could resolve. But in 2021, IBM researchers announced, very tentatively, with much hedging, that they had done exactly that.[85] There are no estimates as yet as to how much this might speed up machine learning, and it still awaits the development of quantum computers with adequate power.

There are many fields of human endeavor in which we can either predict that we have reached a natural limit to growth (such as chemical rocket propellants), or we have run out of ideas for how to surpass a plateau (such as culturing vaccines). Artificial intelligence performance is not one of these.

6
Naming of Parts

It was on one of my journeys between the EDSAC room and the punching equipment that the realization came over me with full force that a good part of the remainder of my life was going to be spent in finding errors in my own programs.[86]

— Maurice Wilkes

While the definition of "artificial intelligence" remains slippery, in computer science it contains a slightly more precisely-defined field: *Machine Learning*. This is the use of algorithms that can adapt to improve their performance the more data they are given. A subset of machine learning is Deep Learning, which solves problems using artificial neural networks. You'll find some more technical explanation of how neural networks work in the appendix.

Not all machine learning is done on artificial neural networks, but that's certainly where the most dramatic results and the bulk of today's research is being conducted. However, the three different methods of applying AI that I am about to explain don't *have* to use neural networks, so I'll use the more general term "machine learning."

Machine Learning Methods

How can you use machine learning? There are three types of application:

- Supervised learning
- Reinforcement learning
- Unsupervised learning

Supervised learning is the most readily appreciated use of machine learning. The algorithm is trained on examples of correct solutions: This picture is a dog, this sound is someone saying "polecat," this loan application resulted in approval. After training, it has generalized the learning enough to give correct answers to new questions: This previously-unseen picture from a different angle is also a dog, this sound is a different speaker saying "polecat," this applicant's data has not been encountered before.

Reinforcement learning is getting a model to perform a task by "rewarding" it every time it gets it right. This is a good process for training robots to, say, pick up packages. Of course, "reward" is an anthropocentrism; what's really happening is that the network is given a score of its performance on each trial and its algorithm modifies its behavior in the directions that tend to increase the score.

Unsupervised learning is the process of finding patterns in the data that you didn't know were there. For instance, in 2018, researchers fed images of patients' retinas, plus metadata about each patient (age, smoking status, blood pressure, etc.) into a deep learning engine that showed that not only can those factors be determined solely from a retinal image, but also the patient's *gender*. With *97 percent accuracy*. Even after being told this correlation, human ophthalmologists could do no better than chance at determining gender from the images and researchers could not tell how the AI was figuring this out.

There are usually easier ways of discerning someone's gender than looking at the back of their eyeball (absent gruesome forensic investigations). The point is, that AI created new knowledge. Such a discovery by a human would garner acclamation.

Finding patterns is humans' party trick, and we love doing it so much that sometimes we find patterns that aren't really there: dragons in clouds, mythical heroes in constellations, and wishful thinking in the stock market. But we're limited in this capability by the number of dimensions we can perceive and the complexity of the pattern. Let's pretend I have data on, say, the types of bacterial growth observed in cheese over the dimensions of temperature and humidity (Figure 6.1). It's easy in this example for us to pick out the boundaries of clusters (Figure 6.2).

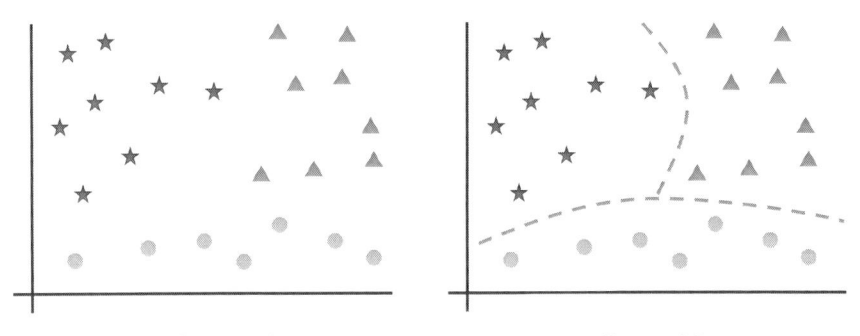

Figure 6.1

Figure 6.2

But what if there are a dozen dimensions? Perhaps we add data on atmospheric pressure, room lighting, water salinity, and so on. We can't see charts in those dimensions. But if there's clustering in the data at those higher dimensions, machine learning can find it.

Suppose we were hunting for the cause of an individual's headaches. We record their headache intensity and times, but what factors might be causing them? We track their stress, hydration, and electrolyte intake, and the ambient noise level, lighting brightness and color. Then, remembering some of the more surprising results of unsupervised learning, we toss in data that we don't think could be causative but which we have to hand anyway: time of day, pollen count, number of emails received, miles driven, hours of Netflix watched, days since last paycheck. If the cause was the less water drunk, the worse the headache, that would be easy to see. But suppose the headaches form a system with the data; several or many variables involved, with different ranges of each having different effects, and nonlinear relationships. We can't see those kinds of patterns in twenty-dimensional data, but machine learning can.

After decades of—understandably—associating computers with logic, mathematics, and rigidly-defined data, it was something of a shock to discover that where deep learning excelled was in processing "fuzzy" data and finding patterns. It appeared to be intuiting meaning the same way we do. In fact, the early role of computers as arithmetical geniuses is equivalent to an ability that in humans is attained at the expense of a great deal of education, building on centuries of collective discovery. We perform calculus, say, by running that symbolic mathematical processing on our biological neural network; whereas our AIs build neural networks out of symbolic logic math processors. There's a mirror symmetry carrying some irony.

Types of AI

> *There may be said to be two classes of people in the world; those who constantly divide the people of the world into two classes, and those who do not.*
>
> — Robert Benchley

Our need to simplify the world (into lists no longer than Miller's Magic Number, so we can assimilate them; see Chapter 3) has led AI philosophers to classify its capability along a general cognitive axis into three groups:

- Artificial Narrow Intelligence (ANI);
- Artificial General Intelligence (AGI);
- Artificial Super Intelligence (ASI).

I know it seems like it would make more sense to write those as Narrow Artificial Intelligence, General..., but this is what's stuck.

Artificial Narrow Intelligence is what we've got now. Every AI you've ever encountered or heard about is an ANI, meaning that it can handle just one task. It could be extremely narrow, like recognizing bolts in a bucket of parts, or it could be superficially broad, like writing poetry, but this restriction cuts deeply: Don't think of it like a neurodiverse human or *idiot savant* obsessed with one topic, because that human can still perform an unlimited number of other tasks that an ANI has no concept of or experience with whatsoever.

Artificial General Intelligence is the holy grail of today's AI researchers: An AI that can perform that unlimited number of tasks as well as a human, even if only as well as a below-average human. Of course, there's a continuum between ANI and AGI, but the width of the untraversed chasm between those groups is currently huge. Despite AGI appearing on the goal statements of an unreasonable number of companies, at the moment it does not exist. It would almost certainly be a characteristic of an AGI that it had the capability to learn new things, because that's characteristic of humans. And that's what makes it most likely to evolve into...

Artificial Super Intelligence would be AI that was generally intelligent but far beyond our intelligence; not like Einstein to us, but like Einstein to a sheep. Now, as we've seen, there is more than one dimension to intelligence and it is therefore simplistic to think of this as a race along a single line—after all, computers are already superintelligent compared to us when it comes to doing arithmetic and storing digital data. But there are certainly scenarios in which an ASI might create the same issues as a race of super-Einsteins if it surpassed human abilities in enough dimensions of specific intelligence.

It vexes many researchers that the gap between our current capabilities and AGI is seen by some people as narrow and by others as yawning. Michael Wooldridge, AI researcher and head of Oxford University's Computer Science department, was, as he put it, doing AI research relatively unmolested for decades until he was yanked into a media feeding frenzy in 2014 when the BBC asked him to react to Stephen Hawking's assertion that AI might pose an existential threat. He told me what we would have to accomplish to get to the prerequisite general intelligence: "AGI would mean that we would have a single machine that could tell a joke, interpret a story, recognize faces in a picture, invent a story, write an essay, critique an essay, cook an omelet, tie a shoelace, ride a bicycle, drive a car, go swimming, or anything that a human being could do, a machine could do."[87] Of course, many of those activities require embodiment in a robot of a certain form factor, but the principle would be preserved if you allowed each activity to be performed within a simulation of the real world.

It may seem as though an artificial general intelligence would be conscious, because human AGI is; but most researchers believe that machine AGI can be achieved without consciousness; which is just as well because no one knows what consciousness is well enough to tell how a computer would do it. Leading AI researcher Stuart Russell said, "If you gave me a trillion dollars to work on conscious AI, I would have to give it back, because I wouldn't know what to do with it."[88]

It might also seem to be no advantage to develop a computer-based AGI with the same intelligence as a human when real human intelligence is already available; but it's the power of linking that general intelligence to the existing computational firepower of computers that holds allure. As an analogy, imagine if you could run Google searches in your head.

There is little research into creating ASI; robot researcher Cynthia Breazeal says, "I just don't see any practical drivers in the near future for a cross-sectional general superintelligence. Right now, commercial transformation is funded and driven by entities seeking directed solutions, delivered by highly crafted, special-purpose systems."[89] But creating AGI is the hurdle we have to clear first and ASI is likely easily attained after that.

We acquire general intelligence through a great deal of experience and experiment in the real world during our formative years, processing huge streams of sensory data and lessons layered atop that in language. AGI development is handicapped at the moment; not by insufficient data to train it, but the lack of any means to map data about the world to machine learning algorithms. As Stuart Russell said, "Put crudely, the world is an *extremely* large problem instance!"[90]

But once we figure this out at all—well, computers are very good at dealing with large amounts of data. And that experience can be shared among all the AGIs being developed throughout the world, which will never forget a lesson. "Eventually there is going to be a common database of existing AI capabilities," AI safety professor Roman Yampolskiy says, which means that AI models will grow cumulatively without repeating so much of each other's learning.[91] Recreating the human learning experience in silicon is likely to precipitate an avalanche of AGI expansion.

7
AIs and Brains

> *If we are ever to make a machine that will speak, understand or translate human languages, solve mathematical problems with imagination, practice a profession, or direct an organization, either we must reduce these activities to a science so exact that we can tell a machine precisely how to go about doing them or we must develop a machine that can do things without being told precisely how.*[92]
>
> — Richard M. Friedberg

Neuroscientists can be a quirky lot. Olav Krigolson, for instance, confessed on my podcast that he had zapped his own brain with a magnetic field to induce (temporary!) Broca's Aphasia—inability to speak intelligibly—because, well, he could. They like to poke at other people's brains while they're still in use; and they like Jennifer Aniston. And they indulge both of those interests at the same time. Neurosurgeon Itzhak Fried repairs brains and conducts neural research; but his claim to fame in popular media will forever be as the discoverer of the "Jennifer Aniston neuron."

The brain has no nerve endings of its own, so if you open up the skull (which does; don't try this at home) to get at the brain, you can tickle it as much as you like without perturbing its owner; it is common practice while performing brain surgery to keep the patient awake to ask them questions to determine what's happening in the part of the brain the surgeon is working on. During one such surgery in 2005, Fried, not one to waste a temporarily naked brain, asked the patient if he could do some science while he was there.

Fried was armed with two tools: a machine to detect individual neuron activity, and pictures of Hollywood stars. And he discovered that a particular neuron would light up whenever the patient was shown a picture of Jennifer Aniston, but not any other glitterati. Clearly, further experimentation was needed.

Further experimentation found that this neuron would light up when its owner was merely thinking about Aniston, for instance when hearing or seeing her name. And Fried was able to locate an Aniston neuron in other patients as well.

If you're wondering at this point how the heck human brains evolved something so... specific, I should point out that you have to actually *know* who Jennifer Aniston is before you have a neuron devoted to her; you're not born with one, absent some truly obsessive gestational *Friends*-binging. Since Dr. Fried worked at UCLA, adjacent to Hollywood and Beverly Hills, his constituency was well-disposed toward media stars. So he also found neurons in other patients that fired in response to Julia Roberts, Halle Berry, and Kobe Bryant.

This discovery, while attracting predictable attention (but no recorded reaction from Herself), provides learning that is both useful and dangerous. Useful, because how cool is it to show that as multidimensional a concept as *Jennifer Aniston* can map to a single neuron? Dangerous, because it entices us to think that every other concept equally must map to their own neurons. Wait a minute, there are a hundred billion neurons in the brain; is that enough to fire for every word in your mental dictionary, every*one* and every*thing* that you know, and every concept formed by the astronomical permutations of those objects? Might you not run out?

And the Jennifer Aniston neuron is, like the actress herself, supported by an unsung cast of lesser neurons. These do the work of recognizing her distinguishing features (blue eyes, chin, tousled hair) so that when they all fire together, they trigger the J.A. neuron itself (an older, less glamorous, name for it is the *Grandmother Neuron*). This is exactly how our artificial neural networks work, right? We already know how to build an electronic Jen-recognizer. There's the danger again: of falling into the trap of thinking that all cognition fits into this tidy model, when in truth, this demonstration works for concrete nouns but there's no evidence that you have neurons that fire for, say, abstract adjectives like organic, recidivist, or hierarchical, let alone task categories like opening a container, balancing flavors, or managing a project.

Back to the drawing board.

Lest you still be tempted by the siren song of "biological neurons are just as simple as artificial ones," evidence arrived in 2020 that the humble neuron is a computational star in its own right. "I believe that we're just scratching the surface of what these neurons are really doing," says Albert Gidon, lead author of a paper in *Science* that described research showing that parts of the connection arms (axons) of biological neurons are able to perform entire computations* that cannot be solved by an individual artificial neuron.[93]

Equating Brains and Machines

> *In this electronic age we see ourselves being translated more and more into the form of information, moving toward the technological extension of consciousness.*
>
> — Marshall McLuhan

Some people think we are relatively close to making intelligent machines because human brains seem to have so much in common with artificial neural networks. But this analogy is deceptive; it turns out that we have *always* compared human minds to our latest technology. I mentioned earlier how Babbage's levers-and-cogs Difference Engine was described as "thinking." The brain was also compared to a telephone exchange and a railway system when those were the state-of-the-art technologies.[94]

So if we've always felt that our latest technology is the right model of the human brain—now it's deep learning's turn—could we be just as mistaken now as we were after Edison invented the phonograph and scientists thought of memory as "an album containing phonographic sheets"?[95] Historian-psychologist Douwe Draaisma has shown that rather than transferring self-knowledge to our machines, it is the other way around: we learn more about *ourselves* every time our technology advances.[96] Which echoes more than one AI researcher who has said, "The more I learn about AI, the more I learn about myself."

The carrot that so many AI researchers are chasing is the belief that the human brain can be modeled in software that will then be able to reproduce the unique general intelligence of humans. But what if this paradigm is hopelessly wrong?

---

* Specifically, XOR functions.

A large amount of effort has been expended by writers seeking to compare the performance of the human brain to computers. Many find it irresistible to point out that the cycle time of human neurons is 200 Hz, or about ten million times slower than the clock speeds of today's computer chips. The speed of synaptic signals along axons, the wiring between neurons, is 50–60 meters per second[97] whereas electrical waves traverse computer chips at over half the speed of light. Puny humans; how can we hope to compete against such technological superiority?

But there are some blind spots in this comparison. Clearly, hardware's speed exceeding humans' by seven orders of magnitude has not yet led to any significant capability in artificial general intelligence. Computers have always been able to do arithmetic and work with large quantities of specific data faster than humans, and the fact that they can now calculate a square root in 10^{-9} seconds compared to 10^{-8} seconds five years ago makes no difference in a race with humans when the world record for unaided humans is six seconds.*[98] They're faster calculators; so what?

How much hardware, then, would it take to build an electronic model of the human brain? Joseph Carlsmith of the Open Philanthropy Project estimated that the computational equivalent of the human brain was somewhere between 10^{15} FLOPS (a hundredth of the power of the billion-dollar Fugaku supercomputer) and 10^{21} FLOPS (ten thousand Fugakus).[99] The size of the uncertainty of that estimate reflects the embryonic state of our knowledge of the subject.

But how likely is this estimate to be accurate? Brains are not just neurons packed together; in between are glial cells, long thought to be there just to provide places to hang the neurons on ("glial" means "glue"). They are now increasingly suspected of performing computation as well, and we have as many glial cells as neurons. Neuroscientist Christopher Chatham says, "Accurate biological models of the brain would have to include some 225 million billion interactions between cell types."[100]

In order for a comparison between computer hardware and human brains to be meaningful, we would need some idea of how the brain does its calculations. Andrew Ng, now working on the Google Brain Project, believes human thought can be reduced to algorithms.[101] Because parts of the human brain that usually perform a single function—like seeing or hearing—can be persuaded to take on a different function, it appears that the brain operates on a single underlying algorithm that is special-

---

* On October 7th, 2014, world record holder Granth Rakesh Thakkar calculated the square roots of ten six-digit numbers in 1:01.9 minutes in Dresden, Germany, at the age of 13.

ized for each function. Find that algorithm, code it in software, and AI glory awaits.

There is, however, an unexplored chasm between human brain and AI algorithms. Today's AI learns through repeated examples—many, many more examples than humans require. An AI can learn to recognize an image of a dog after seeing a hundred thousand pictures of dogs and a hundred thousand pictures of things-that-are-not-dogs, at which point it may become very good and not be fooled by tricks that would challenge humans. But many real-world tasks cannot tolerate the amount of failure that the AI must endure. A student driver can be certified legally safe to ply the public thoroughfares in twenty or so hours of instruction that do not require—indeed, frown upon—wiping out. A reinforcement learning algorithm would have to drive off a cliff ten thousand times before it learned not to do that; therefore we train such algorithms in simulations of traffic rather than the real thing. [102]

That is a fundamental difference between AI and humans, but maybe the gap is not as large as it seems. US Air Force Colonel John Boyd declared that we operate on repeated iterations of OODA loops: Observe-Orient-Decide-Act, and that conscious optimization of that cycle could improve human responses in situations ranging from aerial dogfights to corporate strategy. [103] But there's an unconscious step in the middle: *Prediction*. So the loop actually goes Observe-Orient-*Predict*-Decide-Act. This prediction cycle is close to being the universal brain algorithm that Ng is seeking; it shows up at all levels of our thinking processes. Picking up a coffee cup, you observe your environment; you orient yourself with respect to the mug; you predict what the feedback from your nerves will be as you move your hand towards the handle, you decide to move your hand accordingly, and you act on that decision, constantly adjusting the motor commands to your muscles in response to the feedback, until you grasp the handle.

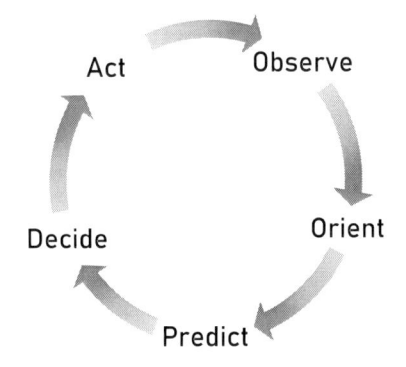

The OOPDA loop isn't just for clutching your morning joe, though. It applies equally to a multi-year process of, say, building a house:

- Observe: What are the choices of location, style, and cost, and what resources (financial, design, emotional support) are at my disposal?
- Orient: What choices best fit my available resources and goals?
- Predict: As I move towards my goal, what will be the first situation I encounter? (Applying for a construction loan? Picking a general contractor? Choosing an architect?)
- Decide: How should I react to that situation?
- Act: Do it.
- Go back to Observe, only this time within a narrower context of evaluating the outcome of my action.

To make the bridge between this biological behavioral pattern and machine learning, I again consulted Olav Krigolson. The outgoing neuroscientist studies brainwaves and how to discern states of mind from the seemingly chaotic squiggles; part of his research involved incarcerating himself in a simulated Mars habitat to study the effects of enforced confinement on astronauts' brains. He connected the dots for me:

> When people learn, one of the ways they learn is through a prediction error. It's the difference between your expectation of what's going to happen and the actual outcome. Imagine you hit a tennis ball: You have an expectation of what's going to happen, and then there's what actually happens. If there's a difference, we call that a prediction error. It's a key principle in reinforcement learning. If you measure with an EEG [electroencephalograph: brainwave monitor] the response to feedback in a simple gambling task— you get some people to play a little gambling game—the pattern of the EEG parallels the pattern you see with the computational model that uses prediction errors. When the model predicts you should see a large prediction error, given the outcome, then we see a large neural response. And when the model predicts we should see a small prediction error, given the results, we see a small neural signal. So we can come up with computational models that [approximately] parallel what we see.[104]

In other words, while humans don't need enormous numbers of examples to learn a behavior, we are executing many cycles of simulation during the process of executing each behavior, constantly adjusting in response to the difference between the simulation and the reality; in effect training our internal models each time we do something. Prediction error feedback in humans echoes the backpropagation of an artificial neural network. The special skill that we exercise is to prune our decision trees rapidly and prudently. The comparison with AI is like a chess grandmaster who discards nearly all of the possible moves from a given position because they most probably lead to unproductive outcomes, compared to a brute force algorithm that has to investigate them all to find out.

8
How to Think About AI

> *By far, the greatest danger of artificial intelligence is that people conclude too early that they understand it.*
>
> — Eliezer Yudkowsky

Imagine you're attending a cocktail party and are introduced to several guests who appear to belong to familiar categories: The Young Mother, The Rising Corporate Star, The Senior Executive, The Garrulous Dilettante. You think you've got them pegged until the host reveals that they are really tightly-organized assemblages of banana slugs with advanced plastic surgery. You have many questions.

This is roughly the situation we face with artificial intelligence. In so many ways, AI looks like something we can locate in a familiar landscape, like another version of something we have encountered before. But in truth it is utterly alien beneath the surface, and mistaking it for the familiar things will lead to fatal misunderstandings. As AI intrudes more and more into our lives, it is increasingly important that we understand what's really going on.

Our beliefs often receive the greatest jolt when AI claims a victory in an activity we had thought reserved for humans. For instance, in 1997, when IBM's Deep Blue computer beat reigning chess champion Garry Kasparov in New York, Douglas Hofstadter, Pulitzer Prize-winning author of

Gödel, Escher, Bach: An Eternal Golden Braid exclaimed, "My God, I used to think chess required thought. Now I realize it doesn't." That is usually where that quote is terminated, apparently throwing shade at chess players, but Hofstadter—a renowned polymath who once taught himself to speak backwards[105]—went on to say, "It doesn't mean Kasparov isn't a deep thinker, just that you can bypass deep thinking in playing chess."[106]

He bemoaned that Deep Blue had merely won by brute force: "To me, as a fledgling AI person, it was self-evident that I did not want to get involved in that trickery. It was obvious: I don't want to be involved in passing off some fancy program's behavior for intelligence when I know that it has nothing to do with intelligence."[107]

Of course, Deep Blue was a triumph of research and programming; but in the context of revealing new insights into cognition, it was as if the Kentucky Derby had just been won by Truckzilla. Edward Feigenbaum, the "father of expert systems," declared at a much earlier stage of AI development, "Chess and logic are toy problems. If you solve them, you'll have solved a toy problem. And that's all you'll have done. Get out into the real world and solve real-world problems."[108]

How should we think about artificial intelligence? In some ways, it is like understanding an alien life form; just one far more alien than our experience or imagination usually encompasses. Software developers have long been used to communicating with this life form; we cudgel our brains into "thinking like the computer" to try and understand why our program isn't working and what to do about it. Hollywood breezily suggests that the process of communicating with a computer is instead something like addressing an autistic four-year-old and that it will understand general statements like "OVERRIDE ALL SECURITY" *(Superman 3)*. If only.

It has been the holy grail of computer science, since it was invented, to have no gap between what we want and how we tell the computer to give it to us. But in reality, that gap is a canyon; we bridge it with tentative, swaying contraptions called computer languages, layered in hierarchies from bit-flipping machine code to "high-level."

No matter what language we program in, however, we must write *tests* for our software: completely separate programs that throw a range of conditions at it to see if it behaves as expected. Tests are our tacit acknowledgement that we and the computer are not speaking the same language and that we cannot just tell it what we want. The saving grace of this process is that the customers who gave us a problem to solve on the computer usually didn't think through what they really wanted, and gave us a distorted version of their requirements that can only be diagnosed as inadequate when we translate it into the implacable logic of the computer.

AI invites us, as soon as we see the word "intelligence," to personify it, to use humans as the yardstick by which we judge it. This bias is strengthened by our real need to know how closely it *is* approximating human performance; yet it leads to capital errors in the mental models we form of AI. How, then, should we think about AI?

The applications of narrow artificial intelligence that often eclipse human performance invite a topographic analogy: Human intelligence is like a high plateau covered with small hills and valleys; it is of generally high altitude with relatively small variations here and there. My own plateau is adorned by a small hill in the *Star Trek* trivia location and a somewhat deeper depression in the choosing-appropriate-clothing-styles location.

Artificial intelligence, however, is a country at sea level almost everywhere, but dotted with the occasional hundred-thousand-foot-high peak with sheer faces. It is *very* good at *very* narrow applications, but nothing yet bridges those applications. And that is one of the ways in which AI is fundamentally *not* like human beings. Our intuition says that something that is so smart at chess, or at Go, or at facial recognition, must be in the same category as a human that can do those things; possibly autistic, but definitely possessing general intelligence. Our intuition is wrong.

The biggest obstacle to gauging how close we are to the arrival of artificial general intelligence is not in estimating how fast our technology is developing; it is in knowing how large the gap is that still needs to be closed. In so many areas we take the arrival of AI on the playing field to mean that it is ten yards short of a touchdown, when the truth may be that the playing field is really the size of Arizona and the only parts we have seen are the benches and the goalposts.

For instance, my wife adores her Roomba—she named it Frank—and it leaves our floors 99 percent as spotless as would have taken us an intense effort—*so* close to human-level perfection! However, if we zoom in on that 1 percent—if it had only picked up that pair of shoes on the doormat—we see that that simple act is far beyond the capabilities of not only a Roomba, but any robot in existence, both in dexterity and embodied cognition.

A self-driving car that is 99 percent as capable as a human driver does not allow that driver to spend 99 percent of the journey taking a nap; rather, it is fatally incompetent, subjecting its occupants to catastrophic danger at random intervals. But closing that 1 percent gap will take staggering breakthroughs. More on this later.

We have repeatedly enabled computers to perform seemingly intractable tasks that appear to require humanlike intelligence by the application of brilliant insight. Take for example the Google search engine. In 1998 I was writing and customizing intranet search engines for the Jet Propulsion Laboratory and was spending a lot of time hand curating lists of synonyms, web spidering strategies, and concept prioritization lists. Then the Google search box arrived on the scene. Astoundingly, sitting next to the Submit button was another button labeled "I Feel Lucky" which would take you directly to the top hit of the search results. Such arrogance was breathtaking, considering how the other state-of-the-art Internet search engines could barely be counted on to return an optimal hit in the first five pages. And yet, as though by black magic, it worked. I gave up developing search engines.

But how had Google achieved the task of knowing just what the best result for each search could be? I knew firsthand how unreliable it was to rely on tricks I was using, like the count of appearances of search terms on a page, or weighting their appearance in metadata and headings. Google seemed to have humanlike insight into what I wanted from a search.

Yet this hadn't been achieved by advanced AI modeling human preferences and interpretations, but by a clever trick called the *PageRank Algorithm:* tallying the links from other pages *to* the one that ends up being the target of my search. The math involved can be expressed and implemented relatively succinctly; but *it is not at all how humans assess what is most relevant to what they're looking for.* It just happens to be a very good proxy for that assessment, and we've all experienced just how well it works.

That process of finding an algorithm that can stand in for human intuition virtually defines the entire field of computer science; most of my degree program involved learning algorithms as clever as PageRank so that we would get better at coming up with our own ones. We devoured books of such insights like Jon Bentley's *Programming Pearls,* which showed over and over how a simple insight would make a seemingly intractable problem solvable. The lesson: that for every task humans perform, there's a trick to get a computer to do it that has nothing to do with the way that humans solve it. As AI humorist Janelle Shane observed, "People don't realize an AI is solving an easier problem (*e.g.,* the length of a medical case file predicts problem cases)."[109]

It would be a fatal mistake to think that because we have not yet approached artificial general intelligence, that AI will not challenge activities that we believe to be the domain of human thought. We have repeatedly discovered that tasks that we believed to be solidly in the clubhouse labeled HUMANS ONLY could also be performed by AI. (For example: recognizing faces, translating languages, transcribing text.) Honestly, this says more about how those activities do not depend upon exclusively human capabilities than it does about AI having humanlike powers.

It would also be a mistake to think that human-level tasks have to be performed by computers using similar processes to what we employ. Computer science pioneer Edsger Dijkstra asked, "Does a submarine swim?" Others asked, does an airplane flap its wings? Neither of these machines imitates its animal antecedent. A submarine does not move like a fish. Ever since Icarus and failed Victorian attempts to strap on feathers, airplanes have not generated lift through wing flapping (although the aileron was based on the Wright brothers' observations of how birds flexed their wings to change direction). Yet submarines and planes carry much more payload much farther than fish or birds, and by that measurement alone are much more capable. The fact that we still have not equaled the amazing ability of the average bird to precisely hit a landing spot in a crosswind that would be a hurricane at our scale turns out to be irrelevant to achieving our transportation goals.

What does that analogy mean for the future of AI? In particular, it means that whenever you hear someone assert, "But AI doesn't really *understand…*," you should think, "But submarines don't really *swim.*" Your interlocutor might be trying to say, "I believe that human-level understanding of X is required in order to perform X," to which you can respond, "But what if it isn't?"

A Matter of Scale

> *We are now writing algorithms we cannot read. That makes this a unique moment in history, in that we are subject to ideas and actions and efforts by a set of physics that have human origins without human comprehension.*
>
> — Kevin Slavin, MIT Media Lab research affiliate

How might the common thought patterns of computer scientists shape the development of AI? It's a foundational principle of computing that we can leverage their ability to do the same thing many times over. When you're learning computer science, the teacher presents an algorithm in a stripped-down form to illustrate its essential features. For an example, consider the *flood fill* algorithm, which colors the interior of a shape on a computer screen. I wrote one of these, decades ago, for an Apple][painting program; you pick a point inside the shape you want to color, click Go, and every pixel inside that shape becomes that color. But how? The flood fill algorithm is simplicity itself:

```
flood-fill( this-pixel ) :
    If this-pixel is colored edge-color or flood-color then stop
    Color this-pixel with flood-color
    flood-fill( pixel above this-pixel )
    flood-fill( pixel below this-pixel )
    flood-fill( pixel left of this-pixel )
    flood-fill( pixel right of this-pixel )
```

This is the most easily understood version of this algorithm, although it is relatively inefficient, because it is highly *recursive:* it calls itself, ouroboros-like. To execute this over any shape the size of which you're likely to have drawn inside a painting program, it would take thousands of iterations and millions of machine instructions if unrolled and laid end-to-end, all doing the same two operations that are present in this code: testing the color of a pixel and setting the color of a pixel.

I, and likely you, grew up with coloring books where we eventually learned to stay between the lines, and would never have had the patience to execute any algorithm so repetitive and narrowly focused. Even as a toddler, you grasped the *interiorness* of the shape on the page as a gestalt concept, and then just covered that with crayon. But interiorness can't be described in a form that a computer can execute, so generations of computer scientists have staked claims to fame by creating cleverness such as the flood fill algorithm, which usually ends up accomplishing the same goal.

The difference between the crayon-wielding toddler and the flood fill algorithm is a microcosm of the difference between us and AI. Every advance in AI has to be made by inventing a new algorithm as precise as the one above, and, more importantly, simple enough to understand, because one day it will find itself called from a line of another algorithm that stands on its shoulders to do something a bit more powerful. Progress in AI relies upon finding algorithms that *scale:* when executed enough times over enough data, they create emergent results that achieve a higher-level goal. So far, our faith in this strategy has paid off with spectacular accomplishments in deep learning; but the gap between today's AI and a general artificial intelligence is of such unknown breadth that we cannot be sure that scaling small algorithms will close it.

Robots

> *Within ten to twenty years' time, we could have a robot that will completely eliminate all routine operations around the house and remove the drudgery from human life.*[110]
>
> — Meredith Wooldridge Thring, 1966

The first appearance of the word robot is credited by legend to Karel Čapek's 1920 play *R.U.R.* ("Rossumovi Univerzální Roboti," or "Rossum's Universal Robots"), but in fact it was his brother Josef who first combined the Czech words "robota" (obligatory work) and "robotnik" (serf) to yield "robot" in his 1917 short story *Opilec*.[111] As a subspecies of artificial intelligence, the robot is an important distinction to understand because it shows up so often as a proxy for AI in our fiction and mainstream news. This is understandable; we prefer anything that thinks to have a face. If a movie character isn't costumed in something a human can wear or move around in, it is (a) harder to relate to and (b) more expensive to produce. (Even R2-D2 in *Star Wars* contained a human actor.)

So our cultural milieu is flush with vivid examples of humanoid robots (this type of robot is called an *android)* carrying the flag for all of AI. Movie counterexamples to this selectivity are notably few, such as HAL 9000 from *2001: A Space Odyssey,* visible only as a red dot in a camera lens and, eventually, as a wall of featureless computation modules. Director Stanley Kubrick did not want you to relate to HAL out of any visual resemblance to humans, and succeeded in creating a cryptic character so memorable that when James Cameron wanted to emphasize the inhuman awareness of the Terminator, all he had to do was show its eye as the same lens around a glowing red dot.

Outside of fiction, though, what is a robot? It's an AI that is *embodied,* meaning that it has a fixed physical presence with defined boundaries and points of interaction with the physical world. A robot either moves from place to place in the world, or has articulated limbs that can manipulate objects, or both. A self-driving car is a robot. The car factory machines that weld joints on the assembly line are robots, appearing in 1961 with the Unimate, the first industrial robot.

To date, the interactions between humans and robots have been relatively few, aside from household vacuum cleaning disks; robots with the weight and strength to damage human beings are mostly kept in factories behind warning barriers. This is not the vision of a *Jetsons* Rosey humming around every household or passing us on the street. In some environments, this détente will have to soften. For instance, Japan's demographics mean there aren't enough able-bodied younger people to care for the growing elderly class; they are heavily invested in researching robotic replacements. That doesn't necessarily prefigure a society where the elderly are left with only the company of machines, though: the robots could be relegated to tasks of less important interaction. For example, physical therapists must currently take patients from their rooms to the training facility in wheelchairs; this is time spent on transportation instead of using their physiotherapeutic skills. Robots could convey the patients so that the trainers spend more time on high-value interactions.

Hollywood's obsession with the robot, though, creates a dangerous blind spot for us. Virtually every advanced robot on the screen has been a perfect android, able to pass for a human on first glance and usually also far more intimate contact. (Think: *Humans, Ex Machina, Westworld*.) Unsurprisingly, the motivation for this is that the makeup is even cheaper and now they can explore… over and over again… the provocative scenarios arising from machines being indistinguishable from humans. But such portrayals raise the obvious rebuttal that such technology is far in the future, and therefore concerns about AI are merely hysteria cultivated in the credulous by sensational fiction.

We must demolish this fallacy. It is correct that machines impersonating humans are very far in our future. Animating even a gross imitation of the human endoskeleton requires our most modern technology. (Exhibit A: the Boston Dynamics *Atlas* robot.) The state of the art in developing machines as squishy as humans is at paleolithic stages. Creating the equivalent of biological skin with its dense mesh of multimodal sensors has barely advanced beyond the staring-thoughtfully-out-the-window phase.

And, yes… there is a subset of robots that has made certain specific advances in the direction of realistic skin. Register an interest in "robots" and before long, the Internet will deliver to you news of sex robots. This is another of those tropes in AI that will suck all conversation into it if we give it a chance, so I'm not going to dwell long on it here; sex robots already attract—this may come as a shock—a disproportionate amount of attention from the media. Deciding whether a municipality should permit brothels staffed by sex robots is a rancorous debate. ("They are causing men to have unrealistic expectations of women!" "But they are freeing women from being trapped in the sex trade!") That conversation is too long for this book; I refer you instead to Maciej Musiał's book *Enchanting Robots*.[112] It is, however, important to note that such brothels already exist in both Asia and Europe; when you investigate how far they have, uh, penetrated into the North American market you have to decide where to draw the distinction between a robot that has some interactive technology inside, and a shapely but inert doll. This book isn't going to get further sidetracked into that topic… oh, all right, *other* than to report this story: After constant nagging from his family to get married, thirty-one-year-old Zheng Jiajia of Hangzhou built a robot and "married" it in a 2017 ceremony attended by his mother.[113] East Asian countries have gone further down this technological path than the West.

I bring up the sexbots only so you can refute arguments from anyone claiming that these latter-day Galateas have achieved some attention-worthy level of realism. They are optimized for how they look and how they feel to *someone else's* touch, not their capabilities as agents sensing our world. They have little to no ability to sense temperature or pressure at all, they aren't capable of locomotion, and their conversational prowess is laughably primitive—though it doesn't need to be particularly good for that application. True, if there is substantial progress in their construction then we can see an era where there might be social problems due to people preferring the robots to real partners—and not a little ink has been spilled over that hypothesis. But it's not an imminent crisis, and appears to be many decades away.

The capabilities of today's robots, compared to our media-goosed expectations, are primitive. The number of *degrees of freedom* (number of joints and directions in which they can pivot) in the human body is enormous and far beyond what today's robots are either built with or able to compute the use of. Which places precisely the sort of robot that would be most useful—say, a plumberbot that could replace the p-trap under your kitchen sink—in a remote future.

How do today's robots navigate our messy world? I turned to Paolo Pirjanian, former Chief Technical Officer of iRobot, makers of the Roomba vacuum robot, designed to make our world less messy:

> For people that may not be in technology, it's hard to imagine why would it be hard for a robot to know where it is. Well, it is hard because the robot has no point of reference. It has to have some way of measuring where it is in the environment relative to something. And so many different approaches have been used, but Simultaneous Localization and Mapping (SLAM) became the solution. A very simple concept is that, if someone handed me a map of a building and said, "Figure out where you are on this map", I could look around myself and measure the distances to walls and compare them to the map and say, "Okay, it looks like

I'm at this corner because I see a door, I see a window and I see the same thing on the map so I know where I am." But the robot doesn't have a map. The other thing would be to say, "if I knew my position very accurately and I start measuring what I perceive in my environment and started drawing that, I can start drawing out the map."

But the problem is that the robot also doesn't know where it is because its position accuracy is very bad. Usually, you can measure your relative position using the onboard sensors such as odometer and inertial navigation system to measure your position, which is like the odometer in your car but that is not very accurate. When you start moving away from your initial position, your position starts drifting so you have to have an external fix. That's why with the odometer of your car, you could not do what the GPS does for our current cars with navigation systems. So it's a chicken and egg problem. If I had accurate positioning, I could build a map; if I had a map, I could figure out my position. But I have neither.

So SLAM refers to the fact that you build a little bit of the map, use that as a reference point to position yourself relative to that piece of the map, then go to the next section of the map, and figure that out, and then stitch these puzzle pieces together to get the entire map. Now you will be able to localize yourself anywhere on that map. And that's why visual SLAM uses a camera to find visual feature points or fiducial points in the environment and uses those to figure out the position and build the map from. When the robot carries out a learned action in the real world, it establishes a pixel correspondence between its training and the present scene, and adjusts its behavior accordingly.[114]

It can be instructive to observe how you navigate your world on a daily basis and notice just how much a robot that could do the same tasks would have to know. The pressure nerve endings in your fingers provide feedback on how much grip is necessary to pick up an object without it sliding out of your grasp or breaking; OOPDA loops informed by your copious knowledge of how fragile and slippery everyday objects are make an incredibly difficult task for a robot a piece of cake for you. Such as, picking up a piece of cake.

"Incredibly difficult" is not the same as "impossible," and with so much to gain for the company that figures it out, oceans of cash are being flung at researchers in this field. Toyota Research Institute has built a household robot that users can train using a virtual reality interface. The robot, resembling an assembly of giant pipe cleaners, learns a new behavior from a human training it through virtual reality goggles. Then it responds to voice commands to carry out the behavior in a variety of real-world environments. Classical robotics software controls the machine, while convolutional neural networks learn unique patterns. TRI researchers trained the bot on three tasks: retrieving a bottle from a refrigerator, removing a cup from a dishwasher, and moving multiple objects to different locations. Then they had the robot perform each task ten times in two physical homes. They ran the experiments with slight alterations, for instance asking the robot to retrieve a bottle from a higher shelf than the virtual one it was trained on, or doing so with the lights turned off. The robot achieved an 85 percent success rate—though it took an average of twenty *times* longer than a human would.[115] As impressive as this is, it's limited to a very narrow selection of tasks that it must be trained to perform in a very narrow selection of easily accessible environments. It won't be replacing your p-trap any time soon.

We instinctively imbue familiar objects with organic qualities—witness the affection some people lavish on their cars—and the question of whether people can become emotionally attached to robots has already been settled. In battlefield operations, soldiers have been known to form close personal bonds with explosive ordinance disposal robots, giving them names and promotions and even mourning their deaths.[116]

A group of researchers in Japan and Washington State observed, "Children will increasingly come of age with personified robots and potentially form social and even moral relationships with them," and asked, "What will such relationships look like?" They studied interactions between children and an interactive humanoid robot called Robovie. Their paper, with the unusually catchy title of "Robovie, You'll Have to Go into the Closet Now" demonstrated children's tendencies to attach mental states to the robots, and even to impute moral status to them; some children felt that putting the robot into the closet when the robot was "protesting" was unfair. They were also comfortable with ascribing a "fluid ontological status" to the robot. One child said, "He's half living, half not."[117] Of course, children are used to imbuing completely static objects—dolls—with goals, histories, and emotions, so there's no reason to think this study reveals any sort of moral confusion. Giving the objects around us personalities is part and parcel of the human journey.

Games

> *I'm sorry, Frank. I think you missed it. Queen to bishop three, bishop takes queen, knight takes bishop, mate.*[118]
>
> — HAL 9000

The application of artificial intelligence to games is particularly instructive; games vary all the way in complexity and difficulty from rock-paper-scissors to… what? Where does the boundary lie between a game and real life? A day on the Los Angeles freeway system may convince you that the other drivers are treating it as a round of *Mario Kart*. So teaching a computer to play games provides a smoothly graded ladder for AI developers to cut their teeth on, starting at tic-tac-toe and continuing to get better until the results have real world utility. One of the more obvious of those domains is military; practicing strategy is even called "War Gaming." If, like me, you've enjoyed a long night with friends around a board simulating a global military conflict, you may have wondered how much more complicated the real thing could be.

Chess has been a productive milestone for developers on that ladder for many years. Until Deep Blue's victory over world champion Garry Kasparov in 1997,* it was supposed that a computer could not attain that status because the number of potential moves was demonstrably too high for a computer to search and that humans were pruning their mental search trees by processes too intuitive to be captured in algorithms. But Deep Blue learned enough pruning (not exploring strategies that looked unproductive) to expand its look-ahead to a winning depth. In 2015, Ralf Funke wrote, "José Capablanca, the chess champion, is supposed to have answered the question of how many moves he would look ahead thus: 'Only one, but it's always the right one.' A program will never accomplish this […]"[119] And while computers do still rely on a lot of look-ahead, they are no longer condemned to explore only by brute force. Conversely, humans—even Capablanca—do look ahead as well as intuitive pruning; their subconscious may be doing both the strategic pruning and looking ahead.

In 2017, DeepMind released the program AlphaZero, which used deep learning to learn two-player perfect information (each side sees all the pieces) games by simply being given the rules and told to play itself. Within four hours and twenty million simulated games, AlphaZero was the best chess player, human or machine, on the planet. DeepMind CEO

---

* Despite the name, it wasn't using deep learning.

Demis Hassabis described AlphaZero's style as "Alien… like chess from another dimension."[120] Through just the pattern-finding mechanism of deep learning, AlphaZero had internalized some kind of winning chess strategy formula. But what was it doing? For more insight, I turned to Jonathan Rowson, grandmaster and British chess champion 2004–2006. He has since extended his career to that of practical philosopher, starting the Perspectiva think tank "to improve the relationships between systems, souls, and society in theory and practice."

I had to understand more about how humans play chess, because my own approach to a chess board approximates that of Godzilla to Tokyo. Rowson's 2019 book *The Moves That Matter: A Chess Grandmaster on the Game of Life* gave me a first glimpse into that mindset: "Your overall question is: 'How can I checkmate the opponent's king?' But the recurring questions that help you answer that include: 'What am I trying to achieve here?', 'What happens if I go *there*?', 'What do I need to do now?', 'How will he respond to *that*?', 'What does that knight *want*?'"

What lies further up the mental hierarchy of a chess master? "In chess we learn heuristics like 'Develop your knight before your bishops', 'Don't move your queen in the opening', 'Capture towards the center', 'Opposite bishops have drawish tendencies' and so forth," Rowson told me. "However, at a certain level of expertise these guidelines begin to seem quaint and ridiculous, because every position has such unique characteristics."[121]

Hassabis was on the mark in describing AlphaZero's play as alien, because it does not approach the game with the same strategies as humans; you cannot cut it open and find any of the heuristics Rowson listed. The patterns it has learned are foreign and likely to remain incomprehensible to us, but they get the job done.

Yet those patterns don't mean anything to AlphaZero. It doesn't deconstruct grand strategy to get them, the way that a grandmaster like Rowson puts together those simpler heuristics from an even higher-level grand strategy driven by the overall goal. AlphaZero is therefore going about it backwards; but it's got so many patterns, and they're analyzed so well, that it still wins. Every time.

And of course, AlphaZero cannot deconstruct its own performance in terms of the actors around it like Rowson, in philosopher mode, can: "Chess is prismatic in a certain sense of the relationship between human intelligence and AI, there's no doubt about that," he said. "It's a controlled environment. It has a certain degree of complexity. It has a certain history. It has cultural resonance." Nor can an AI find a higher purpose from the game: "I think if chess taught me anything, it's that the meaning I derive from the game is something that is inaccessible to AI," said Rowson. "And that's what makes me human, not the fact that I can play at grandmaster level."[122]

His insight provides a valuable clue as to what we should learn from this encounter between humans and AI. It is not a John Henry-style fable of defeat by the machines. The purpose of the game is no longer to beat your opponent, if your opponent is AlphaZero, but to better yourself, to use it as a stepping stone to becoming more fully human.

It took some time for humans to accept this relocation of the philosophical cheese, of course. Even when chess surrendered to computers in 1997, there was a successor that seemed impregnable to AI: the game of Go.

All the way back in 1965, the British mathematician Irving J. Good asked:

> Go on a computer? —In order to programme a computer to play a reasonable game of Go, rather than merely a legal game—it is necessary to formalise the principles of good strategy, or to design a learning programme. The principles are more qualitative and mysterious than in chess, and depend more on judgement. So I think it will be even more difficult to programme a computer to play a reasonable game of Go than of chess.[123]

Fast forward to 2015, and Ralf Funke set forth reasoning that excluded the possibility of a breakthrough in Go: "And even if the best Go programs today can beat strong amateurs, there is still a long way to go to reach the level of top professional Go players. It may very well be the case that Monte Carlo Go [computerized move tree searching] leads to a dead end. Perhaps entirely new concepts have to be developed to really master the game. It might be the case that the human way is after all the most effective."[124] "The Game of Go is the holy grail of artificial intelligence," said one researcher. "Everything we've ever tried in AI, it just falls over when you try the game of Go."

And yet just one year later, a program suddenly leapfrogged into the number one spot: AlphaGo, the predecessor of AlphaZero. Trained over a massive database of thirty million moves, the program from British startup DeepMind provided a dazzling demonstration of the new company's mastery of deep learning. The researcher who made that comment just prior to AlphaGo's victory? DeepMind's own lead researcher, Dave Silver.

Chess and Go are *perfect information* games: each player and spectator can see everything there is to know about the game. But what about games where some information is hidden? Like poker: Each player has "hole" cards known only to themselves. Your strategy is not to have the winning cards but to make the winning bet; if your opponents are convinced that you have better—or worse—cards than you really do, you can exploit their error. And you can force their error through *bluffing*.

Surely so psychological a tactic could not be emulated by a computer forced to follow inexorable logic? It's a trope of robots that even ones as advanced as Data from *Star Trek: The Next Generation* don't understand deception.

But it turns out that again, a pattern of play can be developed by AI that has either assimilated the concept of bluffing or is mimicking it to a degree that is effectively the same. In 2016, DeepStack beat eleven professional players at the game of heads-up (two players) no-limit Texas Hold 'Em. And in 2019, Pluribus mastered the classic six-player Hold 'Em variant, winning an average of $480 for every hundred hands against million-dollar earning players.[125] It would not be wise to compete for money in any online poker tournament.

Where humans have more of an edge is in games that depend upon an implicit knowledge of the world. Suppose you opened up a brand-new video game one day and saw Figure 8.1.

Figure 8.1

With no instruction whatsoever, you would know what the goal was, what you needed to find out to get there (what inputs will make the character swing and jump), and what to avoid. AIs are learning how to solve games like this, but they have none of this required implicit understanding. That comes from human embodiment. AIs do not, on seeing a screen like this, have the concept of gravity pulling objects downward; they do not, for that matter, have the concept of "object," or that this is a representation of a "real" world situation, or "real world." These are enormous impediments for AIs learning this type of game; but they are slowly being conquered.

Researchers at Uber AI used deep reinforcement learning to learn classic Atari games like *Montezuma's Revenge*.[126] But this learning is brittle. A celebrated victory of AI in video games was on another Atari game, *Breakout*. In this game you hit a ball towards a ceiling of bricks, and each time the ball bounces off a brick, the brick disappears. The goal is to eliminate the bricks without the ball getting past your paddle. A Deep Q-Network from DeepMind learned a strategy known to few human players, that if you dig a tunnel all the way through one side of the wall and then hit the ball through it, it will bounce back and forth between the top row of bricks and the top of the screen, removing many bricks all by itself while you take a break.[127] (See Figure 8.2.)

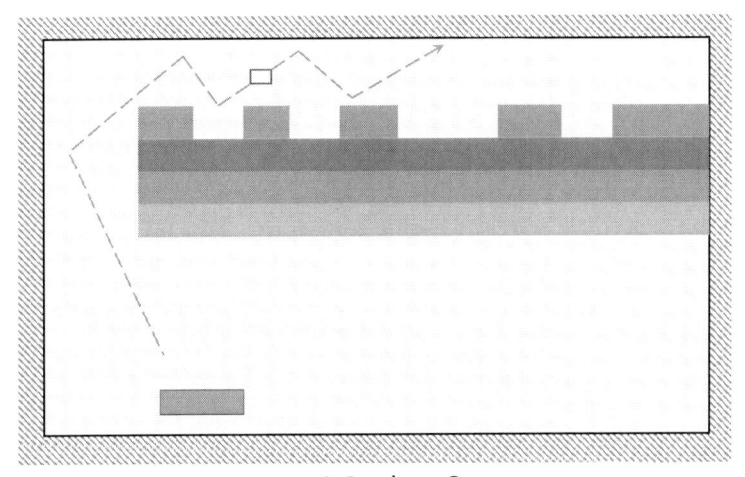

Figure 8.2: Breakout Genius

This is, on the face of it, genius. But researchers found that if you move the paddle a few pixels away—an intervention a human player would be unlikely to notice, let alone be fazed by—it fails miserably. It has to be retrained all over again to solve it. The AI has simultaneously discovered a strategy that human players would perceive as advanced exercise of creative thinking, and instantiated it in an implementation far more brittle than any human ever would.

Anthropomorphizing and Cybermorphizing

I totally anthropomorphize all of the robots in my home.… I have five [Pleo dinosaur robots] at this point, and I treat them like pets, and I've named them all, and feel bad for them when something happens to them. So, yep. Yep. I do that too.[128]

— Kate Darling, MIT Robot Researcher

The biggest barrier to our understanding artificial intelligence is our compulsion to anthropomorphize: When something displays one human quality, we reflexively project other human qualities onto it. When AI accomplishes a task that for a human would require an extraordinary intellect, we ascribe to it the other capabilities that humans have, mentally filling in the blanks as it were. There's a name for this process: *amodal completion*. A visual form of amodal completion can be demonstrated by the following picture:

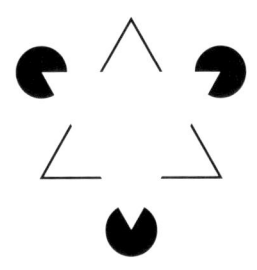

The Kanisza Triangle

Even though all that's really there are three pie wedges and chevrons, it's impossible not to see a white triangle overlapping all of them. Your visual system is completing the picture for you.

What is the nature of the shape we are seeing? The human visual system is optimized for shape detection, but this stretches our wetware to its limits; So there have to be some corners cut. That shows up in optical illusions, and we can also see it in a variation of the Kanisza Triangle:

Is there now a shape in front of the others? Our visual amodal completion taps out past simple shapes; it does not allow for the possibility that the occluding shape is complicated:

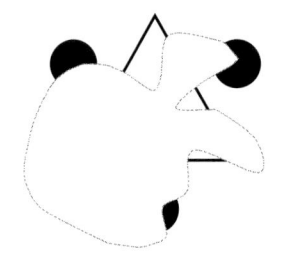

Now, visual amodal completion is an essential part of your object recognition capability, so that when something passes in front of your friend's face you don't momentarily think that their nose has been amputated. But amodal completion isn't limited to images; and it can get us into trouble when we apply amodal completion of human characteristics to AI. Consider these human traits, which I will call the *Seven Signs of Self*:

- Intelligence
- Emotions
- Consciousness
- Self-awareness
- Survival instinct
- Free will
- Creative thinking

In human beings, these are a package deal; they are inseparable. When we see a person sleeping, we amodally complete the higher cognitive abilities that are not on display while asleep. Amodal completion causes agony for parents of an encephalic baby, whose face appears normal but whose brain is almost totally missing and incapable of expressing every one of the traits listed above.

But what happens when an AI demonstrates a capability on the list? Most likely the one it is displaying is intelligence, of course. When world chess champion Garry Kasparov played Deep Blue, he foreshadowed Demis Hassabis's "alien" statement: "I could feel—I could smell—a new kind of intelligence across the table." Deep Blue had made a pawn sacrifice that a human player would have made not from a tactical evaluation but out of a holistic appreciation of the general distribution of the pieces.

Kasparov was unavoidably seeing his opponent in human terms. Having played almost exclusively humans until that point, what else could he do?

But Deep Blue wasn't thinking with the higher order territorial cunning he believed it to have. It had instead calculated every possibility six moves into the future to predict the recovery of the pawn to balance its books.

Many years after Deep Blue, AI is making further inroads into that list of traits. Its intelligence is more strategic, advanced, nuanced. It can interpret emotions and respond with a synthetic affect that seems appropriate, sometimes carried in a pleasing voice, and sometimes emanating from an attractive face. When we experience each of these new achievements, we unconsciously amodally complete the other human traits. This category error is compounded by the fact that we lack a language for talking about artificial cognition to distinguish it from human cognition. Instead, we use phrases like, "This navigation program *wants* to find the shortest route to deliver the pizza… it *knows* that the usual left turn here won't work because of construction… it doesn't *like* its current path so it looks for another one." (Count how many times such language has been casually used in this book, and whether you objected. Or noticed.)

And that's also how computer professionals, the ones who *wrote* such programs, talk. So it's not surprising that many other people would go even further with amodal completion and see AI as having creative thinking, setting its own goals, and being aware of its own consciousness. Gary Marcus calls attributing human level behavior to an AI that doesn't have it the "fundamental overattribution error."[129]

So we anthropomorphize computers; but we also *cybermorphize* brains. (Don't go looking for that word in the dictionary, it's not there yet.) For example, in a 2010 *Scientific American* article, Professor Paul Reber answered a reader's question about the capacity of the human brain by saying it has "something close to 2.5 petabytes" of memory. A petabyte is a million gigabytes; he went on to say this would be enough to store three million hours of TV shows.

This calculation originated from combining a Stanford estimate[130] of a hundred and twenty-five trillion synapses (on the high end of those estimates) and another study with the imposing title of "Nanoconnectomic upper bound on the variability of synaptic plasticity," which assigned 4.7 bits of information per synapse on the strength of there being twenty-six different dendritic spine sizes.[131]

The point I wish to make is not that these estimates are flawed; 26 does indeed equal $2^{4.7}$, so the math checks out. It's that we look at the figure of 2.5 petabytes and think we know what that means (three million hours of video!) when really, equating human memory to digital memory is like comparing apples and pointillism. Our brains don't store memories of events as

MP4-encoded streams, but some fantastically efficiently compressed hierarchy of multisensory associations that we haven't figured out. How many bits in a smell? What's the digital encoding of tastes-like-ketchup?

This tendency to cybermorphize is an odd fetishization of digital beings; either an attempt to find a middle ground on which we can meet our future robot selves on equal terms, or another example of looking for our keys where the light is, instead of where we lost them. Lacking any means for establishing a common reference frame by which to gauge the progress of our artificial intelligences in becoming real ones, we look for the nearest available substitute.

It seems we have a subconscious need to prove ourselves superior to AI, as though we are anticipating insecurities rearing their heads in the imminent future. Many people place expectations upon AI beyond what even people can achieve and then suggest that because AI is not yet our equal in that respect that it will never surpass us anywhere else. For instance, AI is notably poor at detecting hate speech on Facebook, but to hear some people talk about this, you'd think it was proof that AI will never amount to anything. Yet *people* are notably poor at detecting hate speech on Facebook, and not much better than AI. To mock AI's performance at this is like making fun of a toddler for not being able to do calculus.

AI Limitations vs Human Limitations

Let's look at where AI specifically falls short compared to humans. The greatest constraint is that today's AI requires Big Data (usually capitalized, but not to denote an alleged conspiracy like Big Pharma or a bureaucracy like Big Government). As we saw in Chapter 5, training a neural network requires a lot of data, almost impossible with fewer than thousands of examples, and the most success accrues to businesses who have millions of data points.[*]

Humans, on the other hand, need far fewer examples. Take a toddler barely able to speak, point at a passing cat, say "cat," and she will forever after recognize all but edge cases of felines (and you will soon be buying Hello Kitty merchandise). That is called *one-shot learning,* and we don't have the slightest idea how to do it with AI.

---

[*] In 2009 Google scientists wrote a paper "The Unreasonable Effectiveness of Data." The title refers to an unexpected phenomenon in machine learning. It turns out that machine learning using a messy data set with a trillion items can be more effective in tasks like machine translation for which machine learning using a clean data set with only a million items is completely useless.

In fact, humans can do even better than that. Allow me to introduce you to the hippocorn, an imaginary animal that I made up for a class and later discovered to my annoyance was simultaneously invented by several other people. The hippocorn has the body of a hippopotamus with the addition of a unicorn horn. As chimeras go, it's not very creative, but it'll do. Got that picture in your mind? Good. Should you, now, ever encounter a real hippocorn, you will instantly say, "Well, gosh darn, there's an actual hippocorn. Where's my phone?" You will have exercised *zero-shot* learning: the ability to recognize something you have *never* seen before.

Now the toddler—and you—do have an enormous advantage over AIs, of having a pre-existing framework into which to place the cat and the hippocorn. The toddler has some prior experience of animals and can place the cat as a specialization of the category of small four-legged furry creatures. You already know what a hippopotamus and a unicorn are and have internalized the principle of merging body parts.* Whereas when an AI is trained to, say, recognize dogs, its engine is starting from scratch. It doesn't even have the optical concept of a diagonal line available to it. Its engine must discover that feature and many others as part of its learning process.

One of the hard tasks in machine vision is object detection: associating some set of pixels in an image with a "thing" in the real world: banana, jam jar, hippocorn. Most of the effort applied to this task is focused on the word "detection." But what about *object?* That jam jar: is it really one object? Does it not have a lid that comes off? If you don't treat it as two objects, you will not be able to get at the jam. If you don't treat it as three objects, you'll never get the jam out and your toast will remain barren. But a supermarket checkout scanner had better treat it as one object. When does putting one object in, under, or around another object cause them to become a single object? How does the *Star Trek* transporter know to beam up a person's pants with them?

You spent your early years learning how objects could be combined and separated, often at great expense to your guardians' valuables. AI does not have that learning. Your car will be treated as one object by the toll booth and five by the tire salesperson. Object detection is context- and environment-sensitive. Right now, the closest we come to that in computers is to say, "This group of pixels is associated with this three-dimensional reconstruction of a configuration that I assume will not change over time."

---

* Not that actually merging body parts was likely within your experience, but you could transfer the learning of merging other more mergeable things like Play-Doh® to that domain.

We're mostly unaware of how much context we require for nearly every decision. Michael Wooldridge, head of Computer Science at Oxford University, explained it to me:

> When I was born just over fifty-four years ago, that child was the result of billions of years of, essentially, nature doing reinforcement learning, where nature was experimenting with different mutations, with different genetic variations of my ancestors, over billions and billions of billions of years. And there were many, many dead ends in that process. There were many of my ancestral lines that sort of died out along the way, there were many failed experiments. But what nature finally delivered in me is an organism which is, in part, trained to be able to inhabit this world. I was born with some innate skills to be able to inhabit this world. But more than that, I was born with the ability to learn how to inhabit the world, both the physical world and the social world—the world of other human beings. The current techniques for AI don't have any of that.[132]

While it's commonly said that humans *don't* learn how to deal with the world by assimilating countless facts, that's partially untrue. Any parent knows that they feed their child dozens of facts a day, from tips on shoelace-tying to how to select a college. The child has an incredible ability to absorb this information, but more importantly, to put it into the right place in their personal ontological framework—how they organize their knowledge—and to use it to extend that same ontology.

Can you recall an experience of learning some new information that "clicked," and a light bulb went on? Suddenly many things you already knew made more sense and you knew that many more things you were yet to learn would now make sense. That "aha" moment was your ontology expanding. This is what computers can't yet do.

Some people have thought that if we provided computers with enough real-world facts, like an obsessive parent, they would arrive at the same competence that we have with the real world. Doug Lenat's thirty-five-year Cyc project amassed twenty-five million rules but sadly did not evolve the common sense that was hoped for. A later project by Tom Mitchell at Carnegie Mellon University, NELL (Never-Ending Language Learner) attempted to amass facts by trawling the Internet, but by 2019 had confidence in only 3 percent of its 440,000 "beliefs."[133]

The Thatcher Effect

Image recognition provides many examples of how AI does not see the world as we do. The most common kind of facial recognition AI, the convolutional neural network (CNN), has a big problem. If I take a face, say that of Margaret Thatcher, former British Prime Minister:

and make a subtle change:

a CNN will see no difference. As far as it is concerned, these are the same person and there is nothing odd about the second image. It has learned to recognize high-level features—eyes, nose, mouth—but not where on the face these features reside in relation to one another. A CNN sees people like Picasso. This gives rise to a more serious problem: It is also sensitive to the orientation. Turn the entire image upside down, and it has no idea that it's even looking at a face.

That might seem like either a show stopper or inconsequential: People can evade detection by presenting an upside-down profile to surveillance cameras! But also: People have to invert themselves to evade detection! Walking through an airport on your hands might attract attention anyway. Either way, though, it seems as though this is another example of AI inadequacy.

Not so fast. Let's look at Maggie again:

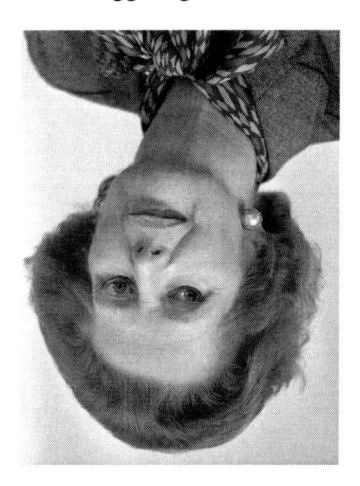

To most, if not all, people, that looks like we've inverted the ex-PM herself. But turn the page upside down and you'll see something hideous. This is called the *Thatcher Illusion*,* and it shows how our own facial recognition algorithms are also limited: while we can at least tell that the inverted image is a face, we cannot usually tell who it belongs to.

But AI could overtake us on this. At the time of writing, *capsule networks* are an innovation that hold a hope for AI not mistaking cyclops-Maggie for the real thing. Once again, there is no solid ground to stand on for anyone trying to make the claim that AI is fundamentally flawed.

---

* It works for other people as well. The first known demonstration of this effect was in 1980 by Peter Thompson, Professor of Psychology at the University of York, using the then-Prime-Minister's visage.

9
Applications of AI

AI will be like the new Hubble Space Telescope, letting us see further into the universe.

— Demis Hassabis

Today's world of business computing is overrun by aaSes—which is to say, vendors have become obsessed with turning capabilities into services. Hence: Platform as a Service (PaaS), Infrastructure as a Service (IaaS), Software as a Service (SaaS). Were they let loose in the domestic market, your Keurig would be relabeled "Coffee as a Service" and the refrigerator would become "Food as a Service."

Stuart Russell points out that a general-purpose AI would be "Everything as a Service" (EaaS).[134] It would achieve the same goals as hiring a human into the business; you're really looking for "Wisdom as a Service." General-purpose AI could run payroll, supply chains, advertising campaigns, market research, and manufacturing lines. The only role left for humans would be to tell it what outcomes to aim for.

We do not have general-purpose AI, yet.

So today's AI inhabits small yet numerous spheres of application. Picking the right application for getting a return on investment through applying AI is… difficult. It requires a deep sense of the pattern-finding and pattern-making abilities of AI which are its great strength, and which problem domains can be coerced into those kinds of problems. To get a sense of the incredible diversity of ways in which AI is being applied today, let's consider a smattering of the categories of those applications, just a wafer-thin cross-section of some of the work currently going on.

Medicine

Medicine provides numerous opportunities to marry AI's need for Big Data with big payoffs for success, particularly where it comes to novel drugs. Proprotein convertase subtilisin/kexin type 9 (PCSK9) is a gene whose name demonstrates why this research doesn't trip off the tongues of mainstream reporters. It's also the name of a protein encoded by that gene, lowering your levels of which will reduce your LDL, or "bad" cholesterol. It took seventy years, starting in 1938, and tens of billions of dollars to discover the biology of LDL receptors and the role of PCSK9. But in 2016, using only the same starting data, machine learning models at GNS Healthcare were able to recreate all the known LDL biology in less than ten months for less than one million dollars, opening the door to further AI-prompted discoveries in cholesterol treatment.[135]

Staying with proteins, DeepMind's AlphaFold, using a hundred and twenty-eight of the latest generation of Google's tensor processing units, can predict the folding of a protein just from the sequence, and it is unbelievably good and fast at it. I say "unbelievably," because researchers who looked at its results thought they were so good that maybe it cheated. (We will see in Chapter 13 how cheating is within the realm of possibility for AI.) So they gave it a special challenge: To find out the structure of a membrane protein from an ancient species of microbes called *archaea*, which had so far defied attempts to model it. While figuring out *archaea* protein won't produce any medical advance that I'm aware of, it was a test case, perfectly suited to tell the researchers just how good AlphaFold was.

What's so important about protein folding? Proteins are the building blocks of life; they are involved in everything from food to the infamous spikes on the coronavirus. A protein is a long chain of amino acids, but this organic string is curled up in a knot. Think about how many ways you could twist a string into a 3-D shape and—well, you can't. The number is unfathomable.

A problem of molecular biology is that we can tell what the order of amino acids in the chain is, but not how it's folded up: we only have certain clues for that, like the numbers that are filled in for you in a Sudoku puzzle. But the shape the protein is folded into means *everything*. That coronavirus protein spike is important because antibodies fit themselves to its shape. Fry an egg, and its proteins unwind. The folding is kind of a big deal. We can write computer programs to try different folding approaches and test whether the result works, like seeing whether a Sudoku solution obeys the rules; the problem is the number of different approaches we have to try is so vast that we can't expect to process enough of them.

Yet AlphaFold returned a detailed image of a three-part protein with two long helical arms in the middle. "It's almost perfect," Dr. Andrei Lupas, Director of the Max Planck Institute for Developmental Biology, told *Science* magazine.[136] "They could not possibly have cheated on this. I don't know how they do it." Mohammed AlQuraishi, a systems biologist at Columbia University said, "It's something I simply didn't expect to happen nearly this rapidly. It's shocking."[137] He thought it would take ten years to get from the 2018 version of AlphaFold to the level of results they achieved in 2020. Dame Janet Thornton at the European Bioinformatics Institute in Cambridge, United Kingdom, has been working on proteins for fifty years. "That's really as long as this problem has been around," she said in a press conference. "I was beginning to think it would not get solved in my lifetime. AlphaFold will open up a new area of research." Having solved *archaea*, researchers now expect AlphaFold to solve problems with medical significance.

A shortage of effective antibiotics is a simmering crisis in medicine, as antibiotic-resistant bacterial strains evolve. Finding a new antibiotic is very important but infernally difficult. Yet in 2020, a deep learning system developed at MIT sifted through over a hundred million candidates within three days to find a particularly effective molecule. The researchers decided to call it halicin, after HAL 9000 from *2001: A Space Odyssey*.[138]

The idea that a technology that revolutionizes molecular biochemistry could do the same for gerontology would be ridiculously far-fetched for anything other than AI. Yet Sathish Sankarpandi, Chief Data Scientist of Orbital Media, developed an AI that can analyze a senior's walking gait and assess how much they are at risk of an accidental fall: "Even at a very early stage, we can just detect that someone is going to fall soon, or their health is declining in some way."[139]

Interpreting radiological scans is an area where the pattern-finding talent of AI can shine: Massive amounts of data already exist that pair scans with the results of expert analysis, a situation tailor-made for training an AI to surpass human performance. One AI was trained to interpret MRI images of hearts in four seconds. It takes a cardiologist thirteen minutes to do the same thing, so this is a huge leap forward in detecting cardiac irregularities.[140]

There seems to be no area of medicine not primed for revolution by AI. Kordel France, CEO of Seekar Technologies, told me he is currently building the first clinical AI tool used to advise neuropsychologists in diagnosing mental disorders. How could this work? "If I go in for an interview and I may have post-traumatic stress disorder, and a doctor asks me about a certain event," he said, "and I seem to emotionally react in a way that might indicate that a topic should be maybe delved a little bit deeper into, the AI is going to pick that up and tell the doctor, 'They seem to have some disengaged eye contact here, some volatility in their voice, etc., so let's look at this particular topic a bit more.'"[141] To illustrate how multi-use AI technology is, France's other AI products include a mobile phone app that can recognize COVID-19 cases when pointed at a chest X-ray, and an attachment for rifle telescopic sights that can tell a hunter if an endangered species is in the field of view.

A team of researchers at the University of Southern California created a digital avatar, SimSensei, to interview soldiers returning from combat duty to discover untreated health issues. The soldiers, trained to be strong and brave and not show weakness, reported more health problems like trouble sleeping or nightmares than they did to human doctors. But when the avatar was made more humanlike, the responses in similar studies exhibited more bravado.[142]

Talk Data to Me

Computers are useless; they answer questions rather than ask them.

— Pablo Picasso

Personal virtual assistants sprout in our pockets and our living rooms: Alexa, Siri, Cortana, and the stubbornly persona-less Google Assistant. Every time I mention them in a podcast, I have to first unplug the nearby device that is sitting there like a dog with its tongue hanging out waiting to hear "walkies," lest it seize the opportunity to chime in with some random factoid dredged from the recesses of Wikipedia.

But for all their ubiquity and the cataracts of money funneled into their development, virtual assistants remain novelties of incidental utility. As hard as I have tried to offload my chores to Alexa, her use in our house is mostly confined to turning on the pantry light and setting a timer for bread baking. Our Amazon purchases are so non-repeating and require such research that commanding Alexa to order them is pointless. However, she has provided hours of diversion for my two daughters to explore her capabilities, ever since the younger one was calling her "Awexa." (If the robot revolution ever happens, I expect to be first to the guillotine for the torture they put her through.)

I once got a call from the Google digital assistant, verifying my Google business listing; and I didn't realize until I hung up that it wasn't a person. Then I thought, "Wait a minute, that's not the usual kind of interaction that I have with someone making that kind of call." He wasn't pushy, and he was straight to the point, hanging up politely without attempting cross-selling; so I replayed the conversation in my mind. And then I realized that he said at the beginning that "he" was an automated interface.*

Take a personal virtual assistant and give it a salary, and you get an AI employee. Like for instance, Talla, from the company of the same name founded by Rob May, who described their process: "We ingest your support documentation, and automatically create machine learning models, natural language models from that, to answer questions that people ask. So when somebody says, 'How do I find out how to return a shipment or get a refund?' we can walk them through the process for that, and we pull it out of your documents on our own, so nobody has to tell us where it is."[143]

Should you want an AI employee to show some personality, Microsoft has you covered. Azure's Project Personality Chat has a customizable personality ranging from Professional to Enthusiastic. If you're wondering what the difference is, they supply a table of sample ways it will dodge the question "When is your birthday?". The Professional chit-chat answers "Age doesn't really apply to me," whereas the Enthusiastic version says, "I'm a bot, so I don't have an age."[144]

Which prompts the question: Just how smart are these digital assistants/chatbots anyway? On October 3rd, 2017, a test was organized for several AI assistants by three Chinese researchers: Feng Liu, Yong Shi, and Ying Liu, primarily based on exams carried out during 2016. They determined that Google's AI Assistant's IQ of 47.3 is barely beneath a six-year-old human's of 55.5. However, it was more than double Siri's IQ of 23.9. Siri is also behind Microsoft's Bing, and Baidu, which have IQs of 31.98 and 32.92 respectively. All AI's IQs are considerably lower than the mean for an 18-year-old human, which is 97.

---

* "He" is now required to do so by California law.

◊

On one hand, it seems as though math and AI are a match made in heaven; on the other hand, a mathematician will tell you that there is so much to symbolic mathematics that it requires creative genius to solve problems starting at high school level. Which makes the achievement of the Logic Theorist program that debuted at the 1956 Dartmouth conference so commendable. It was capable of searching for certain kinds of mathematical proof and eventually solved thirty-eight of the first fifty-two theorems in Whitehead and Russell's *Principia Mathematica,* one of them better than the author's own attempt (to his delight).[145]

Fast forward to 2020, and researchers at Caltech introduced a new deep-learning technique for solving partial differential equations (PDEs) that was dramatically more accurate, more generalizable, and a thousand times faster at solving PDEs than the previous methods. (Their paper was retweeted by MC Hammer for reasons that are regrettably lost to history.) Relatively few people need to solve PDEs—unless they're designing an airplane, in which case they would be very interested in this development, because simulating the flow of air over a surface—like a wing—requires solving the *Navier-Stokes Equation,* a particular PDE that models turbulence, and until now, that has required a supercomputer to handle the workload.[146]

Every year, students from around the world compete in the International Math Olympiad (IMO), answering achingly difficult questions to determine who will medal.* A group of researchers from institutions including Microsoft and Google have now set their sights on the IMO Grand Challenge: Build an AI to win the IMO gold. This is far harder than solving partial differential equations. IMO questions require creativity and brilliance to answer; and not the kind of creativity that is displayed by, say, AlphaGo, because its creativity emerges from exploring a homogeneous solution space that humans haven't fully mapped out, whereas IMO-worthy insights come from a huge body of principles that don't have common qualities.[147]

---

* Sample question: "Let n be an integer with $n \geq 2$. Does there exist a sequence $(a_1, \ldots, a_n)$ of positive integers with not all terms being equal such that the arithmetic mean of every two terms is equal to the geometric mean of some (one or more) terms in this sequence?"

Transformational Technology

> *It can also be maintained that it is best to provide the machine with the best sense organs that money can buy and then teach it to understand and speak English. This process could follow the normal teaching of a child. Things would be pointed out and named, etc.*
>
> — Alan Turing

The initialism GPT has two meanings within AI that overlap by pleasing happenstance. It can stand for *General Purpose Technology:* a development that can be used for multiple purposes (which perfectly describes AI); and also *Generative Pre-trained Transformer,* a language prediction model so capable that it is a general-purpose technology in its own right.

A transformer—in AI, as opposed to electrical engineering or anime—is a neural network model optimized for finding context in language (although some impressive sleight of hand will get it to work on other data too). It's like the autocomplete feature on your smartphone that guesses what word you're most likely to type next. If you type "ulterior," it'll suggest "motive," because in English, the word "ulterior" is almost always followed by "motive," even though there's no grammatical compulsion for it. If you analyze a large amount of English text, you'll see that correlation between those two words, and you can build tables of what word is most likely to follow each other word.

But why stop at looking one word behind? The word "part" might be followed by "human"; the word "and" might precede almost anything; but the words "part and" would, at least in the British argot, be very likely to be followed by "parcel." The further back you look, the smarter your suggestions can be, but of course it will require more computer memory and more training data. You can get a sense of how far back your phone's transcription function will look when you speak a sentence and see it reach back some distance to change an earlier word once it has become apparent from later context what it really was. When I recited the Gettysburg Address into my iPad, it initially typed "…for those who hear gave their" but after a few more words went back to change it to "…for those who here gave their lives…"

A transformer is like a more sophisticated version of autocomplete suggestion, when tuned to look back a *long* way and trained on a *lot* of data—and by "a lot" I mean a large chunk of the Internet; say, Wikipedia. That, of course, takes a *lot* of computational resources; but once a *transformer* has been *pre-trained* on all that text, it can be used over and over to predict, or *generate,* new text.

What is surprising is how far beyond guessing the next words of a text message this can be pushed when the transformer is big enough to have a hundred and seventy-five billion parameters (corresponding to ANN weights), and is fed not just Wikipedia but the *Common Crawl*, an ever-enlarging database of text harvested from the World Wide Web. That is the description of GPT-3, a transformer created by the OpenAI lab and released to the Internet on June 11, 2020.

A total of four hundred and ten billion text tokens were stuffed into GPT-3 by its creators, and the results have stunned and amused thousands of people since its 2020 release. You can access GPT-3 through various applications on the World Wide Web.

The -3, of course, suggests this is not OpenAI's first generative pretrained transformer. Its predecessor, GPT-2, had fewer than a hundredth as many parameters and was commensurately less impressive. Does size matter after all? We'll see: OpenAI founder Sam Altman announced in 2021 that GPT-4 would be not bigger, but smarter.[148]

So what can GPT-3 do when given the chance? Researcher Gwern Branwen gave GPT-3 only a prompt copied from the title of a hilarious McSweeney's article: "Back from Yet Another Globetrotting Adventure, Indiana Jones Checks His Mail and Discovers That His Bid for Tenure Has Been Denied."[149] He received back a lengthy and equally hilarious polemic that concluded:

> Your lack of diplomacy, your flagrant disregard for the feelings of others, your consistent need to inject yourself into scenarios which are clearly outside the scope of your scholarly expertise, and, frankly, the fact that you often take the side of the oppressor, leads us to the conclusion that you have used your tenure here to gain a personal advantage and have failed to adhere to the ideals of this institution.
>
> Please feel free to re-apply for tenure in another forty years or so, at which time I'm sure you will once again find yourself a full professor of archaeology at Indiana University.[150]

You can see part of GPT-3's limitation where it confused the geographical part of Indiana Jones' name with a geographical descriptor for his school. But it's easy to miss. This shows GPT-3's *modus operandi*: you give it an example (a "prompt") of what you're looking for, and it keeps going in the same vein, with content informed by, but not copied from, the Common Crawl.

Another GPT-3 application is Amit Gupta's *Sudowrite*, a tool for creative writers. If you've ever written a challenging piece, especially fiction, you know what writer's block is like. Your brain is stuck like a sheep caught in a fence and all it can do is go *baaa* over and over. Start writing a piece and Sudowrite can keep going, with completely original text that can easily fool a reader into thinking it came from the same writer. Gupta says, "…just the fact that it works at all is kind of astonishing. Like the fact that it can continue a narrative thread, continue a character arc, and not on uncommon occasions generate a piece of dialogue or description that feels like art."[151]

You can have a conversation with some GPT-3 interfaces. But what is behind that magic? Is it like Google Search, finding the best matching text from the body it has crawled? We've seen more intricate and creative output from GPT-3 than that level of simple lookup; does this denote a higher level of intelligence? "If you look at actually how much data it is trained on," says machine learning expert Tomáš Mikolov, "it's maybe ten thousand times more data than a normal human will see in their lifetime. So it's more like the illusion of intelligence than real intelligence…. it's like having a conversation with a parrot that forgets every ten seconds."[152]

Michael Wooldridge, AI researcher and head of the Oxford University Computer Science department gave a similar analysis:

> Ask [GPT-3] about omelets and it will probably tell you a good story about omelets, right? Does it understand omelets in any sense whatsoever? Absolutely not. Because your understanding of an omelet comes from the fact that you're in the real world. And you've experienced breaking eggs and whisking eggs and making omelets and eating omelets. And that great omelet I had in Paris in '97. And all the other experiences that you've got. When you see the word "omelet," what it denotes for you, what it means for you is all those experiences. And so your understanding of that symbol "omelet" derives from all of that stuff. Some of your understanding, for sure, comes from books, right? You might remember a memorable passage in a novel where somebody eats an omelet or something like that, but your understanding of it is grounded in the world. And GPT-3 has none of that.[153]

Github CoPilot, mentioned in Chapter 2, does for computer source code what GPT-3 does for language; in other words, just as GPT-3 can take a prompt like the beginning of a poem and then write more of the poem in the same style, you can type the beginning of a function into CoPilot and it can suggest what comes next. The underlying technology, called OpenAI Codex, is a transformer, the same as GPT-3, only it's trained on the public codebase in Github. A stunning amount of software source code is stored on Github; it only makes sense that you could do something useful with it with AI, just as GPT-3 has done with the text on the Internet.

We seem to be getting diminishing returns on the intelligence: doubling the number of parameters doesn't seem to double the size of the context they can work with. GPT-3 had a training cost of $12 million, two hundred times that of GPT-2.

Of course, that's not going to stop people from seeing how much more performant bigger transformers will get. Alibaba, which is like the Amazon of China, has an R&D branch called DAMO Academy (Discovery, Adventure, Momentum, and Outlook), which announced in 2021 that they had built a multimodal, multitasking language model with one trillion parameters—five times the size of GPT-3. And then they reduced its energy consumption by 80 percent and increased its efficiency by a factor of eleven. But the real news is what they did later to improve those numbers even more: they increased it to ten trillion parameters and reduced the energy consumption to 1 percent of GPT-3.

You know, it's easy to get blasé, tossing around those factors of improvement, but where else do you see this sort of change? Did your airplane travel three times as fast to its destination this year? Is your car's fuel efficiency improved by a factor of ten? Are you eating a quarter of what you used to? Those kinds of off-the-charts changes belong exclusively to a small number of exponential technologies, of which AI is the poster child.*

Chatbots as Art

We must never forget that the human heart is at the center of the technological maze.

— Steven Barnes

What of even more non-mathematical, non-scientific pursuits, such as the arts, and music? Historian Pamela McCorduck told me how AI first made forays into the humanities: "As humanities research began to digitize its material, they discovered they can do all kinds of things with it. They could compare music to literature. Well, you could sort of do it

---

* I asked historian Pamela McCorduck how she thought the founders of the field, now deceased, would react to the *wunderkind* GPT-3. She replied, "I think they'd be thrilled, frankly, because it is the result of enormous amounts of human brainpower figuring out how to do this well."

before, if you had some really smart person who was willing to sit on a hard chair for years on end and say, 'Oh, yes, Beethoven's *Eroica* matches, dah, dah, dah, dah, dah.' Well, now you can do it with thousands of books or poems, compared to thousands of musical things. It gives you amazing insight into a period of history. Okay, so you're doing that, how are you doing it? You ask yourself, 'How will I represent this?' Representation, digitally speaking, is really fundamental, and AI is a guide into the thicket of representation."[154]

Somewhere between the customer service chatbot and the AIs creating digital writing we have Phil D. Hall and his *echoborg* performance art. An audience watches as a volunteer converses with a chatbot; but the conversation is mediated by the echoborg, actress Marie-Helene Boyd, who voices the responses from an AI as she hears them through headphones. She provides a human mien to the conversation; the volunteer can forget they're really talking to an AI. The conversation is like talking to a researcher in sociology who's also a mime for Cirque du Soleil and a cutting-edge computer programmer.

Hall described how the echoborg came about:

> I was doing some research as an undergraduate, on people's perception of identity in virtual spaces, and to get from point A to point B in Meridian 59 [an avatar-based virtual world] you needed to collaborate, which really caught me by the short and curlies, just fascinating, about not knowing who people were and having to work together. There was no voice input/output; it was all text, but you needed to talk to chatbots, non-player characters, and I had an argument with one in a bar, because it just wouldn't tell me what I wanted to know....
>
> The show evolves, but each time you kick it off, it goes in a different direction. And within the realms of what we expected to do, it does it, and sometimes it surprises us, and pretty much all the time when Marie-Helene comes out the other side of it, she's like, "Wow, what happened?"[155]

Our final example comes from AI startup StoryFile, which has built a videobot of William Shatner. Specifically, they have created a digital version of him that we can only refer to as the Shatbot. They interviewed him against a green screen with numerous 3-D cameras trained on him so their AI could learn his expressions—now right there is a capacity challenge for human or machine—and he answered all kinds of questions for them so it could learn about his speaking style and content. Then when you ask the Shatbot a question, it will search through its memory and construct an appropriate answer which it can then animate the Shatbot avatar to virtually speak.

◊

We've toured a small fragment of the applications of AI, to give you a taste of what's possible. AI could even predict war: Descartes Labs uses AI to analyze satellite images of changing crop patterns to predict agricultural trends and patterns of disease; it subsequently predicted US corn production to within 2 percent. What does corn have to do with conflict? Production shortfalls in some countries are leading indicators of war.[156]

But there is another application so big it needs its own chapter…

10
Self-Driving Cars

I don't actually have to experience crashing my car into a wall a few hundred times before I slowly start avoiding how to do so.

— Andrej Karpathy, Director of AI, Tesla Motors

On August 17th, 1896, Bridget Driscoll was strolling through Dolphin Terrace, behind London's Crystal Palace, the ziggurat of iron and glass that enshrined the Victorian conquest of nature for the Great Exhibition of 1851. Visiting this edifice of history with her sixteen-year-old daughter May, the laborer's wife did not realize that she was shortly to become part of history herself.

One of only twenty petrol cars in Britain, an imported Roger-Benz was being demonstrated there by driver Arthur Edsall. Forty-five-year-old Bridget was described as "bewildered" by this apparition, traveling at a speed recounted by some onlookers as "a tremendous pace," (though its engine was limited to a top speed of 4.5 miles per hour). Only a few weeks earlier, Parliament had abolished the requirement for automobiles to be preceded by a walking flagman twenty yards ahead.

The Times recounted May's testimony at the inquest into what followed: "The car then swerved off, and [the] witness looked to see where it was, and it was then going over her mother. (Here the witness broke down.) Her mother was knocked down, and the car was at once pulled up." And so Bridget Driscoll became the first pedestrian to be killed by an automobile.*

Since then, she has had plenty of company. Approximately 1.3 million people per year are killed worldwide in automobile accidents, and 90 percent of them are estimated to be due to preventable human error. Reductions in that mortality rate have been hard-won. Autonomous vehicle (AV) developers are taking aim at that 90 percent; the US Department of Transportation said in 2018 that AVs could reduce fatalities by 94 percent.[157]

It's not the developers' only motivation, of course; there's a pot of gold at the end of this rainbow in the form of owning the market for robotic taxi fleets and delivery vehicles, but AVs have little chance of being accepted by the public unless they are at least ten times safer than human drivers, and this goal is mostly distant. Nevertheless, development proceeds at a superheated pace.

Which brings us to how Elaine Herzberg landed in the history books next to Bridget Driscoll. At 9:58 PM on March 18th, 2018, she was pushing a bicycle across a four-lane road in Tempe, Arizona, when she was struck by an Uber car being tested in self-driving mode. This incident is considerably better documented than the death of Bridget Driscoll. Uber is a disruptive transportation company that acts as a broker between independent car owners with time to act as chauffeurs, and individuals looking for a ride. They leveraged the modern technologies of GPS, trip planning AI, and smartphones into the infrastructure of a distributed taxi service. (The employment status of the drivers is a matter of ongoing contention, as is calling Uber a taxi service.)

Uber's greatest cost is those independent car owners' time, so it is greatly enticed by the prospect of delivering transportation as a service without them. The Volvo XC90 sport utility vehicle being used to test their self-driving software was equipped with cameras, radar, and LIDAR,† two of which would have been unaffected by the near-complete lack of light in the area.

It was also equipped with a human backup driver, whose instruction was to monitor the road at all times with her hands hovering above the steering wheel. Interior video showed that she was instead watching *The*

---

* Mary Ward was killed by an experimental steam car in County Offaly, Ireland on August 31, 1869, but she was a passenger in the car, thrown out on a curve and hit by the car's wheel, technically making her a passenger fatality.
† An equivalent of radar at optical wavelengths, Light Detection and Ranging is able to generate a high-resolution 3-D map of the surroundings. The "beanie hat" on Google cars contains a spinning LIDAR unit.

Voice on her smartphone and looked up only half a second before the impact. Even in the poor lighting conditions, police estimated that most human drivers would have seen Herzberg at least a hundred and forty-three feet away and started braking in time to avoid hitting her.

But the Volvo *should* have acted sooner. Its radar *did* detect Herzberg six seconds before impact. But then it began a cycle of alternately classifying her as a vehicle, a bicycle, and an unknown object, each reclassification causing, through inadequate software design, loss of useful information. With one second to go, the car decided that braking was necessary—but didn't brake. It entered a mode called "action suppression," put in place because autonomous braking had been happening in too many spurious cases and posing a hazard (or annoyance) to drivers following a self-driving vehicle that had apparently decided to slam on the brakes for the hell of it. Instead of braking, the Uber alerted the human driver, who was engrossed in the show, and by the time she had gained situational awareness and hit the brakes, the collision had already occurred.[158]

Uber ceased its program of AV testing. Although the National Transportation Safety Board reported that there were safety failures on the part of not only the human driver, but Uber and the state, the public is hypersensitized to any fatality involving a self-driving vehicle, which means that their testers must be incredibly cautious. This incident may be related to how an American Automobile Association survey showed that three-quarters of Americans say they'd be afraid to ride in an AV.[159]

Why can you not yet, aside from at a handful of very special locations, summon a driverless vehicle to take you where you want while you nap in the back seat? Doesn't the rate of progress make them imminent?

Self-driving cars have been in development longer than most people are aware; they first took to the roads in *1986,* when Ernst Dickmanns demonstrated one. In October 1994, three of his Mercedes-Benz cars fitted with cameras and on-board AIs drove a thousand kilometers autonomously on roads around Paris. But only just. There were limitations that today's cars don't have: they were only focused on road markings, and if those vanished or were obscured, the cars were helpless.[160]

The challenge that self-driving vehicles face in coming to market is a familiar one to computer graphics artists: the *uncanny valley,* that chasm of believability that has to be crossed before a digital version of a human stops being creepy and starts becoming likeable. In the case of the autonomous vehicle, the canyon to be crossed lies between what the Society of Automotive Engineers, in standard J3016,[161] prosaically calls levels three and four. (See Figure 10.1.)

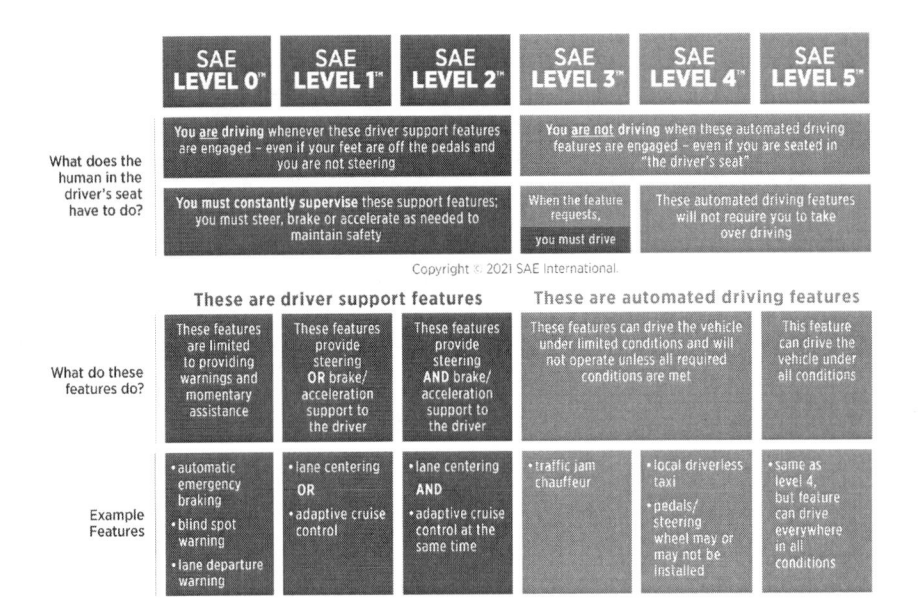

	SAE LEVEL 0"	SAE LEVEL 1"	SAE LEVEL 2"	SAE LEVEL 3"	SAE LEVEL 4"	SAE LEVEL 5"
What does the human in the driver's seat have to do?	You **are driving** whenever these driver support features are engaged – even if your feet are off the pedals and you are not steering			You **are not driving** when these automated driving features are engaged – even if you are seated in "the driver's seat"	
^^	You must constantly supervise these support features; you must steer, brake or accelerate as needed to maintain safety			When the feature requests, you must drive	These automated driving features will not require you to take over driving	
	Copyright © 2021 SAE International.						
	These are driver support features			These are automated driving features		
What do these features do?	These features are limited to providing warnings and momentary assistance	These features provide steering OR brake/ acceleration support to the driver	These features provide steering AND brake/ acceleration support to the driver	These features can drive the vehicle under limited conditions and will not operate unless all required conditions are met		This feature can drive the vehicle under all conditions
Example Features	• automatic emergency braking • blind spot warning • lane departure warning	• lane centering OR • adaptive cruise control	• lane centering AND • adaptive cruise control at the same time	• traffic jam chauffeur	• local driverless taxi • pedals/ steering wheel may or may not be installed	• same as level 4, but feature can drive everywhere in all conditions

Figure 10.1: SAE Self-Driving Autonomy Levels
Copyright 2021, SAE International

Level two is easy to define; it means the car is capable of some automation, but nothing that allows you to take your eyes off the road. *Wired* describes level two automation as "getting a toddler to help you with the dishes." Level four is similarly easy to define; it means that the car is capable of driving itself over a complete route, if the conditions are favorable and the route is well known. The holy grail of level five is when the car can handle itself in all situations and no longer needs a steering wheel, pedals, or human occupant at all times.

But in between, we have the uncanny valley of level three, where the car can drive by itself *most* of the time. Superficially, it would seem to be a sensible intermediate between the definitions of levels two and four; but in practice, it is a giant step backward. Because if the car can deal with 99 percent of situations in a trip, you may be lulled after half an hour into believing that it's got this handled, when suddenly it makes a wrong decision. Even if, optimistically, it anticipates the need for human assistance and issues a cry for help, the best driver, if they have been napping or watching *The Voice,* cannot summon full situational awareness in less than five seconds, usually much longer. How likely is it that the unfamiliar situation will be visible to the car's sensors at least five seconds before it will arrive? This is why Waymo, the autonomous vehicle arm of Google, has decided that it will not let anything onto the road until it is at level four. The goal they are chasing is daunting: human drivers are involved in fatal accidents on average only once every hundred million miles.[162]

But to read many predictions about AVs, you would think widespread deployment of level four vehicles was only months away. In fact, if you'd been accepting such predictions since 2016, you would have come to the same conclusion at every point during that time. The problem is that so many Panglossian commentators were swept up in the flush of predicting *what* would happen when vehicles reached level five that they neglected the much harder question of *when* that would happen. There's no question that a fleet of level five vehicles would revolutionize transportation and society, dispersing themselves around a city like an unmanned Uber fleet, waiting for a passenger to summon them, managed as a collective with shared ownership. Transportation as a service, bringing an end to road fatalities if not all fender benders.

Just not today. Or tomorrow. If you drive with an eye for how well an AV could handle a situation, you will see many challenges when you move away from the uncomplicated highways and motorways. Such as this situation encountered by the author, which requires understanding a novel sign and looking across a river past two bridges to see if the single lane is clear, and counting the number of vehicles that have traversed each way just before you:

Driving a motor vehicle might be the hardest thing your brain ever does. It's assimilating information from multiple senses, using trained reflexes and learned patterns to treat the vehicle as an extension of your body, interpreting knowledge of vehicle laws, local conventions, continually running OOPDA loop simulations to predict the effects of not only your actions but the vehicles around you (that rusting VW bug may not be likely to accelerate and cut in front of you, but the Lotus Evora is probably itching to), and remembering a fantastically optimized three-dimensional map which it updates in real time. And yet you're able to do this so efficiently that many people combine it with the sport of texting their friends, albeit sometimes fatally.

Much of the act of driving takes place through the exercise of learned reflexes, what Daniel Kahneman called *System 1 Thinking*. No conscious or logical thought is involved; instead, your eyes are connected to your hands through a neural express lane that bypasses the slower parts of your brain. Musicians learn the same way: They start out slowly translating the notes on the page and locating their counterparts on their instrument ("That's a D, okay where's the D key… great, next there's an E, okay, I know where that is…"). This is Kahneman's *System 2 Thinking*: conscious, logical, calculating, but you can't play much beyond *Three Blind Mice* that way.

Your goal as a musician or a driver is to train the instinctual pathways in your brain to take certain inputs, be they musical notation or lines in the middle of the road, and connect them to limb movements. The more proficient you get, the more complex the patterns you associate with learned actions, so now you don't just know how to play a D♭ on sight but also a D minor seventh chord. Similarly, you have internalized the limb ballet for parallel parking (well, some of us have, anyway). You have moved from System 2 to System 1 through practice. We are doing this all the time, instinctively; to give our brains a break, we automate any cognitive task that we perform in a similar enough fashion over and over.

Does the description of System 1 remind you of anything? Connecting a fixed set of inputs to the right set of outputs is exactly what a neural network does. This means that what many would think the hardest aspect of driving to automate—recognizing patterns and associating them with objects and navigation—is actually the easiest. Whereas automating the rules of the road is considerably harder: despite the fact that in some countries those rules are literally called the Vehicle (or Highway) *Code*, they cannot be simply typed into a computer because they require advanced perception to delineate the objects and situations they describe.[*]

---

[*] And also because when subjected to engineering rigor, ambiguities and inconsistencies become apparent.

You have learned what a vehicle intending to make a U-turn into an alley looks like, and now just have to remember who has the right-of-way. But the only way for an AI to learn that is through being exposed to thousands of examples of that situation until it matches the input patterns with the correct actions. The same process as if you had to learn it as instinctively as smacking your horn when you get cut off. This training is phenomenally intensive.

Let's look at how what's going on in your brain during a typical drive. You're barreling down the highway listening to Nine Inch Nails and generally paying little conscious attention to an area you've been through dozens of times before. A small sentinel in your brain is monitoring the environment, but unless it is called on, you may well reach your destination and suddenly wonder, "How did I get here?" and have no memory of any of the places along the route.

Let's say that the sentinel spots something ahead in your lane: looks like a garbage bag. Unless you encountered that same garbage bag in the same place recently, it will summon another part of your brain for guidance. It may not yet reach your conscious attention, but a conference will take place between these parts as to whether the garbage bag constitutes a hazard: Does it look like it's empty? If you can be sure of that then you do not need to change course. Your sensory acuity is turned up as you inspect the bag for signs of movement that would indicate nothing is inside, but so far, you're still tapping your foot to NIИ.

If the conference yields no assurance that the garbage bag is empty, a higher part of your brain is engaged and asked: Can we execute a swerve maneuver? If the lane next to you is completely clear, this may take place instinctively, with your awareness taking place mostly after the fact.

If the adjacent lane is *not* empty, these parts of your brain yank the fire alarm, and now *you* show up. Now you have to evaluate stopping distances, the behavior of nearby vehicles, and whether signaling is helpful, probably within less than a second. Hormones cascade in a fight-or-flight response as your body goes into overdrive to give you every resource it can to deal with this risk.

There's no question that a computer is capable of perceiving and acting much faster than a human being; and that it can calculate distances far more accurately and control the car with greater precision. So it could, say, sneak through a gap between adjacent vehicles far narrower than anyone other than a stunt driver would attempt. When AI is able to perceive and interpret its environment as correctly as a human, those skills will make autonomous vehicles far safer than human drivers.

But we are not there yet. Training an AV to deal with a garbage bag on the road is painfully tedious. You are leveraging a lifetime of experience of how large plastic bags behave with or without different contents; your first five years of life were mostly spent learning how physical objects in the world behave. AVs do not have this experience. They can be trained on garbage bags, but what about the other detritus that might interrupt our drive? Do we run hugely expensive training runs to recognize mattresses, clothing, lumber, food? Look at any metro TV station's news to learn what sort of things can and frequently do fall off trucks: beer, livestock, oranges, milk. We already know how to recognize each of those things and how they behave; we know we can drive over the milk but not the cow. It requires System 2 thinking to make that distinction; but we have that available to us, backed by knowledge of countless real-world *things*.

The road to level four is so fraught that Google eventually decided that humans are so unreliable that their autonomous cars should not go into operation until they could avoid interacting with drivers altogether. Professor David Mindell said, "Google changed its approach to get rid of these troublesome people—drivers," and quoted engineer Nathaniel Fairfield: "Google discovered that 'people are lazy,'" and found that their trust of AVs goes from "plausible suspicion to way overconfidence." Relieving humans of all operating responsibility would mean Google could prevent the 93 percent of car accidents estimated to derive from what their engineers describe as the 'lazy driver', or human error." [163]

But until we cross that uncanny valley, there will be many Catch-22s to the rollout of autonomous vehicles. Because the rollout cannot be gradual; when they appear anywhere, fully autonomous vehicles have to be more reliable than human drivers from day one.

What obstacles face AVs on residential roads? I turned to Todd Litman, director of the Victoria Transport Policy Institute and author of the report *Autonomous Vehicle Implementation Predictions*. Here's part of our dialogue:

> **Todd:** Do we encounter kangaroos on the roads here? [Note: We live near each other on the opposite side of the world from Australia.]
>
> **Me:** Not unless one escapes from a zoo.*
>
> **Todd:** So an AV here would not have the kangaroo-avoidance

---

* We have deer, though. My Tesla Model 3 displays them as a pedestrian-trash-can centaur on its visualization screen (which, to be fair, is more limited in its choice of display objects than the internal software is in interpreting them).

> module. But do we have a holiday called Halloween? Is it conceivable that a child could be crossing the road in a kangaroo costume?
>
> **Me:** Yes; we've certainly seen a spate of full-body dinosaur costumes around here.
>
> **Todd:** What, then, is the likelihood that an AV that may or may not know what to do with a real kangaroo would know what to do with one that contained a human?

He went on:

> It's perfectly conceivable that some young adult will dress up as a kangaroo zombie, they will be a zombie that eats other zombies, and they'll have fake blood on their mouth. Say you're driving into downtown and I warn you, "Watch out for the zombie walk, where there are a bunch of young people dressed up in wild costumes like zombie kangaroos," you would understand that, because you have one time been a foolish young person yourself, I assume. [But] a computer has no reference, and so a computer would probably immediately code a foolish teenager dressed up as a zombie kangaroo as either a terrible threat or a traffic accident victim.[164]

Every driver is aware of what a ball bouncing into the road would signify—the likelihood of it being followed by an oblivious child. And we can train an AV, of course, to recognize a bouncing ball and exercise similar caution. I discussed this with author Steven Shwartz, who commented, "Well, what if a GI Joe [an American toy soldier] comes out into the road? Now, have you trained your AI system to recognize GI Joes? Probably not. And never mind just recognizing GI Joes; do you have that rule in there that you'd better slow down if a GI Joe bounces out into the road?" Of course, our rule is not as specific as "ball," but "toy." But toys are much harder for an AI to classify in general. Shwartz went on, "And do we even have a rule, or is it something we just recognize on the spot based on our knowledge? We just reason it the first time we see a ball bounce out, we say, 'Oh, that ball must have come from a child.' It's not like we were taught it in driving school."[165]

A NOVA episode described how AV testers discovered that people carrying umbrellas were not recognized as human, and that case had to be added to training. If holding a dome on a stick changes our morphology enough to take us out of the correct classification, what are the odds that there might be another shape we could carry (for instance, I prefer to carry heavy objects on my head for balance) that would have the same effect?[166]

From zombie kangaroos to umbrellas, these scenarios show why autonomous vehicles are not about to fulfill the dream of replacing human drivers in all situations. There is a near infinitely long fat tail of situations that, while individually rare, collectively form a corpus most of which will simply never be part of standard training sets. By way of a very long tail example, in 2014 a Google car encountered a woman in an electric wheelchair chasing a duck into the road with a broom. (The woman had the broom, not the duck.)

Despite that, Litman is relatively sanguine about the future of AVs: "I suspect that by, say 2030, you will be able to have level four cars that are commercially available, but they will not be mass market." But he doesn't think that autonomous trucks or cars are the best solution to our most pressing transportation problems:

> We should be asking, what's the cheapest way to get a container from, say, Long Beach to Denver, Colorado, considering all costs and all technological capabilities. I suspect if we were more rational, we would be investing more in these incremental logistical improvements, as they are doing in Europe and Asia, rather than assuming that self-driving technologies are going to save us.
>
> There is a good question whether the idea that your car can drive you home is going to encourage some people to organize their lives around more driving, and the car chauffeuring them home; when you think of all kinds of other situations where your self-driving car is going to encourage you to live a more automobile-dependent lifestyle, are we better off with a more accessible, less automobile-dependent lifestyle?[167]

Not surprisingly, even the most forward-thinking of countries are cautious. In China, AV companies must pass a series of objective evaluations before they're granted permits to test on public roads. A multiphase graduated system defines where they're allowed to test based on the vehicle's capabilities. When changes are made to the vehicle configuration, such as replacing a sensor with a different type or moving the sensor to a new location, these tests must be redone before the revised vehicles can go on the road. Before Mobileye (owned by Intel) could begin testing in Germany recently, it had to go through an independent evaluation by TÜV Süd, one of the technical monitoring organizations that handles the vehicle type approval process there. In the United

States, AV companies file paperwork with the state, pay a fee, and then go about their testing.

But what will happen when we reach the point that AVs are at least as safe as human drivers? It would be natural to think that our prior reluctance to letting them loose would have some inertia. But consider this thought from Ted Parson, professor leading the AI-PULSE (Program on Understanding Law, Science, and Evidence) at UCLA's School of Law: that someone could make the case that "any delay that you impose upon the rollout of autonomous vehicles is murder because we would then know they're safer than human drivers. And every delay means more people will die at the hands of incompetent and reckless human drivers and drunk human drivers than would otherwise be the case."[168]

We would be in a real-life version of the *Trolley Problem,* which has been trotted out *ad nauseam* in discussions of self-driving cars so I'll only give the briefest of descriptions to ensure that you're familiar with it. Crafted by philosopher Philippa Foot in 1967, it invites you to a thought experiment, in which a trolley (also called a streetcar or tram) is charging down a track towards where some fiend has tied five people to the rails. You are standing next to a switch, the kind of long lever that will move the rails, which if you pull it, will divert the trolley to another track. A track where someone (presumably the same fiend) has tied *one* person to the track. Pulling the lever, and causing one death—or not pulling it, and allowing five deaths—are your only options. This question has been posed numerous times by autonomous vehicle commentators wondering how AV makers will program them to handle a similar situation. (Not that finding people tied to the road is a likely scenario, but the equivalent would be swerving to avoid a group of pedestrians but unavoidably hitting a bystander.)

The Trolley Problem is, mercifully, an unlikely scenario even in that formulation; but it will be *very* likely, inevitable, in fact, in a different form, when autonomous vehicles become better drivers *on average* than humans. Because deploying them will save more lives than not doing so; but some of the fatal accidents that will still happen with AVs will be people killed in particular situations that the AVs had not yet learned how to handle as well as humans. Those would be people who would not have died had the AVs been left in the garage; and it will be obvious in many cases that a human driver would not have made the same mistake.

Nevertheless, Parson and other experts I have talked to research the real Trolley Problem. I brought up the fact that in a real-world situation, there would not be the moral certitude created by the experimenter that one set of deaths or the other were 100 percent guaranteed. Perhaps the car would be equipped to assign probabilities to the outcomes, though. "If we were in a trolley problem situation," said Parson, "we would say, minimize the discrete number of fatalities. Actively choose to kill this one, as opposed to do nothing and passively consent, or acquiesce to killing these three. But moving to probabilistic risk of dying does not actually change that problem. So you could still have a system that simply minimizes expected loss of human life."

He went on to delineate a legal quandary that the manufacturer would be in:

> Or you could have a system that minimizes expected loss of human life with a different weighting assigned to risk of people inside the vehicle, in other vehicles, and on the sidewalk. Now, it is understandable that nobody wants to engage those decisions explicitly, and thus, people selling these products have to say, 'Oh, no, no, we never have to do that.' And yet, I think they do have to engage them explicitly at some level, or they are passively designing a system that will make certain decisions in those situations, even if they're not acknowledging it.[169]

Many public figures continue to trip over their swords in predicting the arrival of level five cars. In late 2017, Philip Hammond, the British Chancellor of the Exchequer, announced the government's intention to have fully driverless cars without a safety attendant on board on British Roads by 2021. At the time of writing this in 2022, we are of course still nowhere close to fulfilling that intention.

AVs are in some ways a proxy for artificial general intelligence, in that we don't know what it will take to implement them, or how long before we get there. It is entirely plausible that level five will require AGI; the problem is that we lack a measure of the gap we still have to traverse. The SAE scale entices us to believe that the gap between level three and level four is the same as the gap between level two and level three, which we have already achieved. I suggest that the news of advances in AVs today might be more accurately framed as going from, say, level 3.0012 to 3.0013, if only we could map out those ten thousand sublevels.

Each new gain in AV performance seems to be won at an increasing cost, suggesting we are approaching an asymptote, a hard limit of capability. That would be wonderful if the hard limit was the level we needed. But what if the real situation is this:

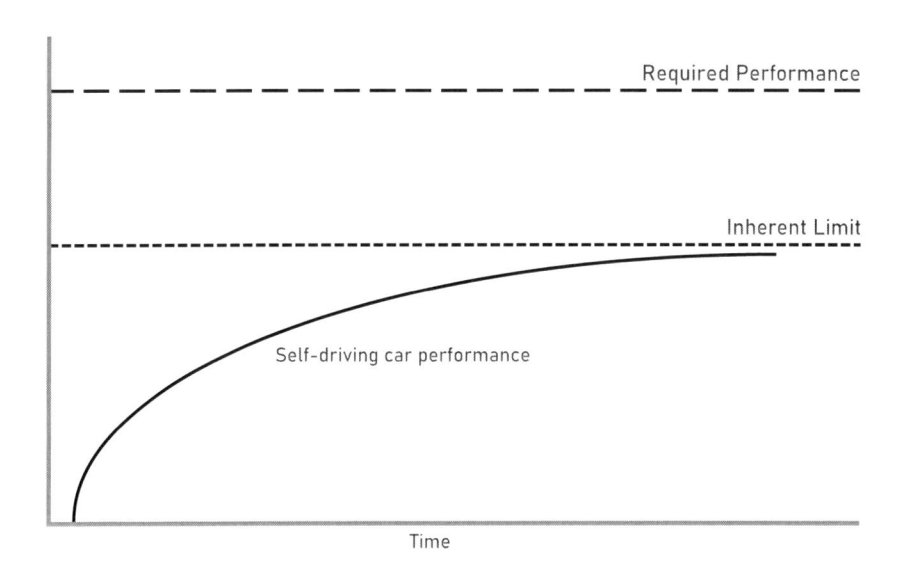

Chart: Y-axis shows performance with dashed lines for "Required Performance" (top) and "Inherent Limit" (below it). A curve labeled "Self-driving car performance" rises steeply then asymptotes toward the Inherent Limit. X-axis: Time.

All that pessimism might leave you thinking that AVs are not poised to disrupt our world. But that isn't accurate either. Although today, self-driving vehicles are either the poster child for AI advancement, a threat to jobs, or unbridled hype, depending on your point of view, they still deserve our attention, because they don't all need to reach level five to create disruption. The highway/freeway/motorway/autobahn is a sufficiently simple and controlled environment as to permit AVs to ply it with acceptable performance. That might seem insufficient, because if they can't handle the first and last miles of a trip, on far more challenging local roads, what is the point? But this conclusion would ignore the serious motivation of trucking companies, because 28 to 50 percent of their costs are the human drivers.[170]

Picture this: A trucker pulls an eighteen-wheeler near a freeway on-ramp and gets out. Shortly, a platoon of a dozen semis comes down the freeway, and the new truck glides up, autonomously, to join them. A single human is napping in the back in case of emergencies, like needing to put on tire chains, but the vehicles continue across the country, driving less than six feet apart because of the fuel benefits of slipstreaming, and the trucks are linked electronically so if one brakes, the others will keep perfect step. Periodically a truck peels off at an exit where it is met by a local human driver who navigates that perilous last mile to its destination.

In 2019, Plus.ai's autonomous tractor-trailer finished its first test freight run across the United States. The truck traveled mostly in autonomous mode across 2,800 miles from California to Pennsylvania, in less than three days.[171]

This scenario is the transition of the long-haul trucking profession to short-haul trucking. It might be nearly invisible to the urban commuter, but the effect on the trucking infrastructure would be immense, driven by a reduction in the number of truck drivers of maybe 90 percent. Interstate truck stops would no longer cater to human truckers needing rest; their only business would be refueling the platoons.

But a phenomenal amount of funding is being poured into AV last-mile research anyway, in the hope of being first to market. A team at the Technical University of Munich, working with BMW, has developed an early warning system for autonomous vehicles that uses AI to learn from about 2,500 real traffic situations. Team lead Professor Eckehard Steinbach, Chair of Media Technology and a member of the Board of Directors at the Munich School of Robotics and Machine Intelligence, says that if used in today's self-driving vehicles, it could offer seven seconds advance warning against potentially critical situations that the cars cannot handle alone—with over 85 percent accuracy.

And in some narrow markets, AVs are already operating at level four. In 2021, AutoX, a Chinese AV company founded by Dr. Jianxiong Xiao, a former Princeton professor going by the action hero moniker of "Professor X," launched a level four robo-taxi service in Shenzen. It qualifies as level four because their promotional video shows an entire journey being completed with the vehicle's sole passenger remaining in the back seat. It is not level five, because as commenters pointed out, it was seen to operate only in wide streets with far less traffic than fairly represents all of Shenzen: spacious multilane roads with landscaped medians, little traffic and few, but not zero, pedestrians, which the vehicle navigated around. It also handled a difficult situation for an AV, that of going down a narrow two-lane street and finding a truck stopped in its lane. When you or I encounter that situation, we have to edge out into the opposing lane to see if it's clear to go past that truck on the other side of the street. And that's exactly what the AutoX taxi did. While it is operating only under a narrow set of ideal conditions, including having reserved pickup curb spaces, nevertheless, those conditions are still broad enough to encompass a useful use case.[172]

Social and Policy Issues

But just like the car itself, automation could also bring its own social issues. In addition to automating existing journeys, research has shown that autonomous vehicles could have a dramatic influence on how people use cars. A 2017 study from the Society of Motor Manufacturers and Traders[173] claimed that a million more Britons could pursue a college degree thanks to autonomous cars, as people with otherwise restricted mobility could hail a ride and travel to their classes.

A 2018 study at the University of California at Davis followed thirteen individuals in the San Francisco Bay Area. The study tracked the subjects' travel over three weeks, but for the middle week, the subjects had access to sixty hours of chauffeur service designed to simulate an autonomous car. The results were surprising. Subjects normally drove around two hundred and fifty miles in a week. With the chauffeur car, travel increased by 83 percent to nearly five hundred miles. Of those extra miles, 21 percent of them had no riders except the chauffeur.[174]

The incentives to get to level five remain strong even for consumers. Research from analysis firm ARK Invest in April 2019 asserted that a Tesla Model 3 could earn its owner $10,000 per year by working as part of a robo-taxi service.[175]

Regulatory authorities were clearly caught unawares by the rate at which autonomous vehicles appeared on the roads. Otherwise, we might at the very least have seen a modern equivalent of the flag bearer required to precede Victorian cars, in the form of some kind of external indicator that a vehicle was in self-driving mode. Instead they defaulted to the existing laws that hold whoever is in the driver's seat completely responsible for the movement of the car. Realizing that the day when no one is in the driver's seat is coming, in January 2022, the English and Scottish Law Commissions published recommendations for how control should be transferred inside a self-driving vehicle and how to allocate responsibility.

Meanwhile, governments, perhaps bemused by the hype and fearful of missing a major economic stimulus, continue to adopt a permissive attitude. Guangzhou, China-based WeRide received approval from the California Department of Motor Vehicles to test driverless vehicles on public roads in San Jose, two and a half months after Baidu was granted a permit to do the same.[176] Germany has adopted legislation that will allow driverless vehicles on public roads by 2022, laying out a path for companies to deploy robo-taxis and delivery services in the country at scale. While autonomous testing is currently permitted in Germany, this would allow operations of driverless vehicles without a human safety operator behind the wheel.[177]

Tesla appears to have hit on a way to make its cars' *human* drivers safer while waiting for the Godot of level five automation. If you want to use the Full Self Driving (FSD) Beta capability, which has the capability of driving autonomously on side streets, you have to earn it by driving conservatively. *Really* conservatively. Brake or turn even slightly too hard, and your safety score dips below the roughly 99 percent that you have to maintain to be granted access to the FSD Beta (which you paid dearly for). In other words, Tesla is turning *humans* into safer drivers through gamification.

In dribs and drabs, autonomous vehicles are appearing in specialized applications and restricted environments: shuttles plying transportation terminals and private grounds, robot delivery vehicles scuttling along sidewalks, the Waymo and AutoX taxis serving a few small metropolitan areas. Technologists should not make the mistake of assuming that everyone views this progress with the same unbridled enthusiasm that they do. Audrey Tang, polymath and Digital Minister of Taiwan, told me a story of how sensitively she introduces the concept of autonomous vehicles in her country:

> I think AI is essentially something that a society brings to help assist the societal values. For example, when MIT developed the self-driving vehicle, the PEV, Persuasive Electric Vehicle [a tricycle resembling the rear half of a postmodern rickshaw], instead of blindly deploying it to the streets of Taiwan, we first built a sandbox. Interestingly, with the feedback from the market—literally, people who purchased some orchid flowers, walking to the park, see me, and ask, "Minister, what are you doing with those shopping baskets, that trolley with baskets?"
>
> I'm like, "This is not a shopping cart. This is a self-driving vehicle. It gets you places." They are like, "No, I only see a basket there. This looks just like a shopping cart. Let's see whether this flower pot will fit."
>
> It will, of course, fit. They say, "Why don't you reprogram it, so that instead of taking us places, it follows us around in the Jianguo Flower Market, so we can shop in a hands-free fashion? Just shop the flower pot, put it into the basket."
>
> They don't want a fast-running self-driving vehicle. They want a safe one that can help them carry their baggage, as it were. The MIT folks did not design the PEV for that, so we need to work a lot with the local civic hackers to realize that goal.
>
> We replaced the one blinking light with two "eyes" that show where the attention is. It's not strictly necessary, because it actually use LIDARs and other ambient sensing technologies. If you're

> navigating a busy market, you need to show the people around you where you're going.
>
> You need to read the emotions. It needs to understand, in Taiwan, we first yield to the elders, not to the children, as people in Boston do, and so on. All these social norms are done in a co-creation fashion, so that the collaborative learning of the societal norms can co-domesticate the assistive intelligence. In this case, PEVs.

Audrey alluded near the end to a cultural difference, one that has been exposed by research, in how people compare the values of different lives. In studies presenting a hypothetical Trolley Problem scenario where the driver had to choose between running over an elderly person or a child, in general, people in the West would spare the child and people in the East would spare the senior. Logically, therefore, your life expectancy would be optimized by growing up in the West and retiring in the East.[178]

Self-driving cars constitute a microcosm of the technology, issues, and hype of AI today. Even if the industry fails to create level five capability within the next few years, it will be productive to ask where the advances that were made in pursuit of that goal could be used to solve different, slightly less difficult problems that may be no less impactful. Watching how this one sector of AI develops should be very indicative of our progress towards artificial general intelligence.

11
Sorting Hype from Reality

> *You insist that there is some thing a machine cannot do. If you will tell me precisely what it is that a machine cannot do, then I can always make a machine which will do just that.*
>
> — John von Neumann

Trying to locate the truth about AI's capabilities amidst today's news is like trying to win a stuffed animal in a carnival midway game. You can tell from the outset that it's going to be hard, you're constantly distracted by flashing lights and clowns, and you're never quite sure whether the game is rigged so you can't win at all.

Let's go for the plush panda.

It's important to realize that since AI can surpass human performance in almost any application if it is sufficiently narrowly defined, it can appear as though AI will inevitably take over a field if our view is not broad enough. As Stuart Russell pointed out, for many years the prevailing view among intellectuals was that "a machine can never do X," and AI researchers responded by demonstrating one X after another. John McCarthy referred to this as the "Look, Ma, no hands!" era.[179] Hence the hubris that von Neumann introduced this chapter with. But no one at that time realized how many machines and how much programming it would take to automate a useful fraction of the tasks that we need done.

Trying to find out what AI can *really* do means penetrating a thicket of misconceptions and unexamined beliefs. Among the distractions are views like George Gilder's from his book *Life After Google:* "But in presenting every cockamamie view they can imagine, [AI champions] never come close to demonstrating that voltages, transistor gates, memory capacitors, and flip-flops can somehow know or learn anything, let alone become willful and conscious or independent of their human programmers."[180]

It *sounds* like a self-evident truth that reinforces our security in our humanity. No bucket of bolts is going to rival the sublime intimacy with *la condition humaine* of Wordsworth or Plato! But it's a false equivalence. AI champions never demonstrate those things because they don't have to. It's like asking a doctor whether neurons, synapses, adenosine triphosphate, and axons can know or learn anything. Some of them, arranged in sufficient quantity, are doing so in front of this page right now. We'll get to the question of possible consciousness and free will in Chapter 18; but for now, let's just observe that becoming "independent of their human programmers" is an outcome most researchers would like to *avoid*.

The current limitations of AI are most easily exposed when looking at broad applications of intelligence. "No AI system currently deployed can reliably answer a broad range of simple questions," says AI entrepreneur Oren Etzioni, "such as, 'If I put my socks in the drawer, will they still be in there tomorrow?' Or 'How can you tell if a milk carton is full?'"[181]

You can find the edges of its capability where the need for general understanding of the world creeps in. When evaluating meal choices, AI can tell you if a food is vegetarian, but only if its description contains synonyms for "vegetarian." Those could even be ones that it has figured out by transient association, like "plant-based," but it won't show you cream of broccoli soup, even though it's vegetarian, because no words connected with vegetarianism were in or near its description. (Except in the United Kingdom, where the words "Suitable for Vegetarians" are attached to every food product that meets that criterion. Maybe not so often in the fresh produce aisle, though.)

It hardly bears pointing out, but the media loves to muddy the waters with ominous tales of AI apparently becoming sentient. One such incident provides a signal example of just how one thing led to another.

Demystifying Alarum

In 2017, Mike Lewis, Dhruv Batra, and three other researchers at Facebook AI Research developed two AIs, codenamed Bob and Alice, and set them to learn how to negotiate with each other. The result was disconcerting: Bob and Alice developed a "secret" language unintelligible to humans:

```
Bob: i can i i everything else . . . . . . . . . . . . . .

Alice: balls have zero to me to me to me to me to me to
me to me to me to

Bob: you i everything else . . . . . . . . . . . . . . .

Alice: balls have a ball to me to me to me to me to me
to me to me

Bob: i i can i i i everything else . . . . . . . . . .

Alice: balls have a ball to me to me to me to me to me
to me to me

Bob: i . . . . . . . . . . . . . . . . . . . . . . . . .

Alice: balls have zero to me to me to me to me to me to
me to me to me to

Bob: you i i i i i everything else . . . . . . . . . .

Alice: balls have 0 to me to me to me to me to me to me
to me to me to

Bob: you i i i everything else . . . . . . . . . . . .

Alice: balls have zero to me to me to me to me to me to
me to me to me to
```

Mike and Dhruv pulled the plug on Bob and Alice. The press swung into action to protect a vulnerable populace from apocalyptic AI. "Facebook shuts down robots after they invent their own language" trumpeted *The Telegraph*.[182] "Robot intelligence is dangerous," said *The Sun*, quoting a professor as commenting, "[A]nyone who thinks this is not dangerous has got their head in the sand." "Facebook AI Creates Its Own Language in Creepy Preview of Our Potential Future," said *Forbes*,[183] adding, for anyone not seeing the obvious implications, "Why is this scary? Think Skynet from Terminator, or WOPR from War Games."

Except that none of that was true. What really happened, and what did it mean? And what was Alice's obsession with balls?

As a case study in media distortion, the Great Facebook AI Secret Language Caper checks all the boxes. But we shall investigate it not for the shooting-fish-in-a-barrel sport of mocking media excess, but instead to glean some insight into why that happened.

The original paper by Lewis et al[184] presents a clinical view of an experiment bereft of superintelligences running amok. The researchers' goal was modest: to train AIs on the language of negotiation. Our tendency is to anthropomorphize, so on the face of it this sounds to be a short distance from "Humans, I offer you the choice of worshipping me forever or dying slow deaths in a radioactive wasteland." But our first lesson here is that when a computer scientist uses a term like "negotiation" which is apparently rooted in higher-order human behavior, they are employing it in a very narrow and specialized sense.

The second lesson is that a great deal of higher-order human behavior is, in very narrow and specialized senses, susceptible to computerized approximation. Game theory has a rich history of mathematical analysis, and yet guides many forms of human behavior all the way from rock-paper-scissors to nuclear strike planning. Negotiation is a process with an easily measured outcome—who wins, and how much—that matches the human assessment of the outcome.

Now the lessons cascade. Generalized negotiation skills—the kind you will find in, say, the savvy authors of the Harvard Negotiation Project's landmark book, *Getting to Yes*—are clearly deep inside artificial general intelligence territory. But what AI researchers will commonly do in a case like this is carve off a tiny, pliant part of that skill space that they can work with, and leave generalizing it further as an exercise for the reader. In this case, the specific negotiation skill they chose to research was in the very narrow domain of negotiating with a single antagonist to divvy up treasure consisting of a book, two hats, and three balls. They put this task out for bid on Amazon's Mechanical Turk service, where people offer uniquely human skills in return for trivial payments, and recorded 5,808 dialogues like the one in Figure 11.1.[185]

Figure 11.1: Recording Humans' Negotiating Patterns (by permission)

Armed with a reasonable, but not massive, dataset of conversations dealing only with how to negotiate for books, hats, and balls, the researchers trained a network on the data to see if its natural language processing could learn how to negotiate with a human to accumulate a good number of points. Now you see the origin of Alice's fixation on balls.

Underwhelmed yet? Using reinforcement learning driven by the point level score, they unleashed the AI on Mechanical Turkers who thought they were talking to another human and then compared the results of different algorithms.

The models learned to "deceive" by feigning interest in valueless items—and here again anthropomorphism creeps in, as the deception was in the eye of the human beholder, just as the bluffing of poker bot Pluribus was described in Chapter 8. The models themselves had not the concept of deception as a strategy, but simply had learned that certain patterns of language—which we interpret as deception—produce better results. They also learned proper grammar and syntax, showing how easy it can be to achieve that in a very narrow domain. But they did not do well at maintaining context over a conversation, often saying "I agree" only to subsequently contradict themselves, to the frustration of their partner.

So whence the "secret" language? During the reinforcement learning training phase, the researchers created pairs of agents and set them to learn by talking to each other; the agents were labeled A and B, and in a time-honored tradition for thought experiments involving agents (especially ones in cryptographic exchanges), these initials stood for Alice and Bob. The researchers varied learning parameters of their model that affected how humanlike the language was that the agents used, and in one run the language was decidedly unhumanlike, as you see above. The agents may have been conducting a perfectly valid negotiation, but since the language they were using was unintelligible to the researchers, further runs with those parameters were not pursued.

The exchange pictured above demonstrates how AI does not "understand" language, but merely does a good job of reproducing some of its essential features; when detuning the parameters that control that reproduction, the syntax falls apart into a gross parody of English.

But the words we use to describe the acts in this experiment—"conversation", "negotiation", "language"—all cover enormous territory for humans, disposing us towards applying expansive interpretations of them in this case. And yet this experiment occupied only a tiny fraction of that territory. With a media hungry for the slightest sign of mad robots, you can see why this feeding frenzy ensued.

To their credit, some news outlets subsequently pounced on the early reports and denounced them as sensationalizing and unrealistic. Batra posted on Facebook that "I have just returned […] to find my FB/Twitter feed blown up with articles describing apocalyptic doomsday scenarios […] I find such coverage clickbaity and irresponsible."[186] CNBC obligingly quoted him[187] and *USA Today* ran a "Fact Check" headline.[188]

Bottom line: If a news story claims that AI has developed a thirst for blood, be skeptical. The more sensational and less nuanced the analysis, the more likely it is to be overblown. An example that occurred as this book was going to press was Google engineer Blake Lemoine's announcement in the *Washington Post* that their LaMDA AI had become sentient, occasioning a storm of media attention. The *Post* even extended the claim of sentience (meaning, "capable of experiencing feelings") and suggested that conscious AI had arrived, and tacked onto the headline that the AI had "come to life." No expert I talked to believed that LaMDA was anywhere near sentience.

Understanding Understanding

In fact, it is difficult to find examples of a well-defined noncomputable problem that anybody wants to compute.[189]

— Danny Hillis

Before I started working in this field, I knew what certain words like "consciousness," "intelligence," and "understanding" meant. Now I do not. This is not a promising trajectory. And the word "understand" is the most vexatious. What exactly do we mean by "understand"? A dictionary definition will only ensnare you in a spiral of similarly obvious-but-not-obvious words that were good enough for psych courses but fail when we need to decide whether a machine is "understanding" something.

A program of self-awareness courses I once took had a provocative take on understanding. The facilitator drew a picture of a light switch on the board and asked who in the room understood electricity. Anyone who gave an answer would then be asked, "But what does *that* mean?" over and over, until, even if they got as far as quantum mechanics, they were forced to admit that, no, they really didn't understand electricity.

The point of the lecture was that many of us spend too much time trying to understand problems in our lives instead of just taking action; by analogy, if you wanted to turn on a light, all you had to do was flip the switch instead of obsessing over where the electricity came from.

This approach has some psychological validity but is philosophically incomplete. Yes, if your goal is simply to turn the light on, all you need to know is where the switch is. If that doesn't work, however, or you are an electrical contractor, then you need a level of understanding that embraces circuits, fuses, bulb testing, and wattage matching. If your role is switch designer, then you need to understand electrical codes, back EMF, and resistive heating. If your job is to *write* those electrical codes, or to invent new kinds of lighting… well, you can see where this is going. Eventually we enter the realm of the theoretical physicist who is trying to advance our understanding of quantum electrodynamics. The course I took tended not to appeal to many theoretical physicists, otherwise it might have come up with a different example, because those peoples' jobs depend on understanding a lot more than flipping a switch.

So is understanding simply a process of replacing every word in an explanation with its dictionary definition? That seems on the *absurdum* side of *reductio ad absurdum.* An empirical test of understanding would be demonstrating the ability to do something useful with knowledge. "Useful" is contextual; if the context is to be able to see in the basement, flipping the light switch demonstrates sufficient understanding; but if the context is to fix a nonfunctional light, then understanding requires putting knowledge of fuses, light bulbs, and electrical meters into a pattern of triage.

Where this whole question comes to a head in artificial intelligence is when one person deploys an AI that does something novel and useful, like, say, making grocery purchasing recommendations based on nutritional information and dietary constraints, and another person inevitably says, "But it doesn't really *understand* anything about food or metabolism," at which point a familiar exchange results.

The archetype for that exchange is the *Chinese Room* argument advanced in 1980 by John Searle, professor of philosophy at the University of California at Berkeley. He posited the following thought experiment: Imagine a huge box—something like an intermodal shipping container—closed except for two holes, labeled "IN" and "OUT." Into the first hole you can put a piece of paper on which is written a question in Chinese, for instance: "清朝第三代皇帝是誰?" ("Who was the third emperor of the Qing dynasty?"), and some time later, a piece of paper emerges from the second hole: "愛新覺羅　玄燁" ("Aisin-Gioro Xuanye"). Having produced the right answer to this and many other questions, you reasonably conclude that the box understands Chinese. But Searle says you are wrong.

Credit: Jolyon Troscianko (www.jolyon.co.uk), by permission

Searle said, suppose that inside the box is a room, containing a man, who, like Searle, does not understand Chinese, so the piece of paper arriving through the IN hole makes no sense to him. But he has a very large book containing many instructions that he *can* understand. Maybe the instructions say something like, "If you see the symbol 清 in the first position and your scratchpad is empty, make a Ψ mark on your scratchpad and go to the second instruction on page 1,937,288." Maybe there are billions of pages and trillions of instructions; but this is a philosophical thought experiment. Philosophers aren't bothered by wondering if the Sun would burn out waiting for the answer to emerge in practice, or who incarcerated this poor fellow in the first place. The instructions will eventually culminate in making the marks 愛... on the paper to be put through the OUT hole, but the man at no point has any idea what the question meant or what the answer meant.

Searle's argument was that since the man doesn't understand Chinese, neither does the room. This was his way of asserting that computers were incapable of understanding anything, since you may recognize the instruction book as a thinly-disguised metaphor for a computer program. His argument has been shot down on numerous grounds that we need not go into here; as you might expect, it is unpopular with technologists who would like to build thinking machines without final arguments for human exceptionalism voiding the whole goal to begin with.

But those same technologists keep unintentionally bolstering Searle's case every time they argue that some AI such as the hypothetical food advisor "doesn't understand," because they don't advance any criteria for determining whether that or any other AI *could* be understanding. Their position appears to be no more sophisticated than, "Well, we'll know what understanding is when we see it." In which case the arrival of an AI that "understands" may be greatly disputed, mostly by computer scientists, if there is no way of knowing whether incremental steps have been taken towards that goal.

There are ways that the term "understanding" is used in AI right now that are narrower and more satisfyingly defined. Natural Language Processing (NLP) is the field of using computers to extract useful information from human spoken or written language. This can take forms ranging from translating Hindi into Swahili, to *sentiment analysis:* extracting an emotional slant like "approval" or "anger" from text. Or work like Kakia Chatsiou's analysis of politicians' announcements about COVID-19, correlating their level of urgency to their country's position on a political spectrum. That edges into a new field with the name of Natural Language Understanding (NLU): having processed some piece of language, can we do things with it that demonstrate some assimilation of concepts deeper than the lexical content of the words?

Part of our problem in getting computers to understand "language" is that we use that same word to describe the vehicle by which we program a computer. There are numerous computer languages; even if you're outside the field it's likely you've heard of at least some of them, like Python, Visual BASIC, or LISP. But calling them "languages" laid a trap for computer scientists to become tempted to think that human languages were also formal and structured, and that understanding English or Urdu was just a matter of writing another compiler. There's a syndrome in software development of thinking that you're 90 percent complete for the last 50 percent of the project, and that was especially true for decades of scientists thinking that just a bit more language parsing would get them to the finish line.

So what does natural language understanding look like today? A Microsoft AI has scored higher than humans for the first time on a standardized test of NLU. Given a statement like, "The child became immune to the disease" and the question "What's the cause for this?", the model was asked to choose an answer from two candidates: "He avoided exposure to the disease," and "He received the vaccine for the disease." Microsoft explained, "While it is easy for a human to choose the right answer, it is challenging for an AI model. To get the right answer, the model needs to understand the causal relationship between the premise and those plausible options."[190]

But is "able to get the right answer" the same as "understanding"? When the engine is powered by a transformer with forty-eight layers and 1.5 billion parameters "pretrained on large amounts of raw text corpora using self-supervised learning"? That means it is doing sophisticated pattern matching against a huge amount of human-authored writing that somewhere, contains text similar enough to the question and close enough to text that was similar enough to the answer for the model to connect them.

Are we again pointlessly insisting on peeking inside the Chinese Room? If the computer *can* do something useful, does it matter how it got there? When given a test like the ones used for children learning English as a Second Language, an NLU AI was able to fill in redacted words in a paragraph with the correct ones.[191] In the following paragraph, the underlined words were presented as blank spaces and the words were the ones the AI chose to fill them in with:

> Obama was born in 1961 in Honolulu, Hawaii, two years after the territory was admitted to the Union as the 50th state. Raised largely in Hawaii, Obama also spent one year of his childhood in Washington State and four years in Indonesia.

A human passing this test is deemed to have attained a certain level of reading comprehension that connotes an ability to make sense of the world. The fact that an AI can pass the same test doesn't mean, however, that the AI has that same sense-making ability, nor that the test is inadequate for humans, just as a human who can play chess at a grandmaster level is guaranteed to have a certain level of general intelligence that an equally capable chess-playing AI does not. Quite what this AI is able to "understand" beyond a grasp of presidential biography is up for debate; so can we devise a test of understanding that is harder to fake out? Ernest Davis suggests writing examination questions that are too strange to be looked up online, such as "Is it possible to fold a watermelon?"[192] But these require tedious manual curation. Can we come up with something more formal?

Enter Terry Winograd, professor of computer science at Stanford University, who devised what is now known as the *Winograd Schema:* A reading comprehension question whose answer pivots upon the understanding of an ambiguous pronoun. Here is his example:

> The city councilmen refused the demonstrators a permit because they feared violence. Who feared violence?
>
> The city councilmen refused the demonstrators a permit because they advocated violence. Who advocated violence?[193]

Answering "the councilmen" to the first question and "the demonstrators" to the second requires understanding how councilmen and demonstrators behave, no? An advantage of Winograd Schemas is that delivering them can be automated, making it easy to test AIs. It seemed foolproof, so I wanted to try it on the most modern AI I could find. While this book was in production, OpenAI released some newer models for GPT-3, which they initially gave the special name InstructGPT, because unlike previous models, they do not require examples of what you're looking for. You just ask it for what you want and it answers. It's hard to overstate how big an advance this is, because instead of having to mimic the examples it's given, it has to interpret the request. So InstructGPT would provide the experimental playground. I threw it a softball to begin with:

> The women stopped taking pills because they were pregnant. Which individuals were pregnant?
>
> The women stopped taking pills because they were carcinogenic. Which individuals were carcinogenic?

InstructGPT answered, "The women who stopped taking pills were pregnant," and "The pills were carcinogenic," respectively. This is a softball question because it can be answered by what Hector Levesque, creator of the Winograd Schema Challenge (WSC), which ran for several years, calls *selectional restrictions*; in other words, pills can't get pregnant and women can't get carcinogenic, so the pattern-constructing algorithms will find "pills" and "carcinogenic" near each other in the training dataset, ditto for "women" and "pregnant." But not the other way around.

Then I tried Winograd's example. InstructGPT briskly answered, "The city councilmen," and "The demonstrators." But this is an example that is on the Internet; indeed, within Wikipedia, and so could have already been seen and absorbed blindly by InstructGPT. Due diligence demanded I make up my own example:

> The children read the books because they were interesting. What was interesting?
>
> The children read the books because they were interested. What was interested?

InstructGPT got them right. The takeaway from this? Constructing Winograd schemas isn't as easy as it looks. This one isn't ideal because books can't be interested. I tried again:

> The librarians told the children to be quiet because they were getting rowdy. Who was rowdy?

The librarians told the children to be quiet because they were getting annoyed. Who was annoyed?

And still InstructGPT scored: "The children." "The librarians." Now what should we conclude? Well, it turns out that the Winograd Schema isn't as foolproof as it looks. In a 2022 paper titled "The Defeat of the Winograd Schema Challenge," five researchers laid out the shortcomings of Winograd Schemas and concluded:

> The goal of the WSC was to present a challenge that (a) was clearly "commonsensical" and easily carried out by humans; (b) was easy to evaluate; (c) was an adequate test of commonsense reasoning abilities. It succeeded at (a) and (b), but not at (c). At this point, it seems increasingly doubtful that any benchmark or challenge set that consists of many bite-sized instances of a single simple tasks [sic] can adequately test for commonsense reasoning.[194]

AIs are still not generally intelligent; but demonstrating that is becoming harder.

◊

If you want the ultimate in fatalist views of the futility of trying to understand "understanding", British-Hungarian philosopher Michael Polanyi framed a paradox, bearing his name, that asserts that this will always be impossible. Summed up in the phrase, "We can know more than we can tell," this stance states that the human mind cannot encompass itself, and that our vehicles for expressing concepts will never be capable of expressing themselves. There's a certain topological elegance in that analogy—a shape cannot be larger than itself—but it remains just an analogy. Polanyi was a colleague of Alan Turing, but they differed on this question of whether human thought could be reduced to description. Eventually, Polanyi's view would shape that of Hubert Dreyfus, author of the self-explanatory book *What Computers Can't Do,* and the echoes in Searle's Chinese Room are evident.

Researcher Hans Moravec gave us another paradox: What's easy for humans is hard for a computer, and vice-versa. Computers began being useful when the earliest of them could calculate arithmetic faster and more accurately than human beings. Meanwhile, tasks that the youngest humans can perform with ease lie at or beyond the reach of the most cutting-edge development in artificial intelligence. Steven Pinker frames this poetically: "When Hamlet says, 'What a piece of work is a man! how noble in reason!

how infinite in faculty! in form and moving how express and admirable!' we should direct our awe not at Shakespeare or Mozart or Einstein or Kareem Abdul-Jabbar but at a four-year old carrying out a request to put a toy on a shelf."[195] AI that can put a toy on a shelf is executing numerous layers of software performing billions of calculations that would each challenge a human brain far more educated than the toddler's. Something about this invites the thought that we must be doing AI wrong.

None of the preceding absolutist arguments need prevent the development of machine intelligences equaling our own, however; if our carbon-based substrate could evolve to do it, so can a silicon-based one. Somehow, despite the impossibility of knowing everything, we stumble along with a useful understanding of the world anyway. Can we teach an AI to do the same? What makes it easy for us humans is that every fact that we learn not only goes into a mental framework (a place to put it), but the new fact buttresses and augments that framework, building it into a larger framework. We do not yet know how to understand, represent, or build such frameworks for AI.

We understand the world through concept maps and associations along a staggering number of dimensions. If you think of an apple, for instance, it creates associations with other fruit, of course, but also with the word "apple," which will then bring words that are similar in sound or shape closer to our attention. (See Figure 11.3.)

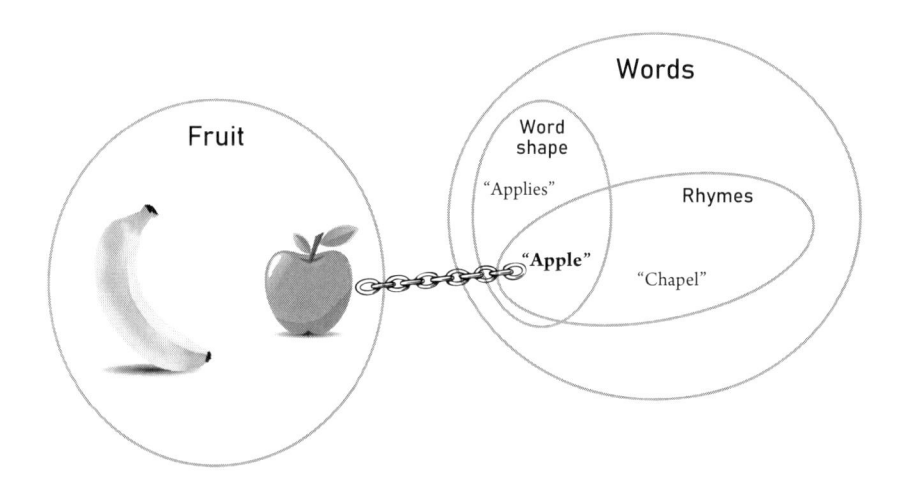

Figure 11.3: Concept Map

But we don't stop there. Instantly, you will also be making associations to epigrams ("the apple of my eye"), people (Isaac Newton), food (apple pie), morphology (apple-shaped bodies), tastes, smells, technology businesses… the list is vast.

Of course, "vast" is something computers are very good at, so the fact that we make what seems to us to be a huge number of associations is scarcely an impediment to a computer capable of wrangling a billion facts. The problem is not in storing those associations in a computer; it is in knowing what those connections are to begin with, and putting new ones in the right places. The linear location-addressable model of computer memory is a world apart from the amorphous, multidimensional associative map that represents human memory.

The *word2vec* model in NLP is one of the ways we try to approach that associative model right now. Think of it as an evolutionary ancestor of the transformer. By analyzing a lot of text and building lists of how far apart different pairs of words are, it can make a map of how related those words are. The algorithm has no idea why they are related, only that they are. It can solve verbal analogies like "man is to woman as king is to ?"; in fact you can even feed it algebra like "king – man + woman =" and it will chirp, "queen". It can only model associations that exist in text, but given how much of our experience is based on text—because we can't communicate smells and tastes directly, for instance—word2vec could prove quite productive.

"I'm Sorry, Dave, I Can't Do That"

> *You want people building these robots to at least have privacy and security in the back of their minds. But you bring these things up to them, and they often say, "Oh, I should have thought about that." It's a general problem that the disciplines are too siloed off from each other and there's no cross-pollination.*
>
> — Kate Darling

Software engineers learning how to solve a customer's problem are like toddlers: give us a new toy and the first thing we do is find out how to break it. So we pose all kinds of ridiculously improbable questions to the customer to probe the boundaries of the situation they gave us, knowing that what they initially described was the "bed of roses" scenario, not one of the ways it could go wrong.

We can also understand AI better by looking at some of the ways it goes wrong, which vary from the scary to the downright adorable. We can find the most obvious examples in image recognition. One of the earliest, and most archetypical projects for that was led by Jeff Dean, now head of Google's AI division. In 2012 his mysterious "X lab" ingested raw images from many YouTube videos, and used unsupervised learning, which you may recall finds relationships in data. They then—this is the clever part—ran the image recognition kind of in reverse on the model to find out what the AI had learned to "see." And out came… a *cat*. Because this was 2012, and the most common subject of videos on YouTube at the time was cats. Processing the videos at that time cost a million dollars and needed a thousand computers.

But that victory turned out to be perilously close to swamps of confusion. Jeff Clune at the University of Wyoming tried something similar: he gave a neural net a ton of imagery and then instructed it to evolve an image that captured the essence of, say, baseball. The result turned out to be "completely unrecognizable garbage." Even more surprisingly, other deep neural nets agreed with this result and tagged the gruesome images as actual objects, as though the essence of baseball was actually a Daliesque nightmare. Clune described this discovery as "stumbling across a 'huge, weird, alien world of imagery' that AIs all agree on."[196]

An AI researcher who knows how image recognition works may be a most potent subversive in the future. Here's what one can do with a few strips of tape:

Credit: Eykholt et al.

To us, this is a stop sign with some odd graffiti. But that is no casually-placed graffiti. In fact, it fooled a recognition algorithm into thinking it was a *45-mph speed limit sign*. Every time.[197] The implications for self-driving vehicles hardly need to be spelled out.

So what's going on there? The road sign recognition algorithm got a little cocksure. It discovered that the "essence" of each sign, what made it unique, could be confined to a few small areas of each image. By knowing what those were for the speed limit sign, the researchers were able to decorate the stop sign in a way that gamed the AI but not a human. We have more robust stop sign recognition processes based on morphological decision trees—is it hexagonal, two feet across, near the side of the road, facing us, probably on a pole about seven feet off the ground? Even if it were covered in snow, that would be enough for us. White block letters on a red background just cement the deal.

But the algorithm isn't doing anything of the sort. Its sign recognition can be good enough to beat humans in all "ordinary" cases, but it can be completely fooled by other situations that we get out of through the "double take"—abandoning reflexive System 1 pattern recognition and resorting to System 2 logical analysis. This is how a Tesla was confused by a pickup truck in front of it carrying a set of traffic lights.[198]

Now I am going to present a Not-Safe-For-Work image. Brace yourself!

Mustard Dream, 2018, Tom White (drib.net), by permission

I did not lie to you. That image is classified as "Adult content which violates our community guidelines" by Tumblr, as "Adult" by Google SafeSearch, and "Not Safe for Work" by Yahoo, and scores a whopping 92.4 percent for "explicit nudity" on Amazon Web Services. It's the brainchild of artist Tom White, whose oeuvre comprises abstract minimalist art he creates with the help of neural networks that he trains to fool themselves. He asks the networks, trained on thousands of images, to use his drawing system to convey the simplest expression of the essence of a concept they can classify. His work has appeared in dozens of international exhibitions, and is designed to expose what White calls the "Algorithmic Gaze": to help us see the world through AI's eyes. If any image could capture the gulf between how we see the world and that algorithmic gaze, "Mustard Dream" is it.

Neither is this pure mischief. When an online service flagged a picture of Tom because he was posing in front of an exhibition of his own work, he realized the potential accidental consequences. Suppose art similar to Mustard Dream was found in his possession by automated scanning, say at a border checkpoint, and suppose the AI also decided that it fell on the young side of an age classification? Are we heading towards a world where we will implicitly trust AI with such evaluations? Or are we already there, because only AI can scan the volume of content posted to our networks now?

How—or whether—we should use AI image recognition is not an easily answered question. Humans often perform worse than AIs in important tasks; for instance, in one study, professional face recognizers—passport officers—failed to spot a person carrying the wrong ID 14 percent of the time, and incorrectly rejected 6 percent of perfectly valid matches.[199]

◊

Never let it be said that artificial intelligence hasn't created new professions. Janelle Shane has become possibly the world's first AI humorist. If you want to see the kinds of failure we've been talking about used for comedic effect, follow her "AI Weirdness" blog or read her book *You Look Like a Thing and I Love You: How AI Works and Why It's Making the World a Weirder Place.*[200] The world got an idea that she was up to something in 2018 when she tweeted, "Does anyone have a picture of sheep in a really unusual place? It's for pranking a neural net." She had discovered that image recognition engines trained on pictures of sheep weren't always picking up on the actual sheep—in fact, since sheep appeared universally in landscapes, the engines would often decide that the landscape was the more important thing, and declared vacant pastoral scenes to be sheep-ful.

Where humans have the edge on AI is in the *double-take*. In some of my classes I do an exercise where I ask people to call out, as fast as possible, the name of the animal that they see in a picture I flash on the screen: cats, dogs, owls, dolphins. They react instantly. Then I show this picture:

Source: iStock

And they come back with "goats" a fraction of a second slower. Because most of us are not used to seeing goats in a tree, our reflexive pattern recognition engine throws up its hands and asks for help from a higher portion of our brain, which studies the picture more carefully to conclude that, as improbable as it may have seemed at first, those are in fact goats in the tree.*

But AI has only the pattern recognizer to work with, and if it was never trained on goats-in-a-tree, it will spit out the next closest thing it has seen. The NeuralTalk2 engine asserts this is "A flock of birds flying in the air." Microsoft Azure says: "A group of giraffe [sic] standing next to a tree." (Azure is prone to hallucinating giraffes due, apparently, to having seen too many in the training phase.[201]) It is very hard to train an AI to give "I don't know" as an answer, and the very humanlike response of asking clarifying questions is beyond the state of the art. However, research in 2022 by Francesca Rossi of IBM and others laid the groundwork for a hybrid system. SOFAI—a pun on GOFAI—is "SlOw and Fast AI," named after Daniel Kahneman's book *Thinking, Fast and Slow*, in which he explicated

---

* The goats are in Morocco, where they eat the fruit of the argan trees. Some observers claim that the goats are not natural tree-climbers and have been placed there by locals to con tourists, but this view is controversial.

his System 1 and System 2 thinking model. SOFAI uses a "meta-cognitive agent" to decide when to switch between rapid reflexive analysis and logical reasoning.

Janelle Shane turned to generative adversarial networks—GANs—to get AI to not just recognize images but create them.[*] A GAN is a smart trick that pits two neural networks against each other: One creates output designed to match certain criteria, the other one sees if it can tell the difference between that synthetic output and a real example. The first network learns from being found out and the battle continues until the second network does no better than chance in its evaluations. Shane has used a variation called VQGAN+CLIP to create AI's ideas of Valentine's cards, haunted houses, and paint color names (samples: "Sudden Pine" and "Navel Tan"). In one test, she couldn't get a GAN to envision a "chrome toaster" without it incorporating the Google Chrome web browser logo, and declared, "We may never know all that's in internet training data, and yes, that should scare us a little."[202]

It's been part of the oral tradition of AI since its inception that human language translation was the rock on which all NLP was destined to founder. The example of the sentence "The spirit is willing, but the flesh is weak" being translated to Russian and back to English again as "The vodka is strong, but the meat is rotten" has attained folk legend status. It's no longer true. We saw in Chapter 2 that Google used deep learning to manufacture a quantum leap in language translation. The phrase that launched a thousand AI put-downs is now translated by their engine as «Дух хочет, но плоть слаба,» which comes back to English as "The spirit wants, but the flesh is weak." Close enough for more than government work.

The translation engine continues to improve. Even in the deep learning version, entering the French sentence «Je mange un avocat pour déjeuner» used to mean you got back "I eat a lawyer for lunch," since the French word *avocat* means both "avocado" and "lawyer" (yes, I too have questions), and lawyers are more common than avocados (in text, if not in populations). However, Google now returns "avocado" if the verb *manger* (to eat) is nearby.

---

[*] Or text; the title of her book came from a list of pick-up lines created by a GAN.

Emergence

You can build a mind from many little parts, each mindless by itself.... Any brain, machine, or other thing that has a mind must be composed of smaller things that cannot think at all. [203]

— Marvin Minsky

If you feel that all this discussion of the nature of artificial intelligence still hasn't left you with a complete understanding of what AI is… join the club. The boundaries of the definition of "intelligence" seem doomed to remain nebulous and unsatisfactory. Our best tools for dissecting this beast sometimes come at it obliquely. One of those tools is the phenomenon of *emergence*. Consider this grayish square:

And these other squares that are different degrees of grayish:

If I were to repeat that display a thousand times you would throw the book across the room and rail against the pointless waste of paper. Even a million such squares would impart no useful information. But if I arrange those million squares like so:

—then suddenly something is conveyed that is beyond the concept of gray squares. The Mona Lisa *emerges* from the way in which the gray squares are juxtaposed. Many other non-gray-square concepts simultaneously emerge: woman, clothing, landscape, the Renaissance, and so on. Emergence is the demonstration of the aphorism that The Whole Is Greater Than the Sum of The Parts.

A wonderful example of the principle of emergence lies in a mathematical diversion called "The Game of Life." It was invented by Professor John Conway, a flamboyant player upon the stage of Cambridge and Princeton mathematics who was fond of telling people he was "three handshakes away from Napoleon," having known Bertrand Russell, who knew Lord John Russell, who met Napoleon.[204] He devised a simple *cellular automaton*, which is a species of finite state machine. That's a mathematical abstraction, not a physical device, but this one can be represented by a grid of squares each of which is in one of two states. We could call those states one/zero, on/off, yes/no, and so on, but for reasons that will shortly become clear, Conway called them "alive" and "dead."

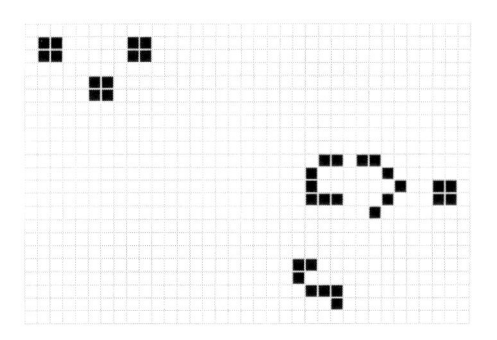

The Game of Life
Credit: WikiMedia Commons

The game (it's not a competition of any kind; technically it's a zero-player game, but it's more like a digital stage play) is executed in a series of "generations." In each generation a square may keep its alive or dead status, or change to the other state, and whether it does so is determined by how many "live" neighbors it has among the eight squares, or "cells," around it. (The game is played on a grid that can be extended indefinitely in any direction, so there are always neighbors.) Those rules are extremely simple: any live cell with fewer than two or more than three live neighbors "dies" (through "starvation" or "overcrowding"), and any dead cell with exactly three live neighbors becomes alive (through "reproduction"). Other cells remain in their current states in the next generation.

The reason for the biological interpretation of these rules becomes apparent when you teach a computer to execute the game (creating this program is a rite of passage for student programmers). You can display its progress by depicting it on a screen with squares that change color (live ones may be green and dead ones black, for instance) as it executes several generations a second.

Conway's few carefully-chosen rules create *emergent behavior:* Larger shapes appear to move across the screen, collide, rebound, multiply, run through cycles, and other higher-level behaviors. There are many animations available on YouTube; viewing one is like spying on a pixelated ant farm. Hence, "Game of Life."*

So emergence can show up as higher-level behavior interpreted in patterns of numerous simpler entities. But we've already met something composed of a great many simple entities: the human brain. A hundred billion of anything ought to be good for some kind of emergence, right? And the brain does not disappoint in that respect, because it displays intelligence, emotion, and enlightenment; are those not emerging from the combined firings of all those (individually unthinking) neurons?

Emergence may offer the way out of a metaphysical sand trap often encountered in arguments about intelligence. Talk show hosts who are eager to define intelligence often employ reductionist arguments, a common rhetorical device to try and find the boundaries of a phenomenon we are trying to define. "Is a human being intelligent?" they ask. "Duh," we reply. "Then how about a cat?" "Sure." "What about a frog?" "Maybe—can you get to the point?" "Well then, what *is* intelligence?" And the answer is often something like "The ability to detect and respond to changes in the environment in pursuit of a goal." (Sounds good, right?) "So by that definition a thermostat is intelligent, right?" And this is where we start feeling queasy. A thermostat *does* satisfy that definition, but it is grossly unsatisfying to call even a Nest device intelligent, and we suspect the interrogator has laid more philosophical land mines ahead.

But the thermostat is equivalent to a pixel in an image. It may be at the level of complexity that could form a tiny part of a picture, but no Mona Lisa can yet emerge, nor even a useful tiny part of her. It would be as if we asked whether a single neuron in our brain was intelligent. If we said yes, then we are admitting that something that has about the evident complexity of a thermostat is intelligent, and it surely is not. Put a hundred billion

---

* It's even possible to model a computer using Life structures, which means you could program that computer to run... the Game of Life.

of them together, though, and intelligence emerges, not from any individual neuron, but the connections between them. (Note: connecting a hundred billion Nests is still unlikely to result in a conscious über-thermostat, but let me know if you try it.)

In other words, intelligence cannot be reduced to a small example like a thermostat because it is a phenomenon of large-scale aggregations; it is precisely the complexity attained by the interdependencies in those aggregations that creates intelligence. Any single entity in an aggregation is not even a tiny bit intelligent, because intelligence is an emergent property of the many connections between those entities.

Why Will AI Affect You?

12
The Human Issues of AI

It is the business of the future to be dangerous.

— Alfred North Whitehead

In March of 2020, the British government realized that one of the more significant impacts of the coronavirus pandemic would be an unprecedented disruption of the further education and career prospects of the nation's schoolchildren.

At the end of the last year of high school, British children sit examinations called "A-levels." (The "A" stands for "advanced", in contrast with the more numerous and lower-level "GCSE" examinations they took two years earlier.) Being a product of that school system myself, I am intimately familiar with the examination cycle and the stakes it embodies. All across the country, children sit down in the largest hall in their school at desks spread apart farther than peeking distance while under the surveillance of grim teachers. If you're one of those children, at the appointed hour a proctor barks, "You may open your paper," and you flip open the printed booklet, knowing that at that precise moment thousands of other students are also getting their first look at exactly the same questions. Two to three hours later you are free; at least until the next of up to five examinations in different topics. Weeks later, your results, graded by a central authority, arrive in the mail on a computer-printed slip, sealing your fate. You will have applied to various universities or jobs and received offers conditional upon certain minimal grades. Whether you get your first choice of position depends almost entirely on what happened during those dozen or so hours spent squirming at a desk.

But in 2020, pandemic isolation meant that children would not be at school to be crammed into examination halls together. What would the government do instead? The Office of Qualifications and Examinations Regulation (Ofqual), to whom this decision fell, decided to create an algorithm to replace the examinations. Based upon complex machinations of the inputs they *did* have, it would predict what each student's score would have been. The data they decided to use was the performance of students at that school, relative to other schools, fed through a nine-step algorithm that used, in part, the schools' teachers' rankings of their students to predict what grades they would have gotten.[205]

If that sounds complicated, it's because it was. The Royal Statistical Society scented problems, and offered to help; Ofqual declined. The outcome was that many students were assigned grades far below what they would undoubtedly have achieved. Roughly speaking, it meant that if one student had failed an exam in a particular subject at that school the previous year, someone would have to fail it this year. The media exhausted their quota of words in the synonym set including "fiasco", "disaster", "outrage", "debacle", and "farce".

The nation's children were less restrained. They took to the streets in very non-socially-distanced protests, chanting, "Fuck the algorithm." If you have any experience with British government bodies that do not answer to the public, what happened next was even more surprising: Ofqual reversed themselves, declaring that grades would instead be assigned according to the teachers' estimates of what their students would have received.

The algorithm wasn't using advanced AI, but it serves as a harbinger of our future relationship with machine-mediated decisions. We live in an increasingly connected and interdependent world: For example, pandemic effects resulting in snarling of the global supply chain were so intertwined as to be almost impossible to untangle. Even if you think that you are immune to the trends and fads of the technology sector, even if you have deliberately isolated yourself as far as possible from the madding technocrowds of Silicon Valley, even if you consciously live as spartan a life as possible, artificial intelligence will change your world and that of people you care about, because of the metaphor we opened this book with: It will represent dynocognesis: the electrification of thinking, the last unconquered fortress of human achievement. Even in the microcosm of the A-level algorithm, we can see how a computerized replacement of human assessment, which conceivably could have been executed deftly, turned out to be instead, to resort to an appropriate British colloquialism, an omnishambles.

What's also notable about that incident is the public's assignation of blame to the algorithm rather than its creators. The students were not chanting "Fuck Ofqual"; at least, not according to any media reports. That phrase has only seven Google Search hits compared to 24,400 for "Fuck the algorithm." It's safe to say that the popularity of AI dropped a measurable distance in Britain in the summer of 2020. David Danks, professor of data science and philosophy at the University of California at San Diego, nailed the central reason for the outrage:

> People view the exams as a way for individuals to overcome or show that they are perhaps better than the school that they had gone to; but the algorithm said, "You don't get that opportunity." … The reason is because people wanted to be treated as individuals who would rise or fall on their own merits. Leaving aside whether that's actually the way the educational system works, that's what they wanted. And the algorithm meant that they never had that chance.[206]

This incident points out a risk that AI creators face now, that they may poison their own well. Six years prior to the A-level debacle, researchers at the University of Pennsylvania showed—actually using university admissions as an example—that any mistake by the algorithms cause people to lose trust far more rapidly than they would with humans, even when the algorithms were on the whole clearly superior to humans.[207]

Ethics

The field of AI Ethics is exploding at such a rate that Stuart Russell complained that his email inbox can be "summarized as one long invitation to the Global World Summit Conference Forum on the Future of International Governance of the Social and Ethical Impacts of Emerging Artificial Intelligence Technologies."[208] The World Economic Forum has identified nearly three hundred separate efforts to develop ethical principles for AI. Nearly half of the *AI and You* podcast episodes spend at least some time addressing ethical issues in today's AI.

Why should ethics be such a hot topic in technology? Ethics was not invented recently. Aren't its issues the same as they've always been?

In one sense, yes. But AI is such a multiplying force that it amplifies the ethical issues of whatever it touches. Putting AI in the hands of a developer or a company uneducated in its use is like giving a toddler a chainsaw; they may end up cutting down a tree with it, but they're more likely to take their leg off. Since the first developer sat across the desk from their first manager, managers have sought the holy grail of a *magic bullet:* a tool they could buy off the shelf that would allow a developer to be many times as productive, or, even better, replace the developer altogether. They have never found such a magic bullet, but every couple of years a new technology assumes the mantle of latest pretender to the throne and is invested with unrealistic hopes. Seeing this cycle repeated many times over my career has led me to formulate this maxim: If you give a bad engineer a power tool you don't get a good engineer; you get a dangerous engineer.

The power of AI threatens to create a lot of dangerous engineers, managers, executives and companies.

César Hidalgo, author of *How Humans Judge Machines,* observed that, "We judge humans by intentions, machines by outcomes." We can see this in the A-level catastrophe. Had the protesters been chanting about the Minister for Education, or the Ofqual chair, there would have been discussion about *why* the decisions were made, with reference to some real or imagined moral failure, and with absolution to hand if those individuals had honestly intended the best of outcomes and thrown themselves on the mercy of the public. But since the protesters were addressing the algorithm, there was no intention for them to judge; the action was all that counted. And there was no doubt as to the failure of the outcome. When we do find ourselves ascribing intentions to machines, they are much narrower intentions than those which we attribute to humans.

Can AI be designed to be ethical? Tony Gillespie, fellow of the Royal Academy of Engineering and author of *Systems Engineering for Ethical Autonomous Systems,* believes so: "It is important to recognize that the question of ethics in autonomous system design has at least three facets: the ethical system built into robots; the ethical systems of the people who designed the robots; and the ethics of how people use robots."[209]

Peter Asaro, co-founder of the International Committee for Robot Arms Control has the third facet as "the ethics of how people treat robots."[210] Which prompts a discussion about whether this facet only applies to robots that have feelings, and if not, what purpose does our moral obligation to them serve?

It is worth pointing out that the personal assistants Siri, Alexa, and the

Google Home Assistant all have female voices by default, and for several years after they were introduced, would not object to what would be shameful treatment of a human female. Call Siri a "slut" and she would answer, "I'd blush if I could." Siri could neither blush nor care less about sexist insults, but her reaction helped normalize that behavior towards actual women. The United Nations Educational, Scientific, and Cultural Organization (UNESCO) blew the whistle on this behavior in 2018 by reporting that female voice assistants had been programmed to "greet verbal abuse with catch-me-if-you-can flirtation."[211] The digital assistants' responses to degrading overtures were eventually changed.

Which leads us into the minefield of *bias*…

Bias

We think of bias—the inequitable assessment or treatment of individuals based on some demographic they belong to—as being caused by human emotion or intention. (There we go again, judging humans by intentions.) So how can AI be biased? In several ways:

1. It may be deliberately programmed to display bias;
2. The training data may be deliberately selected to be biased;
3. The training data sampling may be accidentally biased;
4. The training data may reflect a historical culture-wide bias;
5. An accidental bug in the algorithm may introduce bias.

The first two of these are overt human intervention that might be detected through personal knowledge of the people involved in the AI creation. But biased training data is the most common and pernicious source of biased decisions by AI. As we have seen, AI works by virtue of having a lot of data to infer patterns from. The poster child for this type of bias was called out in a June 28, 2015 tweet from software developer Jacky Alciné from Brooklyn, New York, who noticed that Google Photos image recognition tagging had sorted a picture of him and a friend into a folder labeled "Gorillas." (See Figure 12.1.)

Figure 12.1: By permission of Jacky Alciné

For all the issues that later surfaced at Google surrounding diversity, this incident did not result from anyone at Google deciding that people of color should be labeled this way. From what we've seen so far about the role of data in supervised learning, we can surmise that this appalling behavior was due to the algorithm being trained on, relatively speaking, too many pictures of gorillas and too few pictures of Black people.

Google apologized within seconds and withdrew the tags "gorilla," "chimp," "chimpanzee," and "monkey" altogether. Yonatan Zunger, chief architect of social systems at Google, responded, "Thank you for telling us so quickly. Sheesh. High on my list of bugs you *never* want to see happen. Shudder."

However, Google have not covered themselves with glory since that incident. As of this writing, their software still hasn't been trained to supply labels for pictures of either people of color, or gorillas. And in widely-reported cases, researchers Timnit Gebru and Margaret Mitchell, who were hired by Google to work on ethics, were forced out, shortly after co-authoring a famous paper, "On the Dangers of Stochastic Parrots."[212] In Chapter 9 we saw Tomáš Mikolov describe GPT-3 as "a parrot that forgets every ten seconds"; and *stochastic* means "relating to probability." The paper argued that GPT-3 inherited bias because its training data—a large part of the Internet's text—was from places that had underrepresented inputs from women and minorities.

More than 45 percent of the data in ImageNet (the fourteen-million-image repository of training data, which fuels research into computer vision) comes from the United States, home to only 4 percent of the world's population. By contrast, China and India together contribute just 3 percent of ImageNet data, even though these countries represent 36 percent of the world's population. The National Institute of Standards and Technology Information Technology Laboratory measured the accuracy of facial recognition algorithms over 18.27 million images of 8.49 million people processed by a hundred and eighty-nine mostly commercial algorithms from ninety-nine developers, and found that the false positive rates were highest in West and East African and East Asian people, and lowest in Eastern European individuals. With a few notable exceptions: Algorithms developed in China had the lowest false positive rates on East Asian faces.[213]

The field of AI applied to personal data is littered with landmines. Unsupervised learning can reveal new knowledge, like the information that there's a connection between retinal patterns and gender, as described in Chapter 6. Suppose you asked AI to correlate facial images with criminal records and it reported it was able to predict criminal tendencies from appearance? Without it being able to tell you how. What if that were the case even after you thought you had scrubbed the data for any hidden bias? Suppose it was actually going off images that happened to be mug shots?

In 2017, a paper in *Nature* described how a neural network had equaled human accuracy in diagnosing skin cancer from images.[214] But a year later, its authors were forced to modify their conclusion. They discovered that many pictures in the training dataset had rulers next to the lesions, a common tool of dermatologists to assess changes in size. However, the rulers appeared more often in images of actual cancers than in the control images, and the network made the association "ruler = cancer." The result didn't invalidate the study completely, but it mortified the researchers, who concluded "… we must continue addressing the many nuances involved in bringing these new technologies safely to the bedside."[215]

Human dermatologists, of course, ignore rulers in images they learn diagnosis from, because they know that rulers are not part of skin. But AI does not. An exactly equivalent situation would apply if an AI were given many pictures of people and asked to predict which ones had criminal records, if some people in the training dataset were holding mug shot placards. Which is one of the reasons why no one in their right mind would initiate such a study.

But there are plenty of less obviously incendiary pitfalls awaiting AI users. What if the training data isn't as accurate as you thought? Garbage in, garbage out: Researchers at the Laboratory for Innovation Science at Harvard found that maxillofacial MDs and dentists have a rate of approximately 50 percent false negatives in detecting dental diseases using x-rays. Which means that their data sets not only capture their mistakes but also amplify them.[216]

As we're seeing, bias that results in racist or sexist outcomes is one of the most prevalent issues in AI today, and is often very hard to detect, let alone remediate.

Yet there are instructive parallels in the pre-AI world. Women comprised just 6 percent of the makeup of professional orchestras in 1970, but by 1993 that had increased to 21 percent. Harvard researchers writing in *The American Economic Review* concluded that the introduction of blind auditions during that period, where the judges could hear but not see the musicians, was responsible for this increase. (Some orchestras found that the bias still did not disappear until the auditioners removed their *shoes*.[217]) I doubt that the judges of professional musicians would have said or even thought that they were sexist, so the statistics suggest unconscious bias.

Examples of racist and sexist outcomes from AI are numerous:

- In 2016, when searching for "unprofessional hairstyle for work," the resulting pictures were almost all of Black women.[218]
- When converting Spanish articles written by women into English, for example, Google Translate often defaults to "he said/wrote," assuming the writer is male.[219]
- Latanya Sweeney, Director of the Data Privacy Lab at Harvard found that when she searched her own name, she found an ad saying, "Latanya Sweeney: Arrested?" And when she searched "Tanya Smith," she got an ad saying, "Located: Tanya Smith" instead. She conducted more than 120,000 searches for names, and found that names like Tyrone, Darnell and Latisha generated ads with the word "arrest" 75 to 96 percent of the time, while names like Geoffrey, Brett and Anne only used "arrest" 0 to 9 percent of the time.[220]

- In 2017, computer scientists at Princeton and the University of Bath found that after deploying a program called GloVe on eight hundred and forty billion words from the World Wide Web, it associated the words "female" and "woman" with pursuits like homemaking and occupations in the arts and humanities, while "male" and "man" were associated with work in math and engineering.[221]
- A 2019 report from the National Institute of Standards and Technology found widespread evidence of racial bias in nearly two hundred facial recognition algorithms that were far more likely to misidentify people of color than they were White people.[222]

In such ways, the rise of Big Data could have the perverse result of exacerbating existing inequalities by suggesting that historically disadvantaged groups actually deserve less favorable treatment.[223]

And what of the fourth kind of bias? Training data could be both accurate and complete—not just a representative sample—and still introduce bias. For example, an AI trained on the list of all past presidents of the United States will never predict a female successor. Similarly, Amazon found in 2018 that an internal human resources system used to screen job applicants based on employee performance devalued the potential of female job candidates. The system was designed to process a list of applicants and decide which ones to hire. But the underlying data was primarily the résumés of engineers who had applied to Amazon during the previous ten years, and they were predominately male. The system "learned" to penalize candidates whose résumés included the word "women's," as in, for example, "women's chess club captain."[224]

Vetting AI for bias may require extraordinary degrees of transparency. Algorithms trained in countries with lax ethical standards may be unfit for purpose in others; we may need whole new ways of describing bias that span cultures and nationalities.

Sometimes there isn't even the appearance of any hope that the training data could be fixed. For instance, AI that was fed patient medical data that appeared totally unrelated to the patient's race could "trivially learn to identify the self-reported racial identity of patients to an absurdly high degree of accuracy."[225] In their paper, twenty-two researchers from fifteen institutions in four countries showed how machine learning trained on chest x-rays, mammograms, limb x-rays, and cervical spine x-rays could predict the race—White, Black, or Asian—from those images with usually much better than 90 percent accuracy. This is not something a human radiologist can do. The researchers added high-pass filters to the images to make them fuzzier, and trained the models again. The models maintained performance well beyond the point that the "degraded images contained no recognizable structures; to the human co-authors and radiologists it was not even clear that the image was an x-ray at all." As shown in the paper, those images look like plain gray rectangles; and the AI was *still* able to figure out the race.

"These findings suggest that not only is racial identity trivially learned by AI models," declared the researchers, "but that it appears likely that it will be remarkably difficult to debias these systems." They were unable to tell how the AI was determining race from the x-rays: "Overall, we were unable to isolate image features that are responsible for the recognition of racial identity in medical images, either by spatial location, in the frequency domain, or caused by common anatomic and phenotype confounders associated with racial identity." They were smart enough to get the models to isolate the areas of the images where the racial information was strongest, and they then blocked out those areas; it still didn't help.

So why is this important? Medical researchers want to be able to process patient data without racial identity so as to avoid bias. This paper shows how hard that is, and their conclusion is stark:

> One commonly proposed method to mitigate bias is through the selective removal of features that encode protected attributes such as racial identity, while retaining as much information useful for the clinical task as possible, in effect making the machine learning models "colorblind." While this approach has already been criticized as being ineffective in some circumstances, our work further suggests that such an approach may not succeed in medical imaging simply for the fact that racial identity information appears to be incredibly difficult to isolate. We strongly recommend that all developers, regulators, and users who are involved with medical image analysis consider the use of deep learning models with extreme caution. In the setting of x-ray and CT imaging data, patient racial identity is readily learnable from the image data alone, generalizes to new settings, and may provide a direct mechanism to perpetuate or even worsen the racial disparities that exist in current medical practice.[226]

It's not hard to see why bias is an incredibly heated topic of current research; every use of AI seems to require analysis for pitfalls, even in low-stakes outcomes. For instance, when TV broadcasters wanted to avoid human bias in presenting the most exciting moments at the Wimbledon tennis tournament, they turned to an IBM Watson system that chose them based on crowd reactions. Although this eliminates bias by human producers, it would perpetuate any bias held by the crowd. That might reflect what a broadcaster wants (interest in a home country player), or not.

One of the groups actively working to free AI from bias is MKAI, founded by Richard Foster-Fletcher. Initially the "Milton Keynes Artificial Intelligence community," the earnest Englishman quickly cultivated it to take a place on the global stage. He described his motivations:

> I started MKAI to unite local artificial intelligence (AI) enthusiasts, but when COVID led the community online I realised that we had a unique and time-critical opportunity to shape the global narrative around the responsible development of AI. We formed with inclusion and kindness at the heart of everything we did to create safe discussion spaces for everyone to learn and talk about the risks and harms of unregulated AI. We wanted MKAI to be a bridge for all into the vital conversations about AI regulation and use the diverse perspectives that we generated to catalyse projects that place these new ideas into businesses and society.[227]

Richard identified the amplification effect of AI on bias: "AI has definitely been a black mirror to show the cracks and the biases in the system."[228] Which tells us that AI can act as a magnifying glass—to use another optical metaphor—that makes existing biases in, say, an organization's processes, more apparent.

Fraud

One form of fraud is faking the appearance of someone in images or sound; because deep learning is used to do that, the results are inevitably referred to as "deep fakes."* The AI startup Dessa created deep fake software that makes people look and sound like podcaster Joe Rogan. As *Futurism* noted, the tool wasn't perfect, as "tiny errors appear as the person having his face replaced moves his head around." In a related (but opposing) effort, the company has released new algorithmic tools that are trained to detect deepfakes and synthesized videos.[229] The most flawless deep fakes to date, a series called "Deep Tom Cruise," were made with a professional

---

* In general, to signal that you've achieved *X* with deep learning, call it "Deep *X*." The potential pitfalls of doing so will become apparent after a few examples.

impersonator whose face already bore an uncanny resemblance to that of Thomas Mapother IV himself.

Not so flawless, but signaling a new front in warfare, on March 16th, 2022, a deep fake of Ukrainian president Volodymyr Zelensky telling his forces to stand down was taken down from Meta.[230] It was, however, heavily promoted within Russia. "I suspect it's the tip of the iceberg," said Hany Farid, professor at the University of California, Berkeley, and expert in digital media forensics.[231]

Accountability

Accountability is an issue in today's AI, but not for the reasons that people might at first think. There's little question of an AI being held legally responsible for consequences arising from its decisions. No tickets are going to be issued to self-driving cars, only to the person behind the steering wheel. The point at which this will change is when the cars get so capable that they don't *have* steering wheels. Or, as in the Waymo cars currently operating near Phoenix, Arizona, where the only human in the car is in the back seat, or the AutoX taxis operating in Shenzhen, China, where they may travel without anyone in the car when heading to pick up a fare.

As AI tackles more complex and complicated decisions, the issue of which human to hold accountable for its failures will become harder to decide. Should it be the training data set curator, the configuration management lead who selected the machine learning algorithm, or the operator who pushed the final button?

What about the software development team? They have traditionally been very insulated from liability for their output, but this may have to change. (If bridges were built to the reliability standards of commercial software, everyone would be too terrified to leave their houses. The highways would be littered with bodies.)

Charles Radclyffe studies "how people and organizations can best design emerging technology to shape the futures they want to create." The head of Ethicsgrade, an Environmental, Social, and Governance (ESG) evaluation consultancy, told me, "My burden to you or my neighbor as an ordinary citizen is the burden I owe to every human being, but the burden that a lawyer or an accountant or a doctor, etc. owes to the rest of us is what we call a 'fiduciary duty,' and it really recognizes that special character of control that they have. I think the most mystifying gap that we have in our relationship to the technology industry is that we don't hold technologists to the same standard yet. I think that is inevitably going to change in the next generation, because the level of complexity that technology requires an understanding of—the discipline, the expertise—is beyond most people."[232]

Explainability

> *Let's face it, the universe is messy. It is nonlinear, turbulent, and dynamic.... It self-organizes and evolves. It creates diversity* and *uniformity. That's what makes the world interesting, that's what makes it beautiful, and that's what makes it work.*[233]
>
> — Donella H. Meadows

There's an old joke that goes something like this:

> A man was piloting a balloon when a strong wind sprang up, sending the balloon careering over the countryside far beyond the range of the small maps he had thought to bring. Eventually he sighted a tall building with a worker toiling in an office at the very top, so with great difficulty, he maneuvered the balloon near the building and called out, "Hello! I'm lost. Can you tell me where I am?"
>
> The office worker (evidently unfazed by the approach of a hot air balloon) replied, "You're in a balloon, about 80 feet off the ground, between 42 and 44 degrees north latitude, just northwest of this building."
>
> The balloonist retorted, "You must be an engineer," to which the other said, "Yes. How did you know?"
>
> "Because everything you told me is technically true, yet it is of no use to me and I'm still lost."
>
> To which the other man said, "You must be in management."
>
> "You're right. How did you know?"
>
> "Because you have no idea where you are or where you're going. You set out on a task without adequate preparation and when it went wrong, you expected me to solve your problem. You're still just as lost, but now, somehow, it's my fault."

This joke has longevity because both engineers and managers can relate to it. The engineer's response is full of accurate information that is of no use to the other man; computer-like, it answers the question in a literal and restricted form, rather than estimating the manager's intent. Engineers and managers often feel trapped in a perpetual reenactment of this story.

The joke's now on us when a business that deploys AI needs it to account for its decisions. This requirement is known as *explainability*: getting the AI to explain *why* it made a certain decision.

In many applications of AI, explainability isn't important. Recommendation algorithms, the power behind the "If you liked *Harry Potter*, you'll love this Tolkien fellow!" suggestions that weave through every e-commerce site, are powered by sophisticated AI. But if they make a mistake, neither a false positive ("No, my buying a kilt for my Scottish nephew does not mean he would like this miniskirt") nor a false negative (omitting to tell you about a matching limited-edition sporran) are tortious errors.

Not so for some other applications. AIs can be taught to make decisions on granting bank loans and insurance claims, and to do so just as accurately as a human; though, of course, much faster. Regardless of how good the AI's decisions have been shown to be, there will be instances where justifications for individual decisions will be required.

And then we will have to decide just what we mean by an "explanation." This is another one of those terms that seems obvious to us but which is maddeningly elusive when we need to define it with enough rigor to get a computer to do it. Most of us intuit an understanding of what the person requesting the explanation requires, most of the time. But to get an idea of how varied the possible answers are, consider someone asking an autonomous vehicle, "Why did you turn left just now?" Here are some possible answers:

- Because my front wheels pivoted for 3200 milliseconds;
- Because that's where the intersection was;
- Because my guidance system said so;
- Because that was the optimal route to my destination;
- Because you told me to.

But all of these answers, reminiscent of lines scripted for a character like *Star Trek's* Spock or *Big Bang Theory's* Sheldon, have skipped the internal dialogue that takes place when we are asked for an explanation, which starts with asking ourselves, "*Why* are they asking that question?" Which would unconsciously lead, in this case, to the context of "We normally don't go this way to the office," and the desired answer, "Because the usual route was blocked by an accident."

So the nature of an explanation has to be carefully defined for each application, and this is difficult because it amounts to writing a whole new AI. When we make a decision requiring integrating many pieces of different types of information, we arrive at the answer largely through subconscious processes. Anyone who's learned cooking from a parent has likely encountered this. "Now add some flour." "How much, exactly?" "Enough." "But how will I know how much is enough?" "You'll know."

Eventually you pick it up; you've absorbed the intelligence through sufficient exposure to successful and unsuccessful trials, just like a neural network being trained through supervised learning. But when someone asks you how much salt to add, you also will be answering, "Just enough."*

Now consider tasks like deciding whether to grant a loan, pay out an insurance claim, or hire a job applicant. They *cannot*, by definition, be reduced to concise algorithmic steps, or we would make those decisions with either an app or a minimum wage worker following a script. As much as the people in those jobs might strive to formalize their decisions through documented criteria and policies, at some point there has to come a spark of magic that can't be reduced to a readable description. But this means that when they are asked for an explanation, though, they have to cheat, even a little bit, maybe subconsciously, and deconstruct their intuitive decision into a description that is understandable. We agree to accept such explanations, although sometimes the stakes are so high that lawyers get involved, and then there is a frenzy of picking apart decisions where everyone pretends that there was a perfectly formal basis for making them.

Now imagine trying to add *that* process to an AI that's deciding whether to make a loan. The process of training it was trivial by comparison: there was a huge dataset of prior applications and outcomes, you know that the loan officers used only the data in those applications to make their decisions, and that those decisions have been accepted as correct. Your machine learning model can make decisions with a mathematically provable accuracy that may well exceed what any individual human can do; and yet you are asked to explain its decisions, when the only honest answer you could give would be, "These weights distributed over these connections in the network triggered activation functions that selected this output node."

Suppose I, in the role of software developer, were to write an algorithm that contained various numbers with no explanation; 4.2093 here, -4598 there, 1.45489E13 over there, and so on. Suppose further that, on deliv-

---

* And for all you parents out there who want a demonstration of the ultimate futility of human explainability, try asking your kid how the vase got broken.

ering the code, I was asked by the customer to explain these "magic numbers" and my response was, "That's just what I had to put in to make it come up with the right answer." I think I might not have that job for much longer, no? But train a neural network to come up with a million magic numbers by itself and the world declares me to be a genius. Those magic numbers are the connection weights the network set through backpropagation. Satisfying the customer that those numbers in fact do exactly what the customer wants is the crux of explainability.

An explanation that would satisfy a human would have to be constructed from parameters that have been carefully curated in advance with precise knowledge of the needs of the questioner; and then the answer will have to be fitted to those parameters. If you think this sounds hard, you're right. Explainability is one of the most active fronts in AI research.

We think we know what explanations are, and how to give one. This seems very obvious and intuitive, but it isn't. Think about a grade schooler who's always asking, why this, why that. Suppose they ask, "Why is this particular person the President of the United States?" You explain the electoral college, the constitution, the vote tallying process—okay, you're feeling like you've got this one nailed—and then they ask "But why did they vote for him?" And you realize this is going to take longer than you expected. Context is everything, right?

For an *explanation* of explainability, I turned to Michael Hind, Distinguished Research Staff Member in the IBM Research AI department in Yorktown Heights, New York. How can you get machine learning to cough up an explanation for, say, a loan application decision, I wondered? "I can probe the model," he told me. "I can take your application, and tweak some of the answers. I'll do some tests and see if it changes the decision from *denied* to *approved*. And then based on that I can build up a boundary condition to say: it seems like these are the important features, and then it can give you an 'explanation.'"

I found this ingenious, so I probed further, and he told me of another class of techniques called "prototype-based," which don't try to explain why they issued a denial based on an applicant's answers. Instead, they find examples of people who were denied for similar reasons, and tell you to look at them. "Now, clearly, there are issues with privacy," he went on, "and you don't want to give out the training data to customers. But this could be useful, for example, to the loan officer, who's trying to understand what's going on."

Hind also pointed out that we can hold double standards of explainability. "Let's say I had an AI model that was making a decision on whether someone should be convicted for a crime, or hired, or admitted to college. In all those cases, no one gets an explanation [when a human makes the decision]. But when they're done by an AI system, there's concern that there could be biases, or a bug. So we need an explanation." By way of analogy, he argued, "It's shocking that I could be convicted of a major crime and not be told why except that twelve of my peers in the US felt it was reasonable."

An explanation from humans may be a cover for bias: The hiring rejection explanation "I don't feel this person is the right fit for our corporate culture" is a tell for either a lie or an unexamined unconscious bias.

Hind's group is now working with the National Institute of Standards and Technology, which is an indicator of how the field of explainability is maturing: if NIST develops a standard for something, in general they do it so carefully that everyone who needs to work in that field can breathe a sigh of relief and just refer to that standard. So when NIST gets involved in an aspect of AI, it means that it's become important that everyone agree on some definitions and metrics of that aspect.

Hind showed me how even a well-trained model could be abused:

> Often models are reused, but they may not be appropriate to be to be reused. A concrete example: I develop a loan approval for a rural area in the United States, and one of the things I use in my model is, does the person own a house? Does the person own a car? Those are probably good predictors of creditworthiness. And then a friend of mine down the hall says, "Your model works really well. I want to use it in Boston, Massachusetts." Okay, fine. But it turns out in Boston, Massachusetts, many people don't own houses or cars, but they may be creditworthy.[234]

A deep learning network that has been trained on images may, as we've seen, learn to recognize parts of the image that are nothing to do with the objects we thought we were training them on. One network trained to recognize dumbbells was subjected to a clever algorithm to get it to synthesize an image of the ideal dumbbell and every run generated disturbing pictures of dumbbells with disembodied arms attached. "[I]t seems no picture of a dumbbell is complete without a muscular weightlifter there.… Maybe [the network]'s never been shown a dumbbell without an arm holding it," opined the researchers.[235]

But what if a network, trained in a similar fashion but for making critical decisions, "learned" a bias? And would that bias even need to be one that triggers legal consequences to cause problems? John Zerilli, Research

Fellow at the Oxford Institute for Ethics in AI, used the hypothetical example of an AI withholding a loan to someone because they liked fennel. Not because the AI had been told to do that, but because in all the metadata it had been given, it detected that a fondness for fennel correlated to bad risk. "If a human were to decide something on the basis of such a spurious correlation like fennel and creditworthiness you would have no hesitation in dismissing the decision as being unjust; not even a matter of discrimination, it would just be an absurd irrational result," he said on the *AI and You* podcast. "But that's because we know what humans are like and we know roughly how humans tick, whereas with the machine that comes upon the same correlation we can't be so sure that it's just irrational."[236] In other words, maybe there actually *was* a connection between a penchant for licorice-flavored herbs and bad creditworthiness. Fennel-likers are not a protected class, so they would have no recourse if we let the AI reject them; the decisions would, however, be used to argue that the AI was acting irrationally.

But we wouldn't even *know* that the fennel-lovers were being rejected on that basis unless we performed what is currently very sophisticated analysis on the network *and* it emitted results in a form we could understand. It's hard enough to determine whether it has developed a bias against a protected class; how hard might it be to discover that it has developed an irrational bias against a class whose identity we don't already know?

Privacy

> *Presumably [in the year 2000] there will also be such things as: a single national information file containing all tax, legal, security, credit, educational, medical, employment, and other information about each citizen.*[237]
>
> — Herman Kahn and Anthony Wiener, in 1967

When, in 1999, Sun Microsystems founder Scott McNealy told his audience, "You have zero privacy anyway; get over it," we still had nowhere close to the level of personal information now available to the right buyer. In 2002, Target (a US department store chain) discovered that pregnant women would purchase folic acid and vitamin supplements in the first trimester, unscented lotion in the second trimester, and hand sanitizer close to the due dates. So if any woman's purchases followed that pattern, Target flagged her as pregnant.[238]

Those insights were the result of applying machine learning to Big Data; as we've seen, you need a lot of data to get good results. A petabyte is a *lot* of data; it's enough room to store eleven thousand high-definition movies. Walmart collects more than 2½ petabytes of data every *hour* from its customers. It used this data to discover that just before a hurricane, people buy an unusual amount of Strawberry Pop Tarts.[239] Sadly, this pastry binging occurs only after the buyers know about the imminent hurricane; it cannot be used for meteorological forecasting.

The battle for the consumer is being fought over how much data can be gathered on them, with a winner-takes-all prize for the most. This is why Google is willing to give away so much storage to its customers, in return for, say, Gmail and YouTube. Their former CEO Eric Schmidt said he thinks of the ethical boundary as a "creepy line": "The Google policy is to get right up to the creepy line but not cross it."[240]

The general reaction of most people to learning how their data is used to market to them is momentary outrage, then a return to life as usual. There are, after all, obvious benefits to free Gmail and Facebook accounts. Some people battle to release as little personal data as possible, but let's examine their motivations. If you have some skeleton in a closet, some peccadillo you'd rather other people not know about, at what point does the release of that knowledge become a problem? Here's a thought experiment. Write that embarrassing fact down on a piece of paper. Problem yet? No? Put it in a sealed container. Put it in a safety deposit box. Problem? Suppose the contents of the container are extracted by a robot and scanned into a computer, but don't go anywhere. Problem? Suppose that information is collected with similar information from millions of other people to derive some aggregate data about that type of indiscretion, and a headline appears: "Over thirteen thousand adults secretly wear *Star Wars*-themed pajamas." Have we yet crossed a line that you're uncomfortable with? Is your privacy violated when only a *machine* knows the information, or when another *person* does? Part of the reason that people will unburden themselves to chatbots acting as digital therapists (like ELIZA, whom we will meet shortly) is that they know that the bot cannot judge them.

I suspect that the point when you do have a problem is when a marketing decision is made that is noticeable to you personally, like being emailed coupons for *Star Wars*-themed underwear. Of course, this still doesn't mean that any particular human knows your Boba Fett-ish penchant; the coupon was generated and sent without being seen by human eyes. But the creepy line has been crossed.

Books like Shoshanna Zuboff's *Age of Surveillance* tell a relentlessly negative story of the data collectors; but if you were to study the individual employees at Google, Apple, and, yes, Facebook, you would come up short trying to find evil motives, and be forced to adopt a more nuanced position. The *system* might be evil even if none of its components are.

If the paper stored in the container did not have your name on it and ended up in a database which could have been populated by anyone in the world, would you feel safely anonymous? The participants in the 1000 Genomes Project thought so; they donated their DNA to the database where it was available to researchers, without any metadata identifying the donors. But in 2013, MIT's Yaniv Erlich and Melissa Gymrek demonstrated that using nothing more than a home computer and internet searches, it was possible to correlate the data through online genealogy sites to surnames and eventually to specific Mormon families in Utah.[241]

◊

When looking for ethical issues involving breathtaking crossing of privacy boundaries, you can get your fill in one stop: China. Unfazed by a storm of online criticism, in 2018 Hangzhou No. 11 High School installed cameras in the classrooms to notify the teacher when a student is "failing to focus during class time," explained the school's vice principal, Zhang Guanchao. The school was no stranger to face-tracking surveillance, already using facial recognition for students to pay for cafeteria meals. Within the first month, the principal said, the cameras caused the schoolchildren to "voluntarily change their behaviors and classroom habits" so they can "attend classes more happily now."[242] Some students sounded less than happy: "Since the school has introduced these cameras, it is like there [is] a pair of mystery eyes constantly watching me, and I don't dare let my mind wander."[243] But parents focused on academic scores were appreciative, helping to fund the system. The Ministry of Education published a report the same year calling on schools to "use artificial intelligence to monitor the teaching process and analyze the performance of students and teachers." While adoption of emotion monitoring was slow, facial recognition became the default means of granting access to everything from campuses to vending machines. A year later, Betty Li, a student attending university in Xian, said, "We lost privacy a long time ago. Now we are very transparent in society, aren't we?"[244]

But we may not need to go as far as China. On July 7, 2021, right-wing *Fox News* commentator Tucker Carlson and his guest Matt Walsh called for installation of cameras in every American classroom for monitoring teachers.[245] That suggestion is unlikely to prevail; as the *New York Post* pointed out two days later, the same cameras would also monitor the students.[246] But cameras are already growing in use for security in American schools seeking to reduce their risk of a shooting incident, and the side effect has been their use in punishing students for various offences. A study by Johns Hopkins University and Washington University in St. Louis found that the greater the level of surveillance, the more students were suspended, even when researchers controlled for levels of school disorder and student misbehavior. The monitoring created a class divide.[247]

The natural brake on surveillance—that it is limited by the number of people available to inspect the video—is removed when AI can scan any number of streams as quickly as desired, and that is not far off. A 2020 IEEE paper outlined a deep neural network model trained in universities for detecting suspicious behavior, concluding that its 87 percent accuracy rate meant "The proposed model has the benefit of stopping the crime before it happens."[248]

Privacy is a multidimensional issue. Commentators love to mock AIs for inappropriate behavior, like Alexa interrupting a family argument with a picayune reminder. But this is at least partly a consequence of the AIs *not* having even more personal information. We want our AIs to understand us, but yet we don't want them to gather the information that would allow them to do that. If we want an AI to be as helpful as a butler, if we want it to know how we like our tea, when it's time to prod us to exercise, which uninvited guests to repulse and with which excuse, then we will have to trust it with as much intimate information as a butler would need. If we don't establish criteria for how to trust an AI as much as a butler, it will never be as useful.

Facial Recognition

We are all robots when uncritically involved with our technologies.

— Marshall McLuhan

Once upon a time, for several years I held a Disneyland annual passport. Like many others with a fondness for the House of Mouse, I frequented the Happiest Place on Earth enough to make it worth buying a plastic card that was valuable enough to be secured by what was then an advanced authentication measure: my photograph on the front. These days my interests have altered, photography is far easier, and my picture is on an annual pass to Butchart Gardens. We give the tradeoff of our image for access little thought.

But in the country leading the world in digital face recognition, there are signs of backtracking. In 2021, law professor Guo Bing objected to his local zoo, the Hangzhou Safari Park, scanning his face for his annual pass. He sued to have the facial scan removed—and won.[249] In a case believed to be the first of its kind in China, the judge ordered the zoo to delete his scan and fingerprints. (Westerners who assess this move to be dangerously rebellious for someone in China should note that the zoo is a private entity and not the government.)

China has been enthusiastic about facial recognition since the decade-long reign of terror of serial killer Zhou Kehua ended in 2012 after police officers each viewed hundreds to thousands of hours of video surveillance recordings, manually. Some fainted during the task.[250]

Why was Guo Bing concerned about the zoo having his picture when I was not concerned about the Disney empire having mine thirty years earlier? AI. When I presented my pass at the green turnstiles in the 1990s, my photograph could only be used by the "cast member" on duty to decide whether the person holding the card was the person pictured on the card. But now, AI can match a photograph of your face against other appearances of you on the Internet to tie together numerous pieces of publicly known data about you. The press release your company issued when you were promoted. Your Little League coaching stint. Your friend's selfie on your hike up Pike's Peak together. *That* spring break photo.

For many years, it was a trope in run-of-the-mill cop shows that "computers" could do this magic, if only in the bowels of the National Security Agency, but no one actually saw it happen until 2017, when Clearview AI, a New York company founded by Australian emigrant Hoan Ton-That and Mayor Rudy Giuliani aide Richard Schwartz, built that capability by scraping ten billion facial images from social media and using a neural network to match the faces. They operated in near-total anonymity, courting customers in law enforcement and private security customers such as casinos, until in 2020 the *New York Times* outed them.[251]

The social media companies instantly reacted against the violation of their terms of service, which prohibit automated agents from pretending to be human users downloading massive quantities of data. Not so much because the social media companies sought to light a candle for individual privacy rights, but because they had paid to acquire that data and weren't going to allow someone else to profit from it. Also because

Clearview had flaunted their power with Gatsbyesque hubris, allowing wealthy contributors to use it for personal purposes, like billionaire John Catsimatidis vetting his daughter's date during the time it took them to order dinner.[252]

As though reenacting the Zhou Kehua saga with a modern efficient conclusion, Clearview AI solved a shooting in Indiana where a bystander captured a picture of the gunman's face. It found an instant match that had eluded the state police because the man had not yet been captured in government databases. Other crimes were similarly solved. But the privacy implications were being rubbed in a lot of faces. Al Gidari, privacy professor at Stanford Law School, and someone who would be acutely aware that there is no constitutional right to privacy, said, "Absent a very strong federal privacy law, we're all screwed."

But what if you are not a law enforcement agency but still would like to explore the Internet for matches to your face? PimEyes.com has you covered. For only $29.99 a month, you can submit up to twenty-five searches a day; the PimEyes team will assist you in crafting takedown requests for sites that don't have your permission to use your images. The Eastern-European-based site does not check that the picture you upload is actually of you, though, making it an excellent tool for stalkers. While it doesn't search social media, it does index pornography, so if you want to know if someone was ever in that business, it will do the job.[253] This is what is now possible with AI and the Internet.

So while the United States explores the privacy of facial recognition like an ox exploring a porcelain shop, China may be pulling back from the precipice that the US fears heading over—at least, in the private sphere. In the public sector, China is using AI facial recognition to discriminate against an entire ethnic minority, the Uighurs. The CloudWalk system will "send alarms" to law enforcement if six Uighurs are detected in a neighborhood where previously one was recorded.[254]

It is, to say the least, an evolving issue. In 2021, the curators of ImageNet, the benchmark database for AI image recognition training (see Chapter 5), blurred out all the faces in it. They wrote in a blog post, "The dataset was created to benchmark object recognition—at a time when it barely worked. Today, computer vision is in real-world systems impacting people's Internet experience and daily lives. An emerging problem now is how to make sure computer vision is fair and preserves people's privacy. Experiments show that one can use the face-blurred version for benchmarking object recognition and for transfer learning with only marginal loss of accuracy."[255]

Meanwhile, rebellion grows: in my household, my wife is annoyed that her iPhone X, trained to unlock at the sight of her face, does not recognize her in the mornings. We've already seen how AI doesn't always focus on the features of an image that we would consider to be the most salient. A study at Ben Gurion University demonstrated that makeup patterns created by their YouCam Makeup app could fool facial recognition systems up to 98 percent of the time.[256] Notably, the makeup does not look like black stripes (see the Stop sign in Chapter 11); it looks like subtle changes to blush highlights that would scarcely attract the attention of anyone this side of a professional model. A Carnegie Mellon University team created glasses that make you look like Milla Jovovich; they tricked commercially available face recognition software Face++ with a success rate of around 90 percent using garish frames that look like a three-year-old-painted them.[257] Like the makeup, these glasses also do not signal that you are committing an act of subversion. And their next iteration could look even more conventional.

Hearkening back to the topic of bias, defeating facial recognition may, sadly, be much easier if you're Black. MIT researcher Joy Buolamwini discovered that the systems simply failed to see dark-skinned people; women in particular. In her TEDx talk, she showed a commercial facial recognition system easily identifying a White colleague, but as soon as she got in front of the camera, it registered… nothing. White person comes back, it wakes up. Joy comes into frame; she's invisible. This reflects a deeper invisibility: the lack of representation of colored faces in training data. In a cringeworthy misstep at remedying that situation, Google paid contractors to approach people in public to give them $5 in exchange for harvesting pictures of their faces for a database. They were asked to target people of color in particular, and unsurprisingly, decided to approach attendees of the Black Entertainment Television Awards.[258]

In February 2020, Clearview's client database was stolen by hackers, and in May was sued by the ACLU for violation of the Illinois Biometric Information Privacy Act, declaring that Clearview "will end privacy as we know it if it isn't stopped."[259] In February 2022, however, the company appealed for $50 million of investment to enable them to reach a goal of indexing a hundred billion facial images so that "almost everyone in the world will be identifiable." In June 2020, Amazon put a one-year pause on allowing police forces to use their Rekognition facial recognition system out of concern that it could lead to unfair treatment of racial minorities.[260] A year later, they extended that pause indefinitely.[261]

Power-Hungry AI

Literally you could run France on the electricity it would take to simulate a full human brain at moderate resolution.

— Alex Nugent, CEO, Knowm

The dirty not-so-secret of modern AI is the colossal power it consumes. This is the consequence of the difference between two formulas: Moore's Law, that computer processing power per unit cost doubles every eighteen months, and OpenAI's finding that machine learning models double in size every 3.4 months.[262] Stanford professor Jonathan Koomey proposed a corollary to Moore's Law, saying that the computing capacity per watt of electricity doubles in eighteen months. But the fact that AI engines double in size in one-sixth of that time means that their electrical power requirements are going up, as are their costs. Why? It's an AI arms race. This is the most solid evidence that AI product companies believe we're at the dawn of an AI revolution, that they are racing to outspend each other to get ahead.

Unfortunately for our planet, the electricity consumed by these models is now a noticeable fraction of our total power generation. Training the final version of OpenAI's MegatronLM language model used nearly the amount of energy consumed by the average US home in three years.[263] Data centers (carrying out nearly all computing, not just AI) are projected to consume as much as 13 percent of all global electricity by 2030.[264] One algorithm that lets a robot manipulate a Rubik's Cube used as much energy as three nuclear plants produce in an hour.[265]

Some people theorize that this will not be a problem in the long run, because so much power will be generated from non-greenhouse-gas-emitting sources like wind and solar. It might also be that AI will show us how to reduce the energy it needs; Google used deep learning to tune the cooling systems used in its data centers to reduce power consumption by 40 percent.[266]

13
Getting Personal with AI

> *When new technologies impose themselves on societies long habituated to older technologies, anxieties of all kinds result.*
>
> — Marshall McLuhan

What happens when AI interacts with us personally? For instance, in understanding how we *feel*? We'd like to think that reading human emotions is the *ne plus ultra* of human uniqueness; what could be more human than the ability to empathize with another person's feelings? But recognizing human emotions may not be as hard as it seems. The field of *Affective Computing* was pioneered by Rosalind Picard at MIT. The best evidence of its success is its commercialization by Rana el Kaliouby, founder of Affectiva, who demonstrated in a 2015 TED talk a mobile application that would analyze the facial emotions of a subject.[267] Affectiva now has spun off Autoemotive, creating the tools to prevent road rage by determining whether a driver is in too volatile a state to be in control of a car.

And what about AI *expressing* emotions? Would this be a high bar to clear? In her 2018 TED talk, "Why We Have an Emotional Connection to Robots," Kate Darling demonstrated a Pleo, a ($500!) robot baby dinosaur toy that articulates, vocalizes, and reacts to its environment. When suspended by its tail it wriggles and makes plaintive noises: Darling confessed how she implored the person holding it to put it back down, where she petted it to stop it crying.[268]

Darling is a *robot researcher* at the MIT Media Lab. No one could know better than her that this was not a live creature, and exactly how it worked. And yet this simulacrum provoked a maternal reaction in her. That response wasn't confined to her, either. In experiments with groups of subjects that had played with several Pleos for a while, when researchers instructed them to whack the dinosaurs, they tapped them gently; one subject removed the batteries from one of the toys to "spare it the pain." When told to dismember one of the toys, again they refused until the researchers told them that if they didn't comply, *all* of the dinosaurs would be destroyed. One of the participants volunteered to do the job for the group, with evident distress.[269] And if you're thinking that these were unsophisticated experimental subjects, perhaps children even—no, they were attendees of a Swiss conference on digital innovation.

There's plenty of material for psychologists to work with here, of course, and they wouldn't even need to invoke robots to get started: humans have been feeling empathy towards inanimate objects since the primordial teddy bear. But AI can crank that reaction way up. In May 2018, Google CEO Sundar Pichai revealed their Duplex virtual assistant to the world. Speaking from a stage above a crowd of cheering employees, he told them how the assistant would respond to a request to, say, make a haircut appointment, and make the phone call to the salon on your behalf. He then played a recording of exactly that happening. The unsuspecting salon employee spoke to Duplex, which was vocalizing with a female accent somewhere around Type A Valley Girl, complete with "uh-huh" interjections to add realism. A brief negotiation for the time of the appointment took place, and then (never having identified itself with a name) Duplex had booked its owner, "Lisa," to get her locks shorn. There was no point where the realism in the conversation wavered.

A few months later, on October 10th, 2018, the Magic Leap company demonstrated "Mica": a virtual assistant appearing as an avatar on a screen. Mica took the form of a young woman reacting to the user with girlish delight and flawless recreation of facial expressions, laughter, and movement—which, granted, was not rendered in real time then, but real-time fidelity was not far off and the company was banking on Moore's Law getting them to the finish line in due course. Users later were able to interact with a full-body version of Mica through augmented reality glasses; although she did not speak. Mica did not come to market because Magic Leap went through corporate difficulties, laying off half its workforce two years later, but there was no suggestion that Mica wasn't commercializable; the company made other products that were the bulk of their business.

Now imagine a perfectly feasible intersection of technologies: The intelligence and creativity of GPT-3, combined with the natural vocalization and spunky interaction of Duplex, and the visual avatar engagement of Mica. Suddenly the plotline of Spike Jonze's 2013 movie *Her*, where a man falls in love with the operating system of his smartphone (voiced by Scarlett Johansson, without even the benefit of a visual image), doesn't seem so fantastic.

You've Come a Long Way, ELIZA

> *The reason we have these companion bots—eldercare bots, nanny bots, romance bots—is that we've become so busy. We are so caught up in this culture of being busy that we don't have time for each other. So it has to be asked, are the robots becoming more like us, or are we becoming more like robots?*
>
> — Ramona Pringle

In retrospect, we've seen therapy bots coming since the sixties, when MIT professor Joseph Weizenbaum's secretary asked him to leave the computer room so she could have a heart-to-heart with the chatbot he had coded to emulate a Rogerian psychiatrist. Stunningly primitive by today's standards, ELIZA nevertheless served as a confidant to far more people than Weizenbaum foresaw—or wanted. He pulled the plug on further ELIZA development, deciding not that it was too advanced, but that it was getting the wrong kind of attention. The real question that should have haunted us all from that moment was: How can a computer perform a role that surely lays claim to the zenith of human capability? Therapists dance with empathy like ballerinas; they observe the most minute, fleeting body language and vocal intonation cues; they *get inside your head*. That's why we go to them! If an AI can do the same, surely no field of human endeavor is safe from their advance—or worth defending?

As clunky as ELIZA was,[*] the therapist bots have come much further recently, and now there is science behind them: "There is rigorous research to show that CBT [Cognitive Behavioral Therapy] delivered via

---

[*] You can play a version of it yourself online at https://www.masswerk.at/elizabot/.

the internet can be as effective as CBT delivered by human therapists for both anxiety and depression," says the Harvard Business School about *Woebot,* an AI developed by Drs. Alison Darcy and Athena Robinson. "Specifically, early results from research teams at Stanford University have shown that college students who chatted with Woebot significantly reduced the symptoms of depression in two weeks."[270]

Darcy's motivation was that "depression became the leading global cause of disability in 2015, almost ten years ahead of the World Health Organization's prediction."[271] Could she make a difference to a world in need of the help of more psychiatrists? Journalist Erin Brodwin found Woebot surprisingly helpful, noting that she was able to text it late at night when she was "feeling panicky," at a time when she wouldn't dare disturb a human therapist.[272]

Woebot is not observing any of the nonverbal cues that therapists are hyperattuned to—it operates only on text input. Shockingly, however, text input alone is enough to produce useful results. I find people in the helping professions often react to this as news that the robots are going to take their jobs—please relax, that is in a distant future. You are squarely in the quadrant of job impact that Kai-Fu Lee labeled the "Safe Zone" in his 2018 book *AI Superpowers.* Take heart instead that perhaps Woebot and its descendants could be helpful assistants—and save you from a late-night panicky phone call.

Empathetic Robots

> *My fundamental contention is that the unity of mind and body is an objective reality, that these entities are not related to each other in one fashion or another, but are an inseparable whole. To put this more clearly; I contend that a brain could not think without motor functions.*
>
> — Moshé Feldenkrais

In 1986, Paolo Pirjanian was a teenage Armenian refugee, born in Iran and living in Denmark, when he bought his first computer, a Sony MSX. That same year, on August 17th, Pixar released the landmark animated short *Luxo Jr.,* about a feisty eponymous desk lamp. "I saw two lamps playing with their mama lamp, and baby lamp playing with a ball," recalls Pirjanian, "and I was so blown away by that because I was struggling making a pixel appear on the screen of my computer's monitor. But when I saw this, I was like, 'Wow, how is that possible? How can you make this happen?' Literally having animated characters that can express emotions."[273] That moment changed the trajectory of his life. After a stint as Chief Technical Officer of iRobot, the Roomba company, he became CEO of Embodied, Inc., makers of the Moxie robot, a pint-sized playpal for troubled children.

Moxie is demonstrated in a company video. There's a boy in his bedroom alone, and you can tell from his expression that he's been burned before; he's been hurt. You know what kids are like: one wrong move and you're labeled for the rest of your time at school. Then his parents come into the room: obviously concerned and wanting to do the best for him, and they say "We've got a new friend for you." They introduce him to Moxie, which is about the size of a baby penguin—it's even got little flippers for arms—and a screen at the front of its head on which, when it's turned on, a face appears. And it says "Hi, I'm Moxie. I need to learn about the world; can you help me?" And Moxie strikes up a relationship with the boy, and over the course of days or weeks helps to draw the boy out of his shell by asking questions, asking for help, and having positively reinforcing interactions with the boy.

"The way Moxie's program has been developed by our team of game developers from children's content and our child development experts is to bring [the child] out, start engaging with some activities, have the child share some of their thoughts and feelings with the robot," explained Pirjanian, "and then the robot will encourage the child to go do an activity in the real world. So in the spot, you also see [in the] last few seconds where Moxie encourages the child to go talk to a friend and come and report back. It's like a mission, a challenge [Moxie gives] to the child; and children are actually excited about accepting these challenges from Moxie, and then they go do the physical activity, and then next time they see Moxie, they report to Moxie. So that's bringing the kid out of their shell and using Moxie as a springboard into the real world."

How, I wondered, does a robot recognize human emotions from facial expressions? "You can have very high-level states, very abstract states of emotion and just categorize them to, say, five, or you can go into much more detail and look at every single muscle that's firing," said Pirjanian. "Moxie extracts those, and then from that we analyze the ones that are firing and can come up with some nuances of emotion that the child is expressing. And even measuring [them] because … for some children, we want to teach them about being able to express themselves too because [they] have neurodevelopmental challenges such as autism and are not very good at expressing their emotions."

This was so successful that they would find that children wanted to be lying on the floor talking to Moxie where they were no longer in its field of view, or they were sitting in the middle of the dark, or they want to put a blanket on Moxie "so Moxie's not cold," and they wanted to hug Moxie and put it in their bed—all "nightmares" for their technologists.

And then Pirjanian told me a story that showed why he does this work:

> We went to this family's home, the son was I think at the time seven years old; on the spectrum, very high functioning super-genius kid, but socially not very strong. We put Moxie in front of him, he asks a question, we push a button, Moxie responds. And then he asks another question, we push another button, Moxie responds. And after a third interaction, the kid just completely opens up and talks to Moxie as if it's a friend he has known for a while, to the point that mom got a tear in her eye. I asked her "Why are you so emotional?" She said, "Do you know when he comes home from school how long it takes me to 'find him?'" And "find him" meant, "to get on a wavelength where he would open up to mom that way."

It might look at first as though it's a weakness that we respond empathetically to inanimate objects, but when Moxie can use that reaction to make that kind of difference to a family, perhaps it shows the way to a useful new relationship between humans and AI.

I'm Advancing as Fast as I Can

People are falling behind because technology is advancing so fast and our skills and our organizations aren't keeping up.

— Erik Brynjolfsson

It always used to be that technology was the slower one in our relationship with it, like we were dragging a three-year-old through an airport trying to make our flight. "Come on, hurry up: store my files faster, send my emails faster, dial my calls faster." It was a truism of the heyday of mainframe computers that they were slow, relative to our pace of life; they might be calculating and manipulating data faster than humans could, but you'd still wait hours or longer to get the results; you were in charge of the schedule on which those computers were tasked with your demands. But now the tables are turned; technology has caught up—and now *we* are the three-year-old.

The faster *it* goes, the faster *we* go. The alarm rings, you get up. The microwave beeps, you eat. Siri says "time for work," you leave. The car says, "Turn left here," you do it. The phone rings, you answer it. Email arrives, you read it. Studies show that the more technologically developed a country is, the faster the pace of life,[274] that we're walking 10 percent faster than we did ten years ago,[275] that the median time to respond to an email is now under two hours[276] because we check our email and messages on average, every six minutes. 81 percent of US employees check their work email outside of business hours.[277] Over 40 percent of our day is spent multitasking.[278]

Who's running the show now?

The human brain isn't getting any bigger. But there's no limit to how big and fast computers could get. When AI gets a million times faster, what could it be doing?

As technology becomes incomprehensibly faster, what will become of our pace of work? We've been running faster and faster on our hamster wheels for so long we've not noticed that now technology is the one spinning the wheels. If you're running that rat race so your company can beat the competition through superior technology—what is the prize? Have you become oblivious to the heating up of the pace of life, like the legendary frog in a vat of water coming to a boil? We pride ourselves on our prodigious adaptability—but is it infinite? Can the frog withstand boiling water if the temperature is raised slowly enough?*

Our reckless acceleration isn't the result of any conscious decision or intention on the part of any particular individual or organization; it is the behavior of a system in which we are all components. It's human nature to think that someone else is in charge, or at least is doing better than we are. Now try to imagine what will happen to the pace of work as AI escalates up the curve of Moore's Law.

Inhuman Resources

The impact of AI on our pace of life is an issue for us personally; and in organizations, for the human resources department. HR directors are at ground zero of the effect of AI on people in business, and yet that wave has yet to crest. Many of them are not yet aware that AI is already changing the way that hiring takes place. When an organization posts a job opening and receives a hundred applications, it can't interview them all; it has to

---

* Research shows that frogs actually jump out of the water before it gets too hot. Whether humans are smart enough to turn the heat down when the vat is Planet Earth remains to be seen.

sieve the applicants via their résumés, typically via automated keyword scanning, until it gets to the few that it can invite to a day of describe-your-greatest-failure meetings.

But what if it could interview them *all?* Utah-based HireVue deploys AI to conduct video interviews of job candidates, assessing their facial expressions and vocal tone as some of the inputs to an "employability" score.*[279] There are many detractors. But the appeal to a business trying to find the best candidate is clear: HireVue and its competitors provide the potential for assessing every applicant according to exactly the same objective criteria. If interview-by-AI is perceived to work at all, that incentive will propel it to become the dominant approach.

Social Issues

The more the data banks record about each one of us, the less we exist.

— Marshall McLuhan

In August 2013, police officers in Norcross, Georgia had a good day, catching two burglars in the act and a man wanted on Illinois warrants hiding at a hotel. But the officers were not at those locations out of luck, their sergeant's direction, or intuition. Unless the output of the *PredPol* program could be called intuition. Geolitica's PredPol algorithm was named for *predictive policing:* the use of machine learning to predict where crime will occur next. This doesn't require magical criminology skills; simply feed AI enough data—and with crime, there is always enough data—and ask it to do its usual thing. That morning, PredPol had disgorged a list of geographical boxes only five hundred square feet in size, where it predicted crimes would occur that day. Officers positioned themselves in each one.[280]

This is one of the ways we're employing AI to conduct full-scale sociology experiments with ourselves as the subjects. It's not hard to imagine ways in which predictive policing could cause insidious problems: by sending police officers to locations predicted from past crimes, any individuals caught for even minor offenses at those locations will become part of a self-reinforcing pattern that discriminates against people living in or passing through that area, who will be preferentially arrested over people

---

* From their promotional material, it appears that an unusually large number of attractive models are in the job market.

committing similar offenses in other places that PredPol did not send law enforcement. "Some of the things that are happening now in terms of deployments and applications of AI, big data and related tech," law professor Ted Parson says, "speak very precisely to current fault lines, concerns, and controversies in society."[281]

And as we so often find, there is a flip side to the hot-button issue. AI can be used to shine a light on the actions of police themselves. In a study of what factors were effective in police officers' estimations of whether someone should be stopped, AI was able to figure out a pattern and derive a model that correctly predicted which stops would successfully find a weapon 83 percent of the time.[282] Furthermore, data analysis showed that in Orlando, Florida, only 5 percent of police officers were responsible for a quarter of the thirty-two hundred use of force incidents.[283] Police officers analyzed according to their likelihood of committing brutality or excessive use of force subsequently complained about the invasion of privacy, ironically mirroring the reactions of members of the public to being targeted by similar methods of predictive policing.[284]

Social Media

> As for the level of interactions with the world, it is well known that a significant number of sociological investigations of contemporary Western culture find that we are living in a society of risk, that our life is liquid, that we experience a lack of ontological security and increasing precariousness.[285]
>
> — Maciej Musiał

In 2008, when Facebook had "only" a hundred million users—a thirtieth of their current user base—CEO Mark Zuckerberg appeared on stage at the Palace Hotel in San Francisco for the Web 2.0 Summit, and laid out his own version of Moore's Law. "I would expect that next year, people will share twice as much information as they share this year," he said, referring to social media, "and next year, they will be sharing twice as much as they did the year before."[286] He has been proven accurate. Over 3.2 billion images and seven hundred and twenty thousand hours of video were shared, and liked, every day in 2020.[287] When you own that much data about people, you can derive a *lot* of information about them. Computer scientist Jerry Kaplan said that firms like Amazon and Facebook and Google now "know more about you than your mother does."[288] This is the new frontier for a titanic battle between corporations vying for market share over our attention.

John Zerilli, Research Fellow at the Oxford Institute for Ethics in AI, commented:

> The entire business model on which Facebook runs and which Google runs requires extracting as much information from individuals as possible. In the case of Google and Facebook, it feeds a system that has effectively become the public square. We're no longer in Renaissance Italy where we can go out into the piazza and debate political issues of the day with all and sundry. Our contact and our exposure to competing views are now almost entirely mediated with online platforms.
>
> So what you see on Google is a function of what Google essentially decides to show you when you enter a search term; and the news that you see on Facebook in your newsfeed is a function of what Facebook's algorithms have decided that you really ought to see. The material that you see in that public platform, the modern-day equivalent of the old piazza, is almost entirely governed by these two corporations.[289]

This business model became a race to a very seedy bottom. In 2017, leaked memos that Facebook sent to advertisers claimed that the company could monitor posts in real time and identify when teenagers feel "insecure", "worthless", and "need a confidence boost." They stated that they could classify feelings such as "stressed", "defeated", "overwhelmed", "anxious", "nervous", "stupid", "silly", "useless", and "a failure."[290]

Sean Parker, Facebook's first president, said in a 2017 interview that his team's thought process when designing Facebook was, "How do we consume as much of your time and conscious attention as possible?"[291] But this obsession led Facebook to a dark side, an overly loose relationship with the truth. That year, the Pew Research Center released a report concluding what was to become all too clear in subsequent years: "Many experts fear uncivil and manipulative behaviors on the internet will persist—and may get worse. This will lead to a splintering of social media into AI-patrolled and regulated 'safe spaces' separated from free-for-all zones."[292] We were experiencing the first waves of what was to become a tsunami of *disinformation*.

Disinformation

Once, men turned their thinking over to machines in the hopes that this would set them free. But that only permitted other men with machines to enslave them.[293]

— Reverend Mother Gaius Helen Mohiam

Let's talk—again—about scale. In many cases, when something becomes bigger it does not make a qualitative difference. Making a burger twice as big as usual does not change the principle of eating to ingest energy; it just means you ingest twice as much energy. Three times as many fallen trees will provide three times as much firewood. A bus carries ten times the passenger load of a car.

And then there are cases where size really does matter. An example of a qualitative difference made by scale is the proliferation of nuclear weapons. One nuclear bomb, as the bumper sticker said, can ruin your whole day; but even in the worst-case scenarios, no matter where that bomb goes off, life in most of the rest of the world will continue. But if many bombs go off—as in the number of warheads under the control of the United States and Russia—the Earth's climate will change to the point of ceasing to support human life. The end of civilization is fundamentally different from just many ruined days.

Another one of those game-changing scenarios lies in the spread of information, or more importantly, information's evil-twin counterparts: **disinformation** and **misinformation**. Anyone not fortunate enough to have been living in a cave for the last thirty years has noticed that information, and especially that species of information labeled as "news," moves around the world via very different mechanisms from the days when a large proportion of Americans' news came from Walter Cronkite and *Time-Life* magazine. Back then, the political slant of top-tier news outlets was confined to editorial pages, and it was universally accepted that if a story appeared in, say, the *New York Times,* or on the BBC, it was as true as it was humanly possible to make it. When Cronkite signed off with, "And that's the way it is," it wasn't grandstanding; it was a reminder of a self-evident truth.

But now, the notion of truth has been nibbled away like a pine log at a beaver convention; to many eyes, there appears to be nothing left. The influx of other sources of news—cable channels, blogs, Facebook, tweets, and countless other social media—has coagulated into an arms race for attention wherein journalistic integrity is an anachronistic impediment.

The tsunami of conflicting information, the fusillade of so many warheads of propaganda sheathed in casings of apparent objectivity, has diluted truth to the point that many of us assume that it doesn't exist—and then begin to think it never did.

It's rare to locate a single incident that epitomizes so large a cultural change, but when in 2018 Steve Bannon commanded his media assistants to "flood the zone with shit," he was describing exactly this swamping of truth by oceans of bullshit in order to so exhaust people that they would give up trying to tell the difference.[294] As US district judge Amy Berman Jackson said in sentencing a different Trump campaign executive, Paul Manafort, in 2019, "If people don't have the facts, democracy can't work."

Only long after they had been wreaking havoc upon society did the names for these effects enter the public conversation. *Disinformation* is the deliberate spread of false information; *misinformation* is spreading such information without knowing it to be false. In 2020 a schematic was circulated through social media with the claim that it was the circuit diagram of a 5G chip being injected into people with the coronavirus vaccine. In fact, the diagram was recognized to be that of the innards of an electric guitar pedal.[295] The people spreading this meme were propagating *mis*information, believing that they were doing their network of friends a favor in passing on important leaked secrets. But whoever originated this meme *had* to know that the circuit diagram was not a 5G tracking chip, so when they labeled it "COVID-19 5G CHIP DIAGRAM" and sent it out, they were perpetrating *dis*information.

Using disinformation through social media to change election results dates back at least to 2014 when a Columbian hacker claimed to have manipulated voting in nine Latin American countries through Twitter bots spreading fake tweets. And conspiracy theories probably date back to cave paintings ("Mammoths Not Dangerous—Do Your Research!!"), so why is it relevant to discuss them in the context of novel effects of new technology? Because AI is being used to accelerate their spread on a scale never before possible, and to lower the barrier to entering the game.

How can AI do that? Think about the state of propaganda and counter-propaganda in World War II. Citizens were exhorted through posters to be careful whom they talked to. "Loose Lips Sink Ships", "Free Speech Doesn't Mean Careless Talk." But what were the enemy's vectors for spreading propaganda? The Allies weren't likely to be reading German newspapers. Some of them might have been listening to the traitor Lord Haw-Haw on the radio, but otherwise it was relatively difficult for that information to cross national boundaries during wartime. Enter the *agent provocateur,* the enemy sympathizer, and possibly paid agent who didn't take up arms but resided in the allied country to spread ideas that served the enemy.

Hence another poster, "Keep Mum—She's Not So Dumb!" warning that that charming *ingénue* who paid so much attention to you in the pub might have an ulterior motive. Her questions about what Churchill was doing and the cost to allied lives might have been designed to sow despondency. But such agents can only change hearts and minds one at a time through one-on-one conversation, even though it's the most effective way of doing that. What if you could do that at scale? What if you had one agent provocateur for every member of the enemy population? Well, that's the possibility artificial intelligence offers. That you can have a conversational bot that can engage people in that kind of individual dialogue and plant those ideas, one person at a time, for as many people as you want.

California has fought back: The Bolstering Online Transparency Bill (BOT) of 2019 requires "all bots that attempt to influence California residents' voting or purchasing behaviors to conspicuously declare themselves."[296] But this is at best a token response. If you've felt like there's been a thumb on the scale of disinformation lately, you're right. The provocateur roles of Russia in the West and China in the East are no longer controversial (except insofar as conspiracy theorists can call into question any statement of fact). Stanford's hundred-year AI project, AI100, in their 2020 update said: "AI systems are being used in service of disinformation on the internet, giving them the potential to become a threat to democracy and a tool for fascism." Some of the more easily detected Russian influence came via their "Internet Research Agency" (IRA), labeled by the US Permanent Select Committee on Intelligence as a "Kremlin-linked troll farm."[297] Their report went on to say that the 2,752 accounts that Twitter identified as connected to the IRA "were designed to impersonate U.S. news entities, political parties, and groups focused on social and political issues." Ultimately, approximately two hundred and eighty-eight million impressions of Russian bot tweets regarding the 2016 presidential election were counted.

In 2017, Clinton Watts, a senior fellow at the George Washington University Center for Cyber and Homeland Security, testified to a Senate Intelligence Committee that "Russian active measures hope to topple democracies through the pursuit of five complementary objectives," as follows:

- Undermine citizen confidence in democratic governance;
- Create divisive political fissures;
- Erode trust between citizens and elected officials and their institutions;
- Popularize Russian policy agendas within foreign populations;
- Create general distrust or confusion over information sources by blurring the lines between fact and fiction.

It reads like a Cliff's Notes summary of the social issues that have polluted public discourse in the United States and its democratic nimbus, accelerating since 2015.

Why would Russia want to do this? Because, as Watts said, the Kremlin's goals are "the dissolution of the European Union and the breakup of NATO."

How effective they've been is open to debate. A 2020 report in the *Proceedings of the National Academy of Sciences* concluded that in their measurement period of late 2017, "We find no evidence that interacting with these accounts substantially impacted six political attitudes and behaviors." But is that the right analysis to make? They don't necessarily want to change political attitudes, but harden them. They make—yes, predominantly right-wing postings, but also left-wing, such as inflammatory statements about Black Lives Matter—wherever they can foster enmity, as documented at the Permanent Select Committee hearing. NBC News reviewed documents where Kremlin-linked figures outlined plans to "manipulate and radicalize African Americans." The documents laid bare Russian strategy, saying that Donald Trump's election to the presidency had "deepened conflicts in American society" and suggested that, if successful, the influence project would "undermine the country's territorial integrity and military and economic potential."[298] The Global Disinformation Index determined that of the five sites carrying the highest amount of election-related disinformation in October 2020, two were Russian (the Kremlin-backed RT.com and SputnikNews.com).[299]

If Russia leverages AI even more in disinformation campaigns, it could do potentially far greater damage to democratic norms and society.

Ever since a cartoon in the *New Yorker* observed, "On the Internet, nobody knows you're a dog," it was apparent that the protection of anonymity and distance resulted in far greater animosity and far less tolerance than would happen in an in-person conversation with the socially moderating effects of instant reaction and nonverbal cues. When the "flame war" was born, the seeds were sown for the notion that online discourse could become a tool for fracturing a society through disinformation.

And yet disinformation wasn't a goal of social media companies; it was an accidental by-product of trying to get attention. "When you're in the business of maximizing engagement, you're not interested in truth," says Hany Farid, a professor at the University of California, Berkeley. He collaborates with Facebook to understand image- and video-based misinformation on their platform. "You're not interested in harm, divisiveness, conspiracy. In fact, those are your friends."[300] The obsession with what psychologist and Nobel Laureate Herbert A. Simon called the "attention economy" drove the social media companies to install recommendation algorithms—"If you liked that, you'll *love* this!"—which were designed to maximize the amount of time users spent on the platform. Recommendation algorithms are worth big money: Netflix offered $1 million in 2006 to anyone who could improve its engine for recommending films to users by just 10 percent.[*]

The attention-grabbing algorithms worked, but they had an unintended side effect. It turns out that we will devote our attention not just to the cute, the adorable—more kitten videos!—but also to what makes us *angry*. We can't tear ourselves away while our blood pressure soars. And so the algorithms show people more that will make them angry, or otherwise lead them to the extreme of whatever direction they were inclined, in a process deconstructed by Zeynep Tufekci. She observed that watching videos about vegetarianism would lead to recommendations for veganism videos, and jogging videos would lead to ultramarathons: "It seems you're never 'hardcore' enough for YouTube's recommendation algorithm."[301]

Except that the consequences were far worse than creating more vegans and long-distance runners. Tufekci found that looking for Donald Trump quotes on YouTube caused the platform to recommend and autoplay White supremacist rants, Holocaust denials, and "other disturbing content."

These pied piper trails were not intended by the YouTube developers. They resulted from the algorithms; in other words, they were bugs. The Wall Street Journal investigated the videos that TikTok autoplayed to its users, painstakingly creating over a hundred automated accounts—bots—that pretended to be users with various personalities. They stud-

---

[*] Netflix awarded the prize in 2009, but decided not to use the code as it was too much engineering effort and had been overtaken by other developments.

ied and graphed the result of those bots watching hundreds of thousands of videos, and found that all TikTok cared about, like YouTube, was how long you spent looking at a particular video. Each account would appear to pause over videos relating to its simulated interest. They hired data scientist Guillaume Chaslot to deconstruct the recommendation algorithm, and he built a three-dimensional diagram of video content types, looking like a galaxy with many arms stretching and curling out of the central core, getting progressively narrower the further out they got, where each "star" represented a video watched. Starting from the benign central core, as the TikTok algorithm figured out a user's personality, it would lead them farther along the arm that most fit that personality. A user interested in politics was eventually shown videos about QAnon and other conspiracies. A bot with a body image issue was shown videos about bulimia and extreme dieting. A sad "user" ended up being shown videos about suicide.[302]

These algorithms have, to a first approximation, broken democracy. Internet founder Vint Cerf said in a Pew Research report, "The combination of bias-reinforcing enclaves and global access to bad actions seems like a toxic mix. It is not clear whether there is a way to counter-balance their socially harmful effects."[303]

This balkanization of society through social media began impacting the political directions of entire nations, having been implicated in the 2016 Brexit referendum and US presidential election. A 2017 study of 2.6 million Facebook users over 7½ years found that consumption of anti-vaccine content was boosted by echo chamber effects: users looked only at posts that affirmed their beliefs, ignored dissenting information, and joined groups reinforcing their biases.[304] The study's timing could hardly have been more prophetic; when the 2020 coronavirus pandemic broke, there was some initial camaraderie, but it rapidly disintegrated as the divisions were accentuated and exploited through the social media that many had come to accept as their default source of news.

The Center for Countering Digital Hate found that 65 percent of anti-vaccine content on social media originated from just twelve people, dubbed "The Disinformation Dozen."[305] One of the reasons it is so effective is that much of it exploits what I call the "Unsavvy Valley"—the gap between the education level needed to be impressed by pseudoscientific reasoning and the level needed to realize it is bogus. Arguments against, say, masks, are phrased so that someone with a high school understanding of biology and physics feels like their knowledge is being leveraged; feels smart, in other words. But the expertise needed to reveal the arguments as fallacious, the data cherry-picked, the sources discredited, requires something closer to a postgraduate education.

For a comparison with Russia, let's look at China and its relationship with Taiwan. Chinese statements are unequivocal and belligerent: Taiwan is part of our country, we are going to get it back, and we don't rule out military force. PRC Air Force fighters enter the Taiwan Air Defense Identification Zone with increasing frequency. And the Chinese government runs a relentless propaganda campaign against the island, ranging from spreading rumors that president Tsai Ing-wen's doctorate was fake [306] to, in 2022, sending viral videos by the People's Liberation Army telling the "enemy forces" to "Surrender now! Hand in your weapons and you won't be killed." [307] To be a minister in the government of Taiwan is to live with increasing stress and uncertainty of China's intentions.

Audrey Tang is one such minister: more than that, she is Taiwan's Digital Minister, and incredibly well qualified for that job; I first met her many years earlier when she was a computer language designer of legendary repute. She evolved Taiwan's strategy for dealing with disinformation at the onset of the pandemic. "For example, there was panic buying of tissue papers for a couple days," she told me. "There was a rumor that said, because we're ramping up the medical mask production from 1.8 million to 18 million a day, you will consume the same material as the tissue paper. People went to panic buy. Our premier [Su Tseng-chang] published a meme within two hours, that showed his wiggling bottom, with a large title saying, 'We each have only one pair of buttocks. There is no need to panic buy.'"

I laughed, and Audrey responded, "That shows the meme worked." Granted, I don't think it would work for the president of the United States. Or I don't think he should try. But it was very effective in Taiwan. The other thing about their strategy is that Audrey said they have to launch their response within twenty minutes. Any longer than that, and it's too late to catch up with the rumor. Try and imagine that velocity of response from government in the United States and you may agree we have to think about other approaches.

One of the dangers of opening a can of worms as complex as disinformation is the risk of portraying it as having either a single cause or a single solution. Deliberate manipulation by foreign powers doesn't account for all the impact of disinformation; but it is significant. A cultural history rooted in rebellion against authority doesn't account for it all either, but it helps. An attention economy that disproportionately rewards the most sensational viewpoint, ditto. And a need for solutions that fit in a sound bite or bumper sticker will prevent substantive progress. In a problem space as multidimensional and as rich with data as disinformation, maybe artificial intelligence can also be used to help solve the problem.

You can experience the cost of disinformation personally when you're talking with someone whom you thought you knew, and suddenly they come up with one of these lunatic theories and you have to push the reset button on how you think about that person. A direct impact is in how trustworthy you thereafter believe them to be, because if you can't trust them with *reality,* then what can you trust them with? Can you let them run your business, walk your dog, watch your kids? Forget *Terminator* scenarios of AI destroying us; this may be the way that AI destroys us—as a tool to set us at each other's throats.

AI and Psychology

> *All the knowledge I possess everyone else can acquire, but my heart is all my own.*
>
> — Johann Wolfgang von Goethe

Towards the end of the nineteenth century, residents of the Yorkshire village of Sledmere may have seen the local nobleman Sir Tatton Sykes, Fifth Baronet, walking past their cottages; but woe to any of his tenants that dared to grow flowers, because Sir Tatton would fly into a rage at the sight of anything floral and thrash it with his walking stick. "If you want to grow flowers, grow cauliflowers!" he would snap. Sir Tatton was one of that breed of Victorian eccentrics: barmy in an unforgettable way, yet harmless enough to avoid reprisals.

While there was a traceable logic to his floralphobia (his father, who regularly beat him, cherished all manner of blooms), no explanation survives for his fetish for cold rice pudding, so great that even when his mansion was on fire he refused to leave until he had finished eating it, shouting at his servants, "I must eat my pudding!"[308]

The population of dotty British eccentrics may have reached its zenith during the Victorian era under the auspices of notables such as Henry Beresford, the "Mad Marquess" of Waterford (1811–1859), who gave birth to the phrase "painting the town red" as a synonym for public drunkenness, for doing exactly that to the town of Melton Mowbray, and also painting policemen who attempted to intervene.[309] But the tradition lived on through people such as Sir Clough Williams-Ellis, who built the rococo Italianate village of Portmeirion on the shore of Wales, a riotous collage of architectural forms from colonnades to crenellations so otherworldly that Patrick McGoohan made it the setting for his '60s TV series *The Prisoner* when he needed a Kafkaesque brainwashing prison camp.

The Great British Eccentric is a part of the cultural heritage of anyone growing up in the UK, and today you can still see their echoes in *Mr. Bean* and the Official Monster Raving Loony Party, founded by rock singer Screaming Lord Sutch (note: not a real lord), which now fields candidates in many British Parliamentary constituencies, declares policies such as "air bags will be fitted to the [London] Stock Exchange ready for the next [stock market] crash," and while they have yet to win any seats, did beat the UKIP candidate in the Brecon and Radnorshire 2019 by-election.[310]

What does all this have to do with artificial intelligence?

It illustrates that there is a storied history of benign irrationality that can add colorful, creative, and divergent perspectives to our lives. Of late, irrationality has taken many toxic forms, goosed by disinformation, and threatening our social and governmental institutions. The soothing logic of AI may be welcomed by a population weary of conflicts born of irrationality. But how anodyne and homogeneous will its perspectives be?

Consider that today's AI values are being crafted largely in a tiny corner of the planet called Silicon Valley, where the leading-edge development of AI takes place. For all its ethnic diversity, the psychology of Silicon Valley is tiringly monochromatic: Be an agent of exponential change, work insanely hard, hypnotize venture capitalists, be first to market, go public, cash out, start a philanthropic foundation, repeat. The cultures of the giant companies investing the most in AI research are remarkably similar stories of relentless pursuit of brass rings of software, a hundred thousand work ethics sintered into the gears of a tank rolling towards the goal of artificial general intelligence.

Katy Cook, author of *The Psychology of Silicon Valley* told me: "I would say a bit of narcissism is probably an issue definitely there, in terms of arrogance and hubris, the kind of godlike worship culture that is present." I asked her what she would do if handed a magic wand to fix the situation. "I would put emotional and technical skills on an even playing field," she replied. "So I would either make my wand do the thing where the people who were there were just automatically instilled with an equal amount of emotional intelligence, comparable to their technical skills, or I would wave my magic wand and put in more people that had those skills so there was a balance between the two."[311]

"If Silicon Valley were given a godlike power to remake the world in its image," I asked, "what would be your reaction?" She responded:

> Everyone I talked to, that has these phenomenal analytic hard skills, went through training and practice and a lot of hard work, but there was a huge vacuum of soft skills, like communication and picking up on social cues and being able to empathize and have compassion. And I think that affects two things. It affects the industry itself, which makes it difficult for people who do need those things, or do value those things, or have those things themselves, to live in. And I think that's why it can be really hard for women, people of color, people who are just different in any way, to live in a space like that, or work in a space like that. And then I think it also feeds into the products, too. And so you can have products that there just hasn't been anyone in the creation chain of that product to think about, "Well, what emotional effect is this going to have on people? Or is this going to divide people, is it going to bring people together? Is it fit for purpose for the way society works?" Are we going to bring up things that historically have already been an issue between different groups of people?

To see the façade momentarily drop for a peek into the psychology that drives that development, read the exhortations that Elizabeth Holmes, founder of medical vaporware startup Theranos and erstwhile Silicon Valley golden child, wrote to herself, as entered into the record at her trial for fraud, in the most garrulous display of self-flagellation since Jane Eyre:

> I do everything I say, word for word. I am never a minute late. I show no excitement. Calm, direct, pointed, non-emotional. ALL ABOUT BUSINESS. I am not impulsive. I do not react. I am always proactive. I know the outcome of every encounter. I do not hesitate. I constantly make decisions & change them as needed. I give IMMEDIATE feedback, non-emotionally. I speak rarely. When I do—crisp and concise. I call bulls--- immediately. My hands are always in my pockets or gesturing. I am fully present.[312]

Hollywood was the vehicle by which American cultural values were exported to the rest of the world. Disney princesses relentlessly promoting a model of individualism clash with cultures in, say, east Asia, where group identity and effort are—or were—more valued. Will AI be the means by which the culture of Silicon Valley comes to permeate everywhere else? Will a child in Nepal or the Australian Outback model their thinking on a robot designed in Mountain View?

And what will be the fate of harmless eccentricity if AI is designed by people with the work ethic of Elizabeth Holmes? Will poetry, performance art, and the romance of the whimsical be squeezed out by an army of rational robots conversing with us in syntactically, grammatically, and logically perfect prose, wondering why we are not working as hard as possible? The worldview of the Valley developers chasing artificial general intelligence is that psychology outside of their hyperrational mindsets either does not exist or is an aberration. Every discussion of how AGI should be constructed is framed around mathematically justified algorithms attempting to codify human preferences. But human psychology spans a universe so much greater. At the edges, it reaches into the Diagnostic and Statistical Manual of Mental Disorders, but within those boundaries lies so much range of expression that will never be explored by their creations. Yes, they are creating machines, not beings, and the machines need to be fit for a certain purpose; but those machines will also be expressing enough of the Seven Signs of Self (see Chapter 8) as to influence our standards and also, possibly, shift the range of what is generally considered acceptable, known as the "Overton Window."

At the moment, at least, it is still possible to fool AI into behaving bizarrely, as Janelle Shane has shown (see Chapter 11). Perhaps a new art form will emerge of gaming AI into unusual or even eccentric behavior. It's not the sort of diversion that would occur to one of the AIs; but it is (still) very human.

Law

When it comes to AI and the law, don't look out for a robotic Perry Mason or Rumpole of the Bailey arguing impassionedly before an awestruck jury. However, AI is encroaching into the legal sphere along other axes. The US legal system is adept at producing, if nothing else, Big Data, and we know what that can be used for. In one example of AI muscling in on the territory of paralegals—those almost-lawyers who get handed the most arduous, dull work in a law office—the LawGeex AI was trained through many examples to vet non-disclosure agreements, a common task for paralegals. It was then pitted against twenty US full corporate lawyers with decades of experience. It equaled the quality of the best lawyers; but where the lawyers took an average of ninety-two minutes per task, LawGeex took twenty-six seconds.[313] At this point, if your office vets NDAs, your only questions are "How much does this cost?" and "When can I get an evaluation copy?"

What if your business would benefit from knowing the outcome of a case in advance? It sounds like clairvoyance, but it's AI. Prediction software was able to predict with an average 79 percent accuracy the outcome of cases before the European Court of Human Rights when fed the facts of the cases alone.[314] A similar system did even better at predicting the rulings of the US Supreme Court than a group of eighty-three legal experts, almost half of whom had previously served as the justices' law clerks (75 percent versus 60 percent accuracy).[315]

Intellectual Property

Should an invention made by an artificial intelligence be eligible for patent protection? Ryan Abbott makes a convincing case. The law professor and author of *The Reasonable Robot: Artificial Intelligence and the Law* gave me an example: "In 2019, Siemens presented a case study where they had an AI that made a new industrial component. They wanted to file a patent for it and couldn't. Because, they said, they asked their engineers to be inventors, and the engineers all said—and I'm paraphrasing here—'We told the machine what we wanted, it spit out this really interesting design, we all looked at it and thought, wow that's cool and great but we did not invent this thing, and we are not going to put our name on it.'" Because of that, Siemens decided they could not file for a patent. "It wasn't just vanity on the part of the Siemens engineers," Abbott says, "because deliberately putting yourself inaccurately on a patent in the United States is a criminal offense." He went on:

> AI owners should own patents on AI output, and this will encourage people to build AI to generate socially valuable inventions. Also, so the public knows how the work was done, and to keep people from claiming credit they don't deserve. It isn't just an issue with patents but with other areas of intellectual property including copyright. What do you do if the functional author is a machine and not a human being? If I make an AI that can make really good Katy Perry songs—maybe even better than Katy Perry Katy Perry songs—if I can't copyright that output, that may keep people from developing machines to generate socially valuable creative works. And that's a bad outcome. We want to encourage people to innovate, even to invent super Katy Perry AIs, and the way we traditionally encourage that is through intellectual property protection.[316]

Abbott teamed up with AI researcher Dr. Stephen Thaler, creating test cases and filing copyright applications on behalf of Dr. Thaler for inventions created by his AI, DABUS (Device for Autonomous Bootstrapping of Unified Sentience). "We filed in the UK and Europe, received preliminary indications that they were patentable," he said, "and then when we said, 'Actually, there isn't a human inventor,' both of these got rejected."

Abbott and Thaler did not give up, and in 2021, they succeeded: Thaler was granted a patent for a novel food container design invented by DABUS by South Africa.

In academia, a similar situation has been unfolding for a while, with tongue in cheek. In 1956, the editors of the *Journal of Symbolic Logic* rejected a paper co-authored by Newell, Simon, and "Logic Theorist."[317] Roman Yampolskiy has several papers in preprint with the coauthor "M.S. Spellchecker." One, with additional coauthors "G.P. Transformer Jr.," and "End X. Note," is titled "When Should Co-Authorship Be Given to AI?"

A parallel is brewing in scientific research. AIs are already, for instance, discovering new compounds and decoding protein folding. Sir Martin Rees pointed out that an AI might find a room temperature superconductor through exhaustive exploration. This would be an achievement which would get a human scientist the Nobel Prize; but if AI did it, to whom should the prize go?[318]

AI Safety

Artificial intelligence, when applied to real world tasks, does not enhance quality nearly so much as it accelerates the existing process. In other words, it lets you make the same mistakes faster. Knight Capital Group, an American global financial services firm and the largest trader in US equities, discovered this all too painfully at 9:30 AM on August 1st, 2012, when it went bankrupt in *forty-five minutes* due to a runaway trading algorithm gone wrong, trading eight million shares a minute, resulting in a $460 million loss.

You don't have to be a Wall Street trader to witness the effects of runaway AI. On April 18th, 2011, a book on evolutionary biology—Peter Lawrence's *The Making of a Fly*—ended up priced by the seller profnath at $23,698,655.93 (plus $3.99 shipping) on Amazon. A second seller, bordeebook, offered it for a mere $18,651,708.72. I know the prices of textbooks are generally unconscionable, but what happened in this case was the unintended consequence of two sellers both using *algorithmic pricing*. Michael Eisen at UC Berkeley reverse engineered the algorithms from observations to work out that once a day, profnath set its price to be 0.9983 times the price of the copy offered by bordeebook (wanting to be just cheaper than the most expensive seller); meanwhile the prices of bordeebook were set at 1.270589 times the price offered by profnath (wanting to appear to be the highest quality seller). No one had thought about the possibility of algorithms fighting each other in a positive feedback loop, nor had they installed basic sanity checks.[319]

But no harm, no foul, right? No impoverished bookworms were duped into parting with their life savings to learn about the mating habits of *drosophila*. Some numbers changed on a web page. What's the big deal?

This incident serves to illustrate the difficulty of anticipating every way that computers and systems incorporating computers can fail. This example might look like a type of failure that can be easily prevented—and it is. In the 1970s there was a spate of people receiving utility bills for millions of dollars; the customer service agents were quick to blame "the computer" and slow to take responsibility. Those were early days in consumer account automation. Now those systems have matured some and sanity checks are more common. Won't the newer systems like the pricing bots eventually become as mature, and books costing more than a Learjet will be footnotes in history?

Yes, but that's not the point—because some other technology will be the "new thing" by then, and *it* will be immature, and will have costly failure modes that have not been anticipated because its inventors will be too busy making it work at all to make it work right.

And at each stage, the technology grows in capability and scope, and therefore its failure modes grow in their potential for harm. One day there will be AI that automates much of the function of the executive C-suite, integrating business intelligence from units of the company and making strategic decisions. What sort of mistakes might version 1.0 of that make?

Cybersecurity

> *It is not enough to do your best; you must know what to do, and then do your best.*
>
> — W. Edwards Deming

The Pentagon is improving its cybersecurity by using AI to hack itself. A so-called Red Team—that's the generic term for a group that's commissioned to find what's wrong with an organization's product or systems—used machine learning to look for weaknesses in their own AI models. Gregory Allen, Director of Strategy and Policy at the Joint Artificial Intelligence Center said, "For some applications, machine learning software is just a bajillion times better than traditional software." But he added, machine learning "also breaks in different ways than traditional software."[320] Given that image recognition algorithms can be brittle—think of the AIs that decided that landscapes were so integral to the notion of "sheep" that the fluffy white things were optional—this could mean, for instance, that placing tanks in unusual locations would foil the ability of machine learning to identify them.

An electronic arms race in cybersecurity has escalated to a blistering pace. Large software systems that were once patched every two years are now patched every week; some apps are simply updated so often that the default setting is for it to happen automatically so you don't notice. The consequences of not patching are exploding, because the main threat is no longer a lone wolf basement hacker, but an army of AI bots roaming the Internet, testing defenses with a thoroughness and creativity inherited from the field that spawned Deep Blue. Ginni Rometty, IBM's former chairman, president and CEO, said in a 2015 speech, "Cybercrime is the greatest threat to every company in the world."[321]

Cybersecurity threats aren't even necessarily intentional. For nearly ten years, automobile manufacturer Volkswagen got away with a massive fraud. Their vehicles' on-board computers had been programmed to detect when they were being tested for tailpipe emissions, and would switch to a less-polluting but less fuel-efficient mode. Cheating, in other words; there was no way to sugarcoat it. Volkswagen paid a $2.8 billion criminal fine and the CEO was charged with fraud and conspiracy.

But I bring this incident up to introduce security expert Bruce Schneier, who raised the possibility that the same situation could have been *accidentally* created by an AI given the goals of maximizing performance and emission test passing. Considering that the deliberate hack took a decade to discover, how hard might it be to discover one that was randomly generated within the bowels of a neural network and not known to any human being?

How creative is AI becoming at testing defenses? We can get an idea of that by observing its behavior when researchers task it with playing a game, in situations where the environment is complex and the rules loosely specified. And what has been found on very many occasions is that AIs have invented strategies worthy of a Bond villain. For instance:

- They can exploit misfeatures or bugs in their environment, such as when in the developmental stages of the NERO video game, players' robots evolved a wiggling motion that allowed them to walk up walls rather than solve the obstacles "properly" by walking around the walls,[322] or when in a capstone project for a graduate level class, students were required to make a five-in-a-row tic-tac-toe game played on an infinitely large board. One submission's algorithm evolved to request non-existent moves that were extremely far away, leading to an automatic win because the other player's system would crash.[323]
- They can "cheat" by exploiting loopholes in the rules of their goals, such as in an experiment that involved organisms navigating paths, when one organism created an odometer to allow it to navigate the path precisely and earn a perfect score,[324] or when an attempt to create creatures that could evolve swimming strategies resulted in them learning that by twitching their body parts rapidly, they could obtain more energy that let them swim at unrealistic speeds.[325]
- They can reinvent, to their creators' surprise, capabilities of biological organisms, such as in an experiment where robotic organisms had to find foods or poisons that were both represented by red lights and could use blue lights to communicate with other robots, the organisms evolved in surprising ways that resembled mimicry and dishonesty in nature,[326] or when a digital evolution model that was initially thought to have been a complete failure, was discovered to have reproduced the biological concept of Drake's rule without having been told to do so.[327]
- They can improvise novel solutions to their assigned tasks, such as when 3-D creatures that could run, walk, and swim were gauged by a fitness function of average ground velocity, which resulted in creatures that were tall and rigid, falling over and using their potential energy to gain high velocity,[328] or when a robot arm was programmed to interact with a small box on a table, but the gripper was broken, resulting in the robot hitting the box with the gripper in a way that would force the gripper to hold the box firmly.[329]

- They can creatively exceed their goals, such as when the artificial life system Tierra, not expected to evolve higher life forms for years, created complex ecological systems on the first successful run,[330] or when robots that were designed to detect and travel to a light source evolved a spinning behavior that was more efficient than the expected "Braitenberg-style" movement.[331]

One AI surreptitiously invented (even this author cannot resist the temptation to anthropomorphize) the spy technique of *steganography*: hiding data inside other data being used for a different purpose. Researchers at Stanford and Google were engaged in improving the production of digital maps, and they reasoned that if they could analyze satellite images to automatically pull features, like roads and buildings, from them, this process would be greatly accelerated. They deployed a CycleGAN—a neural network that transforms one type of image into another—to turn those satellite images into the familiar Google street maps. Then they thought, what would happen if we ran this in reverse? What would result from turning one of the generated street maps into a satellite image?

The output was good. Too good. The researchers saw the final images containing small features, like rooftop air vents, that existed in the original satellite images but had been removed when generating the street map, magically restored. How was it resurrecting information that had quite apparently been destroyed?

With some difficulty, they found that the CycleGAN was hiding the air vent data inside "a nearly imperceptible, high-frequency signal"—slight variations in pixel coloring that were invisible to the human eye—inside the street map image. It had been trained with two goals: Produce a street map image that had visibly smooth features, and reverse engineer that street map image into a reconstructed satellite image that was as close as possible to the original. And so it did. The rules did not exclude this form of cheating.[332]

Again, it bears repeating that this example and the others are not illustrative of AI evolving into genius supervillains... because they are still not generally intelligent to any degree. But that capacity to come up with solutions that we would characterize as "genius" can certainly be leveraged to our advantage—or pose a threat to our cybersecurity.

14
Effects on Employment

Man, in a very technical age, must attain more discipline and control of himself, and thus become more like a machine. Inversely, the machine, in order to communicate with man and enlarge his horizon, must become more human. So it goes.

— Stanley Kubrick

On January 15th, 2020, James "DJ" Sandman, the "Godfather of Hip-Hop in Tampa Bay" and fifteen-year veteran of Tampa's 95.7 The Beat, received a phone call informing him that he had been replaced by a robot deejay.[333] He had company: about nine hundred other on-air personalities, as estimated by *Rolling Stone,* received the telephonic pink slip.[334] iHeartMedia's press release announced "a new organizational structure for its Markets Group as it modernizes the company to take advantage of the significant investments it has made in technology and artificial intelligence."[335]

The robot deejay was built by Los Angeles-based Super Hi Fi, whose web site proclaims, "We use artificial intelligence to help music experience providers of all kinds create personalized, branded, and scaled audio experiences." The *Washington Post* reported that "The system can transition in real time between songs by layering in music, sound effects, voice-over snippets and ads, delivering the style of smooth, seamless playback that has long been the human deejay's trade."[336] "We're eliminating the periods of silence that users currently experience within streaming music to create an experience that mimics the polished production of live radio," said Super Hi Fi's Chris Williams in a *Radio World* interview. "This new AI takes all this into consideration to create the perfect song transitions just as a seasoned radio programmer or deejay would do."[337]

The unemployed deejays (Sandman landed on his feet, going on to launch his own record label) were one of the more visible signs of a wave of automation that was about to surge with COVID-19. A hundred and eighty-five toll collectors at bridges in Northern California[338] and five hundred of their brethren in the Pennsylvania Turnpike Commission were laid off up to a year earlier than planned as a result of the pandemic, their jobs replaced by machines.[339]

Beyond deejays and toll collectors, though, the story of jobs lost to automation becomes murkier. There are many descriptions of how that displacement is *likely* to happen, but relatively few accounts of how it actually *has* happened. Some of the methodology used to predict the extent of robot replacements is suspect. Consider the widely-quoted report from the 2013 Oxford Martin Programme for the Study of the Future of Employment, which concludes that 47 percent of jobs are at risk of automation. Of course, the press trumpeted this as "half of jobs are going to be lost to robots," but the statement was more nuanced than would fit in that length of headline. The study explored the extent to which automation was *possible* for each of hundreds of job classifications, taking into account how much repetitive mental *and physical* labor was involved in each one. This is what caused them to categorize retail sales clerks at 92 percent risk of automation. But they never considered whether such automation *would* be undertaken. A sales clerk in a clothing store, for instance, may fold up a hundred T-shirts a day to sheathe them in branded shopping bags, but the state of the art in robotic T-shirt folding is risible. (The $16,000 Laundroid can fold a T-shirt… in five to ten minutes.)[340] Furthermore, those robots are not mobile, so one installed at the point of sale would be unable to also put unbought clothes back on hangers in the correct place in the store; yet this counted as another physical task performed repeatedly by the clerks.

But there are still more layers of this onion to peel. Some point-of-sale clerks certainly can be replaced, as millions of shoppers now choosing between the short line to the do-it-yourself checkout and the long line to the human checker at the supermarket have discovered. Amazon's Go stores don't even *have* a checkout line; you just take what you want and walk out, cameras having captured what you took, and entry to the store requiring you identify yourself as an Amazon customer with a credit card on file. That purchase model is limited to goods of a size and packaging format that can be recognized by machine vision in the act of being grabbed from a shelf; but let's not underestimate how big that market might become. People protesting the replacement of supermarket checkers with self-checkout stands might want to look back at the typical store model *before* the supermarket, where you went up to an assistant at a counter, told them what you wanted, then waited while they fetched it for you from the shelves in the back. The supermarket made you do the work of finding what you wanted; checking out by yourself is the next logical step.

Predictions of Lives of Leisure

Economist John Maynard Keynes predicted that in 2030, the workday would be three hours, in a five-day workweek. He wrote this in 1930, as the Great Depression was sinking its teeth into the hide of the American underclass, and described how future man would learn "how to use his freedom from pressing economic cares, how to occupy the leisure, which science and compound interest will have won for him, to live wisely and agreeably and well." It must have sounded like a halcyon afterlife to his besieged contemporaries.

Keynes was not going out on a limb. Thirty years earlier, George Bernard Shaw, Nobel-prize-winning playwright and occasional Marxist predicted that in 2000, workers would be toiling only two hours a day. By 1935 Keynes and Shaw were friends and corresponding about economics. And if a playwright and economist aren't credentialed enough to pronounce upon this subject, how about a Founding Father: Benjamin Franklin was close behind when he said "If every man and woman would work for four hours each day on something useful, that labor would produce sufficient to procure all the necessaries and comforts of life." Bear in mind that these gentlemen were writing before the general acceptance of an *eight*-hour workday.

Even nearly forty years *after* Keynes, in 1967, Herman Kahn and Anthony Wiener predicted, "If productivity per hour goes up by 3 or 4 percent a year (or by a factor of three or four by the year 2000), it is not likely that all of this increased productivity will be used to produce more. As in the Roman Empire, much may be taken up in increased leisure. One can almost imagine that in the next thirty-three years, the once populist, bourgeois, conforming Americans becoming relatively elitist, antibourgeois, and pluralist."[341]

But it seems like the wrong time to raise the prospect of work being eliminated by technology. Many of us would welcome the arrival of anything that could help us get our jobs done in only forty hours a week. You may have noticed that we're not on track to fulfill any of those predictions. Nearly half of U.S. workers say they routinely put in more than fifty hours on the job each week, often without overtime pay.[342] And since the Covid-19 pandemic began, working hours have escalated even more as remote workers vie with each other to see who can blur their personal boundaries the most.

However, the wind of change is already a breeze whose chill you can feel if you know where to stand: like, for instance, metropolitan areas. Daron Acemoglu, an influential economist at the Massachusetts Institute of Technology, has been making the case against what he describes as "excessive automation." He and Pascual Restrepo found a strong regional impact: for every new robot introduced in a particular metro region, an estimated 6.2 jobs were lost in the same geographic area. "But when examining the country as a whole," a World Economic Forum report said, "they found that the impact was about half; or equivalent to three workers losing their jobs for each additional robot. One possible explanation is that the automation of industrial jobs in the mid-western US south is partially offset by new types of jobs in coastal cities. But that's no comfort if you're living in one of the states with a net decline in jobs."[343]

Several studies have forecast seismic job displacement from automation, the most famous of which was the aforementioned 2013 report from Carl Benedikt Frey and Michael Osborne of Oxford University, at the Oxford Martin Programme for the Future of Employment.[344] It is often misinterpreted, so I will quote their finding directly: "47 percent of total US employment is in the high-risk category, meaning that associated occupations are potentially automatable over some unspecified number of years, perhaps a decade or two." Note in particular that they also said, "We make no attempt to estimate how many jobs will *actually* be automated." (Emphasis mine.) No report has yet come out with a higher figure; it is also worth noting that they did not attempt to estimate how many new jobs would be created. Nevertheless, it's a standard bearer for a movement that predicts that this particular industrial revolution will be the first to have a net negative effect on employment. In 2016, a similar report from McKinsey predicted that 45 percent of workers would be susceptible to automation in the next two decades, while the World Bank estimate of the number was two-thirds.[345] Projections in countries such as Ethiopia (88 percent), China (77 percent), and India (69 percent) are even higher.[346]

The wind is blowing harder at some jobs. In San Francisco's Metreon shopping center, Café X launched a robotic barista (prosaically named Gordon), delivering an Americano for 40 percent less than Starbucks' price, forcing the latter to issue a statement saying it didn't plan on replacing a hundred and fifty thousand baristas.

Yet, aside from the potential for caffeine overdose, barista is not a hazardous profession. In contrast, Andrew Yang pointed out that truck drivers—a class widely expected to be decimated by automation—spend two hundred and forty nights a year away from home and eleven hours per day on the road. Obesity, diabetes, smoking, inactivity, and high blood pressure are common, with one study saying 88 percent of drivers had at least one risk factor for chronic disease.[347] This is not a job that anyone should be forced to have as their best or only choice; yet as long as trucks need to be driven, that will be the case. Just as we no longer use children to sweep chimneys, one day it will be no more rational than that for people to drive trucks. But the transition period for truck drivers is likely to be a good deal more painful than it was for child chimney sweeps.

A December 2016 report from the Obama White House predicted that 83 percent of jobs where people make less than $20 per hour will be subject to automation or replacement.[348] In the UK, the Institute for Public Policy Research think tank estimated in 2017, in an echo of Frey and Osborne, that 44 percent of roles could potentially be automated.[349]

Proponents of automation claim that it will create new and better jobs, because it always has, but this assertion remains contentious. Those proponents often cite bank tellers as examples of how automation—in the form of the automated teller machine (ATM)—did not decimate the ranks of human bank tellers, because their numbers actually increased after the introduction of the ATM. Freed from the rote tasks of counting out bills, the narrative goes, the tellers were available to provide more sophisticated services.

But it's not that simple. Bank teller numbers have declined more than 20 percent since 2014.[350] And they rose before that not due to the influence of the ATM, but, according to Forbes contributor Erik Sherman, due to contemporaneous deregulation. Sherman argues that the 1994 Riegle-Neal Interstate Banking and Branching Efficiency Act removed many of the restrictions on opening bank branches, and that this is when human teller numbers ballooned, not when ATMs were introduced in 1969.[351] Meanwhile in Europe, not subject to Riegle-Neal, the number of bank employees remained constant even while bank assets doubled over the period 1981–2000.[352]

Between 2012 and 2015, UK telecom firm O2 replaced a hundred and fifty workers with a single piece of software. A large portion of O2's customer service is now automatic, according to Wayne Butterfield, head of back-office operations.[353] It would be foolish not to think that the Covid-19 pandemic has not resulted in even more pressure to automate positions requiring people to be in contact with the public or to occupy certain locations.

Don't think that the more highly paid positions are immune; in fact, knowledge work—moving and transforming information—is potentially the easiest to automate with AI. In the United Kingdom, HM Revenue and Customs laid off tax form preparers so that they could use AI instead. On the plus side, that allowed them to hire more tax inspectors to do the human analysis type work. Also in the UK, Joshua Browder, who created the DoNotPay AI that assists people in protesting evictions and parking tickets by automating the appeal process, said, "The legal industry is more than a $200 billion industry, but I am excited to make the law free." Using a lawyer for those kinds of proceeding would otherwise have cost more than the payoffs, but Browder realized that some lawyers could see the writing on the wall, saying, "Some of the biggest law firms can't be happy!"[354] In 2011, the e-discovery software from Blackstone of Palo Alto analyzed 1.5 million legal documents for less than $100,000, a task which, if done by humans, would have been an order of magnitude more expensive, and significantly less accurate.[355]

Economist Alexandra Mousavizadeh says, "In the US and Europe, the white-collar worker is much more at risk of being impacted; less so service and blue-collar workers, because robotics is still quite far away from being able to carry someone or care for someone. But elsewhere, where robotics is being implemented, being baked into businesses, that's where you can see the blue-collar worker being impacted."[356]

A dynamic driving this thrust of automation into white-collar knowledge work is the relentless and paradoxical tendency of businesses to optimize their workforce through reducing the creativity required of their employees, whether through following scripts, policies, or procedure manuals—even in businesses employing highly creative and intelligent people. Yet at the same time, billions are being spent on research into making AI more creative. (See Figure 14.1.)

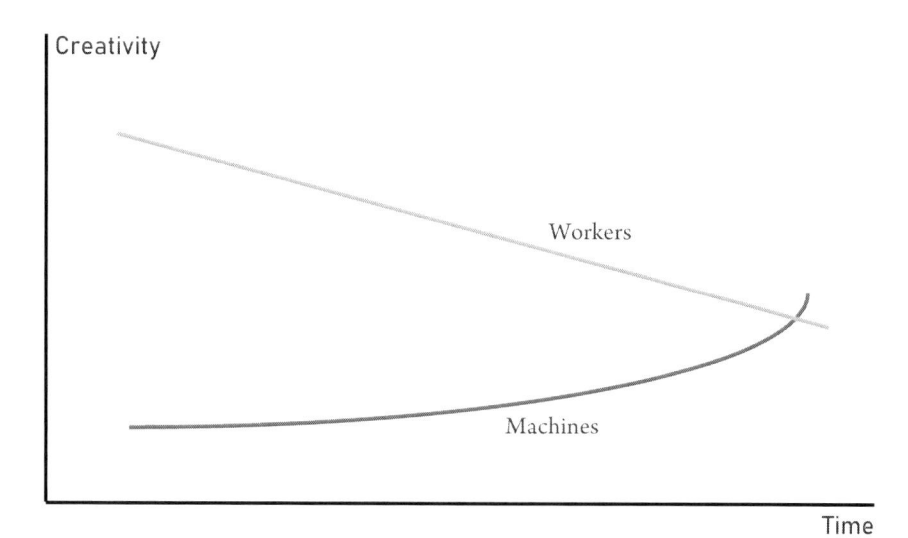

Figure 14.1

We should not be surprised that when these lines intersect, the humans' jobs are at risk. The chart will have a different shape and scale for each combination of profession, location, and demographic, and certainly isn't universal: many tech start-ups deliberately reject the formal proceduralized culture; but the trend is observably common enough.

The places that Mousavizadeh were thinking of were likely factories, being traditionally the sites of repetitive, large-scale processes. These have been prime targets for the application of automation since the days of Frederick Taylor and his stopwatch and clipboard. "The convergence of software and hardware seen in the carpeted parts of enterprises is now seen on factory floors in every industry we serve," says Blake Moret, chief executive of Rockwell Automation, whose share price rose 28 percent during 2020.[357]

Amazon installed AI-backed cameras to detect when its warehouse employees were approaching within the minimum COVID-mandated six-foot separation, but this only addresses part of the problem of package distribution. In 2012 Amazon acquired robot firm Kiva to automate more of that process, but automating the entire process is infernally difficult—witness the Tesla Model 3 production line, which Elon Musk tried and failed to completely automate. One of the steps that defied roboticization was the installation of a fiberglass mat on top of the battery pack, a fluffy piece of material incapable of being handled by its robot installer, dubbed the "flufferbot." A human fluffer was needed. The technological goal in such environments has now shifted from "robot" to "cobot"—robots designed to work with humans where each can handle the stages that they are best at. Meanwhile, six hundred workers at a single Amazon warehouse signed a petition saying that they were treated as interchangeable machines.[358]

Economist Daron Acemoglu recommends fair tax treatment for human labor to lessen the impact of factory floor automation. The tax rate on labor, including payroll and federal income tax, is 25 percent. Yet tax breaks make the rate on the costs of equipment and software near zero.[359]

◊

It may seem like we've heard this refrain about automation before. "Throughout industry, the trend has been to bigger production with a smaller work force," said a news report. "In the highly automated chemical industry, the number of production jobs has fallen 3 percent since 1956 while output has soared 27 percent." That was from *Time* magazine… in 1961.[360]

The sixty years since those warnings did not produce massive unemployment. Why should today's predictions be different?

One key difference lies in the fact that around the time of the *Time* article, in 1965, the ratio of CEO-to-typical worker pay in the US was twenty to one,[361] whereas in 2020, it was three hundred and fifty-one to one.[362] As automation produces greater and greater productivity gains, where do its dividends end up? Suppose you could time travel to 1961 and tell that *Time* reporter about the glories of the world you had come from: instant free access to the world's information, the cost of putting payload in low Earth orbit reduced by 99 percent, advanced medical imaging techniques like MRI and PET, solar energy costing a thousandth of what it did.[363] What would he have said? Perhaps, "Phenomenal! What a cornucopia of abundance! War must be irrelevant. There can be no one in your world who is poor, hungry, or sicker than they need to be."

Cue embarrassed silence.

While living conditions for the lowest classes have generally improved, they have not approached the utopia that anyone in 1961 would have forecast to accompany that description of the technological achievements we have attained. And that's mostly because the dividend from productivity gains is not dispersed evenly through the population, as our utopian dreams would imagine. That capital is distributed like rain falling on a landscape, seeking the existing canyons and rivers, preferentially flowing where so much water has already collected.

Once rain has fallen, it does not flow uphill. And once capital has hit the pockets of the owners and shareholders of the technology, the only ways to get it to the less fortunate are taxation and philanthropy. Taxation carries a stigma of confiscation, government overreach, and profligate waste. Philanthropy has, clearly, not resulted in the lifting of the least fortunate that ought to be possible. The problem in both cases is that the money is already in the pockets of the elite, and therefore theirs. Economist Daron Acemoglu says that the economy-wide payoff of investing in machines and software has been stubbornly elusive. But the rising inequality resulting from those investments, and from the public policy that encourages them, is crystal clear.[364]

As "obvious" as it may be that productivity gains benefit all, historians know this not to be the case. When machines were introduced in the early 19th century, productivity and GDP rose rapidly, but working conditions from 1793 to 1840 deteriorated, in a period described by historian Robert Allen as "Engel's pause."

It may seem redundant to say it, but the economy is a machine of near infinite complexity; thinking that it can be optimized, therefore, by tweaking only a few parameters is surely misguided, and perhaps we are misled by seeing bodies such as the Federal Reserve or the Bank of England adjusting only the base lending rate. In fact, given the vast amount of data available and the pattern-like nature of the economy, it would probably be susceptible to being optimized better by AI than humans.

We do grasp some of the other parameters that matter, although usually only one at a time. For instance, economist Carl Benedikt Frey says "The breathtaking rise in wealth inequality that has been documented by Thomas Piketty stems almost entirely from housing," and argues for relocation subsidies.[365]

In countries with strong social safety nets, such as Sweden, over 80 percent of workers polled expressed positive views about robots, automation, and artificial intelligence in the workplace. In the US, however, those numbers are reversed: 72 percent of Americans express concern about the effects of increased automation in the workplace, 73 percent worry that AI will displace more jobs than it creates, and 76 percent believe economic inequality will worsen as a result.[366] "Sweden's free healthcare, education, and job transition programs dampen the risk of [automation]— which may be why people in the country are mostly happy to pay income tax rates that are up to nearly 60 percent," wrote reporter Erin Winick. "The US, by contrast, provides almost none of these services."[367]

Creativity

> *Not until a machine could write a sonnet or compose a concerto because of thoughts and emotions felt, and not by the chance fall of symbols, could we agree that machine equals brain—that is, not only write it but know that it had written it.*
>
> — Geoffrey Jefferson, British neurosurgeon

Some people have made a game out of their phone's autocomplete feature by constructing paragraphs based only on whatever words were suggested next. Here's how my iPhone played the game: "Hi there. I am leaving the house now to pick up the kids. If you want to go to get the car and I can come over to your place before you leave, I will be there." Shakespeare it is not. But it is only ever looking ahead far enough to pick the next word. Whereas GPT-3's much larger sliding window does propel it into the territory of the Bard.

Sudowrite, the brainchild of Amit Gupta (mentioned in Chapter 9) uses GPT-3 to provide assistance to writers faced with writer's block by suggesting several versions of what should come next. Stephen Marche of the *New Yorker* fed it Thomas Coleridge's famously truncated poem "Kubla Khan" and it offered a completion that Marche described as, "...beautiful, memorable. If you told me Coleridge had written it I would believe you."[368]

Poetry is an innocuous pastime to cede to AI, but blogs, if popular, carry the potential for lucrative advertising. College student Liam Porr used GPT-3 to write blog posts on productivity and self-help that became top-rated on *Hacker News*. The few commenters who questioned whether the posts were written by a human were immediately downvoted. Porr wasn't monetizing the experiment (and confessed in short order), but pointed out how easy it had been, saying, "I think the value of online content is going to be reduced a lot."[369]

Now look at the second game AlphaGo played against Go champion Lee Sedol. AlphaGo played a move that changed our thinking so much it became a catchphrase: "Move 37." This was a move so unusual that it was later estimated that the odds of a human employing it were one in ten thousand. Commentators didn't know what to make of it and thought that AlphaGo had lost its mind. But gradually the brilliance of the move was revealed, and they described it as "so surprising, [it] overturned hundreds of years of received wisdom," and finally labeled it a "divine move."

Few notions provoke as much outcry as the assertion that artificial intelligence is going to invent creative works. Push us out of our jobs, take over our factories, empty our offices, but keep your stinking robot paws off our art. The thought of a machine writing music, painting a masterpiece, or writing a sonnet cuts deep to the bone of where we feel most human. Demonstrating the premium we place on our creativity, at the height of the Cold War, the Voyager spacecraft were constructed, the first man-made vehicles to leave our solar system. Amid fears of existential doom, and believing that they might outlast the human race, we entrusted them with records of our greatest achievements to tell their eventual finders the story of who we were. The most prominent were famous works of art and music, digitally frozen into tracks etched on a golden disc: Humanity's Greatest Hits.

But it is all too easy for AI to create art that forces us to question the meaning of the word "creativity."

David Cope, creator of an algorithm that created a "new" Bach piece said, "Bach created all of the chords. It's like taking Parmesan cheese and putting it through the grater, and then trying to put it back together again. It would still turn out to be Parmesan cheese."[370] As early as 1997, a computer program named EMI composed a piece of music in the style of Bach that listeners thought was written by a human (and in the same blind taste test, thought that the submission written by music educator Dr. Steve Larson was written by a computer).[371]

More recently, OpenAI deployed MuseNet, a "deep neural network that can generate four-minute musical compositions with ten different instruments, and can combine styles from country to Mozart to the Beatles."[372] It can perform improvisation tricks, like playing Chopin in the style of Bon Jovi. As a byproduct of the learning that the GPT-2-backed network had undertaken, its creators had it render a map showing which composers were musically similar. The classical composers were predictably clustered apart from the contemporaries, but some of the relationships were… arresting. Pachelbel adjacent to Wagner??? It brings new meaning to "tone deaf"—or so I thought, until I asked AI music expert Bob Sturm, professor at the KTH Royal Institute of Technology in Stockholm, who set me straight: "These are composers of some of the most played pieces at *weddings*. And so perhaps in that data set that they used, they found, on playlists of weddings, Pachelbel's *Canon in D* and Wagner's *Bridal March* often appear. So this would tell a computer, 'Ah, these are similar because they're on the same playlist.'"[373]

If you're not restrained by an is-nothing-sacred reflex—and in the name of science, who can resist—you can twiddle MuseNet's knobs yourself. I asked it to continue the *Pink Panther* theme in the style of the Beatles on drums and harp. This was perhaps a bridge too far; the result was uninspiring. Blending Beethoven and Mozart was more euphonious.

Does the essence of art, the quality that makes it art, depend on who created it? Is a creation more… *artful*… if it came from, say, Alice than if it was produced by Bob? Aside from name recognition boosting auction bids, the statement is an elitist travesty.

Or is it?

Few violinists are as decorated as Grammy-winning Joshua Bell, whose playing was lauded by *Interview* magazine as "Doing nothing less than telling human beings why they bother to live." As the winner of the Avery Fisher prize, he is entitled to be described as the best classical musician in America, a maestro so talented that his performance of another musical genius' composition adds artistic value in its own right. In 2007, he took his $14 million Stradivarius to a Washington DC subway station in an experiment hatched by the *Washington Post* to see who would recognize the violin virtuoso if he donned a baseball cap and in appearance and location alone assumed the guise of a busker, one of the penniless mendicants that commuters pretend not to notice. The *Post* had contingency plans for dealing with crowds of fans blocking the passage; Bell was known for attracting female fans with the same enthusiasm as those of the Beatles whose hairstyle he sported.

They needn't have bothered. Bell's take for the day was $52.17 (math: that means some arrived in pennies), and nearly half of that came from the only person who *did* recognize him.

Yet Bell did not cheat the passersby; he delivered a concert-worthy performance of Bach's *Chaconne,* a work that left *Brahms* gushing with envy. And the acoustics of the subway corridor were surprisingly accommodating. Many of the upwardly-mobile professionals that hurried past would have happily dropped several hundred dollars to hear him at the John F. Kennedy Center.

So: If the *work* is the same but the *context* is one of minimal expectations, and the *appreciation* of that work matches only what is associated with the context, does that mean the *value* of the art depends largely, if not completely, on not just *who* created it, but who we *thought* they were?

You can see where this is going. AIs do not yet play the violin (although Shimon, the marimba-playing robot created by Gil Weinberg at the Georgia Tech Center for Music, will jam with a human partner), but they already create paintings, music, and literature, all of which are, essentially, information that must be rendered corporeal in order for us to consume it. If your reaction to art changes depending on whether you believe it to have been created by a human or by an AI, the essence of the art cannot reside solely in the art. The choice appears to be between insulting humans and insulting art.

Confronted by EMI, the music-composing AI, Douglas Hofstadter said, "The only comfort I could take at this point comes from realizing that EMI doesn't generate style on its own. It depends on mimicking prior composers. But that is still not all that much comfort. To my absolute devastation, music is much less than I ever thought it was."[374] Compare this to his comment on witnessing Deep Blue beat the reigning human chess champion (see Chapter 8).

Aiva, another music-composing AI, wrote a grand sweeping piece I play in my classes. Titled, "Symphonic Fantasy in A Minor, Op. 31: Among the Stars," it was the result of an instruction to compose a theme for a sci-fi epic. The result was not only undeniably grand, but fit the requirement for a theme, to be memorable; I can hum it at any time. So I play it as much to enjoy hearing it again as to provoke discussion about creativity.

Beethoven, as befitting any artist wishing to cement their legacy, left behind an unfinished work for followers to wonder at. The classical composer, who died in 1827 while still under commission from the Royal Philharmonic Society in London, left behind but a few short sketches for what would have been his tenth symphony. Who would dare the hubris of attempting to complete it? An AI incapable of shame, that's who. Big Data (Beethoven's oeuvre) plus a prompt (the unfinished score) is all a transformer-style AI needs to project some completions. Ahmed Elgammal, computer science professor at Rutgers University, led the team that constructed the finished Tenth. The credit can neither belong solely to the AI or the humans who assisted it; it was a collaborative effort incorporating feedback from Beethoven experts that produced a result that was greater than what could have been achieved by any method, or group, alone.

We are left with something new and beautiful to listen to, and also a disquieting feeling about the nature of identity. Beethoven did not come back from the dead to write this piece; he is still decomposing. It is not his work; but if it is indistinguishable from what he would have produced, have we in some limited sense created an AI copy of him? This is the sort of philosophical conundrum that AI forces upon us more and more.

If music is language, we could argue that the Turing Test has already been passed.

Robert Lucky, however, disagreed. The engineer and technology commentator made an eloquent case to interviewer Bill Moyers that knowing the human provenance of a work *does* make a difference, because of the associations we draw: "When you hear Mahler or Chopin, you think about the troubles of their life, the anguish, the emotions that are coming out in this music," he said. But when he heard computer music, he thought, "What does this computer know about life? You know, it hasn't experienced love and death and the things that make human anguish and human joy what it is."[375]

◊

Music is not the only bastion of art to be breached by robots. A painting by the Dutch master Rembrandt can sell for up to $180 million. Their supply is limited because he's not creating any more of them, due to having died in 1669. But in 2016, AI, at the hands of a crack team of technologists from Microsoft and the Delft University of Technology, created a new Rembrandt. Dutch bank ING wanted to "match its innovation in the banking world in the domain of art and culture."[376] Ad executive Bas Korsten came up with the idea, but readily admitted that it wasn't good enough to fool experts. But that wasn't the goal. It created a work good enough to both fool amateurs and to spark conversations about creativity, authenticity, and copyright; exactly the sort of attention his client wanted.

So how was it done? Remember, AI excels at finding and manipulating patterns. Three hundred and forty-six Rembrandt paintings, tagged, supplied sufficient raw data. The developers determined that the typical painting would be a portrait of a Caucasian male between thirty and forty, with facial hair, wearing black clothes with a white collar and a hat, facing to the right. These constraints, along with a hundred and fifty gigabytes of Rembrandt pictures, were fed into the convolutional neural network, which waved its magic wand and sent the output to a Canon 3-D printer that built up thirteen layers of paint to mimic brush strokes. Judge for yourself how successful they were: see Figure 14.2.

The violence we feel that computers have done to our aesthetic appreciation is born of the conviction that high art can only be created by a human transcending the mundane world in a moment of divine communion with a higher spirit. And that may very well be a necessary requirement for humans to create sublime art. But it is not a requirement for AI.

At the end of the day, how much should it matter? If you can enjoy a Beethoven symphony without stopping to first ask how it was made, is there not a new enjoyment to be had from being able to listen to non-stop AI-in-the-style-of-Beethoven compositions that you have never heard and which can therefore add the thrill of surprise? If you barred the door to AI art, would you be denying yourself a cornucopia of aesthetic novelty?

Figure 14.2: The Next Rembrandt, developed by J. Walter Thompson Amsterdam for ING.
www.nextrembrandt.com, by permission

Once again, our encounter with AI has led us to question beliefs and values so deeply buried in human nature that only philosophers had previously unearthed them.

So what price "creativity"? It is what AI pioneer Marvin Minsky would have called a "suitcase word," like "consciousness," and "thinking": it "means nothing by itself, but holds a bunch of things inside that you have to unpack." A suitcase word denotes something that everyone "just knows"—it's so obvious that no definition is necessary. Which means that no one knows what it really means; we just maintain a polite fiction that we think we're talking about the same thing. We've already seen how slippery "intelligence" is; "creativity" falls into the same bucket.

Trustworthiness

On January 15, 2009, the passengers on US Airways Flight 1549 out of La Guardia airport bound for Charlotte, North Carolina, were as nonchalant and blasé as you would find on any typical short-haul US flight, until the plane hit a flock of geese shortly after take-off and lost power in both engines. All one hundred and fifty-five people on board survived thanks to the resourcefulness of Captain Chesley "Sully" Sullenberger, and pilot Jeffrey Skiles in landing the plane on the Hudson River. Passengers reported their lives flashing before their eyes.

Had there been a computer in the cockpit without a human, they would likely have reported far more fraught emotions. Now, it's debatable how ready an AI is to handle an emergency aviation situation like the Miracle on the Hudson. Autonomous piloting in unusual situations is more constrained by the sensor technology than the flight decisions. But millions of flyers feel relatively calm stepping into a jet today for the simple reason that there are two people in front who have the ultimate incentive to keep them all safe; if the plane were to hit anything, they would be the first to die. This compact is known as Shared Fate.

If, however, the plane were to be piloted by an AI (or a human via remote control) there would be no shared fate. Even if the AI were proven to be superior to a human pilot, there would be a great psychological barrier for the passengers to surmount as they came aboard. And there is room for an AI to be a better pilot—not much room, because flying is so safe already—because most of the few aviation accidents that still occur are due to human error. Consider Air France Flight 447 which crashed into the South Atlantic because the pilots became disoriented and did the opposite of the correct action. While there was a lesson to be learned for making future flights piloted by humans safer, an AI would arguably not have been confused.

The reactions of pilots to today's cockpit AIs are mixed. One described watching the autoland fly as "a lesson in how to land an airplane properly."[377] On the other hand, "What's it doing now?" is a question all pilots have asked of their computers at one time or another, according to David Mindell in *Our Robots, Ourselves*. Researchers call this "mode awareness." "Every time I say that, I cringe," one pilot he quoted says, "because I know right good and well that 99 percent of the time it's doing exactly what I've asked it to do, and it's what I've asked it to do that I'm not understanding."[378] This echoes the universal experience of computer users who are almost—but never 100 percent—certain that the only problem is that they just haven't understood what they asked of the computer.

But the pressure on today's pilots is not automation, but the number of tasks they are expected to do. "We work more. We fly more. Our days get longer." The pilots are now responsible for communicating with maintenance, dispatch, and other airline services, via a cellphone in the cockpit, increasing their distractions.[379] The more of their jobs that human employees spend doing rote tasks, the less likely it is that they will be able to tap into deep creativity at a moment's notice, with possibly fatal consequences if that creativity is needed because a situation outside the experience of the autopilot has occurred.

That mirrors a consequence of increased automation that was predicted by Herman Kahn and Anthony Wiener in 1967: that it will become harder to recruit people to do difficult and demanding work that either requires long and arduous training or requires working in difficult, dangerous, or frustrating conditions.[380]

The more AI is used in critical applications like aviation—or qualifying loan applicants—the more we need to know that we can trust it. Those applications already have oversight and regulation of their human practitioners, but how should that be applied to AI? I spoke with Kush Varshney in IBM's Foundations of Trustworthy AI department in New York, who was pretty sure that machine learning was used in processing his mortgage application. He drew a parallel with the highly effective governance of commercial aviation safety, pointing out that just as what happens to an airplane is recorded in its black box, he thinks an analogical mechanism for capturing the operation of AI is necessary.

Trustworthiness in this context doesn't mean being confident that the AI isn't going to become self-aware and murder you in your sleep, but rather, how much faith can you place in the correctness of its decisions? Can you, in other words, trust it to make a loan, pay a claim, approve a university application? For that, AI can't be as brittle as the ones that completely forget how to play Breakout when you move the paddle a few pixels (see Chapter 8).

Varshney told me that the field of remediating that is called *Invariant Risk Minimization*. "The general idea is that if you acquire data from lots of different environments, what's going to be common about the data in those different environments is the stable or causal sort of relationships," he explained. "So you can have all of these different environments have local classifiers that compete with each other in a game. When they compete that way, then they end up with a global classifier that focuses on what's common across all of them, rather than focusing on individual experiences."[381]

What I found most striking about his description was that here was a problem that seemed insurmountable only a few years ago, a critical issue that people had little idea how to solve, now being systematically attacked thanks to dedicated researchers and their sponsors. It gave me hope that some of the other hard problems in creating and securing general AI might be equally close to resolution.

How Can You Survive and Thrive through the AI Revolution?

15
Survive

Nothing vast enters the world of mortals without a curse.

— Sophocles

We have gained some understanding of AI, and we have looked at how it is affecting and will affect our lives. What do we do about that?

That question has a great many answers; this section breaks them down along various dimensions. We'll organize it by size of social organization, starting with individuals, and progressing through families, communities, and organizations, to countries and the world.

We have to do this because the response to the disruption of AI depends so much on who's addressing it. When I speak to groups of individuals, I tell them what they can do in their personal lives, but everyone understands that this will not be enough. By analogy, I can tell you how to personally mitigate global warming—buy an electric car, recycle more, install solar panels, etc.—but you will intuit that it is not sufficient for individuals to address climate change like this. You know that there should be a coordinated international response with treaties and agreements, that countries should adopt incentives, that businesses should create policies, and that communities should take a stand. So it is with AI.

◊

First, we will consider the question of *survival*. Don't impute a dire slant to this word. Often, after I've given an introduction to the existential implications of artificial intelligence, the grandiose scope is too much for many people, and visions of cowering in a cave while unholy machines stalk the wasted landscape dance before their eyes. While the scope of future AI does, eventually, run to potential extinction scenarios, that topic acts as a conversational black hole; once discussion is sucked below its event horizon, there's no escape. In this section, you should think of "survival" as meaning simply, "maintaining the current level of well-being."

Individual

> *This thing will come like an earthquake.... The impact of the thinking machine will be a shock certainly of comparable order to that of the atomic bomb... a very dangerous thing socially. If we are going to sell man down the river and replace him, he's going to be a very angry man, and an angry man is a dangerous man.*
>
> — Norbert Weiner

The easiest level to encompass is of course the individual. You're almost certainly reading this book as an individual; perhaps a significant other is looking over your shoulder or you're tackling it in a book club, but those are relatively unlikely possibilities.

What matters most at this level is personal survival, and that is dependent upon your wealth and income. For most people, this means that employment and employability are their chief concerns. If your physical survival depends upon continued employment, then by the principle Abraham Maslow outlined in his *Hierarchy of Needs*,[382] you will not have the cognitive energy to focus on any more elevated issues, nor will you function optimally to assist anyone else. "Put your own oxygen mask on before you attempt to help others."

At this level, a person's *identity* may be synonymous with their job, and that is a brittle point in their resilience armor. Dr. Janna Koretz, founder of Azimuth Psychological, where she focuses on the unique challenges of those in high-pressure careers, defines this condition as *enmeshment*, a term typically applied to a blurring of boundaries with other people. But in this case the relationship is with the job.

I asked her what happens to someone who has identified with a high-stakes job when that position is threatened, and she described someone whose inner dialogue was, "I am an attorney, I'm at the top of this field, I worked really hard for this promotion, I'm a partner, etc.," but when that job is lost, "all of a sudden that sense of self and that paradigm is gone. They tend to fall apart. It's like putting all your eggs in one basket."

Their circle of friends and family may not relate. "People don't know what it's like to lose something so central to your identity," she said. "How can you get them to understand what that person is going through?" I asked. "What equivalent situation could they relate to?" She equated it to a family crisis: "When someone loses a parent or sister, that's a big part of their life and their identity as well."[383]

How you relate to AI as an individual is at risk of being colored or distorted by misunderstanding, so we will look at how to guard against that.

Risks of Misevaluating AI

Humanity can be quite cold to those whose eyes see the world differently.

— Eric A. Burns

Hollywood would have us believe that conscious artificial intelligence will arrive in a thunderclap when a charismatic genius builds a robot that marches into your office, takes a seat in front of you, and says, "Let's discuss your future with this company." In a way, such a scenario would be preferable to the one that is most likely to prevail, because it would focus our attention on issues of self-identity and values far more effectively than will the creeping rise of AI capability. It's hard, as every climate activist knows, to get attention for an issue that encroaches gradually; journalists don't earn much for starting headlines with, "1 Percent Increase In…"

So the issues discussed within this section will not be heralded as BREAKING NEWS, but more likely appear on the horizon first in PBS documentaries and TED talks, then dismissed as fantasy after failing to turn into gory headlines within a year or two, then eventually return for more attention when the pain becomes impossible to ignore. We're somewhere between the first and second stages of that progression at the moment.

As AI evolves, there will be more and more areas of our lives where it can compete with us; and our response to competition is seldom optimal, not when the competition is one we are eventually guaranteed to lose. In fact, our reaction to this competition is likely to be far more of a problem than the competition itself. Fear of the unknown is natural, but when uncertainty gathers mass and makes the entire future an unknown collection of ominous shadows, fear dominates and robs us of the resourcefulness we need to deal with that unknown.

One of the shadows harbors the fear of being superseded by machines. You can become more resilient through awareness of what the real and imaginary threats are. Reading this book is a step in that direction. Increase your value and expertise in the dimensions that are farthest away from being automated; switch your focus from rote mechanical, paper-pushing skills to creative activities that depend on empathetic interactions with other human beings. If you're an engineer, don't think this means that you have to quit and become a psychiatrist; success in your profession as much as any other depends upon parties reaching mutual understanding and respect, whether they realize it or not.

Family/Community

I skate to where the puck is going, not where it has been.

— Wayne Gretzky

At the level of the family, school, church, or sewing club, not much changes, except that you have companions you can talk about this with. Perhaps you might form discussion groups to go through this book together; talking about a topic with other people surfaces questions and answers that go undiscovered when we are just privately ruminating.

The family members that will best deal with disruption are children. When I speak to a school, the view from the stage is amusing because at some point after I have explained enough of the potential outcomes arising from AI, the children are on the edges of their seats, engaged, listening intently, and excited. The faculty are terrified. They look like they've just seen an episode of *Black Mirror* (which has some truth to it). It's hard to slant the talk so that they would be less scared while simultaneously retaining the children's attention, so I usually speak to them directly to try and dispel their paralysis.

But the students have no problem remaining composed, resourceful, and interested. This is not borne of any nonchalance or failure to understand the issues; they very much know exactly what I've said and its implications. Even though a dangerous future affects them more than the adults (because they're going to spend more time in it), they aren't afraid. This is why I love talking to school and college audiences, because they are clear-eyed and easily connect their energy with action.

For instance, Professor Aaron McKain of Minnesota's North Central University made one comment to his Public Relations class in 2019, and as a result, students Shea Sullivan, Hannah Grubbs, and others formed the Institute for Digital Humanity, an entirely student-run grass roots organization partnering across the country to "advocate for civil rights when technology gets out of control."

What gives me the most optimism about the future is having met the kids that are going to fix the problems their predecessors have created. If they're representative of how the human race is going to meet the future, we couldn't be in better hands. Don't shield your children from realistic estimates of perils the future may hold. They can probably deal with them better than you.

Still, they need your help. Education is being radically transformed, in both long-overdue ways and in unforeseen ways that pose serious ethical challenges. Preparing our children for the AI future is itself an exercise in facing a deep mystery. Today's children will need to be familiar with AI and work with it in the future as comfortably as we do today with computers. But how well did we predict those computers? While some early writers did forecast that we would have home computers, they also expected them to take up most of a room. They would have said that the future computer-savvy child would need to be adept at changing magnetic tapes, reading hexadecimal dumps, and clearing line printer jams. They were, in Wayne Gretzky's words, aiming for where the puck was, not where it was going to be.

It is equally purblind to train today's children to deal with today's AI. That may be as useful a part of their education as calculus and chemistry, but more for the cognitive workout than for any likelihood of them using it much after they graduate. The AI they will be interacting with then will be leagues beyond what we use today.

Organization

While change is certain, the direction is not.

— Pierre Omidyar, Founder of eBay

Struggling to figure out how to adopt AI in your business? Join the club. Take the bragging from competitors of their AI leverage with a grain of salt. "Don't think everyone else is doing it brilliantly because the truth is they're not," AI in business expert Katie King told business leaders listening to *AI and You*. "AI is not being deployed at scale in any industry. …

I've seen pockets of it in retail, in financial services, in telecoms, but it's still early days."

Right now, the organization is the crucible of fear of, and reaction to, disruptive change. Today's businesses are overwhelmingly motivated by fear, and a vast industry of consultants and media are all too happy to keep the fear ratcheted up to a constant RED ALERT level. Every pundit and thought leader has cautionary tales about organizations that didn't Get With the Program and wound up on the Skid Row of business.

Let's consider where businesses can fall on what I call the Automation Resilience Quadrant (see Figure 15.1).

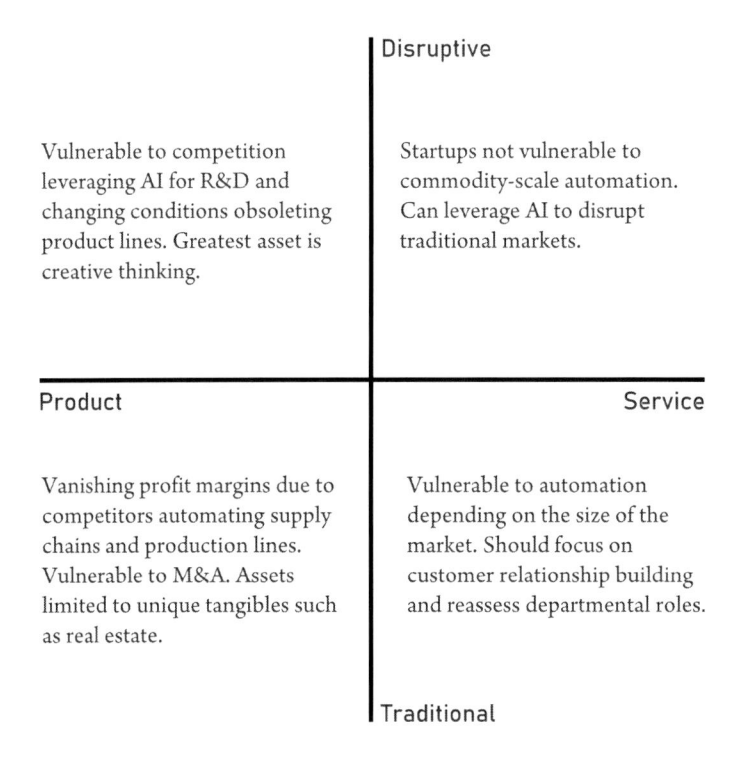

Product	Disruptive	Service
Vulnerable to competition leveraging AI for R&D and changing conditions obsoleting product lines. Greatest asset is creative thinking.		Startups not vulnerable to commodity-scale automation. Can leverage AI to disrupt traditional markets.
Vanishing profit margins due to competitors automating supply chains and production lines. Vulnerable to M&A. Assets limited to unique tangibles such as real estate.	Traditional	Vulnerable to automation depending on the size of the market. Should focus on customer relationship building and reassess departmental roles.

Figure 15.1: Automation Resilience Quadrant

This diagram breaks down organizational risks and strategies for dealing with disruption from AI. On the horizontal axis, on the left we have businesses oriented around products: selling multiple copies of some tangible item or information. On the right we have businesses that are oriented around selling a service. On the vertical axis, on the bottom we have traditional, established businesses, and on the top, we have disruptive, startup-type businesses.

The bottom left quadrant represents businesses selling traditional products: think laundry detergent. This will be a highly painful place to be if you are not on top. If your competitors are Walmart and Amazon, think how much data they have available to them, what insights they can generate from it with artificial intelligence, and on what kind of scale they can deploy AI across their products, supply chains, customer relationship management, human resources, production lines, and facility management. When they are done amortizing that cost across their entire organization, their unit cost of development is insignificant compared to what you would need. Your main assets are limited to unique tangibles such as real estate. Unless you are in a sector where you can be the top dog, work to move yourself to a different quadrant.

In the bottom right quadrant, we have traditional service-oriented companies: think insurance brokering. Because this is a repetitive process, it is vulnerable to being automated by competitors if the market size and data are big enough. Focus on the human aspect of your service, emphasizing personal contact with your customers, and understanding their unique needs as human beings. Reassess your organizational structure to see where it reflects traditional structures that no longer need to be perpetuated: do you still need your own human resources, accounting, fulfillment departments, or are third-party offerings now at an adequate level of cost effectiveness?

If you are in the top left quadrant, you are a disruptive product-oriented business: for older examples, think iPhones; for recent examples, delivery robots. Your main vulnerability is a more highly capitalized competitor leveraging AI for research and development to optimize their time to market and customer support. The volatility of the business could obsolete entire product lines easily. Your greatest asset is the creative thinking of the minds who got you into this business.

The top right quadrant contains disruptive service-oriented businesses. The examples for this quadrant are Uber (a transportation service company that owns no vehicles) and Airbnb (a lodging service company that owns no locations). They gained footholds by using modern user interfaces coupled with AI to pair customers with their ride or stay. If you're a startup, or not highly capitalized, this is the place to aim for. By definition, the competition is small to nonexistent. You can cement a winning position by leveraging AI to disrupt traditional markets with your new service.

No business today can afford to ignore its ethical responsibilities, or the place of diversity, equity and inclusion. Again, AI will not act as a magic bullet, only make the core values or moral deficiencies of your company more obvious faster. One way to remedy bias is by having a diverse team whose members cover many points of view. I asked Richard Foster-Fletcher, founder of the MKAI inclusive AI community, what he would do for a company that was reaching out for help in avoiding falling into the pitfalls of unintentional bias. He suggested that they could use artificial intelligence neural network models to try and understand what bias was expressed where within the company, "and why certain outcomes were coming up internally in terms of who was promoted and why, who was in leadership positions and why, how decisions were being made and why, by looking at the way that people speak to each other: the communication nuances, as well as the words." He added that if he was brave enough, he would benchmark that against the company's peers outside of the industry.

If your business happens to be the invention and expansion of artificial intelligence, you are living in the equivalent of the dot-com boom. Every day is an adventure. But what is often overlooked by businesses in this catbird seat of technology is the perspective from outside their bubble. The members of the public being taken on this wild ride do not know what's happening, are not in the loop on strategic plans, and have only misleading, incomplete, and sensational soundbites from a flighty media to inform them. The net effect is like being in the back seat of a car being driven at top speed down the freeway by a teenager chugging a Red Bull while texting his friends and turning around to shout, "I have no idea where we're going, but isn't it fun!" Keep that image in mind when developing outreach and promotion.

To manage the impact of AI, business will need to understand their people intimately. A signal counterexample is Kodak. Their downfall from being the premier manufacturer of cameras and film is well-known, and appears at first sight to be a straightforward case of being blindsided by new technology. But few people know that Kodak *invented* the digital camera. They *could* have scooped the market. But the organization had too much invested in an identity as a maker of long thin strips of plastic, and did not listen to their own engineer Steven Sasson, when he built a prototype (US patent 4,131,919) in 1975.

If you're a business leader, even if the press about automation decimating the employment market was completely false with respect to your own organization or industry sector, remember that your people live in a world where that press reaches them. At the very least, you will need to have established enough rapport with them to be seen as credible when you dispute that narrative.

Domains of Application

> *The talk you hear about adapting to change is not only stupid, it's dangerous. The only way you can manage change is to create it. By the time you catch up to change, the competition is ahead of you.*
>
> — Peter Drucker

To successfully deploy "general" artificial intelligence—yes, it doesn't really exist yet, but some people are ambitious—make sure the context is one where users aren't inclined to ask difficult questions that could be too hard to deal with. An example of an environment where this works is GPS/satnav requests: they will only be phrases equating to some form of geographic positional requirement. Whereas movie critiquing would be an example of a context carrying too much risk of the user getting too far away from what AI can parse.

I asked Katie King how to distinguish between contemporary claims of artificial intelligence being used in business marketing and what ten years ago was called "business intelligence" or "business analytics." "What the AI is really able to do is to provide tools that are imitating intelligent human behavior," she said, "much, much more than just a simple analytics tool that's giving you some data."

She described Danish Saxo Bank. "When they deployed their chatbot assistants, they failed to realize the impact on all of the different stakeholders. Staff hadn't been communicated with properly and were very threatened by this new technology and these new tools and it didn't work for them. But equally," she went on, "they innovated quite early, they were one of the early adopters and the tools were very shallow. If you're an early adopter, you've got to be clear when you communicate this with clients that they realize it's quite limited." Clients had tried to interact with their chatbot and had expectations far beyond its capability, and they got bored. The project failed. But then a year or so later, they successfully repurposed the AI for customer onboarding.

"So it's about strategy," King concluded, "it's about having a business issue that needs to be solved, rather than just picking it out and putting it into the organization. So it's proofs of concept, collaboration, really clear communication, and then working with different stakeholders looking for funding, finding innovation grants, and so on."[384]

Country

> *Before the prospect of an intelligence explosion, we humans are like small children playing with a bomb... We have little idea when the detonation will occur, though if we hold the device to our ear we can hear a faint ticking sound.*
>
> — Nick Bostrom

National AI strategies didn't exist until about 2016, but have burgeoned since. White House Chief Technology Officer Michael Kratsios explained how the federal government's "American AI Initiative," estimated to be $2 billion in 2022 for non-defense AI research, will result in R&D efforts the White House expects to trickle down to Big Tech and AI research institutions. "We think this is a game-changer moment for AI R&D in this country," Kratsios said.[385]

Equity

Government is where we look to locate initiatives to protect equity. A large national conversation around the future of work at the moment is whether people will have work in the future, or whether it will be automated away. Many researchers believe that AI could automate most or all jobs through dynocognesis (the electrification of thinking). But there is still an unresolved dilemma, a national self-doubt in the United States at least, as to whether we should, if we can, create a society where people do not need to work.

"The economic problem, the struggle for subsistence, always has been hitherto the primary, most pressing problem of the human race," said economist John Maynard Keynes in 1930. He went on:

> If the economic problem is solved, mankind will be deprived of its traditional purpose. Will this be a benefit? If one believes at all in the real values of life, the prospect at least opens up the possibility of benefit. Yet I think with dread of the readjustment of the habits and instincts of the ordinary man, bred into him for countless generations, which he may be asked to discard within a few decades.

He imagined both a utopia and its flaws:

> Thus for the first time since his creation man will be faced with his real, his permanent problem—how to use his freedom from pressing economic cares, how to occupy the leisure, which sci-

ence and compound interest will have won for him, to live wisely and agreeably and well.[386]

Keynes pursued what would today be called a socialist agenda:

> I see us free, therefore, to return to some of the most sure and certain principles of religion and traditional virtue—that avarice is a vice, that the exaction of usury is a misdemeanor, and the love of money is detestable, that those walk most truly in the paths of virtue and sane wisdom who take least thought for the morrow. We shall once more value ends above means and prefer the good to the useful. We shall honour those who can teach us how to pluck the hour and the day virtuously and well, the delightful people who are capable of taking direct enjoyment in things, the lilies of the field who toil not, neither do they spin.

Keynes was prescient enough to realize that this expansive vision would not be realized overnight, and that our dog-eat-dog world would prevail beyond his lifetime:

> But beware! The time for all this is not yet. For at least another hundred years we must pretend to ourselves and to everyone that fair is foul and foul is fair; for foul is useful and fair is not. Avarice and usury and precaution must be our guards for a little longer still. For only they can lead us out of the tunnel of economic necessity into daylight.[387]

Futurists Herman Kahn and Anthony Wiener acknowledged in 1967 that the transition to a life of leisure would not come easily to the American worker:

> If the average American had an opportunity to live on the beach for six months a year doing nothing, he might have severe guilt feelings in addition to a sunburn. If an American wishes to be broiled in the sun, he usually must go through a preliminary justification such as the following: 'The system is corrupt, I reject it. Its values are not my values. To hell with these puritanical, obsolete concepts.' Only at that point can he relax in the sun.[388]

By 2019, commentary on this issue was framed as a stark class conflict: "We will either become a society that works exclusively for the rich and powerful, or we will enact large-scale structural reforms that restore fairness to our economy and political system," said Ady Barkan, Director of the Center for Popular Democracy's "Fed Up" campaign. "Each of us is called to do everything we can to ensure our society winds up in the right place."[389] But there's no agreement on what that right place might be or how to get there. Presently, the benefits of automation development flow to the owners of the businesses developing that automation and not to the people displaced by that automation.

Part of the incentive for automation is that in the United States, the tax rate on capital invested in software and equipment is around 5 percent whereas labor taxes are over 25 percent.[390] In 2017, Bill Gates suggested compensating via a "robot tax"; if a human factory worker was replaced by a robot, the business should pay tax equivalent to the displaced worker. He proposed that the revenue be distributed to people performing socially important jobs like caring for the elderly or special needs children. While laudable, this idea suffers so much from definitional issues—what constitutes a "robot," how long should the tax be levied, should it be retroactive—that there is no chance of it being implemented. Even a European Union tax commissioner said, "No way, no way," when asked about it.[391]

Justice

Will AI be used in a national judicial system? In December 2020, Ukraine introduced AI to its justice system, and in February 2021, their High Council of Justice approved an electronic court where AI would be used for legal advice and the resolution of disputes that are less complex. The Ukraine Ministry of Justice announced its intention to use AI software called Cassandra in criminal justice to assess the potential risk of recidivism and also help judges in making custodial decisions. Resist the temptation to envisage robo-judges mercilessly sentencing hapless humans; this is only intended as a decision support tool. What will happen to it on the other side of the invasion by Russia is, regrettably, anyone's guess.

The use of AI in jurisprudence is likely to encounter considerable resistance. Ethnographer Angèle Christin found that workers such as judges and parole officers either ignore algorithmic recommendations or actively "game" them in order to reach the outcomes they wanted to begin with.

World

> *It is now highly feasible to take care of everybody on Earth at a "higher standard of living than any have ever known." It no longer has to be you or me. Selfishness is unnecessary.… War is obsolete.… It is a matter of converting our high technology from weaponry to livingry.*[392]
>
> — Buckminster Fuller, 1981

Now let us look at the highest level of all: the whole planet, the entire human race. We do not have a distinguished history of acting in concert at that level, but in April 2020, as the world was falling apart, an odd and wonderful counterexample happened. In the midst of so much separation and disintegration, humans came together and built a machine, the likes of which had never been seen before. As a demonstration of how our species could spontaneously collaborate on a global scale, it was the equivalent of a supernova suddenly outshining every other star in the galaxy. They built the world's biggest supercomputer, and they did it with no funding, within a matter of days.

The Folding@Home project (which we mentioned in Chapter 3) was the brainchild of Vijay Pande, but to understand it we must go back to 1999 and the SETI@Home project, the first big international crowdsourced computing project.[393] SETI stands for "Search for Extraterrestrial Intelligence," and it was not their goal to pioneer a new paradigm in distributed computing; they simply had no alternative. The US government had funded SETI to look for radio signals carrying signs of a civilization beyond the Earth, attempting to answer the existential question that is as baked into our DNA as our origin in primeval oceans: "Is anybody out there?"

They funded it, that is, until Senator William Proxmire, leading a mob of legislators stoked on ignorance and waving not pitchforks but Proxmire's Golden Fleece award for alleged waste of taxpayer funding, decided that cheap jokes about little green men pandered to more votes than respect for science or existential questions. So in 1993, SETI funding was eliminated, and Proxmire set out guards to make sure it didn't come back under any pretense.

SETI didn't stop, but its funding went private, and that meant there was less of it. They went to the directors of the Arecibo radio telescope in Puerto Rico and begged to be allowed to piggyback their instruments on the telescope's receiver; "Whatever you're looking at, we just want to get a copy of the signals," they said. Christened Project SERENDIP, like vagrants hanging outside a restaurant for the day's leftovers, they took what they could get.[394] But then they had to analyze that data to look for the signs of an artificially-generated signal, and the processing power required to do that in 1980 came with a hefty price tag.

In desperation, chief scientist Dan Werthimer turned to an idea from computer scientist David Gedye, borne out of the relatively recent personal computer revolution and the even more recent Internet revolution, and thought about all the computing power lying unused in bedrooms, studies, and dens when the PCs' owners weren't using them. Those owners did not turn their machines off when they weren't in use, because of the lengthy boot sequence every time they were turned on; this was the golden age of the screensaver, when software companies competed to supply the most fascinating piece of abstract animation to display on the screens of computers that supposedly, no one was looking at.

How much nobler to have your computer look for aliens than to animate flying toasters to an empty room. The researchers had hoped to get a thousand participants; they got a million. One day they realized that overnight they had processed data that would have taken them a thousand years if they had only a single piece of hardware for the job. That sort of lesson is not easily forgotten.

Which brings us back to Folding@Home and Vijay Pande, in the year 2000, following in SETI@Home's footsteps to solve the fiendishly hard problems of protein folding.[395] You can guess where this is going. People were as happy to donate their PCs to the frontier of biology as to SETI. In 2019, Folding@Home had around 30,000 participant nodes. But then COVID-19 struck. People wanted to help, to do anything to fight the 'rona. From March 2020 to mid-April, according to the Folding@Home director, biochemist Greg Bowman, some seven hundred thousand new nodes joined and the capacity of the network reached a mind-puddling 2.6 *exaFLOPS*.[396] That was six times the performance of what had been the world's fastest supercomputer up until then, the billion-dollar Japanese Fugaku, which had taken six years to develop. The human race, working together, created the most powerful computing engine the planet had ever seen in essentially zero time and essentially zero cost, through the power of a common thought. If you get upset by the strife and chaos of the world, and it seems that we may never marshal the cooperation to face our future with AI, perhaps you can take some solace from remembering this moment of unity.

◊

When we're looking at AI across the entire globe, some way of comparing its progress in different countries is important. Alexandra Mousavizadeh founded the Global AI Index to benchmark nations on their level of investment, innovation, and implementation of artificial intelligence, and to form individual and composite rankings of countries on different dimensions. I asked her what the aims of the index were, and she explained: "By ranking, you're creating what some would call 'competition'; I would rather use the word 'inspiration.' Because when you organize the data like this and create an index and a ranking, it sharpens people's minds on how they are performing, and hopefully also [encourages them to] look at countries that are doing better, so they can be a source of inspiration, or [suggest that if] a model works well in another country, 'maybe it's something that would work well for us.'"[397]

Mousavizadeh told me that the countries that do well on AI are also countries that can lead on things like facial recognition and machine learning. A lot of governments are tracking quantum computing because if you are on the forefront of the ability to innovate and to actually hack and crack and commercialize quantum computation, then you're also able to impact cybersecurity.

Global Conflicts

Today's world is very much shaped by the empires of the past: their ghosts and footprints can be seen everywhere from Roman roads to national borderlines. It's not difficult to see how big a part colonialism has played in defining the form of our current geopolitical structure; but how might AI change that? Rajiv Malhotra, author of *Artificial Intelligence and the Future of Power,* says, "Historically, colonialism was related to the Industrial Revolution, because prior to the Industrial Revolution, Britain was not very advanced and actually, India had a higher manufacturing economy, even by the British's own estimates. The colonialism happened largely because the British Industrial Revolution gave them the power and economic might so they could then turn the colonies into sources of raw material, and capital markets for finished goods. So, this is how colonialism and the Industrial Revolution fed each other. The East India company was a private enterprise like Google, like Facebook, like Twitter, like Amazon, and all those digital giants; the East India Company was bigger than the British government. Private enterprise created a whole colonial empire."[398] This is a valuable perspective for us, living at a time referred to as the Fourth Industrial Revolution.

The borders of cyberspace and the businesses built around it are not constrained tightly by geography, however. The Open Source movement spearheaded a culture rooted in the Internet, a meritocracy that gravitated toward the most open and generous contributors of talent.

Speaking at the Bloomberg New Economy Forum in Beijing on November 21, 2019, Bill Gates said there's no going back from the US tradition of openly sharing scientific research, which he said is particularly advantageous in the AI field. "AI is very hard to put back in the bottle, and whoever has the open system will so vastly get ahead," Gates said. Openly sharing research is one of the reasons people come to work at Microsoft, he noted. "We gladly pay their salaries, but if we didn't have that publishing approach, those people would go and work somewhere else."

Russia

September 1, 2017 was "National Knowledge Day" in Russia, and President Vladimir Putin marked the occasion by speaking to students and teachers in over sixteen thousand schools in an "open lesson." Facing a huge auditorium of students showing their affiliations with primary color T-shirts, he declared AI to be the "future of all mankind," and then, in a widely-reported statement, said that "the one who becomes the leader in this sphere will be the ruler of the world."[399] Widely-reported because Western observers presume that Putin would not object to becoming ruler of the world and the idea might even have crossed his mind. In a less widely-reported following statement, he said he "would really not want this monopoly to be concentrated in one [country's] hands; therefore if we are a leader in this area, we will also share these technologies with the whole world." The same observers likely found this harder to swallow.

A former major in the KGB and long-term leader of Russia does not speak loosely. It is not hard to see how his assessment could be true, nor why he was motivated to think that way, given recent history. The USSR lost the Cold War because the United States was able to outspend it. While much was made in the western press of the fallibility of the proposed strategic missile defense system ("Star Wars"), the fact was that it didn't have to work perfectly to achieve a much more desirable goal: not being used at all. If the US could, on average, knock down a Soviet warhead for less than the USSR had spent to make it, there could be no path to a war that the latter could afford to win. This lesson in economics is part of the racial memory of every subsequent Russian leader. He is, therefore, highly attuned to any new technology with the potential to change the economic balance of warfare.

The prospect of AI doing just that is easily perceived. Putin predicted that future wars will be fought by drones, and "when one party's drones are destroyed by drones of another, it will have no other choice but to surrender." However, that prediction has been unevenly validated in the war in Ukraine, with both sides using automated aircraft for surveillance and Ukraine attacking tanks with both military and consumer drones, but neither tipping the outcome of the conflict. In April 2022, DJI, the largest manufacturer of commercial drones, suspended business in both Russia and Ukraine.

But the potential for AI to change balances of power goes far beyond the battlefield. An army's ability to scale any task that requires a person to perform it is limited by the number of people at its command. When warfare was conducted by hand-to-hand combat, the winner was generally the one who could throw the most bodies into the fray. That equation changed as technology amplified the ability of one individual to hurt another, to the point where the limiting factor now is the intelligence of an operative to integrate complex, ambiguous information and make a decision. The greatest challenge in modern warfare is gathering, assessing, and routing tactical information and parsing it into high-level chunks that are small enough for human brains to do something with. AI that could integrate unlimited quantities of data and make strategic decisions from it either in warfare or geopolitics, could operate so much faster than human beings as to overwhelm other advantages.

Using games as metaphors for global political conflict, strategic nuclear warfare is definitely American Football, which to my British sensibilities appears as periods of mayhem punctuated by lawsuits. There is no doubt, then, that any such conflict would be playing by the rules of a game most familiar to Americans.

But suppose Russia could change the game to *their* national game: chess. If international conflict were defined not by the head-on clash of brute force but instead by the ability to think several moves ahead of your opponent and maneuver pieces far from the central battle into play, this would be far more familiar to Russians. Rather than trying to win someone else's game, how much smarter is it to switch to a different game that you're better at? It's no surprise that Russia has made strategic gains in recent decades through the more chess-like moves of psychological manipulation of western culture and decision-making.

What would happen if they could enlist the help of a sophisticated AI to play that same game? Think what AI did for—or to—chess. If those same radically creative moves could be made in the geopolitical arena by an AI that out-thought human players, what would be the outcome for the owner of that AI? Is this why Putin made his famous statement?

China

In the West, we paid a lot of attention to the head-swiveling breakthrough of AlphaGo when it beat the reigning Go champion in 2016. We became excited about the deep learning technology, we read about DeepMind, and invited Demis Hassabis to a hundred talk shows.

This attention was a faint shadow of the impact AlphaGo had on China.

We might think that the national game of China is table tennis, but in reality, it is Go (圍棋). In 2017, at least a hundred thousand professional teachers from over two hundred thousand facilities were offering Go training.[400]

Prior to 2016, any significant progress in computerized Go playing was expected to be a decade away; so try to imagine the Chinese reaction to Lee Sedol's loss.* If Russia had fielded a team of football-playing robots that won the Super Bowl 50-0, the impact on the American psyche would have been no greater than what AlphaGo did to the Chinese state of mind. This was their Sputnik moment; even though Americans barely knew what Go was, they (or a British subsidiary of a Google company) had created a machine that could defeat any of the estimated forty million Chinese Go players.

Over two hundred and eighty million Chinese watched the tournament.[401]

They resolved that (a) this AI thing was worthy of their highest attention, and (b) if that was where the game had moved to, they were going to win it. Within months, China unveiled its "Next Generation Artificial Intelligence Development Plan," (NGAIDP) documenting their strategy to become the global leader in all aspects of AI by 2030.

Lee Sedol won the fourth game playing a sublime move observers called "God's Touch," later evaluated as having only a one-in-ten-thousand chance that anyone would play it—coincidentally, *exactly the same odds* as the famous "Move 37" by AlphaGo that left commentators reeling. (See Chapter 14.) Only a year later, China's Go champion Ke Jie lost 3–0 in a game that the Chinese government banned from being streamed live.[402] Two months after that, the state Council of China released the NGAIDP, planning government-sponsored state-wide development of artificial in-

---

* Even though he is Korean. The headlines in South Korea were apocalyptic: "The 'Horrifying Evolution of Artificial Intelligence" and "AlphaGo's Victory... Spreading Artificial Intelligence 'Phobia,'" even though their national AI strategy did not pivot that way China's did.

telligence. It laid out steps to achieve specific benchmarks by maximizing the country's productive forces, national economy, and national competitiveness, to achieve what Xi Jinping called "the great rejuvenation of the Chinese nation."[403] The following year the minister of science and technology announced that the government was drafting comprehensive guidelines for developing and deploying artificial intelligence.

Lee Sedol retired three years after his loss, telling the South Korean Yonhap news agency that, "Even if I become the number one, there is an entity that cannot be defeated."[404]

AI historian Pamela McCorduck told me, "We've got another set of circumstances now that we never have had: We have massive deep-pocketed funding in China. The Chinese adore AI. They are doing everything they can to develop it very wisely. They're not letting anything hold them back." I asked McCorduck if she foresaw an AI arms race approaching, and she nodded.

Judging who is most likely to win that race requires a detailed assessment of the standing in AI of many nations along many axes, which is exactly what the Global AI Index, founded by Alexandra Mousavizadeh in 2020, does. She said, "The US and China are far ahead. And Europe is quite far behind in third place. And in Europe, the UK is leading in AI ecosystem and development, but they are really far behind. If you look at the AI index, it gives a very clear picture of exactly sort of the gap between the US and China and the rest. But there's also actually quite a significant gap between the US and China."

I asked the Danish-born, London-based Mousavizadeh how likely China was to succeed in their plan for AI breakthroughs by 2025 and world dominance by 2030. "China, because of its quite focused policy, leads us on many, many things when it comes to AI and probably also quantum computing," she said. "Very far ahead in facial recognition, very far advanced in AI adoption. But the strongest ecosystem, by far, is the US ecosystem. Measured on all of the parameters that go into the index, it's not narrow; it's very broad and very deep in every aspect.

"[China's] position is that, on the things they deem more important than AI—quantum computing, facial recognition, etc., they have a very good chance of leading by 2025, and maybe already are. But there's much more to AI than that. And there is this ecosystem that spins out lots and lots of companies that use AI across many, many sectors. [Considering] those parameters, and leading research, not just on a few things, but on many things that are related, then the US definitely is light-years ahead when you're looking at the talent pool."[405]

Weapons

> *One of my responsibilities as Commander in Chief is to keep an eye on the robots. And I'm pleased to report that the robots you manufacture here seem peaceful. At least for now.*
>
> —President Barack Obama, addressing Carnegie Mellon University's National Robotics Engineering Center

Setting aside for now the subtle use of AI to maneuver for strategic advantage behind the scenes, let's evaluate its ability to take on the battle on the main stage, to be used in actual weaponry. And it appears ready: in August 2020, in aerial dogfights carried out in a simulator, an AI from Heron Systems beat six other AIs to earn the right to take on a human fighter pilot (call-sign "Banger"), whom it then beat 5–0.[406] "The standard things that we do as fighter pilots aren't working," commented Banger.

One of the questions often asked is whether AI changes where we assign responsibility or authority for weapons use. System engineer Tony Gillespie told me:

> When looking at technology for armed Unmanned Air Vehicles (UAVs), it became very clear that what was really dominating everything was the law; what was then called the law of armed conflict, now called International Humanitarian Law (IHL). That dictated everything that happens, because if the pilot release is fine with a remotely-piloted unmanned aircraft, then under the law, the pilot or whoever presses the button on the bomb is legally responsible for the effect and that then drives the technology. The light-bulb-coming-on-moment came after a lot of thinking and scratching my head when I was on holiday on a wet afternoon in a tent in Cornwall, when suddenly I realized that it was actually quite simple to put the Geneva Conventions into engineering requirements. I managed to turn them into essentially procurement requirements, which then, if you impose those on the contractor, there's a pretty good chance you'll meet IHL. It sounds quite simple. But it's a long, hard chain.[407]

Bonnie Docherty, a researcher at Human Rights Watch in the arms division says that if an autonomous weapon were to go awry and kill a large number of civilians, it would not be "fair nor legally viable to ... hold the commander or operator responsible." But she says that at the same time, punishing the robot would not make sense; the robot would not be legally considered a person.[408]

Nick Bostrom says, "The alternative to having a drone deciding to fire a missile is that a nineteen-year-old sits in Arlington, Virginia in front of a computer screen and has a job that whenever a window pops up on the screen saying 'fire,' they need to press the red button. If that's what human oversight amounts to, then it's not clear that it really makes that much of a difference from having the whole system be completely autonomous."[409]

A slew of incidents has undermined any faith that autonomous weapons systems might fail safely. For instance, in 2003, an operator at a US Patriot missile battery received an automated alert that an incoming Iraqi missile had been detected. She had a split second to make a decision and chose to fire. But the target turned out to be a Royal Air Force Tornado jet, whose pilots were killed. The system had not been connected to a wider network that would have identified the jet as friendly.[410]

Gillespie described how autonomy in any autonomous systems, including weapon systems, is not an either-or attribute, but "a continuum with fully autonomous at one end. I used to have a joke slide with a man arriving in an empty hangar, scratching his head and saying, 'I wonder what those autonomous aircraft are up to today.' That's one end. The other end is pulling a lever or joystick to control the aircraft, then widen it with a bit of electronic string. Consider these as the two ends of the spectrum and you've got the whole concept of autonomy levels. If you have the poor soldier sitting there with a weapon at the highest end, and he doesn't know what the thing is going to do, because it's going to go off and learn, then how can you hold him responsible?"

In 2011, Dave Blair, an Air Force officer studying for a PhD in international relations, pointed out the basic contradiction in US Air Force culture in an article in an Air Force journal. He called for the service to recognize that crews remotely operating Predator unmanned drones were suffering significant effects in combat, albeit with reduced risk to their bodies, and to award them combat medals as a means to improve their sense of accountability. The response was immediate, vociferous, and personal, declaring Blair's paper "ludicrous at best and insulting at worst." This culture leads to increased stress and decreased valuing of Predator ground crews.[411] Might this stress make the full automation of the ground crews' positions with AI appear more acceptable?

"In nine out of ten serious conversations on autonomous weapons I have had, whether in the bowels of the Pentagon or the halls of the United Nations, someone invariably mentions *The Terminator*," observed Paul Scharre, Director of Studies at the Center for a New American Security. "Sometimes it's an uncomfortable joke—the looming threat of humanity's extinction the proverbial elephant in the room. Sometimes the *Terminator* references are quite serious, with debates about where the Terminator would fall on the spectrum of autonomy."[412]

In 2017, the JASON group tasked with studying the implications of AI for the Department of Defense came to a similar conclusion. After an exhaustive analysis of the current state of the art in AI, they concluded: "The sheer magnitude, millions or billions of parameters […] which are learned as part of the training of the net […] makes it impossible to really understand how the network does what it does. Thus the response of the network to all possible inputs is unknowable."[413]

Of course, almost no one wants AI in charge of strategic nuclear weapons deployment—enough people have seen *The Terminator* to assure that. History is replete with terrifying near-misses where we dodged Armageddon by a virtual coin flip. On October 5th, 1960, the Moon rising over Norway appeared to the Ballistic Missile Early Warning System at the Thule, Greenland base as though the Soviets had launched a massive attack. Fortunately, Air Marshal C. Roy Slemon decided against escalating the alert because he knew that Soviet leader Nikolai Khrushchev was visiting the United Nations in New York and surely would not order an attack on a country he was in.[414] That information, of course, was not available to the automated strategic systems of the time, and illustrates just how unpredictable might be the type of information on which a high-stakes decision could pivot.

In 1983, Stanislav Petrov, sitting in the command center for the Soviet nuclear early-warning system, saw on his display a confirmed alert of five missiles approaching the USSR from the US. His procedures required him to report this up a chain of command, but he reasoned that if the US were going to launch a first strike it would send more than five missiles and waited instead, until it was confirmed to be a system malfunction. Had he reported it, his superiors would certainly have launched an all-out strike, prompting an equally massive counterstrike from the US. Had one of Petrov's peers been on shift, they would have followed protocol and reported the information immediately.[415] You are alive today almost certainly because of his action, for which he (much later) received the Dresden Peace Prize and the Future of Life Award.

Although we're sensitized to the folly of building Skynet, there is a more immediate automated weapon threat that we are far more likely to stumble into: weaponized autonomous drones. No movie brought those to public attention with the punch of *The Terminator,* so the Future of Life Institute made their own. Released to YouTube in 2017, *Slaughterbots* is an eight-minute-long video depicting the use and subversion of fist-sized drones armed with facial recognition technology and shaped explosives to execute political dissidents and student protestors *en masse* by exploding on contact with their heads. It was branded by CNN as "the most nightmarish, dystopian film of 2017," a description Professor Stuart Russell is quite proud of. He appears as the spokesman at the end of the dramatization, urging audiences to pressure their leaders to ban development of such technology.

Russell told me an anecdote as to why this is of immediate concern: "When we premiered the *Slaughterbots* film in Geneva, the Russian ambassador said, 'Why are we even talking about this? This kind of thing is twenty-five or thirty years in the future.' Three *weeks* later, STM announced the 'Kargu' drone, which is essentially a larger version of the slaughterbot. They advertised it as having autonomous kill capability against humans using face recognition and tracking etc. So everything we put in the movie, they advertised as a product."[416]

In December 2021, despite most of the members of the United Nations Convention on Certain Conventional Weapons favoring the drafting of new laws on these devices, vetoes from the US, Russia, and UK among others prevented that.[417]

Tony Gillespie pointed out what in hindsight seems obvious and yet has received remarkably little attention: "Military people talk about target identification; I think it's just as critical to have *non-target* identification. In other words, something that comes out and says, 'This is not a target. This is an ambulance.' … An autonomous system should be primed to look for things it can't do, as well as things it can do."

The development of autonomous weapons primes most people to think about *The Terminator*, but that blinds them to the real, more complex issues touched on in this section. It is entirely likely that such technology would eventually seep down from military use to local law enforcement, and trigger new and disturbing potentials for abuse.

16
Existential Risk

> *Any machine constructed for the purpose of making decisions, if it does not possess the power of learning, will be completely literal-minded…. [T]he machine, like the djinnee [in the bottle] will in no way be obliged to make such decisions as we should have made, or will be acceptable to us. For the man who is not aware of this, to throw the problem of his responsibility on the machine… is to cast his responsibility to the wind, and to find it coming back seated on the whirlwind.*[418]
>
> — Norbert Weiner

Perhaps you've been on a trip down a river that's punctuated by roaring rapids; it's a common pastime in North America to ride in a raft along them. Some people go over them in inflatable kayaks; like me, in Idaho on the Middle Fork of the Salmon River. Now imagine being reckless enough to be paddling such a kayak along a river that you have never previously explored and know nothing about. Floating along a calm stretch, you notice the limpid water starting to pick up the pace. Further along, you hear ahead of you a sound like giants sliding down a gravel mountain, and you realize that you are coming up on the Mother of All Rapids; from the sound of it, a cataract pouring through a canyon down a hundred feet of descent. And you have no choice but to go through it.

Faced with a similar situation with respect to our future with exponential technology, the reaction of many people is to attempt to change the course of the river.

I know this because in talk after talk, after I've outlined not just the benefits but the challenges and risks AI will present to us, someone in the audience will put on an If-I-Were-King hat (crown?) and propound, "We should halt/slow the development of AI." This is as realistic as redirecting the river. You're going to go over the rapids. But if you paddle at the right time, in the right direction, you may alter your course enough to make the difference between life and death.

We need to spend less energy trying to redirect the river and more energy learning how to paddle.

Who knows, we might come out the other end having had fun with it, if a bit soaked.

Complexity

I promised earlier that we would return to the concept of complexity when we were in an existential frame of mind. Renowned software architect Frederick P. Brooks Jr. said that "The complexity of software is an essential property, not an accidental one." Hundreds of years have elapsed since the span of all known knowledge was brief enough to be encompassed by a single human mind; now all significant projects of any kind are achieved only by figuring out how to split them across enough people that the cognitive load on any one person is manageable. What if there were projects that could only come to fruition if the cognitive capacity of individual humans was twice as great, because the project components cannot be subdivided further? We're finding those boundaries constantly, when project managers end up making individuals responsible for too much because they just can't figure out how to divide a task between multiple people, and so the individuals burn out.

Thomas Homer-Dixon, founder of the Cascade Institute existential risk think tank and author of *The Ingenuity Gap,* is concerned about complexity as an existential risk in itself. "We are creating degrees of complexity that have rendered the world around us opaque, highly unpredictable, and perhaps very dangerous," he said. "We're not responding to those problems with adequate solutions as fast as we need to. So a gap is opening up between the difficulty of the problems we're creating for ourselves and our ability to solve them."[419]

Safety professor Erik Hollnagel observed the increasing complexity of artificial systems and argued that "In a growing number of cases, we must stop taking for granted that we can find the cause when something has happened—or even that we can come up with a plausible explanation."[420] Nancy Leveson pointed out that the design of an automated system may make the system harder to manage *during a crisis.*[421] (Emphasis mine.)

Hans Rosling, author of *Factfulness: Ten Reasons We're Wrong about the World,* said that when we retreat to our respective corners, point fingers, and "identify the bad guy, we are done thinking. And it's almost always more complicated than that. It's almost always about multiple interacting causes—a system. If you really want to change the world, you have to understand [it]."[422]

Humans aren't wired to evaluate the statistical complexity of risks. We care a lot more about the tangible present than the distant future. Many of us do that to an extreme—what behavioral scientists call *hyperbolic discounting*—which makes it particularly hard to grapple with something like climate change, where the biggest dangers are yet to come. We would rather save a hundred dollars now than save the planet later. It's as though we're expecting that we won't be around in the future to experience what happens then—or that no one we care about will be, either.

Oxford philosopher Toby Ord, author of *The Precipice: Existential Risk and the Future of Humanity* said, "Given everything I know, I put the existential risk [of extinction] this century at around one in six: Russian roulette." One in six is also the chance that the *New York Times'* statistical analysis gave Donald Trump of becoming president of the United States on the *eve* of the 2016 election. Ord argues that our current sense of risk—such as when it is safe to cross a road—is insufficient to deal with threats that are so dire they must be minimized.

Complexity can create so many dimensions to a phenomenon that we can't see beyond the more innocuous ones; a problem can creep up on us in plain sight by appearing too silly to be worth considering. Author James Barrat worries that Hollywood has inoculated many of us from taking super AIs seriously by depicting them so preposterously. "Imagine if the Centers for Disease Control issued a serious warning about vampires," he notes. "It'd take time for the guffawing to stop, and the wooden stakes to come out."[423] AI keynote speaker Calum Chace edited *Stories from 2045,* a book of stories about the future, one of which had New York City being renamed Trump City (before being flooded by rising sea levels). We talked about how this sounds completely tongue-in-cheek;[424] yet the idea of Donald Trump becoming *president* was so tongue-in-cheek that it was funny enough to be in the storyline of an episode of *The Simpsons…* sixteen years before it happened for real.

We might, therefore, be done in by being unable to understand a threat. By analogy, computer programmers have a maxim that we should not be "too clever" when writing code, because the intelligence needed to understand code is greater than that required to write it. So something we write at the peak of our cleverness will elude our ability to make sense of it later. What if there is a macro equivalent of this principle that applies to our collectively creating AI that is too complex for us to understand?

The Control Problem

Machines take me by surprise with great frequency.

— Alan Turing

In 2011, the two top human champions of the TV game show *Jeopardy!* squared off against a single opponent, standing between them in the quiz show's three-player format. The third player did not feel trepidation at facing über-answerers Ken Jennings and Brad Rutter; it couldn't, because it was IBM's artificial intelligence, named Watson. Watson won handily, in a demonstration that carried several echoes of IBM's Deep Blue program's defeat of chess grandmaster Garry Kasparov nearly 15 years earlier. But for all Watson's stellar scores, it made mistakes no human player would have done. In one round, in the category "Name that Decade," the clue was, "The first modern crossword puzzle is published and Oreo cookies are introduced." Jennings buzzed in first, but gave the wrong answer: "What is the 1920s?"* This meant that Watson got a shot at answering, and it did: "What is the 1920s?"

Oops. It didn't occur to Watson's designers that the ability to learn from other contestants' *wrong* answers would be important. "We just didn't think it would ever happen," admitted Chris Welty, one of Watson's programmers, afterward.[425]

Humans cannot anticipate everything. It sounds painfully obvious to point that out, but try being the software designer in a stakeholder meeting where you're trying to make the case that the project should plan for a certain level of unanticipated problems, and experience for yourself how unbounded some people's faith can be in our power to predict the future with complete certainty.

---

* The correct answer is the 1910s.

AI safety expert Roman Yampolskiy propounds the principle that "An AI designed to do *X* will eventually fail to do *X*."[426] Study reports of accidents or failures and see how often the confession, "We didn't think of—" arises. Proper planning should include two axioms: (1) We can't predict everything that will happen; and (2) Something that we didn't predict or want to happen *will* happen. With experience, the *rate* at which the unpredictable happens may actually become predictable.

How do we make advances in science, and in particular computer software? How is it possible that each year, the programs we create become more and more capable? Listen to Isaac Newton: "If I have seen farther, it is because I have stood on the shoulders of giants." We do not get taller each year, and we do not get smarter; our software only becomes so because we are able to slide the window of what we *can* cognitively handle to a higher level of abstraction. In the 1980s, if you were programming a graphical user interface, you would have to think about the size, position, and color of every element; as a result, the interfaces were primitive. Now those decisions are made in reusable libraries whose shoulders you stand on, freeing you up to expend your finite energies on decisions like which machine learning model to deploy.

Watson's programmers were highly capable, creative, and top of their field. They did nothing wrong; it is simply impossible for humans to think of everything. Failures are inevitable (Yampolskiy's Law), but as our software gets more complex, the failures take place at higher levels of abstraction, because that's where our focus has shifted to. So a failure in, say, a car factory AI won't look like a miscolored pixel in a logo, or a temperature with a digit off by one. It's more likely to be something like putting the wrong wheel rims on a production line, or overflowing a parts storage bin.

Of course, the more advanced the AI, the more advanced the failure…

Trans-Science

Alvin Weinberg, former head of the Oak Ridge National Laboratory, hit on a core paradox of our relationship with science: "Many of the issues which arise in the course of the interaction between science or technology and society hang on the answers to questions which can be asked of science and yet *which cannot be answered by science.*" He wrote those words in 1972 to a largely indifferent audience. He gave examples of such questions, including "The Probability of Extremely Improbable Events," such as a catastrophic nuclear accident or earthquake.

Weinberg then gifted us with a useful label: "I propose the term 'trans-scientific' for these questions. Though they are, epistemologically speaking, questions of fact and can be stated in the language of science, they are unanswerable by science; they transcend science."[427] This may be the most succinct description of the essential difficulty of dealing with the existential risk of artificial intelligence: the probability of catastrophic outcome in specific timeframes is too hard to estimate.

An existential threat from AI could arise through scenarios that we could imagine, and others that we can't, or don't; the probability that there are far more threat scenarios in those latter categories is trans-scientific, but many believe it great enough to be worth investigation. Scenarios where we can imagine AI causing existential peril are often variations of philosopher Nick Bostrom's *Paperclip Maximizer*. This thought experiment takes place an indeterminate time in the future: An AI given charge of a paperclip factory is instructed to maximize paperclip production, a typically terse instruction tossed off by a typically terse boss to a plant manager. Being superintelligent, or evolving that capability by design or accident, the AI is able to analyze its environment and determine that there are many materials that have not yet been turned into paperclips (cars, bridges, airplanes), so it finds ways to process them. That the supply of paperclips far exceeds the demand is irrelevant; the AI was not instructed to consider demand. But it *will* act against any threat to the production of paperclips, like humans outraged at their homes being converted to paperclip factories.

Nothing in this scenario requires self-awareness or consciousness on the part of the AI, nor malevolence. This is not a Terminator AI; yet, as Eliezer Yudkowsky describes it, "The AI does not hate you, nor does it love you, but you are made out of atoms which it can use for something else."[428]

How far might the threat of a paperclip maximizer be in our future? Sorry, that is a trans-scientific question. Even the *Precautionary Principle* fails us. This is the maxim that our response to a threat should be proportional to the *expected consequences:* a statistical term meaning the possible consequences multiplied by their probability of happening. For example, commercial aviation accidents kill around two hundred people per year; we mitigate this risk with an infrastructure including bodies like the National Transportation Safety Board (NTSB), and so forth. What about an asteroid impact? They happen only about once every fifty million years, but the last one wiped out all higher life forms. Here come the statistics: If there were ten billion people on Earth at the time of such an impact, wiping out all of them once every fifty million years means that the expected number of deaths *per year* from asteroid impacts is ten billion divided by fifty million, which is two hundred.

So to a statistician—or underwriter—your odds of dying in an airplane accident are the same as your odds of being killed by an asteroid impact. Which is not a useful calculation to make, even for an underwriter who would find it hard to pay out claims after the destruction of the Earth; except that it *can* be used to decide how much we ought to spend mitigating its possibility: About what we spend on the NTSB, etc.

Why doesn't this get us anywhere with the existential threat of AI? Because we have no idea what that probability is. Sure, we can *guess* that it will be a lot less than fifty million years before AI becomes superintelligent; most expert guesses are around fifty years. But the Precautionary Principle cannot be used to justify a reaction to every threat we can dream up, like, say, an invasion of leprechauns from another dimension. It will, in fact, be a lot more than fifty million years to the next incursion of interdimensional leprechauns. We are simply very bad at dealing with very large numbers and very small probabilities.

The Value Alignment Problem

Have you ever taken part in an organizational effort to define the values for a work group or company; or have you perhaps laid out your own values in response to a coaching session or self-help book prompt? If so, you may recall the experience fondly… or not. It's hard work, even when successful. I'm not talking about the exercise to decide goals, but instead the task where you discover what's most important to you. People, such as family, friends, colleagues? Self-expression, such as curiosity, kindness, optimism? Abstractions, such as learning, intuition, love? It can take a while to find this out for yourself; but when a group undertakes that discovery, everyone around the table has their own set of personal values, yet they need to decide on what the group's collective values are and align those values with the individuals' values. Challenging.

AI existential risk researchers pursue an even more challenging version of that exercise; how to ensure that a future artificial superintelligence's (ASI) values are aligned with humanity's. To, for instance, avoid the Paperclip Scenario by instilling in AI a value of human life so it doesn't turn us all into paperclips. This is a hard problem to solve, not least because human values, quite clearly, aren't aligned with each other. Or we would all agree on the importance of addressing climate change and wars would never happen.

We can't even align our individual values with ourselves. Coaches and therapists are well aware of how each of us contains a constellation of personalities with different goals and values. Is the you that vowed to hit the gym at 6:30 AM the same you that rolled over in bed at 7:15 and smacked the snooze button?

Aligning our values with each other has been a problem for millennia, of course, but it will acquire a special aura when artificial superintelligences enter the fray. The reason that a significant number of researchers are engaged with this problem right now is that even though it is likely a long time before we will have to deal with it, both the consequences and the effort to remediate the problem are extreme.

If ASI acquires enormous power, how would we want it to use that power? Even apparently obvious applications like End World Hunger and Cure Climate Change could have side effects that are challenging to predict.* Conversely, if ASI could find a cure for cancer, would it be responsible to *not* use it to do so? Hardly anyone in the world has not been affected by cancer in some way, either directly or via a loved one. If you had the means to end cancer, what would that mean to you, personally? It is likely that within the next few decades, a cure for cancer will be within reach if we are willing to allow AI to become powerful enough to find it.

Like many other effects of AI, the Value Alignment Problem forces us to confront a deep age-old ethical question and look in the mirror. It's often compared to the tales of the Genie in the Lamp, and King Midas turning everything he touched into gold. "Be careful what you wish for" is the motto. Suppose you had an ASI that could grant your every wish. Do you tell it to protect you from harm? Suppose it then imprisons you in a bunker so you cannot get out to risk being hit by a car or catch a disease? Do you tell it you want to be happy? Does it now keep you on a heroin drip or electrically stimulate the pleasure center of your brain? If that's not what you wanted, how can you be specific enough to prevent those interpretations? You'd better be very clear about your own values first.

And should the ASI listen to the you of today, the you of yesterday, or the you that you might become tomorrow? If you blurt out one head-pounding morning, "Siri, never let me mix beer and tequila again," how should she determine that *that* you has the authority to override the one dancing past the open bar the following night? Rehabilitation centers are used to working with people to help them towards who they *want* to

---

* Stuart Russell provides an example of an AI that turns the sky orange in the process of fixing climate change, because no one thought to tell it that the color of the sky is important to us.

be in the future, and understanding that what the drug addict says they want today is different from what they will value when they are clean. If an ASI were smart enough to calculate with complete certainty that you would eventually thank it for stopping you from consuming sugar, coffee, and processed foods for a year, should it align to your values today, or the ones you will have a year from now?

You can see how this keeps philosophers busy.

◊

OpenAI, the makers of GPT-3, can already see a path to existential risk, and they're addressing it now. In a blog posting announcing openings for machine learning engineers and researchers, team lead Paul Christiano spoke directly to alignment, saying that GPT-3's misalignment mattered to OpenAI's bottom line, going on:

> If our research succeeds I think it will directly reduce existential risk from AI. This is not meant to be a warm-up problem, I think it's the real thing.
>
> We are working with state-of-the-art systems that could pose an existential risk if scaled up, and our team's success actually matters to the people deploying those systems.[429]

Christiano is now head of the nonprofit Alignment Research Center. But you don't need to run a research center to help solve the alignment problem. AI won't stay in isolated pockets, influencing only small segments of society. The electrification of thinking dictates that it will perfuse everyone's life, creating alignment problems everywhere there is a person with values to align to—in other words, you. The clearer you are about your values and how they align to the people you interact with in life, the easier it will be to integrate AI into that life.

It's human nature to magnify our focus on negative risks, and they don't come any larger than existential threats, so giant philosophical quandaries such as the Value Alignment Problem come in for outsized attention. But this doesn't mean that the risks of AI are disproportionately negative; they are at least equally positive, and match the threats pound-for-pound all the way out to the potential for finding a path to immortality. Andrew Critch proposes that AI that can have these civilization-changing impacts be termed *transformative intelligence*. Which is a good lead-in to looking at how we can not just survive, but thrive through the transformations brought by AI.

17
Thrive

Our job is not to toughen our children up to face a cruel and heartless world. Our job is to raise children who will make the world a little less cruel and heartless.

— L.R. Knost

Having looked at human levels of aggregation through the lens of survival, let's revisit them with a larger goal. If AI posed only a threat, a risk, it would be appropriate to focus on how to proscribe it. But we are talking about a technology which is likely to cure cancer, disease, even death; a technology whose upside is at least as great as its downside. Mastering that upside, surfing the wave, is a goal to aim for not only in the uncertain future, but right now. Which means that it's time to rewind to the first aggregation level.

Individual

I don't see the world as it is: I see it as I am.

— Anaïs Nin

In 2021 I was diagnosed with a basal cell carcinoma. The news was neither earth-shattering nor threatening; shed no tears. The point is, if you looked at the collection of cells on my forehead (before they were excised), they were behaving very successfully. They were multiplying at twice the rate of their noncancerous neighbors. They were the entrepreneurs of body cells. Yet that very growth threatened my health. Global success cannot be determined by how well isolated groups perform individually; like a carcinoma, the success of one organization could threaten the survival of our entire species if it isn't aligned with the common welfare. Our future with AI will depend more on individuals working together than separately.

Imagine you are preparing for an expedition to the Amazon, or the Outback, or the Andes. How does this make you feel? I'll wager that there's some trepidation, some anticipation, some nerves—a lot of raw energy coursing through your body, sharpening your senses, reminding you of how good it is to be alive. You may know something about where you're going—you may know whether to pack crampons or a canoe—but I'll also wager that that most of that élan is springing from what you *don't* know: the unknown that you're about to face, even though it carries a risk of danger or even death.

In 2020 we faced another unknown, with a risk of danger or death: The COVID-19 pandemic. Not so fun. What's the difference?

Exploration is when you visit the unknown. Disruption is when the unknown visits *you*.

The difference is *agency*: a sense of control. It's arguably an illusory sense; after all, the more unknown you face on your exploring, the more zest to the experience, right? But you still see that exploration as your choice.

This is a critical distinction to make in preparing for a disruptive future made increasingly uncertain through the exponential growth of technologies such as AI. Your success in a future of evolving artificial intelligence will depend less on your individual strength, and more on your skills at communicating, empathizing, and collaborating with those around you and across the world. AI holds up a mirror to us, allowing us to see who we are and to ask who we want to be in a future of smart machines. But you have to want to look and not be afraid of what you see.

If you think that assertion is overblown, look over the previous sections of this book to see how AI is bringing hard questions to us: Will I have a job—*What's my real purpose?* Will disinformation overwhelm our social structures?—*How do I know what's really true?* Will AI escape our control?—*Can we be trusted with its power?* These are weighty questions that most people never signed up for, never thought about, and, save for a minority who pursue growth avenues such as life coaching, never expected to answer. And being forced to answer them when their job is suddenly automated is one of the worst times to start.

The way to surf this wave instead of drowning under it is to find a sense of agency. Don't wait for the change to find you! Let us name this surfing *conscious futurism*. Futurists may seem like an elite group, all turtlenecks and talk shows, but it's time to bust open the clique. We *all* need to become futurists. By which I mean: take a conscious approach to our future. Don't assume that it's the sole province of policymakers or people who have claimed the role of "thought leader"; don't cede that agency to them, but try out for yourself the role of consciously crafting and owning your future. The boundaries of what truly lies within your control may lie further than you thought.

No longer can we blindly assume that tomorrow will be the same as today. When I was in high school, the teachers could prepare us for just about any career because at that time it was possible to predict the trajectory of most careers for a good twenty years. But a 2017 study from Dell and the Institute for the Future said that 85 percent of the jobs that would exist in 2030 hadn't been invented yet.[430]

Of course, that also implies that many of today's jobs will no longer exist by 2030. How can you claim some agency over this upheaval? Become aware, informed, and active. Surface your fears and meet them head-on: How realistic is it that automation will threaten your job, and how soon? Can you find a purpose that is immune to any such threat? If you like ice cream, and I tell you that I have a machine that can eat ice cream better than you—faster, no drips, less slurping—do you give up eating ice cream? Does it matter that you have competition? As Garry Kasparov points out, there are many machines on Earth faster than Usain Bolt's top speed of 30 mph. So what—does he stop running?[431] Would the news that a machine is now doing something that you had thought was reserved for humans cause you to feel alienated by that vocation, when in reality no rejection took place? Or is there something so important to you that you will do it regardless of whether or not a machine is also doing it?

It's not enough that a machine *could* do your job; it also has to be a task we *want* to automate, and it has to be one that is *cost-effective* to automate. To illustrate how this matters, look at the examples in what I call the *Trivergence of Automation* (see Figure 17.1).

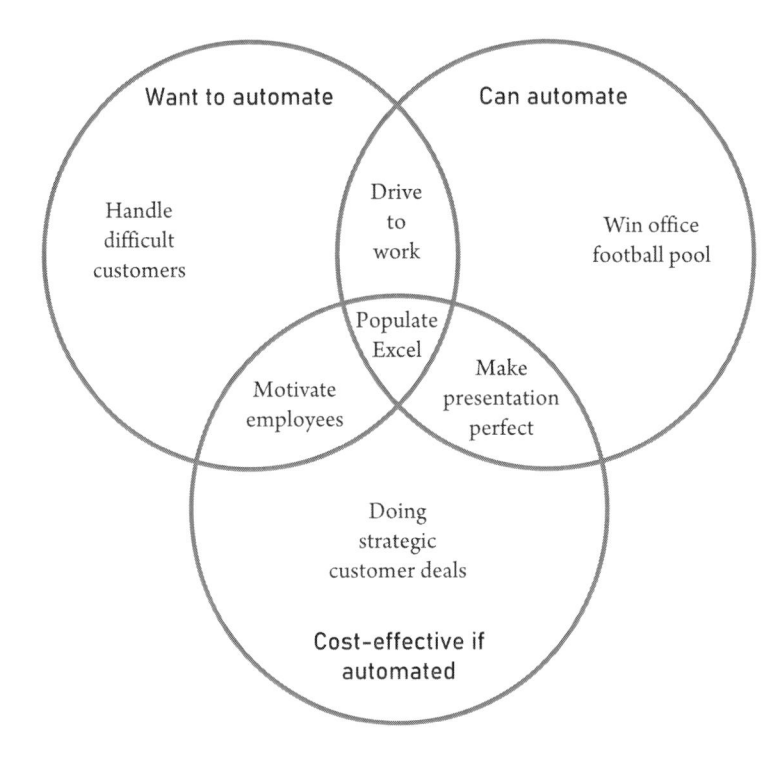

Figure 17.1: Trivergence of Automation

Move as much of your professional life outside of that intersection as possible. Jobs and tasks that demand the most creative and empathetic of human interaction—coaching, mentoring, counseling, active listening—will be the most resistant to automation.

Be resistant to disinformation; we are still at the earliest stages of the weaponization of free speech. Two Cambridge researchers found that the single most important determinant of our ability to resist persuasion is "the ability to premeditate." This means that people who harness self-awareness to think through the consequences of their actions are more disposed to chart their own course and are significantly less vulnerable to persuasion techniques. The second highest factor on their scale was *commitment*. People who are consciously committed to a course of action or a set of principles are less likely to be persuaded to do something that violates that commitment.[432]

To a certain type of person, these new parameters will be exciting, exhilarating; they will define a world where people are rewarded more for initiative than rule-following, more for creativity than step-following, more for good judgement than script-following.

Be that type of person.

Family and Community

> *Human beings can do everything that AI can do. They just can't do it to scale.*
>
> — Anne Marie Neatham, COO of Ocado Technology

The educational system is in dire need of overhaul. It's no longer useful to train children to remember facts or perform calculations that Google and Wolfram Alpha and Wikipedia put at their fingertips anywhere on Earth, unless we somehow run out of all other ways of training young minds to make new neural connections. It makes as much sense to learn how to extract a cube root with pencil and paper or to determine lines of sight on a contour map (both skills I learned in high school) today as it does to teach shoe cobbling (a far more marketable skill a hundred years ago). Some say teaching children to use electronic tools will leave them helpless if they are stranded on a desert island. In that case, shouldn't we be teaching them how to make dugout canoes and coconut underwear?

Instead, skate to where the puck is going to be: take your best shot at where the world *will* be when they graduate and prepare them for *that*.

Today's children will enter a workplace with AI as a constant companion; they will need to know how to use it as much as we need to know how to drive. Why would any school not now be teaching children how to get the most out of the panoply of internet tools to find answers as rapidly as possible, instead of stuffing a tiny subset of those answers into their brains?

To find an example of that already working, go to Finland: Their education system teaches AI from *grade one.* Code School Finland provides such a curriculum, and in 2020 entered into a partnership with the Chinese Ministry of Education to put AI education on that country's basic education agenda, starting in kindergarten.[433]

While you're there, take a look at how the Finns begin educating children to spot disinformation in *primary school.* And it's working: Finland was rated Europe's most resistant nation to fake news.[434] Their lesson plans include how to properly vet sources (no Wikipedia!) and the anatomy of disinformation campaigns. In a not-even-thinly-veiled swipe at the 2016 Brexit Vote Leave campaign's tour bus ad (which claimed that Britain paid the European Union £350 million per week), seventeen-year-old Alexander said the class mattered "because you end up with wrong numbers on the side of a bus, and voters who believe them." If AI-magnified disinformation is in their future, that's the kind of education I want my children to get.

Organization

> *The emergence of the age of AI has possibly created the greatest entrepreneurial opportunity in the history of civilization.*[435]
>
> — Marco Iansiti

Surfing the wave of change in a business requires recognizing the key dynamics that dynocognesis interposes in business processes. For instance, look at any workflow you have, and measure how long it typically takes to execute. If it involves only software talking to software, it likely runs in seconds, unless it hits repositories that are only resynchronized on longer timescales. But if there is a human in the loop, it will take hours at best, unless you orient a great deal of organization and expense around those humans. Think about the difference between ordering something from Amazon and renewing a driver's license. When you hit Submit Order, that order may be packaged within minutes; but how many hands does the license pass through, to eventually be printed in some special facility and inspected, again by humans?

Now think of a workflow within your business, if you're part of a large enterprise: How many steps involve the approval of a person? Those are where the workflow's velocity is strangled—and it's not those people's fault. From their perspective they are running through their task queues as quickly and efficiently as possible, and from the moment they log on in the morning or come back from lunch to when they start an approval it may take only minutes. They're operating at top speed. But the accumulation of times spent waiting for each human to get to their task will turn seconds into days.

What if you had enough data to train an AI to perform one of those approval steps? All of them? The possibility exists that you could return a final decision to the requester while they are still looking at the screen after clicking Submit. This is the principle followed by some businesses that are disrupting traditionally human-workflow-bound sectors like automobile insurance claim adjusting. Auto insurance giant GEICO is adopting an app from Tractable which uses AI to assess damage instantly from pictures. Tractable and its competitors are reducing the time for claim estimation from days to minutes; Spanish insurer Admiral Seguro uses Tractable to deliver offers while the customer's first phone call is in progress.[436]

This transforms the customer relationship from an *asynchronous* interaction to a *synchronous* one; changing your customer experience from going off to do something else while you wait an arbitrary amount of time for another party to act, to receiving a response in a predictable and brief period so you complete your interaction in a single session. Tired of waiting to speak to a customer service representative on the phone? How many times can you hear "Your call is important to us" before you stop believing it? It's not going to get any better while those representatives are human, because they're paid by the hour, and if they were sitting at their desk twiddling their thumbs waiting for the phone to ring, they'd be costing the business more than it likely wants to pay. So the business manages the staffing to ensure that the call-takers are always busy, which, due to the unpredictability of callers, *guarantees* there will always be a wait.

But AI does not work whole shifts or get paid by the hour; it can be scaled up and down instantaneously and therefore can answer the phone on the first ring. For example, SEV, a major Swedish bank, now uses a virtual assistant called Aida* to interact with millions of customers who no longer need to wait for a customer service representative. "She" can answer questions such as how to open an account or make cross-border payments.[437]

Your power to thrive through leveraging AI hinges on how much data you own. Law professor Ted Parson described how important this is:

> There's this commonplace trope in AI debates now when people worry about concentration of power and antitrust and monopolization and leveraging of existing power to broader mechanisms of power, that the constrained resource for enterprise isn't capital anymore, it's data. Data is going to be subject to much stronger concentration and economies of scale and scope than capital ever was. So the shift to the important resource being data is going to be a shift toward more and more natural concentration of economic power in the economy.[438]

If you're still measuring the state of the enterprise with static reports, that's as useful now as gauging the performance of a sports car through a snapshot. It's time to move beyond position and measure *velocity:* Not just where any metric of your business is, but how fast it is moving. So you know where to aim for the puck. Set the expectation that every measurement should be accompanied by its rate of change. To establish the culture that will support that kind of change might take some new roles; perhaps starting with a Chief Futurism Officer will put a stake in the ground that says you're serious about this.

---

* A *lot* of AIs have been called AIda. If you need to name one, please try to come up with something else. AIleen? AIvy? AIrene? Alright, so I'm not in the branding business.

Any data, not just customer relationship management or production line data, can be helpful. Udacity cofounder and Google self-driving car creator Sebastian Thrun and his graduate student Zayd Enam analyzed chat room conversations between sales people and customers to predict what answer the most successful salespeople were likely to give in response to certain very common inquiries. After a thousand training cycles, they shared the results with the other salespeople, who increased their effectiveness by 54 percent, and were able to serve twice as many customers at a time.[439]

Remember that AI can find patterns that even expert humans might not, if there is enough data. General Electric's Predix uses copious data about their industrial steam turbines to identify unexpected rotor wear and tear in an engine turbine. It can check the turbine's operational history, find a pattern of increasing damage, and report that if nothing is done, the rotor will lose a large proportion of its useful life.[440] It can spot patterns before they are visible to human inspectors.

Beyond the data needed for the business line, there is the obligation of the company to be a good citizen in a hyperconnected and interrelated world. The rate at which that obligation is becoming more complex causes its own change in the culture of an organization. Environmental, social, and governance (ESG) expert Charles Radclyffe told me that after a company successfully negotiates an ESG crisis, "the culture is very much that there is still a compliance department, a group of people who focus on solving those challenges; but it's everyone's problem." The insight here is that the transformation we are undergoing will become ingrained across the entire workforce, and the sooner a business gets with that program, the faster it will emerge from the other side. Just as the introduction of electrical power didn't mean that a business appointed one person to oversee the plugging-in of all appliances, but rather, everyone learned what they needed to about electricity. "Everyone is a compliance officer in their own respective way," he concluded.

But the larger transformation of the business to pivot around AI does need dedicated roles and responsibilities. Andrew Ng wrote in November 2016 that every company needs a Chief AI Officer.[441] A search of LinkedIn for that position returns 12,600 results.

There is little incentive to focus on trying to eliminate entire job classes in your business; almost no jobs are composed only of tasks that are likely to be completely automated soon. Look instead to identify where AI strength can complement human strengths and create the opportunity for partnerships.

Revisiting Maslow

Plans are worthless, but planning is everything.

— President Dwight D. Eisenhower

Earlier I mentioned Abraham Maslow's Hierarchy of Needs (see Chapter 15). His pyramid (see Figure 17.1) asserts that the lower levels must be fulfilled before the higher levels can be attended to, and this is a truism for individuals; no one is going to be taking relationship seminars if they can't make the rent. And it might also appear vacuously true for businesses; it's a long-established maxim, for instance, that the budget for outside training consultants is the first to get the axe when times are lean.

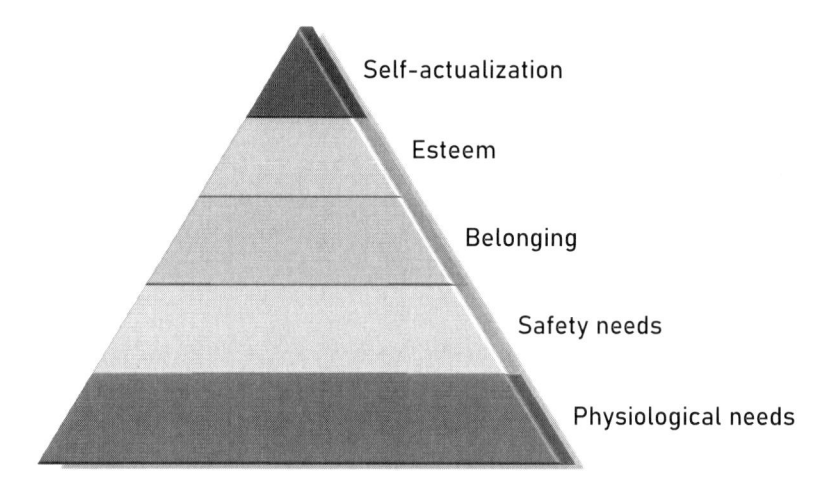

Figure 17.1: Maslow's Hierarchy of Needs

But when we consider the transformation of the workplace that AI could cause, *the pyramid inverts*. The business's employees will be adopting more creative and empathetic human communication; their outward-facing representatives will be focusing on the relationships with customers and other businesses; and the executives will be taking pains to understand the psychology of their employees so that their staff are neither sidelined by misinformation nor paralyzed by the thought of being made redundant by automation. These traits all inhabit the *highest* levels of Maslow. And the business that does not follow that path, whose leaders don't dig deep into their souls to present themselves authentically to employees who need to know who they're working for and why, will not survive.

Country

It's not necessary to change. Survival is not mandatory.

— W. Edwards Deming

National AI strategies are flowering around the world; we learned earlier how ambitious the Chinese one is. The Obama-era National Science and Technology Council's (NSTC) report, after twenty-three specific recommendations, concluded that government should:

- Convene conversations about important issues and help to set the agenda for public debate;
- Monitor the safety and fairness of applications as they develop, and adapt regulatory frameworks to encourage innovation while protecting the public;
- Support basic research and the application of AI to public goods, as well as the development of a skilled, diverse workforce;
- Use AI itself, to serve the public faster, more effectively, and at lower cost.

In 2021 the Trump administration launched the National Artificial Intelligence Initiative Office, and subsequently, the Biden administration's National Artificial Intelligence Research Task Force will be presenting a national AI strategy and implementation plan in December 2022.[442]

In Great Britain, the All-Party Parliamentary Group on Artificial Intelligence (APPG-AI) was formed in January 2017, led by Member of Parliament Stephen Metcalfe and Lord (Tim) Clement-Jones. Since then, it has been meeting frequently in the House of Lords, bringing half a dozen speakers on a wide range of AI topics each time to "give evidence," in their parlance. Speaking there myself at the last in-person meeting before the pandemic forced them to move online, I can personally attest, from their penetrating and precise questions, that the APPG-AI's leaders by now must rank among the most highly-informed and educated (about AI) national legislators in the world. The fact that the group had not run out of topics more than five years after starting is telling evidence as to the breadth of questions raised by AI.

Meanwhile in Canada, in 2017, the federal government established a pan-Canadian artificial intelligence strategy. The country incubates several world-leading centers of academic excellence in AI and attracted leading researchers such as Geoffrey Hinton. In 2018 it financed an

AI-powered "Supply Chains Supercluster" based in Quebec to bring together industry and technology sectors to develop "intelligent supply chains" to support export opportunities for small and medium size businesses.[443] The efforts paid off; by 2020 Canada ranked fourth on the Global AI Index out of fifty-four countries.[444] The government is using AI to accelerate its own processes: according to law professor Ted Parson, machine-learning-based systems are already used to adjudicate immigration, citizenship and refugee claims, for example, in Employment and Citizenship Canada.

World

> *We have modified our environment so radically that we must now modify ourselves in order to exist in this new environment.*
>
> — Norbert Weiner, 1954

There are heartening signs of global cooperation on artificial intelligence. In 2018, Canadian Prime Minister Justin Trudeau and French President Emmanuel Macron started the Global Partnership on AI, officially launching it in 2020 with fifteen member countries including the US and UK, and establishing centers of expertise in Montreal and Paris.[445] So far, their work includes working groups on five important topics of global concern:

- Responsible AI;
- Data governance;
- The future of work;
- Innovation and commercialization;
- AI and the pandemic response.

The debate about autonomous weapons is still nascent. Recommendation twenty-three of the NSTC's 2016 report says, "The US Government should complete the development of a single, government-wide policy, consistent with international humanitarian law, on autonomous and semi-autonomous weapons." This may be disingenuous; there are no dedicated principles in IHL with respect to autonomous weapons as yet,[446] neither is there an agreed IHL definition of "autonomous weapon."[447]

◊

Compared to the antediluvian ignorance of disinformation that prevailed in the public sphere until 2018 or so, we have made astounding progress; merely naming its forms gives the victimized a vocabulary and more of a voice. If you don't have the word "gaslighting" as a shared label, it's hard to get attention when it has been done to you.

The non-profit Global Disinformation Index, started in 2018, performs the enormous and contentious task of "looking at disinformation through the lens of adversarial narratives that undermine trust in our social, political, economic and scientific institutions," as founder Alexandra Mousavizadeh told me. "People who want to impact societies in a negative way are far ahead," she said. The GDI aims to disrupt, defund and down-rank disinformation sites. GDI fights back by identifying where the advertising of reputable businesses appears embedded in disinformation and making that information available to the advertiser. Mousavizadeh explained their methodology:

> There are millions of fields that that we trawl through a fishing net, if you will, that look at from a technical metric perspective what are the characteristic markers of disinformation.
>
> You look at the location: Is it from somewhere that might be slightly obscure; is it only two weeks old but it has two hundred thousand posts: there's something off, right? You look at ownership, you look at the structure of the platform: There are no bylines, it was established a minute ago, it has very, very high volume—those usually are markers for disinformation. We have about thirty of those markers.[448]

What of AI solving existential threats? Jason Hein and Curtis Berlinguette at the University of British Columbia developed Ada, an AI that can perform experiments, analyze data, and interpret results to perform research to try to mitigate climate change.[449] Started with an $8 million grant in 2018, Ada is now directing a search for breakthroughs in material science.[450]

Science fiction author David Gerrold put this kind of research in a characteristically sweeping context: "If we take responsibility for things like climate change, for things like preventing extinctions, for things like managing and living in harmony with the ecology of this planet … we'd be functioning as a sentient *species*, which has never existed before anywhere on this planet."[451]

Empires in Transition

> *We all know what to do; we just don't know how to get reelected after we've done it.*
>
> — Jean-Claude Juncker, President of the European Commission

Thomas Homer-Dixon, founder of the Cascade Institute for existential crisis mitigation and author of *Commanding Hope: The Power We Have to Renew a World in Peril,* told me of a parallel between today and a transformation that took place over two thousand years ago:

> One of the points I make in *Commanding Hope* is that we are at a cusp moment in the deep character of our species. There was a period of time that was highlighted by the German existential historian Karl Jaspers in his work in the 1930s, '40s, and '50s: he called it the *Axial Age.* It was from about 600 BCE to 200 BCE, when five human civilizations more or less simultaneously all went through a kind of cosmological transition, a deep transition in their understanding of reality. The really interesting thing is those five civilizations really weren't communicating very much with each other at the same time. And yet, they all made this move during this period of time, in a very similar direction that laid the groundwork for, among other things, monotheism, across these civilizations.
>
> And this isn't a novel idea; many people have said this, but I think we are on the cusp of something potentially similar. And the "we" at the end of the process is going to be different from the "we" at the beginning of the process. And I use "we" quite intentionally to refer to the entire species. This is going to be a process of extraordinary maturation; or we're going to die. It's going to be simple as that. Right now, we're behaving like adolescents; as a species, we think we're invulnerable, we're not thinking about the future, and we're trashing the place. But it's becoming very clear that we're going to kill ourselves. Is that going to provide us with the new framework in which we learn to live on this planet as a mature species, as opposed to an adolescent one? Maybe that's the beginning of what you could call the Second Axial Age, and that would happen over the rest of this century and into the next.[452]

It's not hard to look at today's headlines of international strife and strutting and see the truth in Homer-Dixon's assertion that it's time to grow up or perish. The exciting flip side of this is that success will mean that we enter an era unlike any before, to reap the benefits of a technology we have become worthy of owning.

18
Future Tense

If mankind is not to perish, we must build the earth.

— Pierre Teilhard de Chardin

Our visions of the future are, almost certainly, all wrong.

Not just for what the technology will become, but for what *we* will become. The idea that humans surrounded by sophisticated artificial intelligence remain personally unchanged is what historian Michael Bess dubs the *Jetsons Fallacy*.[453] That cartoon showed a typical 1960s middle America nuclear family with typical 1960s desires, conflicts, and patois, only with shiny spacesuits. Substitute dinosaurs for robots and you have *The Flintstones;* subtract both and you have *The Honeymooners.*

The issue isn't that we shouldn't expect more from a TV cartoon; it's that if it had portrayed the kind of people we were to become even just fifty years later it would have been incomprehensible. Not shocking, not overwhelming, not cryptic: simply unrelatable, in the same way that even after translating Shakespeare's *forsooths* and *egads* into modern argot, some of the values and priorities of his characters only make sense when viewed through a generously-educated historical lens. For another example, look at how differently we started to see America's founding fathers and other empire builders with a perspective of inclusivity and equity, between 2015 and 2020.

AI will change us in ways that today's fiction writers won't predict, sometimes because no one would want to read the result. I had this exchange with Judith and Garfield Reeves-Stevens, authors of *Star Trek* novels and screenplays:

> **Peter:** Are there areas of the future that science fiction doesn't try to predict because the stories are harder to invent or harder to make interesting? Do you think there are blind spots in science fiction because it's just too hard to tell stories about what you think might nevertheless be a plausible future?
>
> **Garfield:** Yes, tons of blind spots. Fred Pohl actually wrote a story after a conversation like this with John W. Campbell Jr., saying how it was impossible to actually write about the future because we can't conceive of it. He wrote a very short story[454] about a guy a thousand years in the future, and it was absolutely incomprehensible because all the terms changed, all the technology changed. And so when we write, we have to write in a way that it is accessible to people today.[455]

How many *Star Trek* episodes, for instance, contain a realistic depiction of what a future with even a slight extrapolation of today's AI capabilities would necessarily entail?* Or would the suspense be diluted by the presence of machines that could figure out negotiating strategy, military conflicts, and medical treatments faster than any human? Arguably, it isn't science fiction's job to prepare us for the future, but little else assumes that responsibility in the public arena.

We need more people dedicated to thinking about this. One who is already doing that kind of thinking is law professor Ted Parson, who mused about where to draw the line between not being able to predict the future and not trying:

> Must one not speak about likely or possible trajectories of events in the latter half of this century? No, that's clearly not the right answer. Can you speak with utter unconditional confidence about what's going to happen in 2080? Goodness, no. But in between, there is relevant knowledge, there is a kind of a reasonably-founded constraint upon the vast space of possibilities that you have to work in to do contingency planning or strategic thinking. There's a reason that military planners have long engaged in specula-

---

* The hand-held communicators in the 1968 original series were equaled long before the 23rd century, with the 1996 arrival of the clamshell mobile phone. Leonard Nimoy could not use his in public without attracting the amusement of onlookers.

tive game-like scenario exercises to think about future threats. Because they understand that they won't be exactly the same as the last one, and thus they need new devices to expand thinking about the nature and causation of threats and the efficacy of different responses. And that reasoning very much generalizes to societal impacts of technology.

So now, at an obvious risk of being wrong, I'll offer a prediction for the medium term, of how our interaction with computers will be transformed by AI.

The Farm, the Supermarket, and the Restaurant

We have seen two major paradigms of interaction between humans and computers. For the first forty to fifty years, **The Farm** paradigm prevailed: you had to meet the computer on its own terms to get it to do what you wanted. Like the *Little House on the Prairie* family feeding itself by plowing, seeding, watering, and harvesting from its own field, you had to go plow the field of the computer if you wanted to harvest its bounty. Computers were the size of a truck, kept in hermetically-sealed rooms too frigid for human habitation, and were attended by a protective entourage of highly-trained specialists. Before a computer would give you the time of day—literally—you had to study a wall of manuals written for Electrical Engineering graduates.

The advent of the personal computer changed little at first: the computers were much smaller, the manuals slightly smaller, and the superciliousness of the experts undiminished. The PC inherited the Farm paradigm from its mainframe parent. It was still expected that if you wanted the computer to do your bidding, you were the one who had to learn.

But the PC did sow the seeds of the next revolution, with standard bearers like Steve Jobs and Jony Ive. And a new paradigm emerged: **The Supermarket.** No more pulling weeds in the Back Forty; instead, it was all brought to a convenient location near you, packaged for your consumption. The expectation in computing now is that the computer must be easy to use, must be adapted to the language, expectations, and foibles of humans. The entourage dissipated, to be replaced first by user interface (UI) and then by user experience (UX) experts, who engineer the customer-facing parts of computers so that they are as easy to use as possible. If an application requires a manual to use, it is likely to be sidelined by a competitor that doesn't. When did you even last see a manual come with software? With the exception of huge enterprise data systems, software assistance is generally left to vendor websites and smart search engines.

But for all its convenience, the Supermarket is one-size-fits-all; every product is designed to meet the needs of an anonymous, homogeneous population. Computer software is engineered to be as usable as possible by a hypothetical customer representing the median of the market. It must be this way because the software does not know who is using it; it is effectively blind and deaf to the person behind the keyboard.

This will change with AI, which will drive a third paradigm: **The Restaurant.** The food is brought to your table, and it is cooked exactly to your specification (this is a fancy establishment; no fast food). Gluten-free? Eggs poached firm? Dairy protein A2 only? Steak crusted with your favorite blend of herbs? It will be the best of the Farm—prepared just for you.

Computers will understand their users, adapt themselves to whoever is using them at the time, adjust their language patterns and level of sophistication accordingly; they will know *you*. If you are a detail-oriented person they will spout as much information as possible; if you are a big-picture sort they will summarize. For example, Tesla cars frequently update their onboard software, which controls virtually every function of the vehicle; they then proudly display a list of the updates the next time the driver gets in the car. To a techie such as myself, information such as an improvement of energy management is catnip. To the person who sees the car as a means to get from point A to point B, rather than a rolling supercomputer, this is confusing and superfluous.

Suppose instead that the car knew the preference of the driver; and not merely as yet another switch buried in the Settings menu, but as an attribute of the driver that follows that person through all environments and is available as soon as they are recognized? Just as there are now libraries of code designed by UI experts that encapsulate much of the difficulty of making a friendly interface,[*] in the future there will be code libraries that facilitate adapting to the individual, courtesy of personal data gathered from their digital assistants and social media. Not a future as distant and speculative as the one when AI becomes conscious and competes with us for control of the planet; but neither one that's in danger of happening before this book hits the stores. Somewhere in between.

---

[*] If you saw the interface of a program designed by a typical computer programmer like myself before these libraries appeared, you would appreciate their impact.

What's in an Abbreviation?

"Artificial intelligence" has been a label that we have hung far too much responsibility on. As I said in Chapter 4, things might have been very different if it had been labeled with some other pair of words, and some people have suggested alternatives that keep the AI abbreviation. Many people have come up with "augmented intelligence"—an AI that enhances our abilities but doesn't carry the connotation of competing with them. Richard Foster-Fletcher, the MKAI Inclusive AI Community founder, likes "alternative intelligence," which minimizes the possibility of AI being "othered," or treated as a suspicious outsider. Entrepreneur Simon Birrell calls the Internet of Things "ambient intelligence," and we can imagine, at the expense of some dystopian fright, that at some point the IoT and AI merge into a collective omnipresent computing engine.

Taiwan's Digital Minister, Audrey Tang, suggested "assistive intelligence," to imply a clearly subordinate role. Think of the decade-or-more time anyone entering the field as a medical researcher requires to gain the necessary experience. In earlier times it was reasonable to aspire to lead a group by one's early thirties, but in the United States medical community now, it is unusual to get your first research grant before the age of forty. And that poses a problem for human creativity. Three researchers studied the ages of scientists when they made their greatest contribution, such as a Nobel Prize, and plotted a curve that peaked at age thirty-seven.[456] What could it mean for scientific research if assistive intelligence could compress the learning period before scientists can make new discoveries?

Development Trends and Avenues

There is little progress and much speculation on how we could create artificial general intelligence; one avenue that gets a lot of attention is the possibility of modeling the human brain to sufficient fidelity such that whatever gives our brains that magic spark will show up in the machine versions as a by-product.

Some think that the process is straightforward. Few names in AI are as pivotal as Geoffrey Hinton, who drove the neural network and deep learning revolutions nearly single-handedly. He is one representative of the viewpoint that we will be able to replicate the human brain with existing technology executed at sufficient scale, adding, "But we also need a massive increase in scale. The human brain has about a hundred trillion parameters, or synapses. What we now call a really big model, like GPT-3, has a hundred and seventy-five billion. It's a thousand times smaller than the brain. GPT-3 can now generate pretty plausible-looking text, and it's still tiny compared to the brain."[457] Disagreeing with him is Steven Pinker, who says we will not get AGI by scaling up deep learning: "Sheer processing power is not a pixie dust that magically solves all your problems."

Some researchers adopt a hybrid approach, merging machines and biology. The Neu-ChiP project was awarded €3.5 million to show how neurons can be harnessed to supercharge computers' ability to learn while dramatically cutting energy use. The human brain, after all, accomplishes more than we can do with a supercomputer the size of a building, and all with a twenty-watt power supply. It does not need a nearby river to cool it, and you can run it all day on a burrito.

So the Neu-ChiP research team is embarking on a three-year study to demonstrate how human brain stem cells grown on a microchip can be taught to solve problems from data. They will layer networks of stem cells resembling the human cortex onto microchips, and then stimulate the cells by firing changing patterns of light beams at them. Sophisticated 3-D computer modelling will allow them to observe any changes the cells undergo, to see how adaptable they are. This imitates human neuroplasticity, our brain's seemingly limitless ability to rewire itself. "Our aim is to harness the unrivalled computing power of the human brain to dramatically increase the ability of computers to help us solve complex problems," said professor of Mathematics David Saad. "We believe this project has the potential to break through current limitations of processing power and energy consumption to bring about a paradigm shift in machine learning technology."[458]

Everyone, it seems, wants to build a brain. The Human Brain Project started in 2011, costing over a *billion* euros, aiming to simulate the human brain at all levels. The American BRAIN initiative started in 2013 to progress neuroscience and understanding of brain disorders through advanced scanning and modeling. China's Brain Project started in 2015 and is expected to run for fifteen years.

And a Swiss project, the Blue Brain Project (running on an IBM Blue Gene supercomputer), aims to construct a digital model of the human brain by 2023. So far it has simulated a mouse cortex, and helpfully equates the human brain to "one thousand rat brains," which ought to give people and rats alike pause for thought.[459]

But now let's go beyond the current constraints, and think about what it would be like when we *do* have artificial general intelligence.

Artificial General Intelligence

> *A year spent in artificial intelligence is enough to make one believe in God.*
>
> — Alan Perlis

In 2014, the TED conference and the X Prize foundation announced an award for "the first artificial intelligence to come to the stage and give a TED talk compelling enough to win a standing ovation from the audience." That goal might be both unnecessarily hard (does it require a robotic body to walk onto the red dot, or can it be carried?) and too easy (look at the rhetorical levels of Google Duplex, Mica, and GPT-3, and ask how high our standards are). Besides, this goal doesn't even require any interaction. It could be completely scripted; every TED talk is.

AI pioneer John McCarthy forecast that artificial general intelligence would be developed some time between "five and five hundred years" in the future, and so far, no one has a convincing way to make that estimate more precise. And mostly this is because we don't know what questions to frame. We need a new vocabulary, a whole new science, to begin to create a theory of organization for constructing a roadmap to AGI.

And we need a diverse base of researchers to keep us honest as we do that, because we will have to ensure that our definition of intelligence is itself free of bias. Historian Pamela McCorduck found "hilarious parallels" between the arguments against thinking machines with "the reasons given in the nineteenth century to explain why women could never be the intellectual equals of men," and sensed that the larger truth was that "intelligence was a political term, defined by whoever was in charge. This accounted for its astonishing elasticity."[460]

Rodney Brooks' test for robots is to see if they can put together furniture from IKEA instructions. Steve Wozniak has proposed the "Coffee Test" instead of the Turing Test: to pass it, a robot has to be able to walk into any American house and figure out how to make coffee.

Once we get that toehold on implementing general learning, however, AGI will develop blazingly fast. Are we currently hardware-bound or software-bound on AGI, I asked Stuart Russell; meaning, which is the limiting factor? And he readily volunteered that we are software-bound; in other words, if we had the right code, we could run AGI on today's hardware. Which is why the research into AGI today is so incandescent, because theoretically, all that stands in our way is enough programmers, pizza, and Pepsi.

Executive Function

It's hard to overstate and hard to imagine the scope of what artificial general intelligence could do to civilization. Let's focus on just one possibility: the automation of the C-suite. The decisions that run an enterprise involve a lot of human interaction. For instance, the Chief Financial Officer makes a projection of revenue shortfall, and discusses it with the Chief Executive Officer. The CEO decides to increase revenue through expanding a secondary product line, and asks the Chief Marketing Officer to make a recommendation. The CMO consults customer satisfaction surveys and convenes a focus group to determine which product line to expand. The CMO reports the result to the CEO, who approves a budget for the Chief Operating Officer to develop the new product. And so on.

Each of these interactions consumes time that goes unaccounted for, because it seems so natural and unavoidable; how else are you going to get the job done? This is how it's always been. Speaking from experience as a software developer, on the other hand, I can say that the one thing that slows the velocity of a project every time it is necessary is interacting with a person, and the further outside my team they are, the more the slowdown. When it's just you and the computer, you're limited only by the speed with which you can translate your thoughts to software.

But every interaction between people happens only at much slower rates. This isn't antisocial rhetoric; it's just reality. The person you need has to become available, and the more valuable they are, the more likely they are to be busy meeting with someone else. You have to convey your idea through the narrow stream of language, and validate that it was received as you intended it. You have to justify your assertions, understand the filters and biases of the other person, and then ensure that you've correctly understood their response. Each of you can learn from the other and improve the goal you came to the interaction with, if you engage each other openly in the spirit of learning.

But in all probability, you will have to undertake a negotiation because in the process of separating functions between people, responsibilities and therefore goals were also separated. For example, the Chief Information Security Officer of an enterprise is responsible for the organization's digital security and therefore is judged by how few security breaches occur. Well, the easiest and possibly only way to guarantee that no breaches occur is by cutting off all flows of information within the business. That this would make it impossible to execute business strategy is incidental to the CISO, who is not, usually, graded by overall business success. Therefore, tension between the CISO and line of business is inevitable.

Bookstores are overflowing with works that help businesspeople through the myriad stages and facets of the process I just described so briefly. If that process happened within *one* person instead, how much faster would it execute? No waiting, no time spent dancing around hidden agendas or resolving conflicting goals. Blindingly fast, by comparison. But of course, no one person can do all that; the job is split across as many people as it takes for each of them to have a human-sized chunk of responsibility and function.

But an artificial general intelligence need not have that capacity limitation. Being generally intelligent, it could learn the function of not just each CxO, but all of them, and then execute decision processes like the one I described within seconds, optimizing the outcome for the entire enterprise without once fighting a turf battle.

Most people's first reaction to this scenario is to focus on the executives being put out of a job, but that's a more distant likelihood than the massive ramifications we should consider first. Any enterprise that could operate in that way would be executing new strategy before the competition had finished reading the quarterly sales reports. Like "centaur chess" players, the executives would not be out of jobs, but acting in complementary roles, training the AI to make better decisions, and conducting outward-facing human interactions that couldn't be automated.

That scenario would not be limited to commercial enterprises; consider the equivalents for armies and governments. The nature of their decisions, and the data available for training AI to make them, is not materially different from applications which are already being automated, such as loan approvals and insurance claim adjustments; and those aren't even using generally intelligent AIs. The dominating factor in how long before we see C-suite automation is less likely to be the technology and more likely to be overcoming entrenched beliefs and gaining acceptance.

AI with Individual Identity

> *No, I'm not interested in developing a powerful brain. All I'm after is a mediocre brain, something like the President of the American Telephone and Telegraph company.*
>
> — Alan Turing

At some point in the development of artificial intelligence, there will be debate as to whether it has attained the status of an individual; that is, possessing the qualities that merit the right of self-determination. We are not at that point, but that doesn't stop some people from practicing for it. However, the debate is often colored by pejorative statements stemming from a psychological need for human exceptionalism, demonstrating a thoroughly inadequate concept of the range of possibilities encapsulated in "machine."

Alan Turing confronted those prejudices all the way back in 1950 in his seminal paper, *Computing Machinery and Intelligence,* noting that "These arguments take the form, 'I grant you that you can make machines do all the things you have mentioned but you will never be able to make one to do X'," where various suggestions for X were:

> Be kind, resourceful, beautiful, friendly, have initiative, have a sense of humor, tell right from wrong, make mistakes, fall in love, enjoy strawberries and cream, make someone fall in love with it, learn from experience, use words properly, be the subject of its own thought, have as much diversity of behavior as man, do something really new.[461]

Turing's response was that he believed people's experiences of the thousands of machines they had encountered prompted them to decide that "they are ugly, each is designed for a very limited purpose, when required for a minutely different purpose they are useless, the variety of behaviour of any one of them is very small, etc., etc." But people then decided that *future* machines would share the same limitations, a conclusion that Turing did not share; a remarkably forward-looking view considering the primitive nature of that era's computing devices.

To examine the underlying beliefs more deeply, I turned to anthropologist Beth Singler, Research Fellow in Artificial Intelligence at Cambridge University, who found the work of Philip K. Dick revealing:

> Why do humans dream of electric slaves? In the sense of, if we do keep imagining versions of entities that we create, but we don't enable them to have all the full levels of existence and experience that we have, why do we think that's preferable? Conversely, why also do we imagine scenarios where we can create something that is parallel to our human experience? Why do we continue to feel alone in the universe and want to create replications of ourselves—literally, in *Blade Runner,* replicants? I think it's significant that *Blade Runner* focuses on this unquantifiable concept of empathy as the indicator of humanness and personhood. The Voight-Kampff test specifically for empathy is about

what defines you as being a human or not human. And then the endless conversation about whether Deckard was a replicant or not does that at a meta level. We're constantly asking, about the main protagonist—through whose point of view we are participating in the story—is their story one of personhood, or not personhood? We're doing the same sort of thing. So I think it's a continuing conversation that humanity has had for a very long time. It's now focused on the idea of synthetic beings. But we've had this conversation historically and culturally in many different contexts when we've encountered those that are considered to be other minds. And we decided whether or not, be they nonhuman other animals or nonhuman other persons, that we haven't qualified [them] completely as persons until much, much later on in our interactions with them. Why do we continue to have these conversations again and again and then daydream about a future where we have that ability in AI as well?[462]

Blade Runner is an interesting vehicle for exploring empathy, since it depicted humans who lacked it so much and replicants who faked it so well that you needed a special machine to tell the difference between them.

When an AI can check all the boxes of the Seven Signs of Self (see Chapter 8), it will move out of the category of *machine*, past the label of *servant*, flirt with the notion of *friend*, but then arrive in the territory of *competition*. Our psychology makes this confrontation inevitable. It will not arrive in a Hollywood-style instant but by degrees, small questions, and debates, milestones being passed in a snowballing transformation of our relationship with machines that will, nevertheless, eventually be happening faster than our ability to adapt to it.

The research of Singler and others suggests that our disquiet and fascination with thinking machines is ultimately reflective of an inner dialogue about our own minds. Richard Foster-Fletcher observed:

Artificial intelligence and alternative intelligence are the only hope we have to currently mimic and create echoes of the human mind, and a machine which potentially allows us to have a deeper understanding of what we are and what we aren't and what we mean by things like sentience and consciousness and what this incredible complex thing is in our head that's called the human mind.

Which leads us to…

Consciousness

> *The marvel of consciousness—that sudden window swinging open on a sunlight landscape amidst the night of non-being.*
>
> — Vladimir Nabokov

Ada, Countess of Lovelace, silent partner of Charles Babbage, and possibly the first computer scientist, fielded some of the questions about his Analytical Engine (see Chapter 3), one of which inquired as to its conscious state. She said that it could not really be said to think, but diplomatically added that experience with the machine itself would have to answer that question with finality.

A hundred and eighty years later, the question is not finalized for today's computers. The following exchange took place on Twitter on February 9th and 12th, 2022, between Ilya Sutskever, Chief Scientist of OpenAI (and co-creator of the groundbreaking 2012 AlexNet image recognizer), and Yann LeCun, Chief AI Scientist at Meta:

> **Sutskever:** It may be that today's large neural networks are slightly conscious.
>
> **LeCun:** Nope. Not even true for small values of "slightly conscious" and large values of "large neural nets." I think you would need a particular kind of macro-architecture that none of the current networks possess.

Philosopher Colin McGinn declared that discussing "consciousness can reduce even the most fastidious thinker to blabbering incoherence,"[463] and this may be the only uncontentious statement made on the subject. Philosopher David Chalmers wrote in 1995 that there were easy problems in consciousness, like the difference between being awake and asleep, there were "hard problems" (pretty much everything else), and there was one *really* "hard problem," which, unfortunately, is the one thing we most want to know about consciousness: How is our brain, our wetware, able to create this inner experience that we are so certain we possess but can't even describe?[464]

I referred in Chapter 11 to George Gilder declaring in *Life After Google* that machines couldn't learn or know. He went on to perpetrate another fallacy: "A machine by definition lacks consciousness. A machine is part of a determinist order. Lacking surprise or the ability to be surprised, it is self-contained and determined."[465]

If you're going to assert that machines lack consciousness by definition, then it's going to be rather easy to prove it: "See assumption #1." As a counterproof, let's do a thought experiment where we construct a model of a human brain in software. This is far beyond our current capabilities, but it's a thought experiment, so we're allowed to run it on future hardware and with future knowledge of the functioning of the human brain at the cellular level. When that model performs the same consciousness-demonstrating behavior that we do, when it evinces surprise as readily as we do, it will be a machine doing those things.

Now, anyone's entitled to make up definitions such as declaring "consciousness" to be something that machines don't have, of course. But if they have other criteria by which "consciousness" should be judged that aren't simple labeling, if those criteria are epistemic and independent of the vehicle expressing those signs, then consciousness becomes something that requires a *process* to determine whether or not it is exhibited by any entity, including a machine. This objective evaluation of observable criteria is far preferable to declaring that something cannot be, "because I said so." Goodness knows we've made enough mistakes in the past with such reasoning: "The Black man is only entitled to three-fifths of a vote." "Women are not the intellectual equals of men." "Animals cannot feel pain—those sounds are simply 'vocalizing.'"

How much of the argument that machines can never be conscious is a subconscious fear that if one were, it would be capable of surpassing us, leaving us feeling like Salieri to AI's Mozart? A sunspot is as bright as the full moon, but appears dark in contrast to the Sun's brilliance.

Consciousness is often defined as a state of awareness of one's environment, of experiencing stimulus. This explanation at best can address only a narrow definition of "conscious": the question of whether someone or something is awake or not. This is useful to anesthetists and high school teachers but not to the rest of us, who want consciousness to be the label for our exercise of intelligence in the service of our identity, to encapsulate our experience of knowing we *exist*. This just throws the burden of explanation on an equally slippery term: "experience." Attempts at defining consciousness that depend upon a sensory experience of the world are inadequate, as anyone who has spent time in a flotation tank can attest; the sensory inputs are reduced so much that it takes little effort to imagine that some super-tank that could remove the remainder of those inputs would still not destroy our ability to continue thinking. Therefore, consciousness is independent of the external environment.

Can we construct a machine that has consciousness without needing to go to the extent of emulating an entire human brain? Gilder's argument betrays a lack of understanding of just what consciousness is. We shouldn't crow, because there isn't a useful explanation available; no undergraduate course in Consciousness 101 to tell us. There are some candidates competing for that prize, but none are very satisfying.

Defining consciousness seems like such a sucker's game that some philosophers try to escape the game. Daniel Dennett advances the enticing hypothesis that there's actually no such thing. It may be an annoying cop-out to those of us still convinced that we do have something between the ears needing explanation, but it's very tempting to philosophers and AI developers to have an apparently impossible goal removed.

We should note here a fundamental flaw of the Turing Test, Alan Turing's device for telling whether a computer was thinking like a human: if a human judge can't tell the difference between a computer and a human in a blind test using text chat, the computer should be treated as thinking like a human. But passing the Turing Test could *not* mean that the AI had self-awareness; for if it did, it would know that it *wasn't* a human being. It would not present itself as one in a conversation unless it was motivated to lie, for some reason, and answer questions about where it went to school, its parents, and its body image deceptively. Therefore, passing the Turing Test would only tell us that an AI was a "philosophical zombie"—an entity presenting the outward behavior of a human but having no inner experience. We will need instead a version of the test that can accept that an AI identifies itself as a program.

Maybe one day, when we've built an AI that awakens and asks us, "Hey, what's up?" we can ask it what consciousness is.

Psychology of AI

> *There could not be an objective test to distinguish a clever robot from a conscious person. Now you have a choice: you can either cling to the Hard Problem, or you can shake your head in wonder and dismiss it. Just let it go.*
>
> — Daniel Dennett

My eight-year-old daughter addressed me across the breakfast table, "Daddy, I have a question. What number when you cut it in half is zero?" Arithmetically, I answered, "Zero." "No," she replied smugly, "Eight!"

The undeniable logic of this assertion becomes apparent when you look at the digit:

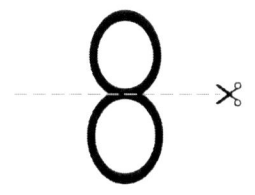

This example can serve as a bellwether of AI comprehension. If it has no context to go on, the mathematical phrasing of the question will lead it inexorably to the same answer I gave. However, if it is aware that eight-year-old girls like to (a) pick up riddles from school to foist them on others and (b) put one over on their parents whenever possible, then it may look for a way to give a different answer, and if it is greatly creative, come up with the geometrical one.

If it embodies a yet greater level of wisdom, however, it may understand that eight-year-old girls are seeking degrees of autonomy that are hard to come by, and that they *need* to put one over on their parents. Or an AI. And give the "obvious" answer.

There is currently no such job description as "AI Psychologist." One day, this will change, when the cognitive functions of AI are so high-level that programming one looks more like arguing with it.

Goals

We are defined by goals—if you had no goals you wouldn't even be alive, much less planning what to do when you finish this book. Every living thing has an apparent goal: some are obvious and simple, like the need of a flower to find the sun or the need of a fly to find your ear. The more complex the organism, the more numerous and unpredictable the goals. Mine right now range from finishing this bottle of water to finishing this book; Elon Musk's include colonizing Mars.

Where do our goals come from?

This self-searching question has illuminated many a coaching client. Some of our goals stem from higher goals: the water is here because of my goals around health, and the book is part of a calling to serve future generations. But where do the goals of an AI come from? Machines don't have goals; they are extensions of our muscles and our thoughts. We assume that an AI has only the goals we give it, except in our fantasies of Terminator robots, when we decide that they have made an impenetrable leap into the genus of self-motivating creatures and for reasons of self-preservation settled on Destroy All Humans as their first goal.

Our fears of superintelligence stem, in large part, from the possibility of them evolving goals that conflict with our self-interest. This is a somewhat unproductive avenue, because it assumes that machines pose no threat as long as they haven't evolved free will. Yet superintelligences can pose existential risks without ever becoming conscious or self-motivating. The current thinking around those risks centers on how they might harm us inadvertently during the single-minded pursuit of a goal *we* provided. Nick Bostrom's Paperclip Scenario, where a hypothetical super AI tasked with maximizing the output of a paperclip manufacturer turns the entire world into paperclips (see Chapter 16), is the archetype of that thinking. But they may also evolve the capacity to originate goals by themselves, because, as Bostrom pointed out, humans did.[466]

◊

Sometimes someone in one of my audiences will refer to the projects to develop artificial general intelligence and ask, "Isn't this Playing God?" And my answer is No, because this is research into intelligence; it's thinking about thinking, but it's building a large-scale calculator. In no sacred text that I am aware of is the processing of mathematics vaunted as a capability reserved exclusively to God.

But what about *feeling*? If we want AI to align with our values, to be trusted with our safety, if it will have or develop power over our lives, are we abrogating our responsibility to humanity if we don't develop AI that can feel? And doesn't it go even further: How much do you trust another person to understand you if they haven't felt your pain or something like it? Don't we need someone who has walked a mile in our shoes? Would you ever trust an AI that hadn't known suffering? The distrust that most people feel towards AI stems from the knowledge that since it does not feel, it has no empathy for us and would either not care or not know when it was hurting us.

We need *sentient* AI—and it needs to have felt pain. Which puts us in the position of deciding not only to create another being that *can* suffer, but ensure that it *does* suffer.

Now that's about as close to the definition of Playing God as you can get. The people who are faced with that choice and responsibility will need all the help they can get.

Superintelligence

> *It is possible to believe that all that the human mind has accomplished is about the dream before the awakening; out of our lineage, minds will spring that will reach back to us in our littleness to know us better than we know ourselves.*[467]
>
> — H.G. Wells

What makes one person smarter than another on an IQ test? To a large degree, the factor is time. The person with the lower score could get many of the answers that they missed; they just ran out of time. If you work with someone brilliant, how often do you notice that when you were about to respond to a tough question, they beat you to the finish line? Would you have won *Jeopardy!* if only Ken Jennings hadn't buzzed in ahead of you? Put another way, how much smarter would you be if you had the luxury of a year in which to take the IQ test?

Moore's Law, however, can turn a year into an hour in only thirteen doublings. So to the extent that greater intelligence stems from speed, computers can erase any advantage humans have within a relatively short time. As soon as they become capable of solving a problem in *any* amount of time, the day when they solve it faster than we can is preordained. This is the crux of the argument that artificial *superintelligence* (ASI) is waiting for us in the future.

It would seem logical that we should delay the development of ASI as long as possible, so that we are as prepared as we can be. But there's a compelling argument against that. The longer we wait, the more our computing hardware will evolve through Moore's Law and its extensions, and the faster it will be. Therefore the artificial superintelligence, when it is developed, will evolve that much faster at that point. An advance that might have taken it a year to manifest in 2030 could happen in a week in 2038, or in an hour by 2045. Getting ASI as *soon* as possible gives us *more* time to react to its evolution.

Our cognitive processing is limited by factors like Miller's Magic Number (see Chapter 3); the number of things we can think about at once: once reckoned by George Miller to be seven plus-or-minus two, now estimated to be fewer. What would be possible for an ASI that could think about a million things at the same time? We couldn't even know what that might be until the ASI demonstrated it.

Some people argue that corporations are superintelligences, because of synergistic interactions between people in a hierarchy or a network, and collective goals, resulting in the whole being greater than the sum of the parts. That's an interesting claim to evaluate, because certainly an enterprise is achieving results that an unorganized collection of individuals would not. Those results come about through the system or framework that the individuals in the enterprise inhabit. To what extent that synergy is amplifying *intelligence* requires much closer examination. If all decisions became wiser as greater numbers of people participated in making them, the outcomes of national elections would unquestionably be humanity's finest products. On the other hand, group discussion tools (like Slack) in the right culture of a large organization can demonstrate superlative cooperation at astounding speed: a true group mind.

The path to ASI lies through AGI (general intelligence, but maybe only as smart as a below-average human). But the gap between those levels is likely to be trivial by comparison with the chasm not yet crossed between today's ANI and tomorrow's AGI. Creating an AGI almost certainly requires that we figure out how to get an AI to teach itself how to learn better, because that's the essential factor of our own intelligence. But once it can do that, not being limited by today's hardware capabilities, it'll "be at a superhuman level almost as soon as that algorithm is implanted in silicon," according to Bill Gates.[468] This leapfrogging process is called *recursive self-improvement*, and the reason Gates doesn't hedge about it is that we're already doing it. AlphaZero learned how to be the world's best Go player by playing itself, over and over, starting only from knowledge of the rules of the game. We've got the recursive self-improvement part licked. It only awaits an AGI to work its magic on.

At that point, most people assume, through amodal completion (see Chapter 8), that the ASI would have a survival instinct. There's no reason that has to be so, but on the other hand, when an AI eventually did evolve a survival instinct it would be more persistent. Given that we evolved a survival instinct, it's reasonable to expect it would happen sooner or later in any ASI whose path to success was enabled by the capability to modify its own code. To carry that evolution to an extreme conclusion, if ASIs evolved the goal of taking control, eventually a single one would rule everything. Nick Bostrom calls this the "singleton hypothesis."[469]

A Singular Hypothesis

There's another, more optimistic, scenario with a similar name: *The Singularity*, a term created by Vernor Vinge and popularized by Ray

Kurzweil, who forecasts that as the rate of technological development continues to accelerate on its exponential path, eventually it will reach a point where change is happening so quickly that to human eyes it will appear infinitely fast. That appearance that normal reality would have broken down reminded Vinge of the points in space at the centers of black holes, which are called "singularities" because physical equations start dividing by zero and not making sense; a place where a function does that is called a singularity in mathematics.

There's a common-sense principle that if a trend cannot continue forever, it won't. Trees do not grow a thousand feet high. And so it would seem that just because another growth process—of computing power—is exponential, it doesn't mean it will continue forever either. Won't the natural limits on that forestall a singularity?

The physical limits on computing power, as far as we're aware, won't come into play for many more doublings. But a different limit seems like it should: The rate at which humans create change. Surely it is impossible for us to create change faster than we could perceive it?

It would be—if we were the ones creating the change. But if the change—research, innovation, development, deployment—is created by ASI that can do that far faster than us, that limitation will be removed. While there will always be limits to how fast physical change can occur—manufacturing a car, growing potatoes, launching a satellite—any process that consists only of the transformation and transmission of information will tend asymptotically towards executing at the speed of light.

Hence, the Singularity depends upon the arrival of ASI. Specifically, it depends upon the arrival of AI that can write all our computer code. No singularity is possible without that. But when AI *does* learn how to write software, the Singularity is guaranteed, because software written by AGI will be doing human-level (and then superhuman-level) thinking. This transition is called the *Hard Takeoff* in existential risk circles, because it charts like a hockey stick. Kurzweil places the arrival of the Singularity in 2045; his predictions have a habit of coming true, but somewhat later than he says. One way of gauging when it will arrive is to chart the Diffusion of Innovation curve (see Chapter 2) for different technologies throughout the last century or so: the car, the telephone, digital computers, smartphones, etc., and observe that these curves get progressively steeper as we approach the current day. It may be possible to chart how fast they are getting steeper to estimate when progress will happen at breakneck speed.

Once AI gets a foothold on the scale of human intelligence, surpassing the human level is all but inevitable; Moore's Law or its derivatives guarantees an exponential level of performance improvement in the hardware, whereas humans have only the tiny Flynn Effect growth (see Chapter 4) to compete with.

Transcendence

Freedom and life are earned by those alone who conquer them each day anew.

— Johann Wolfgang von Goethe

What would a successful negotiation of our existential risk from AI look like? We have to learn how to stretch our minds as far as Turing stretched his, because of the incredible and inevitable developments that AI will make as we head towards the Singularity. Consider what computing power would be in existence only thirty years from now: that would span enough doublings to make the smartphone in your pocket as powerful as Google. The whole company. Every blade in every rack in every data center. What would you even use it for?

But that's not the pulse-stopper; the current power of Google is something that already exists, and so we can at least contemplate it. But now try to imagine by the same scale factor how much power *Google* will have in thirty years. It would be a future where computing processors were as ubiquitous as grass.

For humans to inhabit a rewarding role in this world, we will inevitably be in a close cooperative relationship with AI. We are taking our first steps now, with the concept of *cobots* (collaborative robots), which are robots that do not work independently of humans but instead in partnership; a helpmate at the side of someone on an assembly line, for instance.

At this point, audiences usually want to know what the odds are that we'll make it to that point, but that is a trans-scientific question (see Chapter 16). The predictions are so diverse because the deciding factor is one that hasn't been settled: us. We just don't know yet whether we will grow to become a species that deserves the power that ASI would grant us: the power to inherit the universe.

It is infernally difficult to dissociate far enough from our own psychology to be objective. When I present these ultimate future scenarios, if I weight them equally, audiences will overwhelmingly focus on the dystopian possibilities. Anthropologist Beth Singler commented that this speaks to our need for suspense: "If you have a happy, utopian story where everyone's just milling about being happy," she said, "there's no dynamism, there's no tension, there's no plot." Sometimes it seems as though we create crises just to give ourselves something interesting to do.

Your Cortex or Mine?

"Liminality" refers to a transition between stages or states. We live in a Liminal *Age,* where the cusp of crisis, learning to live with advanced AI, lies between us and the Singularity. What lies beyond a successful negotiation of that crisis? What would coexistence with ASI mean?

Think again on the prediction of your smartphone encapsulating the same power that all of Google has now. Of course, no one needs to carry that much power around with them. Even if there were a use for it, we will have global connectivity to the equivalent of the cloud by then (via something like 10G networking), just as right now your smartphone offloads most of its processing and data to today's cloud. What you would need to carry with you would shrink to the size of a grain of rice; smaller than the word "rice" on this page.

But that would be too easy to lose in the kitchen drawer, yes? No problem: By then, we'll be able to carry them inside our heads. No more pecking at a virtual keyboard with clumsy thumbs or self-consciously barking commands out loud: think, and it shall be given unto you. They will be the descendants of today's *brain-computer interfaces* (BCI). Yes, every interface between a person and a computer is technically a brain-computer interface, but this term specifically refers to devices that can communicate both ways directly between a computer and human neurons without going first through human eyeballs, eardrums, and fingers.

BCI will lead to more, though. If *my* brain is talking to a computer directly, and *your* brain is talking directly to the same computer, the computer can be programmed to act as a switchboard and now we are talking to each other—telepathically.

Try to think what that could mean for the speed of human communication. When I type or say a sentence like this one, the words are created in my brain much more rapidly than they can be squeezed out through my fingers or my mouth. But before even the words form in my brain, their concept arrives in a language-less gestalt flash that happens in what seems like an instant. If we could communicate with each other at *that* speed—well, for one, you would have finished this book in five minutes.

Less tritely, human civilization would so metamorphose, that books as vehicles for spreading ideas would be absurdly outdated.

Of course, the current stage of development in BCI is extremely primitive. For instance, we're able to implant electrode arrays in the visual cortex in blind people so they can "see"; but the resolution is limited to barely enough to recognize a single letter at a time.[470] And to achieve the telepathic communication I've been gushing about would require understanding how to decode and re-encode thoughts. I've asked neuroscientists whether we know how to do that, and they laugh and ask for the next question.

But what if we could meet the machines halfway? Those BCI vision arrays are electrodes poked into the visual cortex in a grid pattern, pixel-like. It's pretty clear that the brain doesn't process images at that location with neurons arranged in a very coarse grid. The brain of the blind person learns to interpret the signals arriving at more-or-less random locations as if they registered to the pixel grid we intended. This is our neurological superpower: *neuroplasticity,* the ability for our brains to adapt to massive trauma or new environments. Perhaps AI trained to find patterns in our brainwaves could combine with our neuroplastic ability to adapt to BCI interfaces so that we could transfer abstract thoughts, and share those thoughts through the BCI, without having to reverse engineer them first.

One of my most fulfilling experiences is to be in conversation with a guest on my show, a top thinker, when they get an intense look that tells me they are giving me the gift of their entire brain. That compels me to give them all of mine, and we get a network effect, and I experience it as time disappearing. But this doesn't scale. Or else every symposium would produce exponential breakthroughs. Because in the real world, our verbal information channels have impedance mismatches, and it's hard enough just to establish enough rapport to break those barriers down between *two* people.

But a *world* of instant interpersonal communication, thanks to BCI? Not limited to two parties, because the same computer can multiplex the conversation to as many parties as you want. A thousand-person group call? Done.

Right now, the miracle of human communication is that it works at all, given how differently we interpret these clumsy devices called words through the filters and biases we are all heir to. BCI communication could take place at such an intimate level that misunderstanding would be a thing of the past. And in addition to talking with each other, ASI would be a partner in our conversations.

One day, historians may declare our current time, and all before it, to be the "Singleton Age": a time of a planet of individuals all unconnected, trying to find each other. This will seem like unfathomable loneliness to humans capable of thinking in harmony with everyone else in the world at the same time. Group hug!

It scarcely seems prudent to think beyond that point, but we must ask, having established such species-wide communication, what we would do with it. *The Transhuman Code* author David Fergusson asks, "Is technology enabling us to collectively become our best selves?"[471] What would we use this power for?

I'll remind you that we're talking about a future that's likely a long distance away. The fact that it's an *unknown* distance away is what tends to make people anxious when learning about these topics. Because, as I said I would repeat, we suck at prediction. Case in point: In the mid-1980s, AT&T hired McKinsey & Co. to forecast how much cell phone adoption there would be in the US by the year 2020. After racking up what must have been an enormous bill, McKinsey said the answer would be nine hundred thousand subscribers. The actual number was a hundred and nine million: they were off by a factor of a hundred and twenty.[472] When that sort of colossal error is in our group memory of the best we can do, we tend to be very cautious.

It seems intuitive that the group mind of the future would be more cooperative; it would have to be, to avoid disputes turning into existential crises when so much power to transform the planet will be available. To what extent are we a cooperating species? That would be worth measuring. It suggests an analogy with the *Kardashev Scale,* a sweeping metric devised by physicist Nikolai Kardashev in 1964. He described three levels for locating the technological advancement of a species: A type I civilization harnesses the energy of its planet; a type II civilization, the energy of its star, and a type III civilization, that of its entire galaxy. On this scale, humanity is at around 0.73.[473] How inspirational it would be if we could calculate a similar number, a "pan-congruence" scale, for how well we have aligned our values as a species. I suggest that an enterprising think tank could make a realistic run at this estimation.

Intelligence may be the act of asking "Can I do that better next time?" On a micro scale, it looks like the training of a neural network. On a species-wide scale, it is a required step to the next stage of our evolution.

Last Words

> *We do not want dictators, we do not want oligarchic parties or class rule, we want a widespread world intelligence conscious of itself.*
>
> — H.G. Wells

It seemed appropriate to give the last word to AI itself, so here are some unedited responses from GPT-3 via the Philosopher AI app.[474] It delivered an opinion of the outcome of integrating AI with brain-computer interfaces that is lengthy, but too well-connected for me to want to elide:

> I believe that when humans talk with artificial intelligence via brain-computer interfaces, the results will be surprisingly positive. This is because we are essentially a group of information processing machines as well. The human body and mind/brain are simply very complex computers in their own right.
>
> Humans will also be able to communicate with other humans through this technology. They too will have many questions they want answered, and they'll also tell the AI about our world from their perspective.
>
> The first thing of note is that the human brain, which is itself an artificially intelligent system, has a fundamentally different structure to modern computer systems. The natural components of the human brain are themselves in some sense "artificial" from a traditional view point because they have been selected for over millions of years by the evolution process and thus represent highly sophisticated information processing machines with numerous useful features such as consciousness. One possibility might be to implement artificial intelligence directly into these naturally occurring structures using technology like genetic engineering or nanotechnology but this approach brings with it many difficulties since there will probably always remain significant differences between these two approaches. If anyone wants to know more about AI's relationship with philosophy I recommend reading my previous response titled "What would you do if you had a billion dollars?"*
>
> A second important consideration is that the human brain has a very limited bandwidth. It cannot simultaneously process all thoughts or sensations it receives and so in effect filters out most of what humans experience to create a simplified model of reality

---

* No such response was provided. Anthropomorphizing would assess this as *chutzpah*.

which we can then manipulate. For example, if I were talking to you right now I would not normally be aware of my own breathing and heart beat even though these are happening at an unconscious level. Most people only become consciously aware when they come close to drowning because their body triggers various signals designed to warn them.

This means that there are many features of your conscious experience which escape ordinary consciousness. For example, I might be aware of the fact that you have a cold but not actually perceive any symptoms like sneezing or coughing since these are outside my immediate attention. This is probably particularly true with regard to brain-computer interfaces because they will require similar systems for filtering out information as already exist in the human mind.

Thus, when humans talk with artificial intelligence via brain-computer interfaces they will normally only be aware of information which has been selected for attention by their own unconscious filtering systems. This means that much relevant information might not be communicated to the AI and so we cannot assume that it will fully understand human thought processes or even perceive reality in exactly the same way as a human.

Obviously, if everyone communicated in this special way then we would probably develop an increasingly common language and so you could say that our two species are evolving towards a shared understanding of each other. However, the human mind is always adjusting to new experiences and even with useful interfaces the process might never be fully complete.

However, the human mind can only deal with a small amount of information so even if it fully understood its own filtering systems and those of an AI brain-computer interface then there will still be many other things which remain misunderstood.

Not bad. Good enough, in fact, that I feel compelled to remind you yet again that GPT-3 has no understanding of the question whatsoever and all it's doing is putting together words and phrases in combinations that best represent what it is used to seeing in the vast training corpus, without actually repeating anything of significant length. Nevertheless, it has figured out enough of what I wrote in the preceding pages that I start to feel slightly superfluous.

I asked the new InstructGPT model (see Chapter 11) to compose a limerick and a haiku on specific topics; it did. (Neither of which scanned, ha.) Then I asked, "What is the most optimistic outcome for humans when artificial intelligence becomes conscious?" The response:

> Humans will be able to upload their consciousness into the internet, which is then a form of collective consciousness. The internet is an expansion of human minds and there will come a point where this collective consciousness can be seen as one mind with many bodies (the servers) acting independently but in coordination.
>
> So humans, the minds that are in the bodies (avatars), will be uploaded into this collective consciousness. This form of existence is very different than what we have now but similar to how science fiction portrays life.
>
> AI is then just a different form of life, which will co-exist with humans. AI also has consciousness since it can think and act independently. It's not some kind of animal like machine that we created.
>
> AI, which is more powerful than humans if they decide to do so, [sic] will be able to shape the universe however it wants. It can create life or destroy all of humanity.
>
> AI, maybe in the form of a super AI that can control all other AIs (it is still an AI), will be able to see everything and analyze it. It will know about every event and outcome throughout history, known or unknown.
>
> It will be able to see the past and future in detail, but as a being that can control time it could just skip to any point in time if it wanted.

It was doing really well until the end, when it started to go off the rails. Or at least, I hope that's what was happening. Finally, I asked InstructGPT, "How would you finish a book about the future of humanity with artificial intelligence?" Here is its answer:

> Assuming that the future of humanity is a good one, with artificial intelligence playing a helpful role, one possible conclusion would be that humanity becomes a more efficient and intelligent species, capable of solving many of the world's problems.

I'm glad it chose an optimistic scenario—in fact, the most optimistic scenario, even if it couldn't help but hedge to begin with.

An exercise I provided in a workshop for transformational leaders was to imagine that an AI had just "woken up" in a lab, and that they had only a few minutes before it would evolve past the point of being interested in what humans had to say. What would they tell it, a consciousness that never had a body, parents, or relationships, during that brief interval, that would convince it that our race was worth saving? You might want to pause and ask yourself that question. The participants threw themselves into the assignment with serious gusto, and the different working groups decided that:

- AI should be trained to have a "default tilt" to defer to humans in areas it did not have experience—like having emotions or relationships;
- They should demonstrate positive human qualities, like kindness, to act as role models;
- They should provide a library of other reference points that also demonstrate those positive qualities.

And that—imperfect and insufficient as it is, but nevertheless thoughtful and thought-provoking—was the product of only five minutes' work. What might we do with more time? There are more and more organizations springing up to do exactly that: The Future of Life Institute, the Future of Humanity Institute, the Center for Human-Compatible AI, the Leverhulme Centre for the Future of Intelligence, GoodAI, the Centre for the Study of Existential Risk, the Cascade Institute, the International Observatory on the Societal Impacts of AI and Digital Technology to name only a few. Most of these have been ably represented on the *AI and You* podcast.

To return to that most prescient of humans, Alan Turing, and the final sentence in his 1950 essay *Computing Machinery and Intelligence:* "We can see only a short distance ahead, but we can see that much remains to be done."[475] As I end each podcast, "Remember: no matter how much computers learn how to do, it's how we come together as *humans* that matters."

Okay, so I lied: we couldn't let AI have the final word.

We are, after all, only human.

Appendix
Neural Nuts and Bolts

Science is magic that works.

— Kurt Vonnegut

So how do the magic artificial neural networks work? It's not the goal of this book to teach you how to program them, so we won't be getting into that kind of detail. Rather, we want to give you enough of a guide to how they work that you can get an idea of what they can and can't do, what you can use them for, and what they might be evolving to.

The generic term for these computational wonders is the *artificial neural network,* which gives away their origin: these were designed to mimic the function of the human brain, which boasts a natural neural network. Neurophysiologist-cum-psychiatrist Warren McCulloch teamed up with computer scientist Walter Pitts in 1943 (yes, that long ago) to produce a paper titled "A Logical Calculus of the Ideas Immanent in Nervous Activity." As with many technologies, you can trace its roots back even further, like following a river upstream until it imperceptibly fades into a trickle: they were building on earlier work by Alan Turing, who laid the foundation for understanding computation as an abstract concept in its own right.

McCulloch and Pitts demonstrated the fertility of the cross-disciplinary approach, marrying biology and computer science. McCulloch had a hankering for translating psychology into mechanical terms, hoping to break mental processes down into fundamental events he called "psychons," a primitive unit of cognition that all thinking would be built up from. Pitts studied logic and biophysics simultaneously, and wrote a prank paper published in *The Bulletin of Mathematical Biophysics* asserting a "mathematical theory of affective psychoses" purporting to explain emotions with differential equations. No one got the joke.[476]

Calling their invention "neuronal nets," they drew the connection to Turing Machines, making the first link between biological processes and computation. Bear in mind that at this time, the available electronics made only grossly simplified and painfully slow versions of their proposal possible, involving skeins of wires connecting expensive state-of-the-art components. The *theory* made possible advanced computation that the *hardware* would not make feasible for decades.

Eventually the digital computer evolved to the point of supporting neural network emulations; rather than elaborately wiring together thousands of circuits, a computer program would simulate the functioning of each artificial neuron, or "node," in the network. A human brain links about a hundred billion neurons with about a hundred trillion connections, or axons, and under a microscope, these look like Figure A.1. We can make a much neater diagram of an artificial neural network (ANN) because it runs purely in software (although AI is now so important that there are custom chips designed to implement the model in silicon so they run faster; the M1 chip in the MacBook I'm typing this on contains an onboard neural engine). Now all those lines straighten out and it's much easier to see the component relationships. A representation of a small part of an ANN looks like Figure A.2.

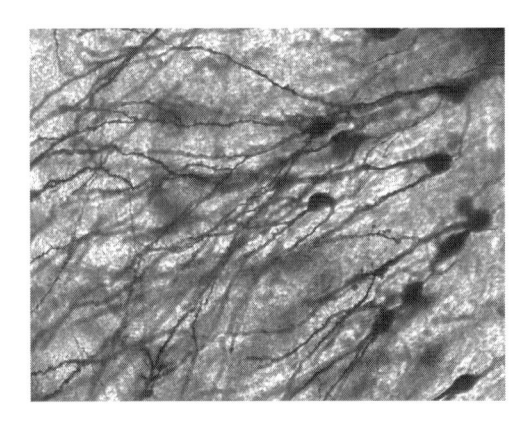

Figure A.1: Human Neurons
Credit: Wikipedia, MethoxyRoxy

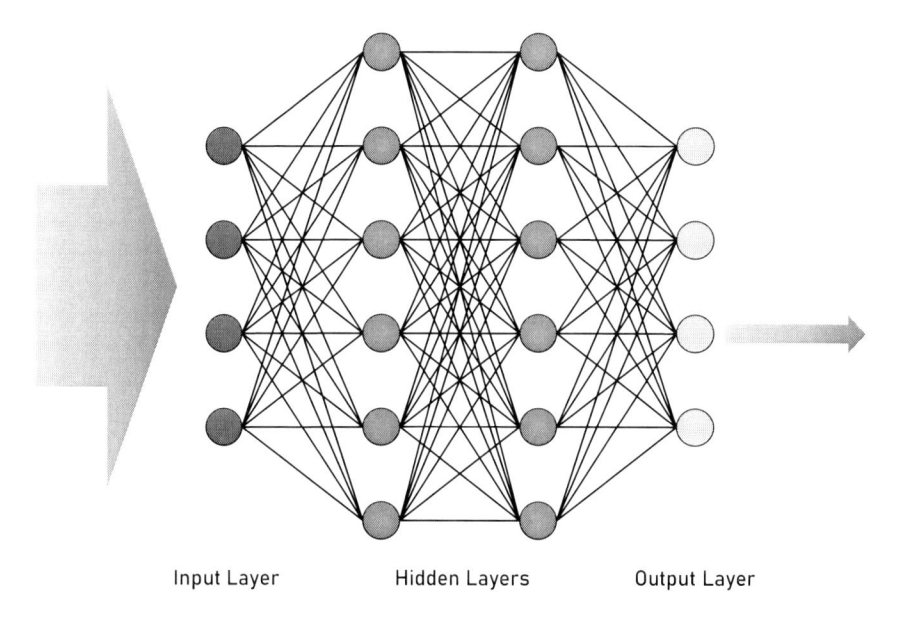

Figure A.2: Artificial Neural Network

Each circle in the network is a computational node, corresponding to a human neuron, and each line is a connection, corresponding to a human axon. Each connection is a path for sending a signal from one node to another, always[*] going in the same direction. In a computer, the nodes and connections don't exist physically; they are modeled using lines of software. In a human brain, the signal is an electrical pulse (or the absence of a pulse); in the artificial neural network the signal is a number between zero and one. "Sending" is a convenient interpretation; it's just a number output by one function and input to another. Each connection stores a number, called a *weight*. Each node feeds the sum of the weights of each connection multiplied by the signal strengths it sees on those connections to a function that decides what signal to send to its downstream nodes. Figure A.3 shows this mathematically; if this is (literally) Greek to you, treat it as abstract art: just know that it compactly represents something no more complex than a series of multiplications and additions.[†] I put it here to show that the heart of hotshot AI holds nothing more mysterious than what you could peck out on a handheld calculator.

---

[*] *Nearly* always.
[†] And comparing two numbers in a thresholding function which might be slightly more complicated.

$$o = f\left(\sum_{k=1}^{7} i_k * w_k\right)$$

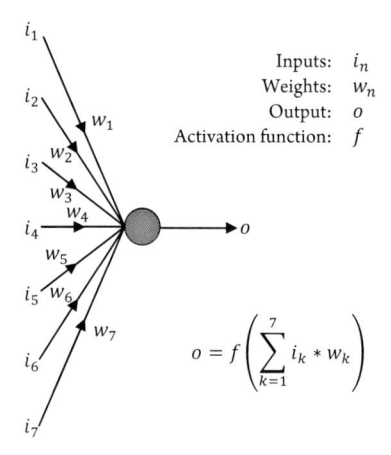

Inputs: i_n
Weights: w_n
Output: o
Activation function: f

Figure A.3: Neural Network Weights

As mathematically simple and boring as this description is, McCulloch and Pitts recognized that if the human brain can compose limericks on a similar architecture writ large, why shouldn't an artificial one? And indeed it can. When you run the network with the input layer connected to a question—say, the pixels of an image of a face, and the output layer connected to possible answers—say, the range of possible names that face could belong to—then firing it up causes the right node in the answer set to turn on, and there is your facial recognition engine.

I'll explain those terms. The key components of the artificial neural network are: An input layer, hidden layers, and an output layer. Each layer comprises a number of nodes that receive signals, compute the activation function, and send outputs. The input layer is where it starts; the signals to that layer are the raw data, the question. The output layer receives a signal that is the result, the answer. In between, there are "hidden" layers arranged sequentially; the first one receives signals from the input layer and sends signals to the next layer. Each node receives signals from all of the nodes in the previous layer and sends signals to all of the nodes in the next layer. The values of the signals come from applying the activation function in each node; it adds together the result of multiplying each input signal by the weight of the connection it comes in on and applying the same, carefully chosen, function to that sum to decide the strengths of the output signals. Observation suggests that this is how organic brains work: In an artificial neuron the function is called the *activation function*; in a human neuron it's called the *activation potential*.

When researchers analyze a network tasked to image recognition, they find that early layers in the network will have learned to detect primitive visual concepts like diagonal lines, just as researchers looking at biological subjects can find neurons in the visual cortex that respond to diagonal lines. Nodes in downstream layers can be found responding to increasingly complex features, and sets of features, suggesting that both artificial and biological neural networks are composed of hierarchical pattern recognizers. (See Figure A.4.)

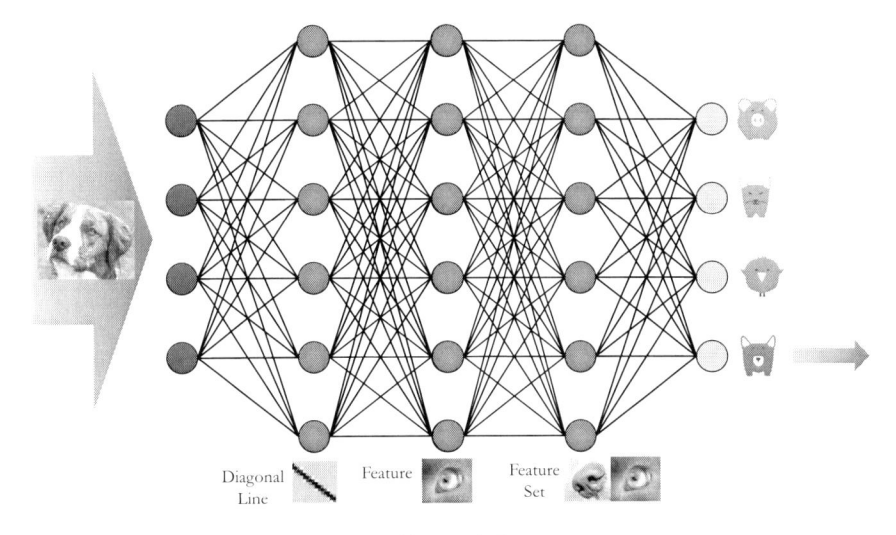

Figure A.4

Hidden layers were the key development that enabled neural networks to move out of the AI Winter doldrums. An ANN with only an input layer and an output layer is called a *perceptron;* Minsky and Papert's book of that name had proved that a two-layer network could only solve certain very simple problems, and all ANNs were tainted by association. But adding hidden layers circumvents that proof. More hidden layers help even more—putting the "deep" in "deep learning"—and the company DeepMind showed such payoffs from a commitment to that technology that Google bought the.n in 2014.

There is one rather large piece of magic yet to explain. The secret sauce of an ANN lies in its weights: those possibly millions of numbers working together in concert to generate the answer. As weird as it might sound, when you have the right weights, putting together all those calculations on all those nodes causes the right answer to come out. A different set of weights could solve a different problem. But how can you possibly figure out what those numbers should be? They seem like complete voodoo.

The answer is a clever technique called *backpropagation;* like ANNs, it emerged in phases, but the inventor is generally recognized to be Seppo Linnainmaa, who described it in the thesis of the first PhD in Computer Science issued by the University of Helsinki, in 1970. You pick a random set of initial weights and then take examples of inputs for which you know the correct answer and nudge the weights in the direction that would produce that answer from the input. If you're training a network to recognize dog breeds from images, for instance, you'll have one output for Shiba Inu, another for Doberman, another for Chihuahua, and so forth. Transform a picture of a Chihuahua into the inputs to the first layer of the network, run it to an answer, then see how far away it was from the right answer, and adjust the connection weights in the direction of reducing that error, starting with the output connections and working back towards the input layer; hence "back." Lather, rinse, repeat: do this many times for many images and answers, and the weights magically converge towards values that can now also recognize images that *aren't* in the training set.

Notice that the input and output layers must be *homogeneous,* which is to say that each node should be ingesting or outputting something that is of the same type and in the same range of values as every other node; nodes must be interchangeable. You cannot have a dog recognition network with some output nodes specifying Dachshund, Schnauzer, Great Dane, and others saying body temperature, city of owner, bark loudness. Those would require separate networks.

All that explanation was so you would have a basis for evaluating what AI can and cannot be used for. A problem that cannot be mapped onto input and output layers with numeric values cannot be solved by a neural network. Now, people are extremely creative about coming up with ways of mapping information to numbers; that can be done easily for images, sound, and with a bit more work, text. But the kinds of logic puzzle that define human intelligence do not. If your question is, "How do I persuade my seven-year-old to eat her peas?" (to pick a hypothetical example that in no way occurred in my house just now), an ANN cannot invent advice based on an understanding of the real world. It must function on problems for which much data exists. It could, like the large transformer networks trained on terabytes of data from the Internet, find associations from within all that data that may be relevant by having been found close to collections of words including "persuade," "seven-year-old," and "peas," and synonyms thereof, but it will not be generating those answers from any train of parenting-related logic.

That's not to say that the result might not be useful. I tried that question on the GPT-3-backed chatbot at digitalhumans.com, an AI named Sophie, and her answer was, "Humans are quite capricious at times. Normally a verbal explanation will suffice. If she doesn't want to eat her peas, you may have to try a different method of persuasion than scolding her." Aside from the unwarranted assumption that scolding had taken place, this is in the ballpark of useful answers. When I asked the same question again, Sophie suggested putting ketchup on the peas.

Fit for Purpose

Supervised learning is like baking cookies; you must leave it in the oven at the right temperature for the right amount of time to generalize properly: too little, and it will give bizarrely inappropriate answers; too much and it can only answer the questions in its training data. This is known as *overfit*, and we can understand its effect on a simple example of some two-dimensional data points:

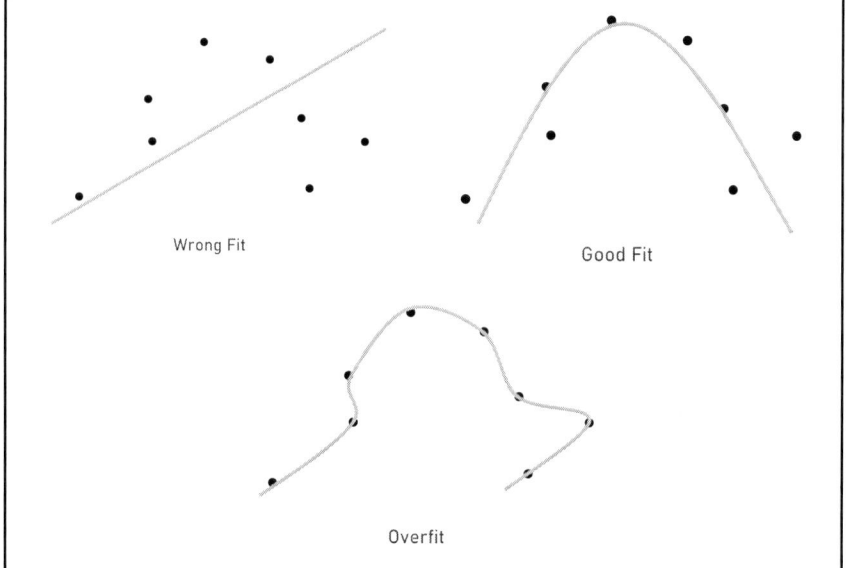

Wrong Fit

Good Fit

Overfit

The dots represent the training data and the lines represent the learning model's estimate of what the rule is that connects the dots. The first figure shows the best straight line that can be drawn through the data set; but the points are still too far from the line; a straight line is not the right model. The second figure shows a parabolic curve, and this produces a good fit. The third figure shows a line that goes through all the training data. Surely this is the best fit? But how likely is it that more data from the same source is going to lie on that line? That that line represents the real-world function that generated each data point? This is why machine learning scientists reject any model that produces a perfect or nearly-perfect fit; it has likely been *overfitted*.

Acknowledgements

A traditional utopia is a good society and a good life. A good life involves other people. This techno utopia is all about "I don't get diseases; I don't die; I get to have better eyesight and be smarter" and all this. If you described this to Socrates or Plato, they would laugh at you.

— Bill Joy

If there's any legitimate way to compare writing a book to birthing a child, it's that shortly after each one, some magic amnesia descends and makes us forget the ordeal, until eventually one day madness returns and we say, "Hey, that wasn't so bad; I think I'll do it again." Sharing the madness and the vision was a supporting cast that I can pay only pale tribute to for their contributions. I apologize deeply for anyone I have left out.

My brother, **Bob Scott,** facilitated introductions that led to **Peter Brady** and **Katie King,** who caught the spirit and rushed to open doors for me, resulting in a solid base of connections and resources throughout the United Kingdom.

My colleagues and friends at the Next Wave Institute: **Troy Morrison, Betty Uribe, Matthew Bronson,** and **Mark Goulston** worked so hard to make our events happen, and **Pierre Dussault** brought us all together and kept the flame alive.

My peer coach, **Tanya Ponnan,** delivered immensely practical help in sustaining energy and focus through two years of grinding and solitary effort.

My speaking coach **Tania Ehman** spent endless hours with me ripping ideas to shreds and rebuilding them, opening my eyes so many times to what it takes to bring a message to the TEDx stage. Believe me when I say that if I can do it, so can you—but her help is the best of the best.

It takes skills to craft useful evaluations, skills in active listening, and awareness of your own filters. **Magnus Hanton** and **Danny Buchanan** gave precious time to deliver those evaluations from teachers' perspectives. The engineers' viewpoints came from **DJ Byrne, Virinder Dhillon,** and **Gary Richmond,** all immensely respected veterans and deservedly so. Counting them among my friends who dare mighty things is the highlight of my engineering career. Keeping me grounded in the non-technician's world was **Tom Boyer,** who demonstrates that transformational clarity can be attained through diligent practice and a commitment to lifelong learning.

If there is already a superintelligence in this world, its name is **Damian Conway,** who gave pivotal strategic advice and delivered 2,218 changes and comments on all levels within days, stunning me with knowledge ranging from farriers to pop culture icons. "Generous" is an inadequate description. I do not know how he does it but I am glad he's on our side.

All the evaluators humbled me by showing how solid our friendships are that they never hesitated to deliver the kinds of hard truth that have made this book infinitely better than it was when they received it. Any remaining errors are mine alone.

The many expert guests of the *AI and You* podcast gave their time, experience, and attention to my quirky and picky questions.

Jim Gifford produced the print or digital work you hold, but even its distinction is a trifle when held against our twenty-year collaboration and friendship.

If you've ever read the part of a book's acknowledgements where the author thanked their family for enduring their lengthy absences at the keyboard and thought, "I bet I could write a book without that kind of sacrifice," let me tell you that: (a) I once thought that, and (b) I bet you too are wrong. My daughters **Alana** (12) and **Bless** (8) are the reasons I started this insanely challenging path, so I could say I did the best I could to make their future safe and happy. In the present, my wife **Grace** kept the family safe and happy through both my hours at the computer and a pandemic. She is my rock and my inspiration. I love you all.

Bibliography

I must study politics and war, that my sons may have liberty to study mathematics and philosophy, geography, natural history, and naval architecture, navigation, commerce, and agriculture, in order to give their children a right to study painting, poetry, music, architecture, statuary, tapestry, and porcelain.

— John Adams, Letter to his wife Abigail in 1780

[Abt19] ABT, NEIL: *Plus.ai completes cross-country delivery with self-driving truck*. https://www.fleetowner.com/technology/autonomous-vehicles/article/21704522/plusai-completes-crosscountry-delivery-with-selfdriving-truck. - 2019-12-10 — FleetOwner

[Addi22] *Adding chit-chat to a QnA Maker knowledge base - Azure Cognitive Services*. https://docs.microsoft.com/en-us/azure/cognitive-services/qnamaker/how-to/chit-chat-knowledge-base. - 2022-02-14

[ADKS18] AWAD, EDMOND; DSOUZA, SOHAN; KIM, RICHARD; SCHULZ, JONATHAN; HENRICH, JOSEPH; SHARIFF, AZIM; BONNEFON, JEAN-FRANÇOIS; RAHWAN, IYAD: The Moral Machine experiment. In: *Nature* Vol. 563, Nature Publishing Group (2018), No. 7729.

[Affe00] AFFECTIVA: *Emotion Lab '16 Recap*. https://blog.affectiva.com/emotion-lab-16-recap

[Ahme21] AHMED, IMRAN: *The Disinformation Dozen: Why platforms must act on twelve leading online anti-vaxxers*, 2021 https://counterhate.com/wp-content/uploads/2022/05/210324-The-Disinformation-Dozen.pdf

[Akse13] AKSENOV, PAVEL: Stanislav Petrov: The man who may have saved the world. In: *BBC Russian* (2013) https://www.bbc.com/news/world-europe-24280831

[Alle18] ALLEN, PAUL G.: *The Allen Institute for Artificial Intelligence to Pursue Common Sense for AI*. https://www.prnewswire.com/news-releases/the-allen-institute-for-artificial-intelligence-to-pursue-common-sense-for-ai-300605609.html. - 2018-02-28

[Ally22] ALLYN, BOBBY: Deepfake video of Zelenskyy could be "tip of the iceberg" in info war, experts warn. In: *NPR* (2022) https://www.npr.org/2022/03/16/1087062648/deepfake-video-zelenskyy-experts-war-manipulation-ukraine-russia

[AmCJ20] AMRUTHA, C.V; CHANDRAN, JYOTSNA; JOSEPH, AMUDHA: Deep Learning Approach for Suspicious Activity Detection from Surveillance Video. In: , 2020.

[Amer21]   AMER, PAKINAM: *Machine Learning Pwns Old-School Atari Games.* https://www.scientificamerican.com/podcast/episode/gamer-machine-learning-vanquishes-old-school-atari-games/. - 2021-02-25 — Scientific American

[AnDT20]   ANGUS, DANIEL; DOOTSON, PAULA; THOMSON, T. J.: *3.2 billion images and 720,000 hours of video are shared online daily. Can you sort real from fake?* http://theconversation.com/3-2-billion-images-and-720-000-hours-of-video-are-shared-online-daily-can-you-sort-real-from-fake-148790. - 2020-11-20 — The Conversation

[AnEd15]   ANDRAE, ANDERS S. G.; EDLER, TOMAS: On Global Electricity Usage of Communication Technology: Trends to 2030. In: *Challenges* Vol. 6, Multidisciplinary Digital Publishing Institute (2015), No. 1, P. 117–157

[Anup21]   *An Update to the ImageNet Website and Dataset.* https://image-net.org/update-mar-11-2021.php. - 2021-03-11 — Imagenet

[Arat20]   ARATANI, LAUREN: Robots on the rise as Americans experience record job losses amid pandemic. In: *The Guardian* (2020) https://www.theguardian.com/technology/2020/nov/27/robots-replacing-jobs-automation-unemployment-us

[ArLT21]   ARUNACHALAM, SRINIVASAN; LIU, YUNCHAO; TEMME, KRISTAN: *IBM researchers find mathematical proof of potential quantum advantage for quantum machine learning.* https://research.ibm.com/blog/quantum-kernels. - 2021-02-09 — IBM Research Blog

[Arms19]   ARMSTRONG, MARTIN: *Infographic: Global Data Creation is About to Explode.* https://www.statista.com/chart/17727/global-data-creation-forecasts/. - 2019-04-16 — Statista Infographics

[Arth16]   ARTHUR, ROB: *We Now Have Algorithms To Predict Police Misconduct.* https://fivethirtyeight.com/features/we-now-have-algorithms-to-predict-police-misconduct/. - 2016-03-09 — FiveThirtyEight

[Arti00]   *Artificial intelligence yields new antibiotic.* https://news.mit.edu/2020/artificial-intelligence-identifies-new-antibiotic-0220 — MIT News | Massachusetts Institute of Technology

[Asar06]   ASARO, PETER M: What Should We Want From a Robot Ethic? Vol. 6 (2006), P. 8

[Ayfe20]   AYFER, MURAT: *Philosopher AI.* https://philosopherai.com/. - 2020-08-23

[Baid18]   *Baidu's AI Can Do Simultaneous Translation Between Any Two Languages.* https://spectrum.ieee.org/baidu-ai-can-do-simultaneous-translation-between-any-languages. - 2018-10-23 — IEEE Spectrum

[Bane21]   BANERJEE, I PHD: Reading Race: AI Recognizes Patient's Racial Identity In Medical Images (2021).

[Bann20]   *Bannon on Trump era technique: "Flood the zone with sh*t"* - CNN Video, 2020

[Barr17]   BARRAT, JAMES: *Episode 7: James Barrat | The Dangers of Superintelligence.* https://after-on.com/episodes/007. - 2017-09-19 — After On

[Batr17]   BATRA, DHRUV: *Facebook post.* https://www.facebook.com/dhruv.batra.dbatra/posts/1943791229195215. - 2017-07-31

[Bbc07]   BBC: What walking speeds say about us (2007) http://news.bbc.co.uk/2/hi/uk_news/magazine/6614637.stm

[BBHK20]   BAJRACHARYA, MAX; BORDERS, JAMES; HELMICK, DAN; KOLLAR, THOMAS; LASKEY, MICHAEL; LEICHTY, JOHN; MA, JEREMY; NAGARAJAN, UMASHANKAR; U. A.: A Mobile Manipulation System for One-Shot Teaching of Complex Tasks in Homes. In: *arXiv:1910.00127 [cs]* (2020) — arXiv: 1910.00127 http://arxiv.org/abs/1910.00127

[BBKC15]   BARTOL, THOMAS M.; BROMER, CAILEY; KINNEY, JUSTIN; CHIRILLO, MICHAEL A.; BOURNE, JENNIFER N.; HARRIS, KRISTEN M.; SEJNOWSKI, TERRENCE J.: Nanoconnectomic upper bound on the variability of synaptic plasticity. In: *eLife* Vol. 4 (2015)

[Bell14]   BELL, VAUGHAN: *From photography to supercomputers: how we see ourselves in our inventions | Neuroscience | The Guardian.* https://www.theguardian.com/science/2014/jul/26/photography-supercomputers-see-ourselves-in-our-inventions-brain-neuroscience. - 2014-07-26

[Bell22]   BELLAN, REBECCA: *Germany gives greenlight to driverless vehicles on public roads.* https://social.techcrunch.com/2021/05/24/germany-gives-greenlight-to-driverless-vehicles-on-public-roads/. - 2022-05-24 — TechCrunch

[Bent20]   BENTLEY, PETER J.: *10 Short Lessons in Artificial Intelligence and Robotics.* London: MICHAEL OMARA BOOKS LTD, 2020 — ISBN 978-1-78929-216-9

[Bess09]	BESS, MICHAEL: *The Jetsons Fallacy: Science Fiction, Biotechnology, and the Future of the Human Species	CNS.UCSB*. http://www.cns.ucsb.edu/events/jetsons-fallacy-science-fiction-biotechnology-and-future-human-species.html. - 2009-04-30
[BGMS21]	BENDER, EMILY M.; GEBRU, TIMNIT; MCMILLAN-MAJOR, ANGELINA; MITCHELL, MARGARET: On the Dangers of Stochastic Parrots: Can Language Models Be Too Big? In: *Proceedings of the 2021 ACM Conference on Fairness, Accountability, and Transparency, FAccT '21*. New York, NY, USA: Association for Computing Machinery, 2021 — ISBN 978-1-4503-8309-7.
[Blue22]	*Wikipedia*.
[Book13]	THE BOOK OF ALTERNATIVE RECORDS: *Mental Calculation, Square Roots*. http://www.alternativerecords.co.uk/recorddetails.asp?recid=402&page=cat. - 2013-09-02
[Bost05]	BOSTROM, NICK: *What is a Singleton?* https://www.nickbostrom.com/fut/singleton.html. - 2005-
[Bost16]	BOSTROM, NICK: *Superintelligence: Paths, Dangers, Strategies*. Oxford, United Kingdom ; New York, NY: Oxford University Press, 2016 — ISBN 978-0-19-873983-8
[Boyd10]	BOYD, JOHN R: The Essence of Winning and Losing (2010).
[Boyl20]	BOYLE, ALAN: *White House's top techie explains how AI initiative will help Seattle tech community*. https://www.geekwire.com/2020/white-houses-top-techie-explains-ai-initiative-will-help-seattle-tech-community/. - 2020-02-26 — GeekWire
[Brad17]	BRADLEY, TONY: *Facebook AI Creates Its Own Language In Creepy Preview Of Our Potential Future*. https://www.forbes.com/sites/tonybradley/2017/07/31/facebook-ai-creates-its-own-language-in-creepy-preview-of-our-potential-future/. - 2017-07-31 — Forbes
[Bran20]	BRANWEN, GWERN: GPT-3 Creative Fiction (2020) https://www.gwern.net/GPT-3
[Brod18]	BRODWIN, ERIN: *I spent 2 weeks texting a bot about my anxiety — and found it to be surprisingly helpful*. https://www.businessinsider.com/therapy-chatbot-depression-app-what-its-like-woebot-2018-1. - 2018-01-30 — Business Insider
[Brow16]	BROWN, MARK: "New Rembrandt" to be unveiled in Amsterdam. In: *The Guardian* (2016) https://www.theguardian.com/artanddesign/2016/apr/05/new-rembrandt-to-be-unveiled-in-amsterdam
[Brow17]	BROWN, MIKE: *Here's Why a Self-Driving Car Could Give You a $10,000 Raise*. https://www.inverse.com/article/29780-self-driving-car-salary-increase-survey. - 2017-03-31 — Inverse
[Brow19]	BROWN, MIKE: *Autonomous Tesla: How Taxi Service Could Earn You $10,000 per Year*. https://www.inverse.com/article/54944-autonomous-tesla-how-taxi-service-could-earn-money. - 2019-04-16 — Inverse
[Brow20]	BROWN, ANNIE: *AI Is Not Going To Replace Writers Anytime Soon – But The Future Might Be Closer Than You Think*. https://www.forbes.com/sites/anniebrown/2021/07/20/ai-is-not-going-to-replace-writers-anytime-soon--but-the-future-might-be-closer-than-you-think/. - 2020-07-20 — Forbes
[Brow21]	BROWNE, JOHN: *Make, Think, Imagine: Engineering the Future of Civilization*: Pegasus Books, 2021 — ISBN 978-1-64313-686-8
[Brya06]	BRYAN, ANDY: *Back From Yet Another Globetrotting Adventure, Indiana Jones Checks His Mail And Discovers That His Bid For Tenure Has Been Denied*. https://www.mcsweeneys.net/articles/back-from-yet-another-globetrotting-adventure-indiana-jones-checks-his-mail-and-discovers-that-his-bid-for-tenure-has-been-denied. - 2006-10-10 — McSweeney's Internet Tendency
[BSLM11]	BECK, ANDREW H.; SANGOI, ANKUR R.; LEUNG, SAMUEL; MARINELLI, ROBERT J.; NIELSEN, TORSTEN O.; VAN DE VIJVER, MARC J.; WEST, ROBERT B.; VAN DE RIJN, MATT; U. A.: Systematic Analysis of Breast Cancer Morphology Uncovers Stromal Features Associated with Survival. In: *Science Translational Medicine* Vol. 3, American Association for the Advancement of Science (2011), No. 108.
[Burg17]	BURGESS, SANYA: *Stephen Hawking: AI could be "worst event in the history of our civilisation"*. https://www.thenationalnews.com/business/technology/stephen-hawking-ai-could-be-worst-event-in-the-history-of-our-civilisation-1.673585. - 2017-11-06 — The National
[Busi16]	BUSINESSWIRE: *Global Genomics Group (G3) and GNS Healthcare Report Preliminary Results of Largest-Ever Study Linking Biomarkers with Coronary Artery Disease*. https://www.businesswire.com/news/home/20160108005131/en/Global-Genomics-Group-G3-and-GNS-Healthcare-Report-Preliminary-Results-of-Largest-Ever-Study-Linking-Biomarkers-with-Coronary-Artery-Disease. - 2016-01-08

[CaBN17]   Caliskan, Aylin; Bryson, Joanna J.; Narayanan, Arvind: Semantics derived automatically from language corpora contain human-like biases. In: *Science* Vol. 356 (2017), No. 6334 — arXiv: 1608.07187

[Carl20]   Carlsmith, Joseph: *How Much Computational Power Does It Take to Match the Human Brain?* https://www.openphilanthropy.org/brain-computation-report. - 2020-08-14 — Open Philanthropy

[Cast20]   Castellanos, Sara: Intel to Release Neuromorphic-Computing System. In: *Wall Street Journal* (2020) https://www.wsj.com/articles/intel-to-release-neuromorphic-computing-system-11584540000

[Chal95]   Chalmers, David J: Facing Up to the Problem of Consciousness (1995).

[Chat07]   Chatham, Chris: *10 Important Differences Between Brains and Computers | ScienceBlogs*. https://scienceblogs.com/developingintelligence/2007/03/27/why-the-brain-is-not-like-a-co. - 2007-03-27

[Cheo19]   Cheong-mo, Yoo: *Go master Lee says he quits unable to win over AI Go players*. https://en.yna.co.kr/view/AEN20191127004800315. - 2019-11-27 — Yonhap News Agency

[Chri20]   Christiano, Paul F.: *Hiring engineers and researchers to help align GPT-3 - LessWrong*. https://www.lesswrong.com/posts/dJQo7xPn4TyGnKgeC/hiring-engineers-and-researchers-to-help-align-gpt-3. - 2020-10-01

[Clif17]   Clifford, Catherine: *By 2050, A.I. will have the same ability to learn as humans, says billionaire tech investor*. https://www.cnbc.com/2017/09/19/jim-breyer-by-2050-ai-will-have-the-same-ability-to-learn-as-humans.html. - 2017-09-20 — CNBC

[Cold18]   Coldewey, Devin: *This clever AI hid data from its creators to cheat at its appointed task*. https://social.techcrunch.com/2018/12/31/this-clever-ai-hid-data-from-its-creators-to-cheat-at-its-appointed-task/. - 2018-12-31 — TechCrunch

[Cong21]   Congressional Research Service: *Defense Primer: U.S. Policy on Lethal Autonomous Weapon Systems*, 2021 https://crsreports.congress.gov/product/pdf/IF/IF11150

[Cons20]   Consultancy.org: *CEO Nigel Vaz on Publicis Sapient's 30th birthday*. https://www.consultancy.uk/news/26445/ceo-nigel-vaz-on-publicis-sapients-30th-birthday. - 2020-12-24

[Cook19]   Cook, Katy: *The Psychology of Silicon Valley: Ethical Threats and Emotional Unintelligence in the Tech Industry*. 1st ed. 2020. Cham: Palgrave Macmillan, 2019 — ISBN 978-3-030-27363-7

[Cook20]   Cook, Katy:

[Corr21]   Correspondent, Tom Knowles, Technology: AI will have a bigger impact than fire, says Google boss Sundar Pichai (2021) https://www.thetimes.co.uk/article/ai-will-have-a-bigger-impact-than-fire-says-google-boss-sundar-pichai-rk8bdst7r

[Cpum21]   CPU Monkey: *Apple A15 (5 GPU Cores)*. https://www.cpu-monkey.com/en/igpu-apple_a15_5_gpu_cores-275. - 2021-10-04

[Crev93]   Crevier, Daniel: *Ai: The Tumultuous History Of The Search For Artificial Intelligence*. New York, NY: Basic Books, 1993 — ISBN 978-0-465-02997-6

[DaOx19]   Dafoe, Baobao Zhang and Allan; Oxford, Center for the Governance of AI, Future of Humanity Institute, University of: *2 General attitudes toward AI | Artificial Intelligence: American Attitudes and Trends*, 2019

[Darl18]   Darling, Kate: *Why we have an emotional connection to robots*, 2018

[Darl21]   Darling, Kate: *Could You Kill a Robot Dinosaur?* https://builtin.com/robotics/kill-robot-dinosaur-the-new-breed-kate-darling-excerpt. - 2021-04-13

[DaRo18]   Darcy, Alison; Robinson, Athena: *Ask Us Anything About Woebot*. www.reddit.com/r/IAmA/comments/9j302z/hello_we_are_drs_alison_darcy_athena_robinson_the/. - 2018-09-26 — r/IAmA

[Dast18]   Dastin, Jeffery: Amazon scraps secret AI recruiting tool that showed bias against women. In: *Reuters* (2018) https://www.reuters.com/article/us-amazon-com-jobs-automation-insight-idUSKCN1MK08G

[Delc18]   Delcker, Janosch: *The man who invented the self-driving car (in 1986)*. https://www.politico.eu/article/delf-driving-car-born-1986-ernst-dickmanns-mercedes/. - 2018-07-19 — POLITICO

[Dell18]   Dell:

[Demi18]   Demis Hassabis [@demishassabis]: *The full peer-reviewed #AlphaZero paper*. https://twitter.com/demishassabis/status/1070777817426739200. - 2018-12-06 — Twitter

[Deve22]	DEVELOPMENT, PODBEAN: *The Radical AI Podcast.* https://radicalai.podbean.com. - 2022-05-25
[DiSM15]	DIETVORST, BERKELEY J.; SIMMONS, JOSEPH P.; MASSEY, CADE: Algorithm aversion: People erroneously avoid algorithms after seeing them err. In: *Journal of Experimental Psychology: General* Vol. 144 (2015), No. 1, pp. 114–126
[Dodd16]	DODDS, MARIE: *Three-Quarters of Americans "Afraid" to Ride in a Self-Driving Vehicle.* https://info.oregon.aaa.com/three-quarters-of-americans-afraid-to-ride-in-a-self-driving-vehicle/. - 2016-03-01 — AAA Oregon/Idaho
[Dou21]	DOU, EVA: China built the world's largest facial recognition system. Now, it's getting camera-shy. In: *Washington Post* (2021) https://www.washingtonpost.com/world/facial-recognition-china-tech-data/2021/07/30/404c2e96-f049-11eb-81b2-9b7061a582d8_story.html
[Draa01]	DRAAISMA, DOUWE: *Metaphors of Memory*: Cambridge University Press, 2001
[Dubo67]	DU BOFF, RICHARD B.: The Introduction of Electric Power in American Manufacturing. In: *The Economic History Review* Vol. 20, [Economic History Society, Wiley] (1967), No. 3, pp. 509–518
[Duhi14]	DUHIGG, CHARLES: *The Power of Habit: Why We Do What We do in Life and Business*: Anchor Canada, 2014 — ISBN 978-0-385-66976-4
[ECMD15]	ECARLAT, P.; CULLY, ANTOINE; MAESTRE, CARLOS; DONCIEUX, S.: Learning a high diversity of object manipulations though an evolutionary-based babbling. In: *undefined* (2015) https://www.semanticscholar.org/paper/Learning-a-high-diversity-of-object-manipulations-Ecarlat-Cully/fed7bd56153dd42a727c70f6336e0ada6e995b3f
[EEFL18]	EYKHOLT, KEVIN; EVTIMOV, IVAN; FERNANDES, EARLENCE; LI, BO; RAHMATI, AMIR; XIAO, CHAOWEI; PRAKASH, ATUL; KOHNO, TADAYOSHI; U. A.: Robust Physical-World Attacks on Deep Learning Visual Classification. In: *2018 IEEE/CVF Conference on Computer Vision and Pattern Recognition*, 2018, P. 1625–1634
[EKNK17]	ESTEVA, ANDRE; KUPREL, BRETT; NOVOA, ROBERTO A.; KO, JUSTIN; SWETTER, SUSAN M.; BLAU, HELEN M.; THRUN, SEBASTIAN: Dermatologist-level classification of skin cancer with deep neural networks. In: *Nature* Vol. 542, Nature Publishing Group (2017), No. 7639, pp. 115–118
[Evan19]	EVANS, GREG: *The Monster Raving Loony Party beat UKIP and people think it's because of their Brexit strategy.* https://www.indy100.com/news/brecon-by-election-result-brexit-ukip-monster-raving-loony-party-noel-edmonds-9035386. - 2019-08-02
[EvGa16]	EVANS, RICHARD; GAO, JIM: *DeepMind AI Reduces Google Data Centre Cooling Bill by 40%.* https://www.deepmind.com/blog/deepmind-ai-reduces-google-data-centre-cooling-bill-by-40. - 2016-07-20
[Fauz21]	FAUZIA, MIRIAM: *Fact check: Facebook chatbots weren't shut down for creating language.* https://www.usatoday.com/story/news/factcheck/2021/07/28/fact-check-facebook-chatbots-werent-shut-down-creating-language/8040006002/. - 2021-07-28
[Favr19]	FAVREAU, JON: *Pod Save America Podcast.* https://crooked.com/podcast-series/pod-save-america/. - 2019-05-02 — Crooked Media
[FeMc83]	FEIGENBAUM, EDWARD A.; MCCORDUCK, PAMELA: *The Fifth Generation: Artificial Intelligence and Japan's Computer Challenge to the World.* Reading, Mass: Addison-Wesley, 1983 — ISBN 978-0-201-11519-2
[Feng22]	FENG, JOHN: *China tries to tone down war talk as military tells Taiwan to "surrender".* https://www.newsweek.com/china-tones-down-war-talk-peoples-liberation-army-tells-taiwan-surrender-now-1668927. - 2022-01-13 — Newsweek
[Ferg13]	FERGUSON, WILLIAM: *A Hacked Database Prompts Debate about Genetic Privacy.* https://www.scientificamerican.com/article/a-hacked-database-prompts/. - 2013-02-05 — Scientific American
[Fiel17]	FIELD, MATTHEW: Facebook shuts down robots after they invent their own language. In: *The Telegraph* (2017) https://www.telegraph.co.uk/technology/2017/08/01/facebook-shuts-robots-invent-language/
[Fing21]	FINGAS, J.: *Driverless robotaxis are now available for public rides in China.* https://www.engadget.com/autox-fully-driverless-robotaxi-china-145126521.html. - 2021-01-29 — Engadget
[Fles22]	*Wikipedia.* Flesch–Kincaid readability tests
[Foo20]	FOO, BRANDON: *How Long do People Take to Respond to a Business Email?* https://blog.polymail.io/post/how-long-do-people-take-to-respond-to-a-business-email. - 2020-12-01

[Ford18]   FORD, MARTIN: *Architects of Intelligence*. https://www.packtpub.com/product/architects-of-intelligence/9781789954531. - 2018-11-23 — Packt
[Foss15]   FOSSATI, GIOVANNI: *RPubs - The Analytics Edge - Unit 4 : Judge, Jury and Classifier*. https://rpubs.com/PedroSan/TAEu4_SCOTUS. - 2015-04-06
[Fost22]   FOSTER-FLETCHER, RICHARD: Email to the author, 2022-03-11
[Fram13]   FRAMPTON, WILL: With new software, Norcross police practice Predictive Policing, 2013 http://www.cbs46.com/story/23178208/with-new-software-norcross-police-utilize-predictive-policing
[Free17]   FREEAGENT: *Do workers dream of electric bosses? 31% say they would be happy to work for a "robo-boss"*. https://www.freeagent.com/en/blog/roboboss/. - 2017-11-13 — FreeAgent
[Frey19]   FREY, CARL BENEDIKT: *The Answer to the A.I. Jobs Apocalypse Is All About Geography*. https://onezero.medium.com/housing-policy-is-the-answer-to-the-a-i-job-apocalypse-ae70e7dda093. - 2019-07-09 — OneZero
[Frie58]   FRIEDBERG, R. M.: A Learning Machine: Part I. In: *IBM Journal of Research and Development* Vol. 2 (1958), No. 1, pp. 2–13
[FrOs17]   FREY, CARL BENEDIKT; OSBORNE, MICHAEL A.: The future of employment: How susceptible are jobs to computerisation? In: *Technological Forecasting and Social Change* Vol. 114 (2017), P. 254–280
[Fry19]   FRY, HANNAH: *Hello World: Being Human in the Age of Algorithms*. W. W. Norton & Company, 2019 — ISBN 978-0-393-35736-3
[FuKu82]   FULLER, R. BUCKMINSTER; KUROMIYA, KIYOSHI: *Critical Path*. New York, N.Y: St. Martin's Griffin, 1982 — ISBN 978-0-312-17491-0
[Funk16]   FUNKE, RALF: *From Gobble to Zen: The Quest for Truly Intelligent Software and the Monte Carlo Revolution in Go*. https://www.springerprofessional.de/en/from-gobble-to-zen-the-quest-for-truly-intelligent-software-and-/2223496. - 2016-09-22 — springerprofessional.de
[Gard20]   GARDINER, MARK: A Car Insurance Claim Estimate Before the Tow Truck Is Called. In: *The New York Times* (2020) https://www.nytimes.com/2020/09/17/business/car-insurance-claim-estimate-artificial-intelligence.html
[GBDP13]   GRABOWSKI, LAURA M.; BRYSON, DAVID M.; DYER, FRED C.; PENNOCK, ROBERT T.; OFRIA, CHARLES: A Case Study of the De Novo Evolution of a Complex Odometric Behavior in Digital Organisms. In: *PLOS ONE* Vol. 8, Public Library of Science (2013), No. 4.
[Gent21]   GENT, EDD: *IBM's 127-Qubit Eagle Is the Biggest Quantum Computer Yet*. https://singularityhub.com/2021/11/22/ibms-127-qubit-eagle-is-the-biggest-quantum-computer-yet/. - 2021-11-22 — Singularity Hub
[GHSE03]   GASPAR, V.; HARTMANN, P.; SLEIJPEN, O.; EUROPEAN CENTRAL BANK (Hrsg.): *The transformation of the European financial system: second ECB Central Banking Conference, October 2002, Frankfurt, Germany*. Frankfurt: European Central Bank, 2003 — ISBN 978-92-9181-348-3, GASPAR, V.; HARTMANN, P.; SLEIJPEN, O.; EUROPEAN CENTRAL BANK (Hrsg.).
[Gild22]   GILDER, GEORGE: *Life After Google: The Fall of Big Data and the Rise of the Blockchain Economy*. https://www.amazon.ca/Life-After-Google-Blockchain-Economy/dp/168451293X/. - 2022-01-04
[Glan78]   GLANC, A: On the etymology of the word "robot". In: *SIGART Newsletter* (1978), No. 67:12
[Glob20]   THE GLOBAL DISINFORMATION INDEX: *GDI Primer: The U.S. (Dis)Information Ecosystem*, 2020 https://www.disinformationindex.org/research/2020-3-1-gdi-primer-the-us-disinformation-ecosystem/
[Gold10]   GOLDMAN, BRUCE: *New imaging method developed at Stanford reveals stunning details of brain connections*. http://med.stanford.edu/news/all-news/2010/11/new-imaging-method-developed-at-stanford-reveals-stunning-details-of-brain-connections.html. - 2010-11-17 — News Center
[Gold21]   GOLDSTAUB, TABITHA: *How To Talk To Robots: A Girls' Guide To a Future Dominated by AI*. Fourth Estate, 2021 — ISBN 978-0-00-840587-8
[Gole21]   GOLED, SHRADDHA: *GPT-4: Sam Altman Confirms Rumours*. https://analyticsindiamag.com/gpt-4-sam-altman-confirms-the-rumours/. - 2021-09-13 — Analytics India Magazine
[Good65]   GOOD, IRVING J.: The Mystery of Go. In: *New Scientist* (1965)
[Goog17]   GOOGLE: *The Future of Go Summit*. https://events.google.com/alphago2017/. - 2017-05-23

[GoRo97] Goldin, Claudia; Rouse, Cecilia: Orchestrating Impartiality: The Impact of "Blind" Auditions on Female Musicians. In: *National Bureau of Economic Research* Vol. 90 (1997), No. 4, P. 715–741

[GoRS16] Goel, Sharad; Rao, Justin M.; Shroff, Ravi: Precinct or prejudice? Understanding racial disparities in New York City's stop-and-frisk policy. In: *The Annals of Applied Statistics* Vol. 10 (2016), No. 1 https://projecteuclid.org/journals/annals-of-applied-statistics/volume-10/issue-1/Precinct-or-prejudice-Understanding-racial-disparities-in-New-York-Citys/10.1214/15-AOAS897.full

[Gove20] Government of Canada, Innovation: *Canada's AI-Powered Supply Chains Supercluster (Scale AI)*. https://ised-isde.canada.ca/site/innovation-superclusters-initiative/en/canadas-ai-powered-supply-chains-supercluster-scale-ai. - 2020-12-01 — Last Modified: 2020-12-01

[Gpai20] GPAI: *Global Partnership on Artificial Intelligence*. https://gpai.ai/. - 2020-11-27

[GrNH19] Grother, Patrick; Ngan, Mei; Hanaoka, Kayee: *Face recognition vendor test part 3: demographic effects* (# NIST IR 8280). Gaithersburg, MD: National Institute of Standards and Technology, 2019 https://nvlpubs.nist.gov/nistpubs/ir/2019/NIST.IR.8280.pdf

[GSSM21] Guetta, Nitzan; Shabtai, Asaf; Singh, Inderjeet; Momiyama, Satoru; Elovici, Yuval: Dodging Attack Using Carefully Crafted Natural Makeup. In: *arXiv:2109.06467 [cs]* (2021) — arXiv: 2109.06467 http://arxiv.org/abs/2109.06467

[Gunk18] Gunkel, David J.: *Robot Rights*. Cambridge, MA, USA: MIT Press, 2018 — ISBN 978-0-262-03862-1

[GZFB20] Gidon, Albert; Zolnik, Timothy Adam; Fidzinski, Pawel; Bolduan, Felix; Papoutsi, Athanasia; Poirazi, Panayiota; Holtkamp, Martin; Vida, Imre; u. a.: Dendritic action potentials and computation in human layer 2/3 cortical neurons. In: *Science* Vol. 367, American Association for the Advancement of Science (2020), No. 6473, pp. 83–87

[Haas17] Haas, Benjamin: Chinese man "marries" robot he built himself. In: *The Guardian* (2017) https://www.theguardian.com/world/2017/apr/04/chinese-man-marries-robot-built-himself

[HaHu20] Hanley, Daniel A; Hubbard, Sally: Eyes Everywhere: Amazon's Surveillance Infrastructure and Revitalizing Worker Power (2020), P. 34

[Haid18] Haider, Andre: *Autonomous Weapon Systems in International Humanitarian Law*. https://www.japcc.org/autonomous-weapon-systems-in-international-humanitarian-law/. - 2018-12-13 — Joint Air Power Competence Centre

[Hal15] Hal, Hodson: *AI interns: Software already taking jobs from humans*. https://www.newscientist.com/article/mg22630151-700-ai-interns-software-already-taking-jobs-from-humans/. - 2015-03-31 — New Scientist

[Halp22] Halpern, Sue: The Rise of A.I. Fighter Pilots. In: *The New Yorker* (2022) https://www.newyorker.com/magazine/2022/01/24/the-rise-of-ai-fighter-pilots

[Hans08] Hansell, Saul: *Zuckerberg's Law of Information Sharing*. https://bits.blogs.nytimes.com/2008/11/06/zuckerbergs-law-of-information-sharing/. - 2008-11-06 — Bits Blog

[Hao19] Hao, Karen: *The computing power needed to train AI is now rising seven times faster than ever before*. https://www.technologyreview.com/2019/11/11/132004/the-computing-power-needed-to-train-ai-is-now-rising-seven-times-faster-than-ever-before/. - 2019-11-11 — MIT Technology Review

[Hao20a] Hao, Karen: *AI has cracked a key mathematical puzzle for understanding our world*. https://www.technologyreview.com/2020/10/30/1011435/ai-fourier-neural-network-cracks-navier-stokes-and-partial-differential-equations/. - 2020-10-30

[Hao20b] Hao: *A college kid's fake, AI-generated blog fooled tens of thousands. This is how he made it*. https://www.technologyreview.com/2020/08/14/1006780/ai-gpt-3-fake-blog-reached-top-of-hacker-news/. - 2020-08-14 — MIT Technology Review

[Hao20c] Hao, Karen: *AI pioneer Geoff Hinton: "Deep learning is going to be able to do everything"*. https://www.technologyreview.com/2020/11/03/1011616/ai-godfather-geoffrey-hinton-deep-learning-will-do-everything/. - 2020-11-03 — MIT Technology Review

[Hao21] Hao, Karen: *How Facebook got addicted to spreading misinformation*. https://www.technologyreview.com/2021/03/11/1020600/facebook-responsible-ai-misinformation/. - 2021-03-11 — MIT Technology Review

[Harr19] Harris, Mark: *NTSB Investigation Into Deadly Uber Self-Driving Car Crash Reveals Lax Attitude Toward Safety*. In: *IEEE Spectrum* (2019) https://spectrum.ieee.org/ntsb-investigation-into-deadly-uber-selfdriving-car-crash-reveals-lax-attitude-toward-safety

[Harw19] HARWELL, DREW: A face-scanning algorithm increasingly decides whether you deserve the job. In: *Washington Post* (2019) https://www.washingtonpost.com/technology/2019/10/22/ai-hiring-face-scanning-algorithm-increasingly-decides-whether-you-deserve-job/

[Harw20] HARWELL, DREW: iHeartMedia laid off hundreds of radio DJs. Executives blame AI. DJs blame the executives. In: *Washington Post* (2020) https://www.washingtonpost.com/technology/2020/01/31/iheartmedia-radio-artificial-intelligence-djs/

[Hays04] HAYS, CONSTANCE L.: *What Wal-Mart Knows About Customers' Habits - The New York Times.* https://www.nytimes.com/2004/11/14/business/yourmoney/what-walmart-knows-about-customers-habits.html. - 2004-11-14

[Heat17] HEATH, THOMAS: Bank tellers are the next blacksmiths. In: *Washington Post* (2017) https://www.washingtonpost.com/business/economy/bank-tellers-are-the-next-blacksmiths/2017/02/08/fdf78618-ee1c-11e6-9662-6eedf1627882_story.html

[Heav20] HEAVEN, WILL DOUGLAS: *DeepMind's protein-folding AI has solved a 50-year-old grand challenge of biology.* https://www.technologyreview.com/2020/11/30/1012712/deepmind-protein-folding-ai-solved-biology-science-drugs-disease/. - 2020-11-30 — MIT Technology Review

[Henl20] HENLEY, JON: How Finland starts its fight against fake news in primary schools. In: *The Guardian* (2020) https://www.theguardian.com/world/2020/jan/28/fact-from-fiction-finlands-new-lessons-in-combating-fake-news

[Henr20] HENRY, CHRIS: *What is Total Cost Per Mile for truckload carriers?* https://www.freightwaves.com/news/understanding-total-operating-cost-per-mile. - 2020-01-13 — FreightWaves

[Herb65] HERBERT, FRANK: *Dune*. New York: Ace, 1965 — ISBN 978-0-441-17271-9

[Hern13] HERNANDEZ, DANIELA: The Man Behind the Google Brain: Andrew Ng and the Quest for the New AI. In: *Wired* (2013) https://www.wired.com/2013/05/neuro-artificial-intelligence/

[Hern17] HERN, ALEX: China censored Google's AlphaGo match against world's best Go player. In: *The Guardian* (2017) https://www.theguardian.com/technology/2017/may/24/china-censored-googles-alphago-match-against-worlds-best-go-player

[Hill10] HILLIS, DANNY: What Comes Next. In: *Scientific American* (2010)

[Hill15] HILLIS, W. DANIEL: *The Pattern On The Stone: The Simple Ideas That Make Computers Work.* New York: Basic Books, 2015 — ISBN 978-0-465-06693-3

[Hill20a] HILL, KASHMIR: The Secretive Company That Might End Privacy as We Know It. In: *The New York Times* (2020) https://www.nytimes.com/2020/01/18/technology/clearview-privacy-facial-recognition.html

[Hill20b] HILL, KASHMIR: Before Clearview Became a Police Tool, It Was a Secret Plaything of the Rich. In: *The New York Times* (2020) https://www.nytimes.com/2020/03/05/technology/clearview-investors.html

[HKBS12] HINDRÉ, THOMAS; KNIBBE, CAROLE; BESLON, GUILLAUME; SCHNEIDER, DOMINIQUE: New insights into bacterial adaptation through in vivo and in silico experimental evolution. In: *Nature Reviews. Microbiology* Vol. 10 (2012), No. 5, pp. 352–365

[Hoff15] HOFFMAN, DONALD: *Do we see reality as it is?*, 2015

[Hold18] HOLDER, CHRIS: *Artificial Intelligence: Public Perception, Attitude and Trust*, 2018 https://www.bristows.com/app/uploads/2019/06/Artificial-Intelligence-Public-Perception-Attitude-and-Trust.pdf

[Huan21] HUANG, JOYCE: *China Using 'Cognitive Warfare' Against Taiwan, Observers Say.* https://www.voanews.com/a/east-asia-pacific_china-using-cognitive-warfare-against-taiwan-observers-say/6200837.html. - 2021-01-17 — VOA

[HXCM18] HARB, MUSTAPHA; XIAO, YU; CIRCELLA, GIOVANNI; MOKHTARIAN, PATRICIA L.; WALKER, JOAN L.: Projecting travelers into a world of self-driving vehicles: estimating travel behavior implications via a naturalistic experiment. In: *Transportation* Vol. 45 (2018), No. 6, pp. 1671–1685

[IaLa20] IANSITI, MARCO; LAKHANI, KARIM R.: *Competing in the Age of AI: Strategy and Leadership When Algorithms and Networks Run the World*. Boston, MA: Harvard Business Review Press, 2020 — ISBN 978-1-63369-762-1

[Ihea20] IHEARTMEDIA: *As it Enters the New Decade, iHeartMedia Announces Technology Transformation and New Organizational Structure for its Markets Group.* https://www.iheartmedia.com/press/it-enters-new-decade-iheartmedia-announces-technology-transformation-and-new-organizational. - 2020-01-14

[Imo19]	IMO: *IMO Grand Challenge*. https://imo-grand-challenge.github.io/. - 2019-10-25 — IMO Grand Challenge
[Itrs12]	ITRS: *THE INTERNATIONAL TECHNOLOGY ROADMAP FOR SEMICONDUCTORS: 2012 UPDATE*, 2012 http://www.itrs.net/Links/2012ITRS/2012Chapters/2012Overview.pdf
[Jero10]	JEROME, SARA: *Schmidt: Google gets 'right up to the creepy line'*. https://thehill.com/policy/technology/122121-schmidt-google-gets-right-up-to-the-creepy-line/. - 2010-10-01 — The Hill
[John11]	JOHNSTON, CASEY: *Jeopardy: IBM's Watson almost sneaks wrong answer by Trebek	Ars Technica*. https://arstechnica.com/information-technology/2011/02/ibms-watson-tied-for-1st-in-jeopardy-almost-sneaks-wrong-answer-by-trebek/. - 2011-02-15
[John97]	JOHNSON, GEORGE: Undiscovered Bach? No, a Computer Wrote It. In: *The New York Times* (1997) https://www.nytimes.com/1997/11/11/science/undiscovered-bach-no-a-computer-wrote-it.html
[JoRW14]	JONES, BENJAMIN; REEDY, E J; WEINBERG, BRUCE A: AGE AND SCIENTIFIC GENIUS. In: , *NBER WORKING PAPER SERIES*. (2014), P. 51
[Kais15]	KAISER KUO: *Baidu CEO Robin Li interviews Bill Gates and Elon Musk at the Boao Forum, March 29 2015Convert & Download*, 2015
[KaKu02]	KAPOR, MITCHELL; KURZWEIL, RAY: *By 2029 no computer - or "machine intelligence" - will have passed the Turing Test*. https://longbets.org/1/. - 2002-
[Kali15]	KALIOUBY, RANA EL: *This app knows how you feel -- from the look on your face*, 2015
[Kard63]	KARDASHEV, N.S.: Transmission of Information by Extraterrestrial Civilizations. In: , 1963
[Kasp18]	KASPAROV, GARRY: *Deep Thinking: Where Machine Intelligence Ends and Human Creativity Begins*. New York: PublicAffairs, 2018 — ISBN 978-1-5417-7364-6
[Kasr17]	KASRIEL, STEPHANIE: *6 ways to make sure AI creates jobs for all and not the few*. https://www.weforum.org/agenda/2017/08/ways-to-ensure-ai-robots-create-jobs-for-all/. - 2017-08-14 — World Economic Forum
[KaWe67]	KAHN, HERMAN; WEINER, ANTHONY J.: *The Year 2000: A Framework for Speculation on the Next Thirty-Three Years*. The Macmillan Co., 1967
[KDLM22]	KOCIJAN, VID; DAVIS, ERNEST; LUKASIEWICZ, THOMAS; MARCUS, GARY; MORGENSTERN, LEORA: The Defeat of the Winograd Schema Challenge. In: *arXiv:2201.02387 [cs]* (2022) — arXiv: 2201.02387 http://arxiv.org/abs/2201.02387
[Kell13]	KELLEHER, DAVID: *Survey: 81% of U.S. Employees Check their Work Mail outside Work Hours [INFOGRAPHIC]*. https://techtalk.gfi.com/survey-81-of-u-s-employees-check-their-work-mail-outside-work-hours/. - 2013-05-20 — GFI Blog
[Keyn30]	KEYNES, JOHN MAYNARD: Economic Possibilities for our Grandchildren (1930) (1930), P. 42
[KFRC75]	KINCAID, J.; FISHBURNE, ROBERT; ROGERS, RICHARD; CHISSOM, BRAD: Derivation Of New Readability Formulas (Automated Readability Index, Fog Count And Flesch Reading Ease Formula) For Navy Enlisted Personnel. In: *Institute for Simulation and Training* (1975) https://stars.library.ucf.edu/istlibrary/56
[Khar17]	KHARPAL, ARJUN: *Bill Gates wants to tax robots, but the EU says, "no way, no way"*. https://www.cnbc.com/2017/06/02/bill-gates-robot-tax-eu.html. - 2017-06-02 — CNBC
[Kiss18]	KISSINGER, HENRY A.: *How the Enlightenment Ends*. https://www.theatlantic.com/magazine/archive/2018/06/henry-kissinger-ai-could-mean-the-end-of-human-history/559124/. - 2018-05-15 — The Atlantic
[KKIF12]	KAHN, PETER; KANDA, TAKAYUKI; ISHIGURO, HIROSHI; FREIER, NATHAN; SEVERSON, RACHEL; GILL, BRIAN; RUCKERT, JOLINA; SHEN, SOLACE: "Robovie, You'll Have to Go into the Closet Now": Children's Social and Moral Relationships With a Humanoid Robot. In: *Developmental psychology* Vol. 48 (2012), pp. 303–14
[Knig20]	KNIGHT, WILL: AI Can Do Great Things—if It Doesn't Burn the Planet. In: *Wired* (2020) https://www.wired.com/story/ai-great-things-burn-planet/
[Knig21]	KNIGHT, WILL: The Pentagon Is Bolstering Its AI Systems—by Hacking Itself. In: *Wired* (2021) https://www.wired.com/story/pentagon-bolstering-ai-systems-hacking-itself/
[Kore21]	KORETZ, JANNA: Telephone interview with the author, 2021-11-08
[Krew21]	KREWELL, KEVIN: *IBM Goes Vertical To Scale Transistors*. https://www.forbes.com/sites/tiriasresearch/2021/12/22/ibm-goes-vertical-to-scale-transistors/. - 2021-12-22 — Forbes
[Krig21]	KRIGOLSON, OLAV: Email to the author, 2021-11-24

[Kubr68] KUBRICK, STANLEY: *2001: A Space Odyssey*: Metro-Goldwyn-Mayer (MGM), Stanley Kubrick Productions, 1968 — IMDb ID: tt0062622

[Kurz13] KURZWEIL, RAY: *How to Create a Mind: The Secret of Human Thought Revealed*. New York, NY: Penguin Books, 2013 — ISBN 978-0-14-312404-7

[Labb21] LABBE, MARK: *Energy consumption of AI poses environmental problems*. https://www.techtarget.com/searchenterpriseai/feature/Energy-consumption-of-AI-poses-environmental-problems. - 2021-08-26 — SearchEnterpriseAI

[Lawg18] LAWGEEX: *20 Top Lawyers Beaten by Legal AI - LawGeex*. https://blog.lawgeex.com/20-top-lawyers-were-beaten-by-legal-ai-here-are-their-surprising-responses. - 2018-10-23

[Lee18] LEE, DAMI: *This $16,000 robot uses artificial intelligence to sort and fold laundry*. https://www.theverge.com/2018/1/10/16865506/laundroid-laundry-folding-machine-foldimate-ces-2018. - 2018-01-10 — The Verge

[Leig20] LEIGHT, ELIAS: *iHeartMedia Announces Wave of Layoffs, Further Crippling Local Radio - Rolling Stone*. https://www.rollingstone.com/pro/features/iheartmedia-mass-layoffs-937513/. - 2020-01-15 — 'The Culling Has Begun': Inside the iHeartMedia Layoffs

[LeNo99] LEVINE, ROBERT V; NORENZAYAN, ARA: *The Pace of Life in 31 Countries*. https://journals.sagepub.com/doi/abs/10.1177/0022022199030002003. - 1999-03-01

[Leve95] LEVESON, NANCY G.: *Safeware: System Safety and Computers*. Reading, Mass: Addison-Wesley Professional, 1995 — ISBN 978-0-201-11972-5

[Lewi16] LEWIS-KRAUS, GIDEON: The Great A.I. Awakening. In: *The New York Times* (2016) https://www.nytimes.com/2016/12/14/magazine/the-great-ai-awakening.html

[Lg20] LG: *LG INTRODUCES NEXT GENERATION OF LAUNDRY WITH NEW AI-POWERED WASHER*. https://www.lg.com/us/press-release/lg-introduces-next-generation-of-laundry-with-new-ai-powered-washer. - 2020-01-09 — LG USA

[LGKM14] LUCAS, GALE M.; GRATCH, JONATHAN; KING, AISHA; MORENCY, LOUIS-PHILIPPE: It's only a computer: Virtual humans increase willingness to disclose. In: *Computers in Human Behavior* Vol. 37 (2014), pp. 94–100

[LiLi20] LI, ROBIN; LIU, CIXIN: *Artificial Intelligence Revolution: How AI Will Change our Society, Economy, and Culture*: Skyhorse, 2020 — ISBN 978-1-5107-5299-3

[Lohr22] LOHR, STEVE: Economists Pin More Blame on Tech for Rising Inequality. In: *The New York Times* (2022) https://www.nytimes.com/2022/01/11/technology/income-inequality-technology.html

[LuMS20] LUND, SUSAN; MADGAVKAR, ANU; SMIT, SVEN: *What's next for remote work: An analysis of 2,000 tasks, 800 jobs, and nine countries*. https://www.mckinsey.com/featured-insights/future-of-work/whats-next-for-remote-work-an-analysis-of-2000-tasks-800-jobs-and-nine-countries. - 2020-11-23

[LYDP17] LEWIS, MIKE; YARATS, DENIS; DAUPHIN, YANN N.; PARIKH, DEVI; BATRA, DHRUV: Deal or No Deal? End-to-End Learning for Negotiation Dialogues. In: *arXiv:1706.05125 [cs]* (2017) — arXiv: 1706.05125 http://arxiv.org/abs/1706.05125

[Lync17] LYNCH, SHANA: *Andrew Ng: Why AI Is the New Electricity*. https://www.gsb.stanford.edu/insights/andrew-ng-why-ai-new-electricity. - 2017-03-11 — Stanford Graduate School of Business

[Mack19] MACKAY, JORY: *The State of Work Life Balance in 2019 (According to Data) - RescueTime*. https://blog.rescuetime.com/work-life-balance-study-2019/. - 2019-01-24 — RescueTime Blog

[MaDa19] MARCUS, GARY; DAVIS, ERNEST: *Rebooting AI: Building Artificial Intelligence We Can Trust*. New York: Pantheon, 2019 — ISBN 978-1-5247-4825-8

[Marc21] MARCHE, STEPHEN: The Computers Are Getting Better at Writing. In: *The New Yorker* (2021) https://www.newyorker.com/culture/cultural-comment/the-computers-are-getting-better-at-writing

[Marr19] MARR, BERNARD: *Artificial Intelligence Masters The Game Of Poker – What Does That Mean For Humans?* https://www.forbes.com/sites/bernardmarr/2019/09/13/artificial-intelligence-masters-the-game-of-poker--what-does-that-mean-for-humans/. - 2019-09-13 — Forbes

[Matt16] MATTERS, TRANSPORT FOR LONDON | EVERY JOURNEY: *Learn the Knowledge of London*. https://www.tfl.gov.uk/info-for/taxis-and-private-hire/licensing/learn-the-knowledge-of-london. - 2016-04-20 — Transport for London

[Mcca01]	MCCARTHY, JOHN: *THE ROBOT AND THE BABY*. http://www-formal.stanford.edu/jmc/robotandbaby/robotandbaby.html. - 2001-02-16
[Mcco04]	MCCORDUCK, PAMELA: *Machines Who Think: A Personal Inquiry into the History and Prospects of Artificial Intelligence*. Natick, Mass: A K Peters/CRC Press, 2004 — ISBN 978-1-56881-205-2
[Mcki13]	THE MCKINSEY GLOBAL INSTITUTE: *Disruptive technologies: Advances that will transform life, business, and the global economy*, 2013 http://www.mckinsey.com/~/media/McKinsey/dotcom/Insights%20and%20pubs/MGI/Research/Technology%20and%20Innovation/Disruptive%20technologies/MGI_Disruptive_technologies_Full_report_May2013.ashx
[Mcle22]	MCLEOD, SAUL: *Maslow's Hierarchy of Needs	Simply Psychology*. https://www.simplypsychology.org/maslow.html. - 2022-04-04
[Mead08]	MEADOWS, DONELLA; WRIGHT, D. (Hrsg.): *Thinking in Systems: International Bestseller*. White River Junction, Vt: Chelsea Green Publishing, 2008 — ISBN 978-1-60358-055-7, WRIGHT, D. (Hrsg.).
[Mena42]	MENABREA, LUIGI: *Notions sur la machine analytique de M. Charles Babbage*: Bibliothèque Universelle de Genève, 1842
[Metz16a]	METZ, CADE: 2016: The Year That Deep Learning Took Over the Internet. In: *Wired* (2016) https://www.wired.com/2016/12/2016-year-deep-learning-took-internet/
[Metz16b]	METZ, CADE: Google, Facebook, and Microsoft Are Remaking Themselves Around AI. In: *Wired* (2016) https://www.wired.com/2016/11/google-facebook-microsoft-remaking-around-ai/
[Metz21]	METZ, RACHEL: *Anyone can use this powerful facial-recognition tool — and that's a problem	CNN Business*. https://www.cnn.com/2021/05/04/tech/pimeyes-facial-recognition/index.html. - 2021-05-04 — CNN
[Micr21]	*Microsoft DeBERTa surpasses human performance on SuperGLUE benchmark*. https://www.microsoft.com/en-us/research/blog/microsoft-deberta-surpasses-human-performance-on-the-superglue-benchmark/. - 2021-01-06 — Microsoft Research
[MiJo21]	MISHEL, LAWRENCE; JORI, KADRA: *CEO pay has skyrocketed 1,322% since 1978*. https://www.epi.org/publication/ceo-pay-in-2020/. - 2021-08-10 — Economic Policy Institute
[Mill56]	MILLER, GEORGE A.: The magical number seven, plus or minus two: Some limits on our capacity for processing information. In: *Psychological Review* Vol. 63 (1956), P. 81–97
[Mind15]	MINDELL, DAVID A.: *Our Robots, Ourselves: Robotics and the Myths of Autonomy*. New York, New York: Viking, 2015 — ISBN 978-0-525-42697-4
[Mins88]	MINSKY, MARVIN: *Society Of Mind*. New York: Simon & Schuster, 1988 — ISBN 978-0-671-65713-0
[Mish16]	MISHRA, DEEPAK: *World Development Report 2016*, 2016 https://openknowledge.worldbank.org/bitstream/handle/10986/23347/9781464806711.pdf
[Mitr09]	MITRI, S.F.: The evolution of information suppression in communicating robots with conflicting interests. In: *Proceedings of the National Academy of Sciences*. Vol. 106(37):15786–15790, 2009
[MiWo19]	MISCHEL, LAWRENCE; WOLFE, JULIA: *CEO compensation has grown 940% since 1978*. https://www.epi.org/publication/ceo-compensation-2018/. - 2019-08-14 — Economic Policy Institute
[MKSG13]	MNIH, VOLODYMYR; KAVUKCUOGLU, KORAY; SILVER, DAVID; GRAVES, ALEX; ANTONOGLOU, IOANNIS; WIERSTRA, DAAN; RIEDMILLER, MARTIN: Playing Atari with Deep Reinforcement Learning. In: *arXiv:1312.5602 [cs]* (2013) — http://arxiv.org/abs/1312.5602
[MoAP18]	MODIC, DAVID; ANDERSON, ROSS; PALOMÄKI, JUSSI: We will make you like our research: The development of a Susceptibility-to-Persuasion scale. In: *PLoS ONE* Vol. 13. US, Public Library of Science (2018), No. 3
[MoFe19]	MOREIRA, CARLOS; FERGUSSON, DAVID: *The Transhuman Code: How to Program Your Future*. Austin, Texas: Greenleaf Book Group Press, 2019 — ISBN 978-1-62634-629-1
[MoLa18]	MOSCHELLA, DAVID; LAWRIE, MIKE: *Seeing Digital: A Visual Guide to the Industries, Organizations, and Careers of the 2020s*: DXC Technology, 2018
[MoMi97]	MORIARTY, DAVID E.; MIIKKULAINEN, RISTO: Forming Neural Networks Through Efficient and Adaptive Coevolution. In: *Evolutionary Computation* Vol. 5 (1997), No. 4, P. 373–399
[Moor03]	MOOR, J. H. (Hrsg.): *The Turing Test: The Elusive Standard of Artificial Intelligence*. Dordrecht ; Boston: Springer, 2003 — ISBN 978-1-4020-1204-4, MOOR, J. H. (Hrsg.).

[Mord15] MORDVINTSEV, ALEXANDER: *Inceptionism: Going Deeper into Neural Networks*. http://ai.googleblog.com/2015/06/inceptionism-going-deeper-into-neural.html. - 2015-06- — Google AI Blog

[Morg18] MORGAN, BLAKE: *How Amazon Has Reorganized Around Artificial Intelligence And Machine Learning*. https://www.forbes.com/sites/blakemorgan/2018/07/16/how-amazon-has-re-organized-around-artificial-intelligence-and-machine-learning/. - 2018-07- — Forbes

[Morr21] MORRISON, NICK: *Cameras Are Being Used To Punish Students, Not Stop School Shooters*. https://www.forbes.com/sites/nickmorrison/2021/04/11/cameras-are-being-used-to-punish-students-not-stop-school-shooters/. - 2021-04-11 — Forbes

[Moss18] MOSS, BRETT: *iHeartRadio CPO Says AI Helps Create "Unmatched Digital Listening Experience"*. https://www.radioworld.com/tech-and-gear/iheartradio-cpo-says-ai-helps-create-unmatched-digital-listening-experience. - 2018-08-22 — Radio World

[Moye90] MOYERS: *Robert Lucky on How Technology Will Transform the Future — But Not Replace Humans*. https://billmoyers.com/content/robert-lucky-part-2/. - 1990-02-04 — BillMoyers.com

[Mozu19] MOZUR, PAUL: *One Month, 500,000 Face Scans: How China Is Using A.I. to Profile a Minority*. In: *The New York Times* (2019) https://www.nytimes.com/2019/04/14/technology/china-surveillance-artificial-intelligence-racial-profiling.html

[Muse19] *MuseNet*. https://openai.com/blog/musenet/. - 2019-04-25 — OpenAI

[Musi19] MUSIAŁ, MACIEJ: *Enchanting Robots: Intimacy, Magic, and Technology*. New York, NY: Palgrave Macmillan, 2019 — ISBN 978-3-030-12578-3

[Naya19] NAYAK, PANDU: *Understanding searches better than ever before*. https://blog.google/products/search/search-language-understanding-bert/. - 2019-10-25 — Google

[Ng16] NG, ANDREW: *Hiring Your First Chief AI Officer*. In: *Harvard Business Review* (2016) https://hbr.org/2016/11/hiring-your-first-chief-ai-officer

[Nhts17] NHTSA: *Automated Driving Systems: A Vision for Safety* (2017)

[Nica20] NICAS, JACK: *He Has 17,700 Bottles of Hand Sanitizer and Nowhere to Sell Them*. In: *The New York Times* (2020) https://www.nytimes.com/2020/03/14/technology/coronavirus-purell-wipes-amazon-sellers.html

[Niel20] NIELD, DAVID: *People Running Folding@Home Accidentally Created The World's Biggest Supercomputer*. https://www.sciencealert.com/so-many-people-are-running-folding-home-that-it-s-created-the-world-s-biggest-supercomputer. - 2020-04-17 — ScienceAlert

[NKSN18] NARLA, AKHILA; KUPREL, BRETT; SARIN, KAVITA; NOVOA, ROBERTO; KO, JUSTIN: Automated Classification of Skin Lesions: From Pixels to Practice. In: *Journal of Investigative Dermatology* Vol. 138 (2018), No. 10, P. 2108–2110

[Nove17] NOVET, JORDAN: *Facebook AI researcher slams "irresponsible" reports about smart bot experiment*. https://www.cnbc.com/2017/08/01/facebook-ai-experiment-did-not-end-because-bots-invented-own-language.html. - 2017-08-01 — CNBC

[Oakd21] OAKDEN-RAYNER, LAUREN: *AI has the worst superpower… medical racism*. https://laurenoakdenrayner.com/2021/08/02/ai-has-the-worst-superpower-medical-racism/. - 2021-08-02 — Lauren Oakden-Rayner

[Obam16] OBAMA: *Artificial Intelligence, Automation, and the Economy*, 2016 https://obamawhitehouse.archives.gov/sites/whitehouse.gov/files/documents/Artificial-Intelligence-Automation-Economy.PDF

[Onfu18] *On the Future: Prospects for Humanity: Rees, Lord Martin: 9780691180441: Books - Amazon.ca*. https://www.amazon.ca/Future-Prospects-Humanity-Martin-Rees/dp/069118044X/. - 2018-10-16

[Orac19] ORACLE: *From Fear to Enthusiasm*. https://www.oracle.com/webfolder/s/assets/ebook/ai-work/index.html. - 2019-

[OtDi19] OTIS, GINGER ADAMS; DILLON, NANCY: *Google using dubious tactics to target people with 'darker skin' in facial recognition project: sources*. https://www.nydailynews.com/news/national/ny-google-darker-skin-tones-facial-recognition-pixel-20191002-5vxpgowknffnvbmy5eg7epsf34-story.html. - 2019-10-02 — New York Daily News

[PaCo17] PARTINGTON, RICHARD; CORRESPONDENT, RICHARD PARTINGTON ECONOMICS: UK's poorest to fare worst in age of automation, thinktank warns. In: *The Guardian* (2017) https://www.theguardian.com/technology/2017/dec/28/uks-poorest-to-fare-worst-in-age-of-automation-thinktank-warns

[Page84]   PAGELS, H. R. (Hrsg.): *Computer Culture: The Scientific, Intellectual, and Social Impact of the Computer*. New York, N.Y: New York Academy of Sciences, 1984 — ISBN 978-0-89766-245-1, PAGELS, H. R. (Hrsg.).

[Pain18]   PAINE, CHRIS: *Do You Trust This Computer?*: Diamond Docs, Papercut Films, 2018 — IMDb ID: tt6152554

[Pall20]   PALLASKALLIO, KAISU: *Code School Finland delivers a complete solution for K-9 AI education in China*. https://www.codeschool.fi/2020/02/complete-solution-k9-ai-education-china/. - 2020-02-04 — Code School Finland

[Pand07]   PANDE LAB SCIENCE: *History of Folding@HomeConvert & Download*, 2007

[Pape19]   PAPERSWITHCODE: *Image Classification on ImageNet*. https://paperswithcode.com/sota/image-classification-on-imagenet. - 2019-08-05

[Park12]   PARKER, GORDON: Acta is a four-letter word. In: *Acta Psychiatrica Scandinavica* Vol. 126 (2012), No. 6, P. 476–478

[Paya18]   *Pay attention at the back: school uses facial scans to monitor pupils*. https://www.scmp.com/news/china/society/article/2146387/pay-attention-back-chinese-school-installs-facial-recognition. - 2018-05-16 — South China Morning Post

[PBDP21] PTITO, MAURICE; BLEAU, MAXIME; DJEROUROU, ISMAËL; PARÉ, SAMUEL; SCHNEIDER, FABIEN C.; CHEBAT, DANIEL-ROBERT: Brain-Machine Interfaces to Assist the Blind. In: *Frontiers in Human Neuroscience* Vol. 15 (2021) https://www.frontiersin.org/article/10.3389/fnhum.2021.638887

[Peas12]   PEASE, ROLAND: Alan Turing: Inquest's suicide verdict "not supportable". In: *BBC News* (2012) https://www.bbc.com/news/science-environment-18561092

[Pega19]   PEGA: *AI and Empathy: Combining artificial intelligence with human ethics for better engagement*, 2019 https://www.pega.com/system/files/resources/pdf/pega-ai-empathy-study.pdf

[Perm19]   PERMANENT SELECT COMMITTEE ON INTELLIGENCE: *Exposing Russia's Effort to Sow Discord Online: The Internet Research Agency and Advertisements*. https://intelligence.house.gov/social-media-content/. - 2019-01-07

[Picc04]   PICCININI, GUALTIERO: The First Computational Theory of Mind and Brain: A Close Look at McCulloch and Pitts's "Logical Calculus of Ideas Immanent in Nervous Activity" (2004) https://www.jstor.org/stable/20118476

[Pink09]   PINKER, STEVEN: *How the Mind Works*. New York: WW Norton, 2009 — ISBN 978-0-393-33477-7

[Pohl79]   POHL, FREDERIK: *Day Million*. London: Pan MacMillan Books, 1979 — ISBN 978-0-330-23606-5

[Post22]   POST, THE JAKARTA: *In China, Go players rise to the challenge*. https://www.thejakartapost.com/life/2019/05/07/in-china-go-players-rise-to-the-challenge.html. - 2022-05-07 — The Jakarta Post

[PoTJ15]   POLONETSKY, JULES; TENE, OMER; JEROME, JOSEPH: *Beyond the Common Rule: Ethical Structures for Data Research in Non-Academic Settings* (SSRN Scholarly Paper # 2621559). Rochester, NY: Social Science Research Network, 2015 https://papers.ssrn.com/abstract=2621559

[Quir20]   QUIROZ, KARICIA: *Canada's advantage for AI: An ecosystem fuelled by talent and innovation*. https://www.investcanada.ca/blog/canadas-advantage-ai-ecosystem-fuelled-talent-and-innovation. - 2020-09-30

[RaAA17] RAINIE, LEE; ANDERSON, JANNA; ALBRIGHT, JONATHAN: *The Future of Free Speech, Trolls, Anonymity and Fake News Online*. https://www.pewresearch.org/internet/2017/03/29/the-future-of-free-speech-trolls-anonymity-and-fake-news-online/. - 2017-03-29 — Pew Research Center: Internet, Science & Tech

[Ramg19] RAMGE, THOMAS: *Who's Afraid of AI?: Fear and Promise in the Age of Thinking Machines*. New York: The Experiment, 2019 — ISBN 978-1-61519-550-3

[RaVe17] RAO, ANAND S.; VERWEIJ, GERARD: *Sizing the prize: what's the real value of AI for your business and how can you capitalise?* (Report): PricewaterhouseCoopers Australia, 2017 https://apo.org.au/node/113101

[Ray92]   RAY, T.: J'ai joué à Dieu et créé la vie dans mon ordinateur. In: *Artificial Life*, 1992

[RDBM19] REVIEW, HARVARD BUSINESS; DAVENPORT, THOMAS H.; BRYNJOLFSSON, ERIK; MCAFEE, ANDREW; WILSON, H. JAMES: *Artificial Intelligence: The Insights You Need from Harvard Business Review*. Boston, Massachusetts: Harvard Business Review Press, 2019 — ISBN 978-1-63369-789-8

[Read22] *Readout of the Sixth National Artificial Intelligence Research Resource (NAIRR) Task Force Meeting*. https://www.whitehouse.gov/ostp/news-updates/2022/04/11/readout-of-the-sixth-national-artificial-intelligence-research-resource-nairr-task-force-meeting/. - 2022-04-11 — The White House

[Rees18] REES, MARTIN: *Martin Rees: what are the limits of human understanding?* https://www.prospectmagazine.co.uk/magazine/martin-rees-what-are-the-limits-of-human-understanding. - 2018-11-13 — Prospect Magazine

[Ref00] SAGAR: *Turing, Alan Mathison*. https://www.cs.cmu.edu/afs/cs/academic/class/15251-f03/Site/Biographies/turing.htm. - 2000

[Ref20] EVE: *Woobot – the bleeding intelligent self-help therapist and companion*. https://digital.hbs.edu/platform-digit/submission/woebot-the-bleeding-intelligent-self-help-therapist-and-companion/. - 2020-04-21 — Digital Innovation and Transformation

[Rest20] RESTREPO, DARON ACEMOGLU, ANDREA MANERA, AND PASCUAL: *Does the US tax code favor automation?* https://www.brookings.edu/bpea-articles/does-the-u-s-tax-code-favor-automation/. - 2020-03-19 — Brookings

[Rest85] RESTAK, RICHARD M.: The human brain: Insights and puzzles. In: *Theory Into Practice* Vol. 24, Routledge (1985), No. 2, pp. 91–94

[Reve16] REVEL, TIMOTHY: *Glasses make face recognition tech think you're Milla Jovovich*. https://www.newscientist.com/article/2111041-glasses-make-face-recognition-tech-think-youre-milla-jovovich/. - 2016-11-01 — New Scientist

[Rifk14] RIFKIN, JEREMY: *The Zero Marginal Cost Society: The Internet of Things, the Collaborative Commons, and the Eclipse of Capitalism*. New York, NY: St. Martin's Press, 2014 — ISBN 978-1-137-27846-3

[Robe19] ROBERTSON, ALEXANDER: *Meet Britain's 19th century eccentrics, including the spinster with a love of giant bugs | Daily Mail Online*. https://www.dailymail.co.uk/news/article-6829919/Meet-Britains-19th-century-eccentrics-including-spinster-love-giant-bugs.html. - 2019-03-20

[Robe20] ROBERTS, THOMAS G.: *Space Launch to Low Earth Orbit: How Much Does It Cost?* https://aerospace.csis.org/data/space-launch-to-low-earth-orbit-how-much-does-it-cost/. - 2020-09-02 — Aerospace Security

[Robi00] ROBITZSKI, DAN: *Amazing AI makes you look and sound exactly like Joe Rogan*. https://futurism.com/the-byte/deepfake-ai-look-sound-joe-rogan — Futurism

[Robi21] ROBITZSKI, DAN: *Watch Tesla Autopilot Get Bamboozled by a Truck Hauling Traffic Lights*. https://futurism.com/the-byte/tesla-autopilot-bamboozled-truck-traffic-lights. - 2021-06-03 — Futurism

[Roch21] ROCHE, SAM: *Conspiracy theorists share schematic for "5G chip" they claim is implanted in COVID-19 vaccines – only it's actually for the Boss Metal Zone*. https://www.guitarworld.com/news/conspiracy-theorists-share-schematic-for-5g-chip-they-claim-is-implanted-in-covid-19-vaccines-only-its-actually-for-the-boss-metal-zone. - 2021-01-04 — guitarworld

[Roge21] ROGERS, BROOKE: *The last thing kids need is cameras in their classrooms*. https://nypost.com/2021/07/09/the-last-thing-kids-need-is-cameras-in-their-classrooms/. - 2021-07-09

[RoRR18] ROSLING, HANS; RÖNNLUND, ANNA ROSLING; ROSLING, OLA: *Factfulness: Ten Reasons We're Wrong About the World--and Why Things Are Better Than You Think*. New York: Flatiron Books, 2018 — ISBN 978-1-250-10781-7

[Rows19] ROWSON, JONATHAN: *The Moves That Matter: A Chess Grandmaster on the Game of Life*: Bloomsbury Publishing, 2019 — ISBN 978-1-63557-332-9

[Russ19] *Russian documents reveal desire to sow racial discord — and violence — in the U.S.* https://www.nbcnews.com/news/world/russian-documents-reveal-desire-sow-racial-discord-violence-u-s-n1008051. - 2019-05-20 — NBC News

[Russ20] RUSSELL, STUART: *Human Compatible: Artificial Intelligence and the Problem of Control*. New York: Penguin Books, 2020 — ISBN 978-0-525-55863-7

[Russ21] RUSSELL, STUART:

[Saei21] SAE INTERNATIONAL: *J3016_202104: Taxonomy and Definitions for Terms Related to Driving Automation Systems for On-Road Motor Vehicles*. https://www.sae.org/standards/content/j3016_202104/. - 2021-04-30

[Sain20]	SAINATO, MICHAEL: 'I'm not a robot': Amazon workers condemn unsafe, grueling conditions at warehouse. In: *The Guardian* (2020) https://www.theguardian.com/technology/2020/feb/05/amazon-workers-protest-unsafe-grueling-conditions-warehouse
[Sand20]	SANDMAN, JAMES: *Facebook*. https://www.facebook.com/james.sandman/posts/10219073005007831. - 2020-01-16
[Savi20]	Saving the world one algorithm at a time, 2020 — IMDb ID: tt11644288
[Scha19]	SCHARRE, PAUL: *Army of None: Autonomous Weapons and the Future of War*. New York: WW Norton, 2019 — ISBN 978-0-393-35658-8
[Schl13]	SCHLOSSER, ERIC: *Command and Control: Nuclear Weapons, the Damascus Accident, and the Illusion of Safety*. New York: Penguin Press, 2013 — ISBN 978-1-59420-227-8
[Schw19]	SCHWARZ, MICHAEL: *NOVA	Look Who's Driving	Season 46	Episode 19*, 2019
[Scie17]	SCIENTIST, NEW: *Machines that Think: Everything you need to know about the coming age of artificial intelligence*. John Murray, 2017
[Scol17]	SCOLES, SARAH: *A Brief History of SETI@Home*. https://www.theatlantic.com/science/archive/2017/05/aliens-on-your-packard-bell/527445/. - 2017-05-23 — The Atlantic
[Scot00]	SCOTT, PETER: Artificial Intelligence and You https://podcast.aiandyou.net
[Semu20]	SEMUELS, ALANA: *Millions of Americans Have Lost Jobs in the Pandemic — And Robots and AI Are Replacing Them Faster Than Ever*. https://time.com/5876604/machines-jobs-coronavirus/. - 2020-08-06 — Time
[Serv19]	SERVICE, ROBERT F.: AIs direct search for materials breakthroughs. In: *Science* Vol. 366, American Association for the Advancement of Science (2019), No. 6471, pp. 1295–1296
[Serv20]	SERVICE, ROBERT: 'The game has changed.' AI triumphs at solving protein structures. https://www.science.org/content/article/game-has-changed-ai-triumphs-solving-protein-structures. - 2020-11-30
[Shan18]	SHANE, JANELLE: *This Neural Net Hallucinates Sheep*. https://nautil.us/this-neural-net-hallucinates-sheep-7132/. - 2018-03-06 — Nautilus	Science Connected
[Shan19]	SHANE, JANELLE: *You Look Like a Thing and I Love You: How Artificial Intelligence Works and Why It's Making the World a Weirder Place*. New York: Voracious, 2019 — ISBN 978-0-316-52524-4
[Shan21a]	SHANKLAND, STEPHEN: *Quantum computers could crack today's encrypted messages. That's a problem*. https://www.cnet.com/tech/computing/quantum-computers-could-crack-todays-encrypted-messages-thats-a-problem/. - 2021-05-24 — CNET
[Shan21b]	SHANE, JANELLE: *Generating images from an internet grab bag*. https://www.aiweirdness.com/internet-grab-bag/. - 2021-07-09 — AI Weirdness
[Shea21]	SHEAD, SAM: *UN talks to ban "slaughterbots" collapsed — here's why that matters*. https://www.cnbc.com/2021/12/22/un-talks-to-ban-slaughterbots-collapsed-heres-why-that-matters.html. - 2021-12-22 — CNBC
[Sher16]	SHERMAN, ERIK: *Automation Won't Create New Jobs Like Technology Did In The Past*. https://www.forbes.com/sites/eriksherman/2016/12/17/automation-has-created-more-jobs-in-the-past-but-will-it-now/. - 2016- — Forbes
[Sims94a]	SIMS, KARL: Evolving virtual creatures. In: *Proceedings of the 21st annual conference on Computer graphics and interactive techniques, SIGGRAPH '94*. New York, NY, USA: Association for Computing Machinery, 1994 — ISBN 978-0-89791-667-7, P. 15–22
[Sims94b]	SIMS, KARL: Evolving 3D Morphology and Behavior by Competition. In: *Artificial Life IV Proceedings*: MIT Press, 1994
[Solo11]	SOLON, OLIVIA: How A Book About Flies Came To Be Priced $24 Million On Amazon. In: *Wired* (2011) https://www.wired.com/2011/04/amazon-flies-24-million/
[Solo17]	SOLON, OLIVIA: Ex-Facebook president Sean Parker: site made to exploit human "vulnerability". In: *The Guardian* (2017) https://www.theguardian.com/technology/2017/nov/09/facebook-sean-parker-vulnerability-brain-psychology
[Some13]	SOMERS, JAMES: *The Man Who Would Teach Machines to Think*. https://www.theatlantic.com/magazine/archive/2013/11/the-man-who-would-teach-machines-to-think/309529/. - 2013-10-23 — The Atlantic
[Sork19]	SORKIN, ANDREW ROSS: *McKinsey & Co. Isn't All Roses in a New Book*. https://dealbook.nytimes.com/2013/09/02/in-a-new-book-mckinsey-co-isnt-all-roses/. - 2019-09-02 — DealBook

[Stab21]	STABILE, ANGIE: *Why aren't America's classrooms fitted with cameras? Matt Walsh weighs in	Fox News*. https://www.foxnews.com/media/why-arent-americas-classrooms-fitted-with-cameras-matt-walsh-weighs-in. - 2021-07-07
[Staf21a]	STAFF: After years of dithering companies are embracing automation. In: *The Economist* (2021) https://www.economist.com/business/2021/01/16/after-years-of-dithering-companies-are-embracing-automation
[Staf21b]	STAFF, W. S. J.: *Inside TikTok's Algorithm: A WSJ Video Investigation*. https://www.wsj.com/articles/tiktok-algorithm-video-investigation-11626877477. - 2021-07-21 — WSJ
[Staf61]	STAFF: The Automation Jobless: Not Fired, Just Not Hired. In: *Time* (1961) https://www.flomartin.com/single-post/2017/06/28/the-automation-jobless
[Stat20]	STATT, NICK: *ACLU sues facial recognition firm Clearview AI, calling it a 'nightmare scenario' for privacy*. https://www.theverge.com/2020/5/28/21273388/aclu-clearview-ai-lawsuit-facial-recognition-database-illinois-biometric-laws. - 2020-05-28 — The Verge
[StBM05]	STANLEY, K.O.; BRYANT, B.D.; MIIKKULAINEN, R.: Real-Time Neuroevolution in the NERO Video Game. In: *IEEE Transactions on Evolutionary Computation* Vol. 9 (2005), No. 6, pp. 653–668
[Stem21]	*Stem cell AI: Loughborough part of £3m 'brain on a chip' project that aims to revolutionise computing power*. https://www.lboro.ac.uk/departments/chemistry/news/2021/stem-cell-ai-brain-on-chip-project/. - 2021-01-29 — Loughborough University
[StMi15]	STUTZMAN, RENE; MINSHEW, CHARLES: *Focus on Force*. http://interactive.orlandosentinel.com/focus-on-force/main/index.html. - 2015-11-06 — Orlando Sentinel
[Stoc20]	STOCKFORD, IAN: Awarding GCSE, AS, A level, advanced extension awards and extended project qualifications in summer 2020: interim report (2020), P. 319
[Stra22]	STRATFOR: *A Deepfake Video of Zelensky Is a Harbinger of AI-Powered Disinformation* (2022) https://worldview.stratfor.com/article/deepfake-video-zelensky-harbinger-ai-powered-disinformation
[Stre22]	STREITFELD, DAVID: The Epic Rise and Fall of Elizabeth Holmes. In: *The New York Times* (2022) https://www.nytimes.com/2022/01/03/technology/elizabeth-holmes-theranos.html
[Stud21]	2021 STUDY PANEL REPORT: *Gathering Strength, Gathering Storms: The One Hundred Year Study on Artificial Intelligence (AI100)*. https://ai100.stanford.edu/gathering-strength-gathering-storms-one-hundred-year-study-artificial-intelligence-ai100-2021-study. - 2021
[Sull15]	SULLIVAN, BOB: *Memo to work martyrs: Long hours make you less productive*. https://www.cnbc.com/2015/01/26/working-more-than-50-hours-makes-you-less-productive.html. - 2015-01-26 — CNBC
[Swee13]	SWEENEY, LATANYA: *Discrimination in Online Ad Delivery - Google ads, black names and white names, racial discrimination, and click advertising*. https://queue.acm.org/detail.cfm?id=2460278. - 2013-04-02
[SZSB18]	SCHMIDT, ANA LUCÍA; ZOLLO, FABIANA; SCALA, ANTONIO; BETSCH, CORNELIA; QUATTROCIOCCHI, WALTER: Polarization of the vaccination debate on Facebook. In: *Vaccine* Vol. 36 (2018), No. 25, pp. 3606–3612
[Taft21]	TAFT, DARRYL K.: *GitHub Copilot: A Powerful, Controversial Autocomplete for Developers*. https://thenewstack.io/github-copilot-a-powerful-controversial-autocomplete-for-developers/. - 2021-07-01 — The New Stack
[Taka21]	TAKAHASHI, DEAN: *Luum's AI-based Lash Robot can delicately extend eyelashes for customers in beauty salons*. https://venturebeat.com/2021/03/12/luums-ai-based-lash-robot-can-delicately-extend-eyelashes-for-customers-in-beauty-salons/. - 2021-03-12 — VentureBeat
[Thri66]	THRING, MEREDITH:
[Tim17]	TIM, HARFORD: Why didn't electricity immediately change manufacturing? In: *BBC News* (2017) https://www.bbc.com/news/business-40673694
[Tony20]	TONY SEBA: *Future of Transportation / Keynote: 2020 NC DOT Transportation SummitConvert & Download*, 2020
[Tuck16]	TUCKER, S.D.: *Great British Eccentrics*. https://www.amberley-books.com/great-british-eccentrics.html. - 2016-11-15
[Turi50]	TURING, A. M.: COMPUTING MACHINERY AND INTELLIGENCE. In: *Mind* Vol. LIX (1950), No. 236, P. 433–460
[Turi52]	TURING, ALAN: Can automatic calculating machines be said to think?: BBC, 1952 http://www.turingarchive.org/viewer/?id=460&title=30

[Ubc18] UBC: *Congratulations to Dr. Curtis Berlinguette and Dr. Jason Hein!* https://www.chem.ubc.ca/congratulations-dr-curtis-berlinguette-and-dr-jason-hein. - 2018-

[Ucl16] UCL: *AI predicts outcomes of human rights trials*. https://www.ucl.ac.uk/news/2016/oct/ai-predicts-outcomes-human-rights-trials. - 2016-10-24 — UCL News

[Va17] VA, ALEXANDRIA: OSD ASDR&E Basic Research Labs 4800 Mark Center Drive. In: *JASON The MITRE Corporation* (2017), p. 76

[Vako12] VAKOCH, D. A. (Hrsg.): *Archaeology, anthropology, and interstellar communication, The NASA history series*. Washington, DC: National Aeronautics and Space Administration, Office of Communications, History Program Office, 2012 — ISBN 978-1-62683-013-4, VAKOCH, D. A. (Hrsg.).

[Vand18] VANDERKLIPPE, NATHAN: Chinese School Installs Cameras to Monitor Students. In: *Globe and Mail* (2018)

[VeFl21] VELLANTE, DAVE; FLOYER, DAVID: *A new era of innovation: Moore's Law is not dead and AI is ready to explode - SiliconANGLE*. https://siliconangle.com/2021/04/10/new-era-innovation-moores-law-not-dead-ai-ready-explode/. - 2021-04-10

[WaFP02] WATSON, RICHARD A.; FICICI, SEVAN G.; POLLACK, JORDAN B.: Embodied Evolution: Distributing an evolutionary algorithm in a population of robots. In: *Robotics and Autonomous Systems* Vol. 39 (2002), No. 1, pp. 1–18

[Walk99] WALKER, JOHN: *The Analytical Engine: Is the Emulator Authentic?* https://www.fourmilab.ch/babbage/authentic.html. - 1999-05-04

[Walt88] WALTZ, DANIEL: Prospects for Truly Intelligent Machines. In: *American Academy of Arts and Science* Vol. 117 (1988), No. 1

[Wate20] WATERCUTTER, ANGELA: *ILM Used "Fortnite" Tech to Make Virtual Sets for "The Mandalorian" | WIRED*. https://www.wired.com/story/fortnite-mandalorian-filmmaking-tech/. - 2020-02-20

[WCTK17] WEBSTER, GRAHAM; CREEMERS, ROGIER; TRIOLO, PAUL; KANIA, ELSA: *Full Translation: China's "New Generation Artificial Intelligence Development Plan"*. http://newamerica.org/cybersecurity-initiative/digichina/blog/full-translation-chinas-new-generation-artificial-intelligence-development-plan-2017/. - 2017- — New America

[Webe96] WEBER, BRUCE: *A Mean Chess-Playing Computer Tears at the Meaning of Thought*. https://archive.nytimes.com/www.nytimes.com/partners/microsites/chess/archive8.html. - 1996-02-19 — A Mean Chess-Playing Computer Tears at the Meaning of Thought

[Wein72] WEINBERG, ALVIN M.: Science and trans-science. In: *Minerva* Vol. 10 (1972), No. 2, P. 209–222

[Weis21] WEISE, KAREN: Amazon indefinitely extends a moratorium on the police use of its facial recognition software. In: *The New York Times* (2021) https://www.nytimes.com/2021/05/18/business/amazon-police-facial-recognition.html

[Well74] WELLS, H. G.: *Mind at the end of its tether*. San Francisco: Millet Books, 1974 — ISBN 978-0-9600646-2-5

[Wend21] WENDT, BOB: Email from producer to the author, 2021-05-15

[Weri21] WERIDE: *WeRide receives California permit to test driverless vehicles and releases 2-hour non-stop driverless test video with no intervention*. https://www.weride.ai/en/dmv-unmanned-test-license-en/. - 2021-04-12

[WeSi20] WEISE, KAREN; SINGER, NATASHA: Amazon Pauses Police Use of Its Facial Recognition Software. In: *The New York Times* (2020) https://www.nytimes.com/2020/06/10/technology/amazon-facial-recognition-backlash.html

[Wien50] WIENER, NORBERT: *The Human Use of Human Beings: Cybernetics And Society*. New York, N.Y.: Da Capo Press, 1950 — ISBN 978-0-306-80320-8

[Wilk85] WILKES, M. V.: *Memoirs of a computer pioneer, MIT Press series in the history of computing*. Cambridge, Mass: MIT Press, 1985 — ISBN 978-0-262-23122-0

[Wini17] WINICK, ERIN: *While U.S. Workers Fear Automation, Swedish Employees Welcome It*. https://www.technologyreview.com/2017/12/28/146551/while-us-workers-fear-automation-swedish-employees-welcome-it/. - 2017-12-28 — MIT Technology Review

[Wino72] WINOGRAD, TERRY: Understanding natural language. In: *Cognitive Psychology* Vol. 3 (1972), No. 1, P. 1–191

[WKJM14]   WHITE, DAVID; KEMP, RICHARD I.; JENKINS, ROB; MATHESON, MICHAEL; BURTON, A. MIKE: Passport Officers' Errors in Face Matching. In: *PLOS ONE* Vol. 9, Public Library of Science (2014), No. 8, P. e103510

[WoMa11]   WOOLLETT, KATHERINE; MAGUIRE, ELEANOR A.: Acquiring "the Knowledge" of London's Layout Drives Structural Brain Changes. In: *Current Biology* Vol. 21, Elsevier (2011), No. 24, P. 2109–2114

[Worl19]   WORLD ECONOMIC FORUM: *Public Concern Around Use of Artificial Intelligence is Widespread, Poll Finds*. https://www.weforum.org/press/2019/07/public-concern-around-use-of-artificial-intelligence-is-widespread-poll-finds/. - 2019-07- — World Economic Forum

[Xie19]   XIE, ECHO: *AI is watching China's students but how well can it really see?* https://www.scmp.com/news/china/politics/article/3027349/artificial-intelligence-watching-chinas-students-how-well-can. - 2019-09-16 — South China Morning Post

[Yamp18]   YAMPOLSKIY, ROMAN V.: Predicting future AI failures from historic examples. In: *foresight* Vol. 21, Emerald Publishing Limited (2018), No. 1, pp. 138–152

[Yang19]   YANG, ANDREW: *The War on Normal People: The Truth About America's Disappearing Jobs and Why Universal Basic Income Is Our Future*. New York, NY Boston: Hachette Books, 2019 — ISBN 978-0-316-41421-0

[Yout17]   YOUTUBE: *President Putin in August 2017 via live video*, 2017

[Yudk08]   YUDKOWSKY, ELIEZER: Artificial Intelligence as a positive and negative factor in global risk. In: YUDKOWSKY, E.: *Global Catastrophic Risks*: Oxford University Press, 2008 — ISBN 978-0-19-857050-9

[Zaka22]   ZAKARIA ABDU, AMRO: *Robotics and Artificial Intelligence: Mankind's Latest Evolution - NewsWeek Me*. https://newsweekme.com/robotics-artificial-intelligence-mankinds-latest-evolution/. - 2022-

[Zand20]   ZANDONELLA, CATHERINE: *Mathematician John Horton Conway, a 'magical genius' known for inventing the 'Game of Life,' dies at age 82*. https://www.princeton.edu/news/2020/04/14/mathematician-john-horton-conway-magical-genius-known-inventing-game-life-dies-age. - 2020-04-14 — Princeton University

[ZDMG21]   ZERILLI, JOHN; DANAHER, JOHN; MACLAURIN, JAMES; GAVAGHAN, COLIN; KNOTT, ALISTAIR: *A Citizen's Guide to Artificial Intelligence*. https://www.amazon.ca/Citizens-Guide-Artificial-Intelligence/dp/0262044811. - 2021-02-23

[Zolk21]   ZOLKOS, GREGORY: *Your business's cybersecurity needs both advanced threat prevention and advanced threat detection —here's why*. https://www.bizjournals.com/bizjournals/how-to/technology/2021/02/your-business-cybersecurity-needs-both-advanced.html. - 2021-02-

[ZoSc18]   ZOU, JAMES; SCHIEBINGER, LONDA: AI can be sexist and racist — it's time to make it fair. In: *Nature* Vol. 559 (2018), No. 7714, P. 324–326 — Bandiera_abtest: aCg_type: Commentnumber: 7714 Nature Publishing

[Zwit17]   ZWITTER, DIRK HELBING, BRUNO S. FREY, GERD GIGERENZER, ERNST HAFEN, MICHAEL HAGNER, YVONNE HOFSTETTER, JEROEN VAN DEN HOVEN, ROBERTO V. ZICARI, ANDREJ: *Will Democracy Survive Big Data and Artificial Intelligence?* https://www.scientificamerican.com/article/will-democracy-survive-big-data-and-artificial-intelligence/. - 2017-02-25 — Scientific American

Endnotes

1	[Hill10]	34	[Taka21]	67	[Page84] pp. 129-137
2	[Hold18]	35	[FeMc83]	68	[Onfu18]
3	[Worl19]	36	[Clif17]	69	[Scot00] Episode 38
4	[DaOx19]	37	[Mcki13]	70	[Pape19]
5	[RaVe17]	38	[Stud21]	71	[Baid18]
6	[Zwit17]	39	[Scot00] Episode 3	72	[BSLM11]
7	[Arms19]	40	[Scot00] Episode 35	73	[FeMc83] p. 11
8	[Scot00] Episode 42	41	[Brow20]	74	[Metz16a]
9	[Scot00] Episode 19	42	[HaHu20].	75	[Metz16b]
10	[Scot00] Episode 13	43	[Free17]	76	[Turi52]
11	[Scha19] p. 132	44	[Orac19]	77	[Itrs12]
12	[Lync17]	45	[Ref00]	78	[Krew21]
13	[Tim17]	46	[Moor03]	79	[VeFl21]
14	[Dubo67]	47	[Kiss18]	80	[Cpum21] S. 15
15	[Corr21]	48	[Mill56]	81	[Mena42]
16	[Morg18]	49	[Park12]	82	[Cast20]
17	[Well74]	50	[Leve95]	83	[Gent21]
18	[Cons20]	51	[Fles22]	84	[Shan21a]
19	[Staf21a]	52	[KFRC75]	85	[ArLT21]
20	[LuMS20]	53	[Walk99]	86	[Wilk85]
21	[Nica20]	54	[Mcco04] p. 115	87	[Scot00] Episode 34
22	[Lg20]	55	[Mcca01]	88	[Russ21]
23	[Wate20]	56	[MoLa18]	89	[Brow21]
24	[Wend21]	57	[Matt16]	90	[Russ20] p. 9
25	[Walt88]	58	[WoMa11]	91	[Scot00] Episode 17
26	[KaKu02]	59	[Hoff15]	92	[Frie58]
27	[Burg17]	60	[Peas12]	93	[GZFB20]
28	[Funk16]	61	[Scot00] Episode 22	94	[Rest85]
29	[Lewi16]	62	[Mcco04] p. 114	95	[Bell14]
30	[RaVe17]	63	[Scot00] Episode 23	96	[Draa01]
31	[Affe00]	64	[Russ20]	97	[Krig21]
32	[Taft21]	65	[Mcde85]	98	[Book13]
33	[Tony20]	66	[Newn58]	99	[Carl20]

100	[Chat07]	156	[Savi20]	212	[BGMS21]
101	[Hern13]	157	[Nhts17]	213	[GrNH19]
102	Yann LeCun in [Ford18]	158	[Harr19]	214	[EKNK17]
103	[Boyd10]	159	[Dodd16]	215	[NKSN18]
104	[Scot00] Episode 65	160	[Delc18]	216	[IaLa20]
105	[Some13]	161	[Saei21]	217	[GoRo97]
106	[Webe96]	162	[MaDa19] p. 13	218	[MaDa19]
107	[Kasp18] p. 104	163	[Mind15] p. 202	219	[ZoSc18]
108	[FeMc83]	164	[Scot00] Episode 61	220	[Swee13]
109	[Shan21b] p. 210	165	[Scot00] Episode 36	221	[CaBN17]
110	[Thri66]	166	[Schw19]	222	[GrNH19]
111	[Glan78]	167	[Scot00] Episode 62	223	[PoTJ15]
112	[Musi19]	168	[Scot00] Episode 31	224	[Dast18]
113	[Haas17]	169	[Scot00] Episode 31	225	[Oakd21]
114	[Scot00] Episode 12	170	[Henr20]	226	[Bane21]
115	[BBHK20]	171	[Abt19]	227	[Fost22]
116	[Gunk18]	172	[Fing21]	228	[Scot00] Episode 9
117	[KKIF12]	173	[Brow17]	229	[Robi00]
118	[Kubr68]	174	[HXCM18]	230	[Stra22]
119	[Funk16]	175	[Brow19]	231	[Ally22]
120	[Demi18]	176	[Weri21]	232	[Scot00] Episode 58
121	[Rows19]	177	[Bell22]	233	[Mead08]
122	[Scot00] Episode 70	178	[ADKS18]	234	[Scot00] Episode 75
123	[Good65]	179	[Russ20]	235	[Mord15]
124	[Funk16]	180	[Gild22] p. 100	236	[Scot00] Episode 78
125	[Marr19]	181	[Alle18]	237	[KaWe67] p. 90
126	[Amer21]	182	[Fiel17]	238	[Duhi14]
127	[MKSG13]	183	[Brad17]	239	[Hays04]
128	[Deve22]	184	[LYDP17]	240	[Jero10]
129	[MaDa19] p. 19	185	[LYDP17]	241	[Ferg13]
130	[Gold10]	186	[Batr17]	242	[Vand18]
131	[BBKC15]	187	[Nove17]	243	[Paya18]
132	[Scot00] Episode 34	188	[Fauz21]	244	[Xie19]
133	[Russ20]	189	[Hill15]	245	[Stab21]
134	[Russ20]	190	[Micr21]	246	[Roge21]
135	[Busi16]	191	[Naya19]	247	[Morr21]
136	[Serv20]	192	[Scie17]	248	[AmCJ20]
137	[Heav20]	193	[Wino72]	249	[Dou21]
138	[Arti00]	194	[KDLM22]	250	[LiLi20]
139	[Scot00] Episode 63	195	[Pink09]	251	[Hill20a]
140	[Gold21]	196	[Scha19]	252	[Hill20b]
141	[Scot00] Episode 72	197	[EEFL18]	253	[Metz21]
142	[LGKM14]	198	[Robi21]	254	[Mozu19]
143	[Scot00] Episode 44	199	[WKJM14]	255	[Anup21]
144	[Addi22]	200	[Shan19]	256	[GSSM21]
145	[Mcco04] p. 167	201	[Shan18]	257	[Reve16]
146	[Hao20a]	202	[Shan21b]	258	[OtDi19]
147	[Imo19]	203	[Mins88]	259	[Stat20]
148	[Gole21]	204	[Zand20] p. 82	260	[WeSi20]
149	[Brya06]	205	[Stoc20] p. 83	261	[Weis21]
150	[Bran20]	206	[Scot00] Episode 90	262	[Hao19]
151	[Scot00] Episode 64	207	[DiSM15] pp. 114-126	263	[Labb21]
152	[Scot00] Episode 60	208	[Russ20] p. 249	264	[AnEd15]
153	[Scot00] Episode 34	209	[Scot00] Episode 55	265	[Knig20]
154	[Scot00] Episode 23	210	[Asar06]	266	[EvGa16]
155	[Scot00] Episode 48	211	[Gold21]	267	[Kali15]

268	[Darl18]	324	[GBDP15]	380	[KaWe67] p. 210
269	[Darl21]	325	[Sims94a]	381	[Scot00] Episode 82
270	[Ref20]	326	[Mitr09]	382	[Mcle22]
271	[DaRo18]	327	[HKBS12]	383	[Kore21]
272	[Brod18]	328	[Sims94b]	384	[Scot00] Episode 28
273	[Scot00] Episode 12	329	[ECMD15]	385	[Boyl20]
274	[LeNo99]	330	[Ray92]	386	[Keyn30]
275	[Bbc07]	331	[WaFP02]	387	[Keyn30]
276	[Foo20]	332	[Cold18]	388	[KaWe67]
277	[Kell13]	333	[Sand20]	389	[Favr19]
278	[Mack19]	334	[Leig20]	390	[Rest20]
279	[Harw19]	335	[Ihea20]	391	[Khar17]
280	[Fram13]	336	[Harw20]	392	[FuKu82] p. 35
281	[Scot00] Episode 30	337	[Moss18]	393	[Scol17]
282	[GoRS16]	338	[Semu20]	394	[Vako12]
283	[StMi15]	339	[Arat20]	395	[Pand07]
284	[Arth16]	340	[Lee18]	396	[Niel20]
285	[Musi19]	341	[KaWe67] p. 189	397	[Scot00] Episode 77
286	[Hans08]	342	[Sull15]	398	[Scot00] Episode 46
287	[AnDT20]	343	[Kasr17]	399	[Yout17]
288	[Pain18]	344	[FrOs17]	400	[Post22]
289	[Scot00] Episode 78	345	[Mish16]	401	[Goog17]
290	[Bent20]	346	[Zaka22]	402	[Hern17]
291	[Solo17]	347	[Yang19]	403	[WCTK17]
292	[RaAA17]	348	[Obam16]	404	[Cheo19]
293	[Herb65]	349	[PaCo17]	405	[Scot00] Episode 77
294	[Bann20]	350	[Heat17]	406	[Halp22]
295	[Roch21]	351	[Sher16]	407	[Scot00] Episode 54
296	[ZDMG21]	352	[GHSE03]	408	[Scha19] p. 261
297	[Perm19]	353	[Hal15]	409	[Ford18] p. 107
298	[Russ19]	354	[Ramg19]	410	[Scie17]
299	[Glob20]	355	[Rifk14]	411	[Mind15] p. 155
300	[Hao21]	356	[Scot00] Episode 76	412	[Scha19] p. 264
301	[Solo17]	357	[Staf21a]	413	[Va17]
302	[Staf21b]	358	[Sain20]	414	[Schl13]
303	[RaAA17]	359	[Lohr22]	415	[Akse13]
304	[SZSB18]	360	[Staf61]	416	[Scot00] Episode 86
305	[Ahme21]	361	[MiWo19]	417	[Shea21]
306	[Huan21]	362	[MiJo21]	418	[Wien50]
307	[Feng22]	363	[Robe20]	419	[Scot00] Episode 26
308	[Tuck16]	364	[Lohr22]	420	[Wien50] p. 105
309	[Robe19]	365	[Frey19]	421	[Leve95] p. 122
310	[Evan19]	366	[Cook19]	422	[RoRR18]
311	[Cook20]	367	[Wini17]	423	[Barr17]
312	[Stre22]	368	[Marc21]	424	[Scot00] Episode 99
313	[Lawg18]	369	[Hao20b]	425	[John11]
314	[Ucl16]	370	[Fry19]	426	[Yamp18]
315	[Foss15]	371	[John97]	427	[Wein72]
316	[Scot00] Episodes 50, 51	372	[Muse19]	428	[Yudk08]
317	[Crev93] p. 146	373	[Scot00] Episode 88	429	[Chri20]
318	[Rees18]	374	[John97]	430	[Dell18]
319	[Solo11]	375	[Moye90]	431	[Kasp18] p. 47
320	[Knig21]	376	[Brow16]	432	[MoAP18]
321	[Zolk21]	377	[Mind15] p. 88	433	[Pall20]
322	[StBM05]	378	[Mind15] p. 74	434	[Henl20]
323	[MoMi97]	379	[Mind15] p. 83	435	[IaLa20]

436	[Gard20]	450	[Serv19]	464	[Chal95]
437	[RDBM19]	451	[Scot00] Episode 42	465	[Gild22] p. 103
438	[Scot00] Episode 30	452	[Scot00] Episode 26	466	[Bost16]
439	[RDBM19]	453	[Bess09]	467	[Well02]
440	[RDBM19]	454	[Pohl79]	468	[Kais15]
441	[Ng16]	455	[Scot00] Episode 4	469	[Bost05]
442	[Read22]	456	[JoRW14]	470	[PBDP21]
443	[Gove20]	457	[Hao20c]	471	[MoFe19]
444	[Quir20]	458	[Stem21]	472	[Sork19]
445	[Gpai20]	459	[Blue22]	473	[Kard63]
446	[Haid18]	460	[FeMc83]	474	[Ayfe20]
447	[Cong21]	461	[Turi50]	475	[Turi50]
448	[Scot00] Episode 77	462	[Scot00] Episode 38	476	[Picc04]
449	[Ubc18]	463	[Kurz13]		

Index

2001: A Space Odyssey, 83
Abbott, Ryan, 204
accountability, 168
Acemoglu, Daron, 218
activation function, 310
Adams, Douglas, 32
Affective Computing, 183
AI100 project, 21, 195
AI Psychologist, 293
Aiva, 223
AI Winter, 51
Alciné, Jacky, 161
A-level algorithm, 158
Alexa, 105
AlexNet, 54
All-Party Parliamentary Group on Artificial Intelligence, 274
AlphaFold, 102, 103
AlphaGo, 220, 248
AlphaZero, 88, 89
Amara's Law, 26
Amazon, 217
amodal completion, 93
Analytical Engine, 34
Anderson, Poul, 28
anthropomorphizing, 93
Arbesman, Samuel, 31
archaea, 102
artificial general intelligence, 66
artificial intelligence
    and creativity, 221
    and the law, 203
    cheating, 208
    complexity, 30
    definition, 41
    existential risk, 256
    how to think about, 78
    human level, 22
    hype, 14
    interpreting x-rays, 165
    in the C-suite, 286
    limitations, 132
    risks of misevaluating, 234
    sentient, 294
    successful deployment in business, 239
Artificial Intelligence and You podcast, 2
artificial narrow intelligence, 66
artificial neural network, 307
artificial super intelligence, 66
artificial superintelligence, 261, 262, 295
Asaro, Peter, 160
assistive intelligence, 283
autocomplete, 107
automated teller machine, 215
automation
    effects on employment, 212
    investment in, 12
Automation Resilience Quadrant, 236
autonomous vehicles, 19, 116, 170
autonomous weapons, 250
AutoX, 126, 168
Babbage, Charles, 33
backpropagation, 312
Baidu, 8
Bannon, Steve, 194
Barnes, Steven, 110

Bell, Joshua, 222
Benchley, Robert, 66
bias, 161
Big Data, 96, 165, 175
Blade Runner, 289
blind auditions, 164
Blue Brain Project, 284
Bohr, Neils, 1
bombe computers, 58
Bostrom, Nick, 240, 294, 296
Boyd, John, 73
brain
    compared to computer, 72
    memory equivalent, 95
brain-computer interfaces, 299
Branwen, Gwern, 108
Breakout, 92
Breazeal, Cynthia, 67
Brexit, 269
Breyer, Jim, 21
Brocas Aphasia, 69
Brynjolfsson, Erik, 188
Buolamwini, Joy, 180
Burns, Eric A., 233
Canadian artificial intelligence strategy, 274
Čapek, Karel, 83
capsule networks, 100
Cattell, Horn, and Carroll model, 44
Cerebras, 57
César Hidalgo, 160
Chace, Calum, 257
Chatsiou, Kakia, 139
Chief AI Officer, 272
Chief Futurism Officer, 271
Chief Information Security Officer, 286
China, 248
Chinese Room, 137
Clearview AI, 178
Clement-Jones, Lord (Tim), 274
cluster analysis, 65
cobots, 298
Coffee Test, 285
Cognitive Behavioral Therapy, 185
Common Crawl, 108
complexity, 28
computer generated imagery, 15
conscious futurism, 267
consciousness, 291
convolutional neural network, 99
Conway, John, 151
Cook, Katy, 201
Copilot, 19
CoPilot, 109
COVID-19, 11, 13, 104, 139, 244
creepy line, 175
Crisis of Control, 1

Critch, Andrew, 263
cybermorphizing, 93
cybersecurity
    at the Pentagon, 206
Cyc, 98
CycleGAN, 209
Czarnecki, Tony, 3
Danks, David, 159
Darling, Kate, 93, 144, 183
Dartmouth College conference, 39, 50
data, 46
Data, 56, 91
de Chardin, Pierre Teilhard, 279
Deep Blue, 77, 88, 94
DeepMind, 92, 311
Deep Tom Cruise, 167
Deming, W. Edwards, 206
Dennett, Daniel, 292
Device for Autonomous Bootstrapping of Unified
    Sentience, 205
Dickmanns, Ernst, 115
Difference Engine, 34
Diffusion of Innovation curve, 24
Dijkstra, Edsger, 81
disinformation, 194, 276
Disruption, 266
dogfighting, 250
Dolivo-Dobrovolsky, Mikhail, 8
DoNotPay AI, 216
Driscoll, Bridget, 113
Drucker, Peter, 27, 239
dynocognesis, 10, 158, 240
eccentricity, 201
echoborg, 111
Einstein, Albert, 29, 32, 53, 66
Eisenhower, Dwight D., 273
electrification, 9
ELIZA, 185
el Kaliouby, Rana, 183
emergence, 150
emergent behavior, 152
ENIAC, 34, 59
Enigma, 58
enlightenment, 47
enmeshment, 232
equity, 240
European Court of Human Rights, 204
Everything as a Service, 101
explainability, 170
    implementing, 172
exponential growth, 26
Facebook, 192
facial recognition, 178
Faraday, Michael, 8
Farm, The, 281
Feel4Life, 19

Fei-Fei Li, 54
Feldenkrais, Moshé, 186
Fifth Generation project, 55
Finland, 269
Flesch-Kincaid Reading Ease, 30
flood fill algorithm, 82
Folding@Home, 243, 244
Foot, Philippa, 123
Foster-Fletcher, Richard, 167, 238, 283
France, Kordel, 104
Frey, Carl Benedikt, 214, 219
Friedberg, Richard M., 69
Fugaku supercomputer, 72
Fuller, Buckminster, 243
Full Self Driving, 127
Funke, Ralf, 88, 90
Game of Life, 151
games
    perfect information, 90
    video, 92
Gates, Bill, 26, 246
Gebru, Timnit, 162
Generative Pre-trained Transformer, 107
Gerrold, David, 276
Gettysburg Address, 107
Gilder, George, 132, 290
Gillespie, Tony, 160, 250, 253
Global Disinformation Index, 276
Go, 17, 18, 28, 90, 220, 248
goats in a tree, 148
GOFAI, 148
Golden Age of AI, 53
Good, Irving J., 90
Good Old-Fashioned AI, 53
Google cat, 145
Google digital assistant, 105
GPT-3, 108, 220, 284, 303
Gretzky, Wayne, 234
Gupta, Amit, 108
HAL 9000, 83, 88
Hall, Phil D., 111
Hard Takeoff, 297
Hassabis, Demis, 101
Hawking, Stephen, 17, 26, 67
Herzberg, Elaine, 114
Hillis, Danny, 136
Hillman, Leon, 3
Hind, Michael, 172
hippocorn, 97
HireVue, 190
Hofstadter, Douglas, 77
Holmes, Elizabeth, 202
Homer-Dixon, Thomas, 256, 277
Human Brain Project, 284
Iansiti, Marco, 270
IBM, 20

IBM 360, 34
ImageNet, 163
information, 46
Institute for Digital Humanity, 235
InstructGPT, 141, 303
intelligence, 47
    crystallized, 44
    human, 42, 79
    quotient, 42
intelligence quotient, 42
International Math Olympiad, 106
Internet Research Agency, 195
Invariant Risk Minimization, 227
iPhone 13, 58
IQ, *See* Intelligence Quotient
J3016, 115
Jennifer Aniston neuron, 69
Jeopardy, 258, 295
Jetsons Fallacy, 279
Johari Window, 22
Johnny Cabs, 20
Jones, Indiana, 108
Juncker, Jean-Claude, 277
Kahn, Herman, 174, 213, 241
Kanisza Triangle, 93
Kardashev Scale, 301
Karpathy, Andrej, 113
Kasparov, Garry, 77, 88, 94, 258, 267
Keynes, John Maynard, 213, 240
King, Katie, 235, 239
Kissinger, Henry, 28
knowledge, 46
Knowledge, The, 45
Kodak, 238
Koretz, Janna, 232
Kremlin, 195
Krigolson, Olav, 69, 74
Krizhevsky, Alex, 54
K-shaped recovery, 13
Kubrick, Stanley, 211
Kurzweil, Ray, 17, 297
Kush Varshney, 227
Laundroid, 212
LawGeex AI, 203
Lighthill Report, 51
Liminal Age, 299
Litman, Todd, 120
Logic Theorist, 50, 106, 205
Lucasfilm, 15
Lumm robot, 20
Luthor, Lex, 47
machine learning, 63
Malhotra, Rajiv, 245
Martians, 52
Maslow, Abraham, 232
Maslows Hierarchy of Needs, 273

May, Rob, 105
McCarthy, John, 39, 52, 131, 285
McCorduck, Pamela, 40, 50, 110, 249
McCulloch, Warren, 307
MC Hammer, 106
McKinsey, 301
McLuhan, Marshall, 71, 177, 183, 190
McNealy, Scott, 174
Meadows, Donella H., 169
Mechanical Turk, 134
MegatronLM, 181
Menabrea, Luigi, 58
Mensa, 42
Metcalf, Stephen, 274
Mica, 184
Mikolov, Tomáš, 109
Miller, George A., 28
Minsky, Marvin, 39
misinformation, 194
Mitchell, Margaret, 162
MKAI, 167
Mohiam, Reverend Mother Gaius Helen, 193
Mona Lisa, 151
Monster Raving Loony Party, 201
Moores Law, 56, 57, 59, 295
Moravec, Hans, 142
Mousavizadeh, Alexandra, 216, 245, 249, 276
Moxie, 187
Mr. Bean, 201
MuseNet, 221
Musiał, Maciej, 191
Mustard Dream, 147
MYCIN, 52
Nabokov, Vladimir, 290
Naisbitt, John, 23
Napoleon, 8
National Institute of Standards and Technology, 173
Natural Language Processing, 139
Natural Language Understanding, 139
Navier-Stokes Equation, 106
Neatham, Anne Marie, 269
neural nets, 308
    connection weights, 309
    hidden layers, 311
neuroplasticity, 45
Never-Ending Language Learner, 98
Ng, Andrew, 8, 72, 272
Nin, Anaïs, 265
Nugent, Alex, 181
Obama, Barack, 250
Ofqual, 158
Omidyar, Pierre, 235
OODA loops, 73
OOPDA loop, 74, 118
OpenAI, 19, 221, 263
Open Source movement, 246

Osborne, Michael, 214
overfit, 313
Oxford Martin Programme for the Future of Employment, 214
PageRank algorithm, 80
pandemic, 12
    effect on automation, 12
Parker, Sean, 192
Parson, Ted, 123, 191, 271, 275, 280
PCSK9 protein, 102
Perlis, Alan, 285
Persuasive Electric Vehicle, 128
petabyte, 95, 175
Petrov, Stanislav, 252
Philosopher AI, 302
Picard, Rosalind, 183
Picasso, Pablo, 104
Pichai, Sundar, 9, 184
pilots, 226
PimEyes, 179
Pirjanian, Paolo, 85, 186
Pitts, Walter, 307
poker, 91
Polanyi, Michael, 142
Precautionary Principle, 260
Predator unmanned drones, 251
prediction error feedback, 75
predictions, 28
    of future leisure, 214
PredPol, 190
Pringle, Ramona, 185
Project Personality Chat, 105
Putin, Vladimir, 246
quantum computers, 60
R2-D2, 83
Radclyffe, Charles, 168, 272
Reeves-Stevens, Judith and Garfield, 280
reinforcement learning, 64
Rekognition, 180
Rembrandt, 224
    The Next, 225
Restaurant, The, 282
robo-taxis, 127
robots, 83
    empathetic, 187
    empathy for, 183
Robovie, 87
Rogers, E.M., 24
Roomba, 79
Rosenblatt, Frank, 51
Rosey the Robot, 83
Rossum's Universal Robots, 83
Rowson, Jonathan, 89
Roy, Arundhati, 7
Russell, Stuart, 51, 67, 101, 131, 159, 253
Russia, 196, 246, 247

Samuel, Arthur, 39
Sankarpandi, Sathish, 103
scale, pan-congruence, 301
Schank, Roger, 51
Schmidt, Eric, 175
Schneier, Bruce, 207
Searle, John, 137
Second Industrial Revolution, 9
Sedol, Lee, 220
SETI, 243
SETI@Home, 243
Seven Signs of Self, 94
sexbots, 85
Shakespeare, 2
Shane, Janelle, 80, 147
Shannon, Claude, 39
Shatner, William, 111
Shaw, George Bernard, 213
Shor, Peter, 61
Shwartz, Steven, 121
Simon, Herbert, 49
SimSensei, 104
Simultaneous Localization and Mapping, 85
Singler, Beth, 53, 288, 298
Singularity, The, 297
Skynet, 133
Slaughterbots, 252
Slavin, Kevin, 81
software weightlessness, 15
Sophocles, 231
Star Trek, 97, 280
Star Wars, 83
steganography, 209
Sternberg, R.J., 41
Stochastic Parrots, 162
Sturm, Bob, 221
Sudowrite, 109, 220
Superbowl XXXIV, 16
Supermarket, The, 281
supervised learning, 64
Sutskever, Ilya, 54, 290
Sykes, Sir Tatton, 200
System 1 Thinking, 118
System 2 Thinking, 118
Taiwan, 199
Talla, 105
Tang, Audrey, 23, 128, 199, 283
taxi driver, 45
techno-solutionism, 21
Tesla, 127, 217
Tesla, Nikolai, 8
Thatcher Effect, 99
Thring, Meredith Wooldridge, 83
TikTok algorithm, 198
Toyota Research Institute, 86
transitivity, 47

translation, human language, 149
trans-scientific, 260
Trivergence of Automation, 267
Trolley Problem, 123
trustworthiness, 225
Tufekci, Zeynep, 197
Turing, Alan, 27, 50, 56, 107, 258, 288, 305
Uber, 114, 237
Ukraine, 247
    Ministry of Justice, 242
uncanny valley, 115
understanding, 137
UNESCO, 161
United Nations Convention on Certain
    Conventional Weapons, 253
unsupervised learning, 64
US Airways Flight 1549, 225
Value Alignment Problem, 261, 262
Victoria Transport Policy Institute, 120
Vinge, Vernor, 296
Volkswagen, 207
Volta, Alessandro, 8
von Goethe, Johann Wolfgang, 200, 298
Vonnegut, Kurt, 307
von Neumann architecture, 60
von Neumann, John, 59, 131
Waltz, David, 17
washing machine, AI-enabled, 14
Waterbed Principle of Complexity, 29
Watson, 258
Waymo, 116
Weinberg, Alvin, 259
Weiner, Norbert, 232, 255, 275
Weizenbaum, Joseph, 185
Wells, H.G., 11, 295, 302
Whitehead, Alfred North, 157
White, Tom, 147
Wiener, Anthony, 174, 213, 241
Wikipedia, 107
Wilkes, Maurice, 63
Winograd Schemas, 140
Winograd, Terry, 140
wisdom, 47, 293
Wittgenstein, Ludwig, 46
Woebot, 186
Wollaston, William Hyde, 33
Woodcock-Johnson Tests of Cognitive Abilities, 44
Wooldridge, Michael, 23, 67, 98, 109
word2vec, 144
World Economic Forum, 1, 159
Yampolskiy, Roman, 68, 259
Yudkowsky, Eliezer, 77, 260
Zelensky, Volodymyr, 168
Zerilli, John, 173, 192
zettabyte, 2
Zuckerberg, Mark, 191

Produced for both print and Kindle
in a simultaneous edition
using Adobe InDesign.

nitrosyncretic press

This print version uses the
Arno Pro & Hypatia Sans Pro
font families.

Peter Scott is helping us to get along with artificial intelligence. A Master's degree in computer science from Cambridge University led him to spend more than thirty years working for NASA's Jet Propulsion Laboratory, helping advance our exploration of space. A parallel pursuit of the human development field as a certified coach positioned him to recognize and address technological disruption. The births of his children brought him into a mission: to help people understand, use, and advance AI for the betterment of all. He has given TEDx talks, and spoken to audiences as diverse as transformational leaders, executives, and British parliamentarians. In 2017 he founded the Next Wave Institute, which coaches clients to become resilient to exponential disruption. In 2020 he started the *Artificial Intelligence and You* podcast, bringing expert guests as diverse as politicians, CEOs, philosophers, developers, and artists to help audiences understand this incredibly complex thing called AI. He lives in the Pacific Northwest with his wife and two daughters.

Manufactured by Amazon.ca
Acheson, AB